International Auditing

PRACTICAL RESOURCE GUIDE

David O'Regan

WILEY

John Wiley & Sons, Inc.

This book is printed on acid-free paper. ∞

Copyright © 2003 by John Wiley & Sons. All rights reserved.

Published by John Wiley & Sons, Inc., Hoboken, New Jersey
Published simultaneously in Canada.

For general information on our other products and services, or technical support, please contact our Customer Care Department within the United States at 800-762-2974, outside the United States at 317-572-3993 or fax 317-572-4002.

Wiley also publishes its books in a variety of electronic formats. Some content that appears in print may not be available in electronic books.

Library of Congress Cataloging-in-Publication Data:

O'Regan, David.
    International auditing : practical resource guide / by David O'Regan.
        p.   cm.
    Includes bibliographical references and index.
    ISBN 0-471-26382-6
    1. Auditing.   2. Auditing—Standards.   3. International business
enterprises—Auditing.   4. International business
enterprises—Accounting.   I. Title.
    HF5667.0673 2003
    657'.96—dc21

2003000568

Printed in the United States of America

10 9 8 7 6 5 4 3 2 1

To Abhishikta and my parents.

About the Author

David O'Regan is the Head of Internal Audit at Oxford University Press in Oxford, England. He has written two audit-related books for the Institute of Internal Auditors (IIA) and has written several articles for such publications as *Internal Auditing, Accountancy, Internal Auditor,* and *Managerial Auditing.* Prior to joining Oxford University Press, he worked for United Technology Corporation and for Price Waterhouse.

About the Institute of Internal Auditors

The Institute of Internal Auditors (IIA) is the primary international professional association, organized on a worldwide basis, dedicated to the promotion and development of the practice of internal auditing. The IIA is the recognized authority, chief educator, and acknowledged leader in standards, education, certification, and research for the profession worldwide. The Institute provides professional and executive development training, educational products, research studies, and guidance to more than 80,000 members in more than 100 countries. For additional information, visit the Web site at *www.theiia.org*.

Contents

Preface

I have designed this book as a guide and reference source for auditors who perform international assignments. Auditing is very much a hands-on activity, and the men and women who practice this profession need practical advice. This book aims to assist both internal and external auditors, as well as anyone whose corporate governance duties have an international dimension. It may also be useful for students of international accounting and auditing.

Chapter 1, "Introduction—International Auditing," briefly reviews the development of the auditing profession, and summarizes recent international developments. Chapter 2, "International Organizations and Their Risks," considers typical areas of risk facing multinational organizations, including economic, political, legal, accounting, and regulatory factors, as well as linguistic and cultural differences. Chapter 3, "Managing International Risks," looks at ways of managing the categories of risk identified in Chapter 2, while Chapter 4, "Organization-Wide Risk Assessment," moves on to discuss broader approaches to organizational risk assessment. Chapter 4 considers both quantitative and qualitative methodologies and suggests ways of achieving a balanced, holistic approach to international risk assessment. At the start of the twenty-first century, the age of globalization has never seemed more dangerous and more fragile, and Chapter 5, "The Logistics of Auditing," discusses logistical matters to encourage effective, efficient, and safe assignments. Chapter 6, "Concluding Thoughts," offers some final reflections on global auditing.

The Appendix offers guidance on individual countries. The information is grouped under headings that include geography, history, demographics, languages, politics, economy, accountancy, and culture. As is clear from this list, the reader will find more than merely auditing information in the country sections. It is my belief that success in the uniquely challenging and rewarding field of international auditing requires a broad understanding of the varied environments in which assignments are conducted, as well as a degree of cultural sensitivity. The auditor visiting Japan, for example, should know that in 2001 the country established a new accounting standards-setting body, and that the new body's Web site has information in English. This is not all: Additional knowledge of Japan is valuable if the auditor is to operate at full effectiveness. An understanding of the complexities of the Japanese writing system and an appreciation of recent Japanese history are examples of the types of information central to a rounded appreciation of a particular country.

Global auditing and risk management is a fascinating subject, and I hope that this book assists auditing professionals in their international duties.

ACKNOWLEDGMENTS

I cannot but feel keenly aware of the gratitude owed to my predecessors, and footnotes and the *Select Bibliography* indicate some of my intellectual debts. However, it would almost take another book to thank all of those who, over the years, have helped me define my ideas on international auditing. In particular, auditing around the world with past and present colleagues at PricewaterhouseCoopers, United Technologies Corporation, and Oxford University Press has been invaluable—there is no substitute for experience in the field.

Thanks are due to Timothy Burgard and Louise Jacob, my editors at John Wiley & Sons, whose advice and perceptive criticism were invaluable, and to Professor Jeffrey Ridley, visiting professor at South Bank University in London, who drew my attention to the increasing importance in recent years of the concept of "assurance" in auditing.

My wife Abhishikta gave valuable assistance with bibliography searches and gave me all the care, affection, and encouragement I needed to complete the book.

Despite this collective help, I remain responsible for any errors or omissions. I invite your comments, corrections, and criticism to ensure the quality and accuracy of any future editions.

David O'Regan
March 2003

Abbreviations

ASEAN	Association of Southeast Asian Nations
BBC	British Broadcasting Corporation
BCE	Before Common Era
CE	Common Era
CN	*Code Napoléon* [the French Napoleonic Code]
COSO	Committee of Sponsoring Organizations [of the Treadway Commission]
CSA	Control Self Assessment
EU	European Union
FCPA	Foreign Corrupt Practices Act
GAAP	Generally Accepted Accounting Principles
GDP	Gross Domestic Product
IAS	International Accounting Standards
IASB	International Accounting Standards Board
IASC	International Accounting Standards Committee
IFAC	International Federation of Accountants
IFAD	International Forum on Accountancy Development
IIA	Institute of Internal Auditors
IOSCO	International Organization of Securities Commissions
ISA	International Standards on Auditing
NATO	North Atlantic Treaty Organization
OECD	Organization for Economic Cooperation and Development
SEC	Securities and Exchange Commission
TI	Transparency International
UN	United Nations

1

Introduction–
International Auditing

EXTERNAL AND INTERNAL AUDITING

Auditing Theory and History

It is appropriate to begin a review of international auditing by defining its terminology and setting out a brief historical background.[1] Auditing is an evaluative process in which the auditor acts as an intermediary between two (or more) parties. The auditor has historically gathered, examined, and evaluated evidence against predetermined criteria, and reported the results to interested parties.

The context in which auditing emerged has often been presented in terms of "agency theory." This proposes that information asymmetry arises when owners of economic resources (principals) delegate the control of those resources to managers (agents). If principals are unable to adequately monitor that agents are fully representing their interests, they may seek the help of outside parties (auditors) to offer independent advice on agents' behavior.

The history of auditing is ancient. It appears that ever since individuals and institutions started to record economic activities, they have felt a need to employ auditors to monitor and oversee them. The classical empires of Rome and China, for example, created elaborate civil services to monitor and report on state finances and to assess taxation revenues. Some commentators even claim that auditing practices date from the very dawn of literate civilization:

"According to earliest Mesopotamian records dating back to 3600 B.C., scribes used to prepare summaries of financial transactions. These were separate from the lists of amounts handled and which others had prepared. . . . Tiny marks, dots, and circles indicated the painstaking comparison of one record with another—marks that have survived the centuries and that auditors still use to tick off their verification of records. Thus were born two control devices still used around the world: division of duties; provision for the review of another's work."[2]

In England in the Middle Ages, many of the parties interested in manorial audits were illiterate and the audit was usually presented orally. As a result, the modern English word *audit* came into use, derived from the Latin verb *audire* ("to hear"). In modern times, auditing tends to be rigorously documented, but the discipline's name still hints back to the era of "audit by ear."[3]

This brief historical sketch suggests that evaluative practices recognizable as forms of auditing have existed since antiquity. Out of the rudimentary practices of the past, modern auditing has emerged as a multifaceted, complex, and constantly developing discipline. The auditing profession today tends to be categorized in two main branches, external and internal auditing, which are discussed in the following sections.

External Auditing

External auditing focuses on the evaluation of financial statements, and it first emerged as a professional discipline in the United Kingdom in the nineteenth century. As we have seen, agency theory argues that the auditor acts as an intermediary between two (or more) parties in situations where the custody, administration, or use of economic resources has been delegated. Such a situation arose in Britain in the nineteenth century, when the creation of limited liability corporations resulted in separation of the providers of industrial capital from the managers who administered it. To monitor that investments were appropriately managed and controlled, the external auditing profession offered providers of capital an independent and objective opinion on the primary record of corporate accountability—published financial statements.

Two early influences on the development of early British external auditing were legislation and the accountancy profession. British legislation on financial auditing was initially patchy, but it progressively increased requirements for the audit of the financial statements of larger corporations and "public interest" organizations, such as the railways. Meanwhile, external auditing's focus on financial statements inevitably led to strong links with accountants. The first institutions of modern public accountancy (from whose ranks external auditors were drawn) first appeared in Scotland in 1854 and England in 1870 before spreading throughout the world. With the establishment of the American Institute of Certified Public Accountants in 1887, external auditing's professional center of gravity shifted to the United States, where it has since remained. Most twentieth-century developments in accounting have originated from the United States, which adapted rather than adopted earlier British models.

In the twentieth century, professional accountancy and auditing associations around the world gradually introduced certification programs for their members. They also developed auditing standards to codify and define the discipline's methodologies, technical base, and ethical foundations. The latter have tended to focus on auditor independence, without which the objectivity of the auditor's opinion is debased.

In addition to the role of professional accountancy bodies, another striking aspect of the external auditing profession has been the rise of powerful auditing firms. The history of early British auditing firms may seem far removed from today's auditing environment, but it is worthwhile to note their astonishing longevity. The auditing firms of nineteenth-century London were the forerunners of most of today's international, multidisciplinary auditing and accounting organizations. Among the names of London auditing firms in 1886 were several that have survived, in various combinations, to the modern era—Cooper Brothers; Deloitte, Dever, Griffiths; and Price, Waterhouse.[4]

Modern external auditing is therefore the result of almost two centuries of continuous evolution. Legislation in most industrialized nations requires the annual external audit of all but the smallest corporations, and restricts auditing to the certified members of professional accountancy and external auditing associations. The practice and theory of external auditing are constantly refined, often as a result of public disquiet over corporate failures or as a result of periodic corporate governance initiatives. Nonetheless, the core of external auditing has changed very little over the years, and has remained the "independent examination of, and expression of opinion on, the financial statements of an enterprise by a qualified auditor."[5]

External auditors seek to provide objective, independent opinions on the accuracy and fair presentation of financial statements. Their reports are not of interest solely to direct investors, but also to many other potentially interested parties and stakeholders—tax authorities, banks, creditors, employees, potential investors, and the wider community.

In the United States, the external auditor confirms that an audit of an organization has been conducted in accordance with generally accepted auditing standards, and gives an opinion on the extent to which financial statements "present fairly, in all material respects" the organization's financial position at the balance sheet date and the results of operations and cash flows for the period under review. The auditor's opinion must also cover the extent to which the financial statements have been prepared in accordance with generally accepted accounting principles. Only if there is no material doubt in these areas does the auditor give an unqualified opinion. In Britain, the terminology differs slightly: The British auditor gives an opinion on the extent to which audited financial statements provide a "true and fair" view and have been prepared in accordance with appropriate accounting standards and legislation.

The English-speaking world generally follows U.S. and British traditions of financial auditing. In recent years, other countries have tended to move closer to the English-speaking world's external auditing culture. For example, in countries such as France and Germany where adherence to fiscal legislation has traditionally driven accounting and external auditing, the notion of "true and fair" has entered legislation through the harmonization directives of the European Union (EU).

Internal Auditing

As its name implies, internal auditing is self-consciously distinct from external auditing, although there can be areas of overlap between the two disciplines. An important feature differentiates the two categories of auditing—the internal auditor's remit is normally far wider than that of the external auditor. External auditing concentrates on financial auditing, while internal auditing covers financial auditing, operational efficiency reviews, fraud investigations, compliance testing, environmental audit, and more.

Another important difference between the internal and external auditor is that the former has traditionally been an employee of the audited organization and reports to its management, while the latter tends to be fully independent, to maintain the objectivity of the external audit opinion. (In recent years, this internal versus external distinction has blurred, as external auditors have increasingly provided internal auditing services to their clients.)

It is notoriously difficult to define internal auditing, owing to the wide range of activities that fall within its remit. Searching for a definition that collapses so many types of activity may seem daunting. As one commentator has remarked: "In addition to financial audits, there are now environmental audits, value for money audits, management audits, forensic audits, data audits, intellectual property audits, medical audits, teaching audits, technology audits, stress audits, democracy audits, and many others besides. . . . What are we to make of this explosion of 'audits'?"[6]

Despite such difficulties, the Institute of Internal Auditors (IIA) has provided a satisfactory definition of internal auditing. The IIA has formulated a Professional Practices Framework for internal auditing that comprises standards, a code of ethics, educational products, and research literature. However, although the IIA has a respected certification program, it does not have exclusivity or monopolistic control in the field of internal auditing. Consequently, many thousands of internal auditors operate outside the IIA's framework. (This situation contrasts starkly with the status of external auditors, whose professional associations normally have exclusive certification within national boundaries.) The IIA's position is therefore somewhat curious, in that its standards and advice are followed by many internal auditors, yet are compulsory only for its members.[7]

Nonetheless, the IIA is a prestigious and highly respected institution with over 75,000 members throughout the world. Since its foundation in 1941, the IIA has been a tenacious promoter of internal auditing as a professional discipline, and has developed an authoritative literature on the subject. Its pronouncements deserve recognition as best practice by internal auditors, whether or not they are formal IIA members. The IIA's body of knowledge has grown to maturity like the topsoil of a forest, by slow accumulation over decades, and it would be unwise to neglect preexisting internal auditing theory of this nature.

The IIA currently defines internal auditing as "an independent, objective assurance and consulting activity designed to add value and improve an organization's operations. It helps an organization accomplish its objectives by bringing a systematic, disciplined approach to evaluate and improve the effectiveness of risk management, control, and governance processes." The IIA also states that internal auditing "reviews the reliability and integrity of information, compliance with policies and regulations, the safeguarding of assets, the economical and efficient use of resources, and established operational goals and objectives. Internal audits encompass financial activities and operations including systems, production, engineering, marketing, and human resources."[8]

This carefully constructed definition is wide, and several of its terms are worth noting. First, the reference to "independent" is not to be understood in terms similar to that of the external auditor, who is generally required to sever all formal links with an audited organization. Internal auditors tend to be employees (and sometimes also stockholders) of their organizations. Therefore, "independence" in the context of internal auditing does not refer to the formalities of financial independence, but to a state of mind characterized by objectivity and rigor.

Second, the reference to "assurance and consulting" indicates internal auditing's oscillation of emphasis between compliance and consultancy. While it is impossible to hold the jar of internal auditing to the light and expect compliance and consultancy to separate like oil and water, it is nonetheless clear that a suitable balance between these two characteristics is at the heart of all internal auditing activity. The precise weighting of the two strands of internal auditing is often a matter of taste, and of meeting the needs of an organization's particular circumstances.

Historically, internal auditors may have suffered from an image as the poor relation of the external auditor, but this has changed in recent years as corporate governance developments around the world have increasingly endorsed the importance of internal auditing. For example, the United Kingdom's 1999 *Turnbull Report* places explicit emphasis on the value of internal auditing alongside other corporate risk-monitoring mechanisms. The *Turnbull Report* requires corporations listed on the London Stock Exchange to assess annually the need for an internal audit function and, where there is an internal audit function, to annually review its scope of work, authority and resources.[9]

Aside from formal corporate governance requirements, the delays between periodic external audits are often deemed too long to respond to the complex, fast-moving management needs of modern organizations. Internal auditing meets this challenge by providing continuous compliance and advisory services to an organization's management.

Cooperation between External and Internal Auditors

A certain degree of overlap between the assurance services of external and internal auditors is probably inevitable. External reviews of the accuracy and fair presentation of periodic financial statements naturally complement continuous internal reviews of risks, controls, and management accounting. An important factor taken into consideration by the external auditor in reaching an opinion on financial statements is the reliability of accounting procedures and controls. Internal auditors are well placed to contribute to an assessment of controls, and the external auditor can clearly benefit from liaison with the internal auditor in this area.

Close cooperation between the two categories of auditors is therefore common, and mutually beneficial. Practical areas of cooperation typically include coordinating audit planning, sharing audit reports, and using complementary auditing methodologies and software tools. The sharing of knowledge of an organization and its risks tends to encourage more focused planning by both sets of auditors, and to eliminate duplication of work in areas where responsibilities overlap. Some activities remain the exclusive field of either the internal or external auditor, but mutual assistance can generally deliver a more efficient and effective overall auditing service.

Internal auditors sometimes perform segments of work on behalf of external auditors. An organization may have several remote international subsidiaries, for example, and the external and internal auditors may establish a shared program of visits to ease the logistical burdens of excessive travel. Internal auditors also frequently undertake periodic inventory counts on which external auditors rely. There are many other examples of internal auditors usefully performing work of an external auditing nature: Internal auditors often undertake transaction-intensive auditing tests, as they generally have time beyond the resources of their external peers to drill down into the details of financial statements. Cooperation of this nature can save an organization considerable audit fees.

Another way in which distinctions have blurred between the two categories of auditing has been the remarkable increase in recent years of the provision of internal auditing services by external auditors. In some countries, regulators have expressed concern that external auditors may compromise their independence by supplying internal auditing services to external audit customers, and have introduced measures either limiting such activity or forcing corporations to disclose the fees charged for nonexternal audit activities.[10]

AUDITING IN A GLOBALIZED WORLD

Globalization can be defined as the international integration of economic, political, and cultural activity. In a sense, limited globalization has occurred periodically throughout history—people, capital, and ideas flowed with relative ease within the empires of the Mongols, the Ottoman Turks, and the Romans, for example. Today, however, the scale of economic and cultural exchange is much vaster, owing to revolutionary developments in travel and communications and important political developments that bind the fortunes of nations more closely together. In the seventeenth century, it could take six months or more for a letter to travel from Europe to India. Today, e-mails can make the same journey in seconds. Indeed, modern India's software houses handle the transactions of many western companies, and it is with only slight exaggeration that India has been described as the "back office" to the world economy.

Regional political developments have also stimulated increases in international activity in recent decades. The collapse of communism in the former Soviet Union and Eastern Europe has opened that region to the rest of the world. Market reforms in China and India have introduced the world's two most populous countries to significant levels of international trade and investment, following around 50 years of aloofness from the global economy. Meanwhile, in Western Europe, the EU is the latest development of the 1957 Treaty of Rome and is increasingly binding to-

gether the nations of that region. There are many more examples of regional political and economic integration: Economic links among the nations of North
America have strengthened since the North American Free Trade Agreement
came into force in 1993, and southeast Asian countries have increasingly cooperated under the umbrella of the 1967 Association of Southeast Asian Nations.

Advances in telecommunications technology and political developments are
only part of the globalization phenomenon, however. Another (arguably more important) aspect concerns changes in outlook and philosophy. Having the technology to shrink distances is one thing, but the technology must be matched by the
desire to fully exploit it. The new spirit of globalization can be seen in activities
as diverse as African theater groups touring the former Soviet Union, Japanese
multinationals establishing subsidiaries in the United States, or European academics attending conferences in New Zealand.

Large organizations—both commercial and noncommercial—operate globally
through networks of subsidiaries and branches. Corporations in particular can find
many advantages in internationalizing their activities. They can tap sources of raw
materials, enter new markets, gain access to local knowledge, and achieve
economies of scale unimaginable in domestic markets. Importantly, organizations
can diversify their overall risk by spreading their operations in territories with very
different risk profiles.

Defenders of globalization claim that the international mobility of people,
finance, and ideas contributes to prosperity and cultural enrichment. In contrast,
skeptics accuse globalization of depressing the already weak economies of developing countries, and of trampling on local cultures by replacing indigenous vital-
ity with bland, internationalized products and services. The intensity of passion
inflamed by globalization debates is reflected in the emergence in recent years of
violent demonstrations at the meetings of international bodies such as the G8
group of industrialized nations. An exploration of the complex and acrimonious
globalization debate is beyond the scope of this book. It should nonetheless be acknowledged that globalization has serious problems, including the rise of violent
local nationalisms, and the exploitation by criminals and terrorists of the ease of
international travel and information transfer.

The rise of the multinational enterprise (or transnational corporation in current
jargon) has triggered the development of international auditing. Where organizations go, auditors follow. To give an opinion on the consolidated financial statements of an international corporation, external auditors need to verify the
underlying data directly, or rely on international colleagues to provide "mini-
opinions" on local accounts. As a consequence, the accountancy firms that audit
the world's largest corporations are themselves huge, multinational firms. Their
international reach offers clients the advantage of a common auditing approach for
subsidiaries around the world.

The professional duties of internal auditors also frequently include an international dimension. Faced with demands for coherent multinational management
structures, international corporations tend to strive for a degree of uniformity
among their remote and disparate entities. Internal auditors conduct assignments

globally to verify the appropriateness of local management practices, procedures, and controls, and to assess the accuracy of periodic management information sent to the parent organization.

The rewards of globalization can be high, as can be the risks. Entities separated by long distances or by significant cultural and linguistic barriers are notoriously difficult to control. Accounting practices, legal differences, and political and economic events can present formidable challenges to the management of an international organization. Even external auditing standards differ between countries. (Despite the promotion of International Standards on Auditing by the International Federation of Accountants, at the time of writing full harmonization of external auditing standards has not yet been achieved.) Similarly, although the IIA's professional standards for internal auditing are intended to be applicable worldwide, thousands of internal auditors operate outside the IIA's Professional Practices Framework: In the author's experience, internal auditing practice varies significantly around the world, reflecting cultural and economic influences.

USING THE BOOK

The Appendix of this book gives specific guidance on individual countries, and the information for each country is grouped under the headings of geography, history, demographics, languages, politics, economy, law and regulations, accountancy, culture, social etiquette, and further information. The author acknowledges that space does not allow full justice to the complexity of the countries covered in the Appendix: The aim is simply to offer a rounded outline of specific countries.

The "Further Information" sections include books on history, politics, and economics, and (where available) the Web pages of governments and national accounting and auditing institutes. All references are to English-language sources, unless stated otherwise. Where no local English-language information is available for accounting and auditing standards, general Web sites such as Deloitte Touche Tohmatsu's IAS Plus Web site (*www.iasplus.com/index.htm*) may be helpful. Chapter 7, "Select Bibliography and Other Sources of Information," includes pointers on where to obtain such information.

We commit astronomical outrage by grouping stars into constellations according to fictions of our own, and in a similar manner, we must give some coherence to the huge, complex, and almost inexhaustible subject matter of the Appendix. First, some selection was inevitable in the choice of country, but the world's major nations have been included. Second, compression and selectivity of material has been necessary for individual countries—condensing 4,000 years of Chinese history into less than 1,200 words requires ruthless editing.

Information in the Appendix is derived from many sources—the "Further Information" sections of individual countries; the books and Web resources listed in the Select Bibliography and Other Sources of Information in Chapter 7; and the author's own experiences of many of the countries discussed. Where sources conflict—on population statistics, for example—the author has reached his own judgment.

A cautionary note is in order for the user of the Appendix. The topics covered are constantly evolving. In politics and economics, things rarely stand still: Wars break out, borders change, countries change their names, and currencies are devalued. Even the accountancy field is in flux: In Japan, for example, a new accounting standards-setting body was established in 2001, with the declared aim of moving Japanese GAAP toward convergence with International Accounting Standards. The links to further information given for each country point toward sources of continuously updated information.

In each geographical region, tax havens have been treated separately. The economic impact of tax havens is wildly disproportionate to their size—they are often small islands or tiny patches of territory at the geographical fringes of major economies, but it is estimated that as much as one-third of the world's Gross Domestic Product passes through them at some point.[11] However, the subject of tax havens is a sensitive one, and the term is often used pejoratively. In recent years, the Organization for Economic Cooperation and Development (OECD) has brought pressure on territories it suspects of facilitating tax evasion and money laundering through lax standards in financial transparency and regulation. Countries targeted by the OECD include major nations as well as tiny tax havens.

In this book the term *Tax Havens and Investment Centers* refers to territories with notable investment-friendly features, and the inclusion or exclusion of a particular territory from this category does not imply any criticism of that territory's policies and practices. Some degree of judgment has been necessary in allocating countries to this rubric. For example, some may disagree with the placing of Singapore as an "investment center." Conversely, Switzerland has been included in the standard country section, while some commentators would classify it as an investment center owing to the legendary secrecy of its banking laws.

Finally, it is commonly acknowledged that international auditors act as unofficial ambassadors of their organizations, and sometimes of their countries. Coping with social and cultural nuances can be tricky, and it is easy to unwittingly cause offense. We may occasionally imagine ourselves peering mournfully at our international colleagues like fishes at the edges of adjacent tanks, with little hope of closing the chasm that divides us. As a modest means of closing this gap, the "Social Etiquette" sections for individual countries provide basic information on things to do, and things to avoid.

NOTES

1. The author does not propose to dwell at length on the theory and history of auditing, as the orientation of this book is principally practical. Chapter 7 includes further sources of information on these topics.

2. Lawrence B. Sawyer and Gerald Vinten, *The Manager and the Internal Auditor: Partners for Profit* (New York: John Wiley & Sons, 1996), 23.

3. William T. Baxter, *Accounting Theory* (New York: Garland, 1996), 347.
4. Derek Matthews, Malcolm Anderson, and John Richard Edwards, *The Priesthood of Industry: The Rise of the Professional Accountant in British Management* (New York and Oxford: Oxford University Press, 1998), 45.
5. Michael Power, *The Audit Society* (New York and Oxford: Oxford University Press, 1997), 17. A fuller definition is offered by Brenda Porter, Jon Simon, and David Hatherly, *Principles of External Auditing* (New York: John Wiley & Sons, 1996), 3: "Auditing is a systematic process of objectively gathering and evaluating evidence relating to assertions about economic actions and events in which the individual or organisation making the assertion has been engaged, to ascertain the degree of correspondence between those assertions and established criteria, and communicating the results to users of the reports in which the assertions are made." This definition was adapted from the work of the American Accounting Association's 1973 Committee on Basic Auditing Concepts.
6. Michael Power, *The Audit Explosion* (London: Demos, 1994), 1.
7. David O'Regan, "Genesis of a Profession: Towards Professional Status for Internal Auditing," *Managerial Auditing Journal*, Volume 16, no. 4 (2001): 215–226.
8. Available from the IIA Web site: *www.theiia.org/ecm/iiapro.cfm?doc_id= 269.*
9. Institute of Chartered Accountants in England and Wales, *Internal Control: Guidance for Directors on the Combined Code* [the "Turnbull Report"] (London: Institute of Chartered Accountants in England and Wales, 1999), section 46.
10. Following the high-profile accounting and external auditing issues that sent Enron and WorldCom into Chapter 11 bankruptcy in 2002, this area is likely to come under further scrutiny. In the United States, the Sarbanes-Oxley Act of 2002 was designed to shore up investor confidence in listed corporations. It resulted in hundreds of chief executives and chief financial officers swearing in front of notaries that "to the best of my knowledge" their latest annual and quarterly reports neither contained an "untrue statement" nor omitted any "material fact."
11. Austin Mitchell, Prem Sikka, John Christensen, Philip Morris, and Steven Filling, *No Accounting for Tax Havens* (Basildon, Essex, UK: Association for Accountancy and Business Affairs, 2002), passim.

2

International Organizations and Their Risks

AUDITING AND RISK

International best practice in corporate governance places significant emphasis on risk assessment and risk management. As a consequence, risk assessment practices have spread beyond their historic heartlands of the insurance and financial services sectors to enter the wider corporate mainstream. Both external and internal auditing are central to corporate governance, and risk assessment has become central to auditing. Professional auditing practice uses risk assessment to prioritize assignments, drive detailed auditing work, and assist organizations in meeting the varied and complex demands of modern corporate governance.

Risk assessment is therefore central to modern auditing. In the case of internal auditing, for example, it has been asserted that internal auditing "has passed through two dominant paradigms and is poised on the edge of a third. The first internal auditing paradigm focused on observing and counting . . . [the second] changed the internal audit paradigm from a focus on *re-performance* to a focus on *controls.* . . . The third paradigm is based on viewing the business process through a focus on risk."[1]

Risk can be defined as "a concept used to express uncertainty about events and/or their outcomes that could have a material effect on the goals and effectiveness of an organization."[2] The Institute of Internal Auditors' (IIA) definition of internal auditing, as we saw in Chapter 1, "Introduction—International Auditing," explicitly refers to the way in which internal auditing "helps an organization accomplish its objectives by bringing a systematic, disciplined approach to evaluate and improve the effectiveness of risk management, control, and governance processes."[3]

All organizations face risks specific to their particular circumstances, and an inventory of potential risks would be vast. Commonly encountered corporate risks include the technological obsolescence of manufactured products, liquidity risks, and reliance on a small number of customers or suppliers. Risks of this nature are faced by all organizations, localized or global. Multinational organizations face a number of additional risks that derive directly from their international activities, and this chapter summarizes some of these common risks.

Few of the risks in the following discussions are stand-alone items. For example, the interplay of economic and accounting risks is often illustrated in countries where experiences of hyperinflation have led to the development of local accounting standards to cope with the phenomenon. In Brazil, for example, the *Conselho Federal de Contabilidade* established accounting standards in the 1970s based on inflation accounting. Multinationals with operations in Brazil have therefore traditionally faced (at least) two risks related to hyperinflation—economic dislocation and accounting compliance. In complex transnational organizations, the interrelationship of risks (as we will see in Chapter 4, "Organization-Wide Risk Assessment") makes organizational risk assessment extremely challenging.

The following discussions on risk make no assumptions about an organization's methodologies or strategies for risk assessment and risk management. Micromanagement of the specific risks discussed here is considered in Chapter 3, "Managing International Risks."

ECONOMIC RISKS

A multinational organization's risk profile is significantly affected by the macroeconomic environments of the territories and markets in which it operates or invests. A multinational corporation's risk profile can differ both between countries and over time in specific markets. Variations in interest rates, for example, can lead to significant differences in the duration of transaction cycles—customer settlement periods can vary significantly both over time and between countries.

Multinational corporations with subsidiaries in mature markets are sensitive to fractional shifts in interest or inflation rates, but in more volatile parts of the world economic "shocks" can halve the value of a currency in less than a month, or send inflation rates to astronomical heights. In late 2001, for example, Argentina experienced the worst economic crisis in its history following several years of apparent stability. This resulted in the end of an 11-year peg of the Argentine peso to the U.S. dollar. In a matter of weeks, the value of the peso fell by 70 percent, unemployment soared, payments of state pensions were interrupted, and up to one-third of the population was plunged into poverty. Food riots and widespread looting occurred.

Sometimes entire regions suffer sudden and severe recessions. The Asian financial crisis that started in 1997 (and whose effects are still felt at the time of writing in 2002) saw free-falling currencies, tumbling real estate prices, corporate bankruptcies, and street violence. Indonesia, South Korea, and Thailand were among the economies badly affected by the "domino" effect of the Asian crisis. The Indonesian rupiah plummeted by three-quarters of its value against the U.S. dollar in the first six months of the crisis.

The effect of international economic risks is not limited to organizations with operations in foreign territories. An organization's operation may be based entirely in the home country, yet it may depend on volatile, risky markets for a large proportion of its revenues. For example, the sales of luxury automobiles nose-dived during the Asian financial crisis, as the middle classes in the affected countries found themselves unable to keep up lease payments on their imported prestige cars.

The preceding examples may be considered extreme. Nonetheless, even less catastrophic economic events can dramatically alter markets in less volatile economies. In the United Kingdom, for example, real estate markets are notoriously sensitive to small changes in interest rates: In 2002, record increases in British property prices resulted from the Bank of England's decision to maintain historically low base rates.

Currency issues often vex multinational organizations, as exchange rate fluctuations and devaluations can seriously affect the performance of specific economies. In Turkey, for example, a financial crisis that began in February 2001 caused the Turkish lira to lose half its value against major currencies, and the country was plunged into its worst recession in 50 years. Volatile exchange rates also affect an organization's decisions on matters ranging from transfer price levels to the timings of the settlement of trading balances.

Another important aspect of international economic risk is the impact of market structure on national economic practices. For simplification, we may distinguish three main types of economic pattern, each with distinctive capital market structures: the *laissez faire* capitalism of the English-speaking world, the *dirigiste* capitalism of continental Europe, and the command economies of socialist countries.

Corporate capital in the English-speaking world has traditionally been channeled through equity markets. Corporations actively make themselves attractive to investors in both primary and secondary security markets, with the result that the mature stock exchanges of the United States, the United Kingdom, and other English-speaking countries are surrounded by sophisticated support services—analysts, accountants, and (of course) auditors who provide assurance on the fair presentation of published financial statements.

In contrast, continental European corporations have tended to fund their activities through corporate debt rather than equity capital. The continental pattern is not restricted to mainland Europe, as it is evident in territories colonized by European powers (e.g., francophone Africa and South America) and in other countries, like Japan, that have traditionally followed European practices. Moreover, while the equity investor has traditionally been seen (until recently, perhaps) as the major corporate stakeholder in the English-speaking world, in continental Europe the major stakeholders have tended to be the debt financier, the creditor, and the state.

Of course, sophisticated equity markets exist in many countries that follow the continental European pattern, but the role of bank lending remains significant. The relative importance of equity markets in continental European and English-speaking countries can be illustrated with statistics—in 2001, equity market capitalization as a proportion of Gross Domestic Product was 2.18 in the United Kingdom and 1.97 in the United States, but only 0.94 in France and 0.61 in Germany.[4]

One consequence of the reduced role of equity markets in countries that follow continental European economic patterns is that the support services of capitalism tend to be less developed than in the English-speaking world. The size of the accountancy profession in different countries is a guide to the importance of equity investment in the national economy. The United States has over 330,000 accountants, and the United Kingdom 130,000, but the statistics for France are 16,000, for Japan 13,000, and for Germany only 10,000.[5]

The economies of communist and socialist states are another distinctive economic category. Planned economies are geared toward the achievement of national targets and are characterized by a "top-down" command culture. These economic patterns are increasingly rare and only a few, last bastions of the pure command economy—such as North Korea—still exist at the time of writing. Many of the former socialist economies have embraced market philosophies to a greater or lesser extent, and their economies follow mixed patterns of command controls and spontaneous markets. For example, China and Vietnam have both implemented economic liberalization (while clinging to rigid, one-party political centralization).

Multinational corporations may struggle to adapt to countries where the investment culture differs from the domestic pattern. For example, multinational corporations based in English-speaking countries may find it difficult to come to terms with some aspects of the "continental" culture, such as the absence of a well-developed local accountancy and external auditing profession. Similarly, corporations accustomed to the continental pattern may have trouble coming to terms with the higher levels of public scrutiny associated with the English-speaking economies—disclosure in financial statements, for example, has traditionally been more onerous in the English-speaking world.

For convenience, the preceding comments distinguished between three types of economic pattern. Naturally, the world is more complicated than this simple analysis might suggest. Many economies are mixed, or are in transition from one category to another. Other economies exhibit uniquely local characteristics. In South Korea, for example, the oligopolistic dominance of the *chaebol* does not fit into any of the economic patterns we have discussed. The *chaebol* are massive, family-controlled industrial conglomerates that enjoy political influence, and are a uniquely Korean phenomenon. Similarly, the economic importance of Chinese communities throughout Southeast Asia (e.g., Indonesia and Malaysia) suggests that some economic structures have a strong ethnic base. Patterns of economic activity vary greatly around the world, and the Appendix includes information on the economic characteristics of individual countries.

POLITICAL FACTORS

The varied political contexts in which multinational organizations operate are a crucial area of risk. Revolution, war, and politically motivated violence can be immensely disruptive, stifling economic and cultural activity. The sheer pace of political events can be disconcertingly swift—as former British Prime Minister Harold Wilson famously remarked, "A week is a long time in politics."

The September 11 attacks in the United States in 2001 are an example of political violence with immense global repercussions. The attacks took a huge human toll and triggered a global response by the U.S. government in which co-ordinated diplomatic, economic, and military pressure was brought to bear on armed militant groups. The economic impact of the attacks was also significant, particularly on the commercial air travel industry. U.S. carriers were the most seriously affected, but the impact of September 11 also pushed several already-troubled European airlines over the brink. The national carriers of Switzerland (Swiss Air) and Belgium (Sabena) had little operational exposure to the United States, as their flight routes were centered on Europe. The events in the United States nonetheless crystallized existing problems, and drove both airlines into bankruptcy within two months of the September 11 attacks.

Multinational organizations can face risks from adverse political events in specific territories. For example, the Iranian revolution of 1979 led to the establishment of a theocratic Islamic administration headed by Ayatollah Khomeini. The revolution was a prelude to an unstable and violent period in Iran's history, including an eight-year war against Iraq. Many western multinational corporations and individuals left Khomeini's Iran, as the political climate turned against the west. (Militant students, for example, held U.S. citizens hostage in the U.S. Embassy in Tehran from late 1979 to early 1981.) Political relations between Iran and the west remain troubled to the present day.

There are many examples of political events interfering with important sources of raw materials and commodities. Diamond-rich Sierra Leone has faced extreme political instability and civil war since the West African country's independence in 1961, and the massive oil reserves of the Mid East are located in a region of immense political volatility. In the Gulf War of 1991, a coalition led by the United States forced the Iraqi army out of Kuwait and preserved western access to the oil-rich Arabian Peninsula, but at the time of writing the region still walks a political tightrope.

Even changes of governments in stable democracies can result in significant economic policy shifts. For example, two parties with opposing ideologies dominate the United Kingdom's political landscape. Alternations of power between the right-leaning Conservative Party and the left-leaning Labour Party result in periodic, radical shifts in political and economic policy, in matters ranging from privatization to tax rates.

The results of dramatic political dislocation are not always negative. The political revolutions of the late 1980s and early 1990s that led to the collapse of the Soviet Iron Curtain in Eastern Europe ended 50 years of economic and cultural semi-isolation. For example, German unification after the fall of the Berlin Wall opened up post-communist East Germany to foreign investment. Similarly, the rise to political power of the anticommunist trade union "Solidarity" opened Poland to foreign investment, while the "velvet revolution" of writer-politician Vaclav Havel brought political and economic freedom to the Czech Republic.

Whether the effects are positive or negative, political change therefore tends to be a significant risk for international organizations. The opportunity costs of failing to benefit from suddenly advantageous political conditions can be huge, as corporations that were slow to enter postcommunist Eastern Europe learned. On the other hand, the effects of a change of political regime hostile to foreign organizations can be disastrous. An abrupt change of regime can lead to the sudden cancellation of contracts with foreign companies, and corporations' assets may be seized in politically inspired nationalization programs, with insufficient compensation. A famous example of the latter was Egyptian leader Gamal Abdul Nasser's 1956 nationalization of the Anglo-French Suez Canal—an event that led to war involving Egypt, Britain, France, and Israel.

The effects of political events can be felt for many years. For example, the German Nazi regime took over a U.S. corporation's automobile plants during World War II and used slave labor in the plants' operations. Half a century later, victims of the human rights abuses alleged that the corporation had benefited from their slave labor, and they demanded compensation. The corporation did not accept responsibility for events during World War II, claiming that it had lost control of its German operations during that period, but it did offer $13 million in compensation to surviving slave laborers. Whether or not the corporation was responsible for its German operations during World War II, the public relations damage caused by the allegations was significant, and illustrated the potentially long-running effects of serious political events.

Political and economic risks are often closely linked. States offer subsidies, tax breaks, financial aid, and other interventionist programs to boost specific sectors. In contrast, boycotts or regulatory hurdles can restrict foreign investment: U.S. sanctions against Fidel Castro's Cuba are a good example of political decisions with major economic impact.

A final area to consider is a country's participation in international political bodies, which can transform trade and cultural exchange. In Europe, a country's membership of the European Union (EU) gives it liberal access to the member countries' markets. Goods, capital, and individuals circulate within the EU with few restrictions. Conversely, the EU's protectionist trade policies vis-à-vis the rest of the world have led to friction in global markets. In 2001, for example, the EU and the United States negotiated an end to the so-called "banana war" following years of acrimonious dispute regarding the EU's alleged preferential treatment of banana producers in former European colonies.

It is clear that political matters are of crucial importance to the investment and operational decisions of international organizations. The Appendix summarizes country-specific political information.

LEGAL AND REGULATORY REQUIREMENTS

Legal and regulatory requirements around the world create both headaches and opportunities for global organizations. To reduce a complex subject to manageable proportions, we will distinguish between three different legal models—the common-law systems of English-speaking countries; the highly codified legal cultures of continental Europe; and the centrally issued directives of communist states. In the earlier section, "Economic Risks," a similar threefold analysis of economic cultures was used; this model is necessarily simplistic and serves only as a starting point for more detailed analysis.

The common-law tradition of the English-speaking world is a "roots-up" legal culture based on custom and precedent. This legal tradition is based on responses to specific problems arising in individual cases, rather than on statements of general legal principles. The common law allows judges not only to interpret and apply law, but also to create it. From their origins in England, common law systems have spread to many parts of the world colonized by the British—North America, Australia, New Zealand, the Indian subcontinent, Ireland, and parts of Africa and the Caribbean. The ever-increasing rise of legislation has eroded many common-law features, yet it remains a powerful force.

Common-law jurisprudence may be seen as an expression of an empiricist and pragmatic cultural philosophy that contrasts with the "top down" legalistic culture of continental Europe.[6] Continental legal systems are derived from Roman law, and in their modern forms they emphasize the codification of legal principles. The best-known embodiment of continental legal codification is the French *Code Napoléon* (CN). The CN has affected not only France, but all European countries (e.g., Italy) where the cultural imprints of the Napoleonic invasions are still felt. In theory, if not always in practice, the codified nature of European legal culture gives less power to judges, who interpret and apply law rather than make it.

The third category is that of the communist world, whose legal culture is very different from the common law and continental traditions. Law in communist societies has tended to be overtly politicized, and has been apt to change at the whim of the ruling political elite. Communist parties have themselves tended to be a source of new law, in the form of directives grafted on to preexisting indigenous traditions. Communist directives have generally been aimed at social and economic control, and have been characterized by heavy bureaucracy, limited individual rights, and the suppression of political dissent. As most of the formerly communist states are currently in various states of reform, the "pure" communist legal system is in retreat (outside one or two remaining territories, such as North Korea). In countries like China, the legal system shows elements of both western-style jurisprudence and traditional "party directives."

Differences in legal culture can affect the efficiency and effectiveness with which international organizations operate throughout the world, and unfamiliarity with any of the legal models discussed previously may cause problems. In particular, business law may be very different between countries. The recovery of customer receivables, for example, has very different legal backing in different jurisdictions. Moreover, privacy laws are at varied levels of sophistication throughout the world—the EU has more onerous requirements than many other countries. Another factor to consider is the speed with which the wheels of justice turn in different countries. In India, for example, civil cases can take literally decades to be resolved. The slow-moving nature of specific legal systems can be a major risk for international organizations.

Before moving on to consider broader regulatory matters, it is worth mentioning that the threefold model does not cover other types of legal culture based on ethnic, religious, or cultural grounds. For example, Islamic Shari'a law forbids the charging of bank interest in many Muslim countries. The Appendix includes country-specific legal information.

The spectrum of regulatory environments is wide. At one end of the spectrum, tax havens have few regulatory restrictions, while at the other extreme some countries groan under heavy-handed bureaucracy. Some postcommunist countries in Eastern Europe, for example, maintain currency controls that require documented state approval of all original invoices relating to foreign currency payments. In transaction-intensive industries, the need to obtain official approval of every invoice before payment can be a serious administrative challenge.

Regulatory hurdles can take many forms. As mentioned earlier, foreign currency controls can present serious obstacles to international business operations, preventing timely settlement of intercompany balances and restricting the repatriation of profits. Contravention of export and import requirements can result in heavy penalties, disruption of an organization's operations, and even seizure of its assets. In 1999, for example, a customs dispute led the authorities in the lucrative Mid East market of Dubai to close retail outlets selling the products of a major French luxury goods firm.

Other areas of potential regulatory difficulty include environmental issues and employment matters. Compliance with environmental laws and regulations can be problematic, not least in terms of adverse publicity for real or perceived pollution. A major oil company suffered adverse publicity in the mid-1990s over its attempts to dump an oil storage structure in the North Atlantic, and it was forced to change its plans following a high profile campaign by environmental activists. The campaign included well-publicized boycotts of the corporation's products.

In terms of both legislation and custom, employment regulations can be a minefield for an organization operating in an unfamiliar country. In post-apartheid South Africa, for example, affirmative action legislation requires employers to achieve an equitable ethnic balance of their employees, and failure to meet quota targets can result in severe fines. An example of a customary employment practice is the provision of staff loans in some developing countries—an organization may have a general policy against such practices, but it may have to be flexible to adapt to the customs of specific territories.

Collective bargaining is common in countries with strong syndicalist traditions, such as France. Going over the heads of trade unions may be dangerous, as inappropriate behavior may lead to strikes that severely disrupt operations and damage the organization's reputation. Another dangerous area in employment matters is the use of intermediary organizations in developing countries. By subcontracting employment contracts, an organization can easily become embroiled in exploitative practices such as child labor. Even if an intermediary organization is directly to blame for such activity, public opinion may hold a multinational organization ultimately responsible.

Activists monitor very closely the behavior of multinational corporations in developing countries. In early 2002, for example, the international aid agency Oxfam Community Aid Abroad released a report—"We Are Not Machines"— that publicly criticized conditions at Indonesian factories supplying major western sportswear manufacturers. Whether or not such allegations are well-founded, adverse publicity of this nature is extremely damaging to international corporations.

TAXATION

International organizations must grapple with the taxation requirements of the countries in which they operate. Taxation systems and tax rates differ significantly around the world, and keeping up with shifting fiscal legislation can be difficult, especially in countries in transition from command to market economies. Penalties for tax errors can be punitive.

National tax authorities and the influential Organization for Economic Co-operation and Development (OECD) are also taking an increasing interest in transfer pricing arrangements, which are often used to manipulate the distribution of taxable income around multinational organizations. Tax authorities are increasingly demanding evidence that transactions relating to the transfer of goods and services around international groups are priced on an arm's length basis.

Effective tax planning can reduce international liabilities, and tax considerations can affect where an international organization operates, where it raises capital, and how it remits profits to the parent organization. Some parts of the world—notably the EU—are well known for relatively heavy taxation. Tax havens offer potential tax savings, but they are currently under pressure from national and international organizations. Following the September 11 attacks of 2001, the U.S. government in particular has taken a keen interest in the potential use of tax havens as channels for the finance of illegal activities. In 2001, the Patriot Act was designed to combat money laundering.

In 2000, the OECD drafted a list of 35 "non-cooperative" countries and territories, which it criticized for allegedly poor standards of financial transparency, tax regulation, and exchange of information. Most of the territories subsequently committed to improvements in regulation and transparency, but in 2002, the OECD identified seven territories for further criticism. The OECD backed up its criticism with the threat of "defensive measures" by its 30 member states. These "measures" may involve the estrangement of specific territories from global financial systems. International organizations should therefore be careful before choosing to operate from a particular low tax territory, should the OECD subsequently deem it an "uncooperative tax haven."[7]

In many countries—above all in Western Europe and the former colonies of European powers—tax laws often drive accountancy practice. In Germany, for example, commercial accounts and tax accounts are the same, while in the English-speaking world tax accounts are normally prepared separately from commercial accounts. This topic is reviewed in more detail in the following paragraphs.

GENERALLY ACCEPTED ACCOUNTING PRINCIPLES

The rise of multinational organizations and the effects of global market forces have increased pressure for the international harmonization of accounting practice. However, at the time of writing, Generally Accepted Accounting Principles (GAAP) still vary significantly around the world. A number of organizations, including the United Nations and the EU, have attempted to encourage regional or global accounting harmonization, but by far the most significant body in this field is the International Accounting Standards Board (IASB).

The IASB has replaced the International Accounting Standards Committee (IASC). Established in 1973, the IASC's founding members were the accounting professions of the United States, the United Kingdom and Ireland, Australia, Canada, Japan, West Germany, France, Holland, and Mexico. The focus of the IASC was to produce International Accounting Standards (IAS) to encourage global accountancy harmonization. The IASC had mixed success in promoting global accounting harmonization. One reason for slow acceptance of IAS was a perception in some parts of the world that the London-based IASC leaned too heavily toward the accounting practices of the English-speaking countries.

After the IASB succeeded the IASC in 2001, the momentum of IAS acceptance appears to have gathered pace. For example, a major coup for the harmonizing project has been the EU decision to adopt IAS for listed corporations by 2005. In some EU countries—the United Kingdom, for example—standards-setting bodies are preempting the 2005 deadline and are already redrafting national standards in line with IAS. The interest of the International Organization of Securities Commissions (IOSCO) in removing barriers to the effective functioning of international capital markets has led it to support the work of the IASB.

However, for a variety of reasons—including inertia and nationalism—progress around the world in harmonizing accountancy practice has been slow. The standards-setting bodies of many countries have declared their intention to conform local GAAP to IAS, yet have reserved the right to adapt standards to suit local circumstances. This has inevitably led to continuing discrepancies between the GAAP of various countries. (The Appendix outlines the approaches of individual countries' standards-setting bodies to international GAAP harmonization.)

Another important organization in global accountancy harmonization is the International Federation of Accountants (IFAC). The IFAC aims to develop the accountancy profession worldwide, and to promote international consistency in its practices. The IFAC's activities are wide, and cover guidance on education, ethics, and management accounting. The IFAC also issues International Standards on Auditing (ISA), intended to encourage international harmonization in external auditing.

Another notable voice in the harmonization field is the International Forum on Accountancy Development (IFAD). The IFAD was established following the devastating impact of the Asian financial crisis of the late 1990s, and its members include IOSCO, the IFAC, and major international financial institutions such as the World Bank and the International Monetary Fund. The IFAD's aims include the harnessing of the resources of the accountancy profession and international financial institutions to promote transparent financial reporting in accordance with sound corporate governance, and to develop the accounting and auditing capabilities of developing countries.

This chapter has so far suggested a threefold analytical structure to differentiate between the world's economic and legal cultures: the models of the English-speaking world, continental Europe, and the command economies. This threefold structure is also valuable in outlining international GAAP differences, as it separates three distinctive streams of accounting methodology.

As discussed in Chapter 1, the modern accountancy profession first developed in the English-speaking world. From its early days in Britain, the torch was passed to the United States, as evidenced by the survival of the names of early British pioneers: "Such founding fathers of U.S. accounting as Arthur Young and James Marwick (whose names are now incorporated into the names of the firms Ernst & Young and KPMG, respectively) were expatriate Britons."[8] As a result, the motor of accountancy development has remained in the English-speaking world, and it is unsurprising that the English-speaking countries tend to possess the most sophisticated accountancy professions. This has led to the international dominance of the large Anglo-American external auditing firms, and the greatest theoretical work on formal accounting practice has emerged from the standards-setting bodies of English-speaking countries.

GAAP in the English-speaking countries tends to be more flexible than elsewhere in the world: The aim is to "present fairly" in the United States, or to reach a "true and fair view" in England. Accounting standards tend to promote the financial substance of transactions over their legal form, and they permit a fairly wide degree of judgment in the preparation of financial statements.

GAAP under the continental European pattern is generally less judgmental than its English-speaking counterpart. Some commentators describe the European pattern as "conservative," to the extent that it subordinates the role of subjective application of accounting principles and fair presentation to narrowly defined adherence to tax rules. This reflects traditions that the main user of financial statements in the English-speaking world has traditionally been the equity investor, while continental financial statements have traditionally been prepared with the debt financier and tax authorities in mind.

Tax regulations have therefore been historically important in driving continental accounting practice. For example, in the United Kingdom the amortization of property and equipment tends to be based on estimates of assets' useful lives and residual values. For tax purposes, the judgmentally derived amortization rates are replaced by fixed "capital allowances." In the United Kingdom, therefore, corporations tend to produce two sets of financial statements—the "true and fair" accounts for use by investors and other stakeholders, and tax accounts for the fiscal authorities. In contrast, in Germany only one set of financial statements is prepared to cover both commercial and fiscal purposes, and amortization rates follow tax rules.

The traditionally flexible approach to accountancy of the English-speaking world therefore contrasts with formulaic continental European practices. The European approach to legal codification that is reflected in the *Code Napoléon* (as discussed in the section "Legal and Regulatory Requirements") is evident in another characteristic of European-style accounting—the use of nationally determined charts of accounts. Unlike the flexible approach to account numbering systems in English-speaking countries, European charts of accounts are intended to ensure that organizations follow systematic account numbering. For example, the French *plan comptable général* (general accounting plan) exists in slightly different formats for different industries, and provides definitive account numbering patterns that are used as the basis for preparing tax returns. In the use of charts of accounts, one can perceive the all-pervasive importance of taxation and national macroeconomic planning as motors of European accounting practice.

In recent years, EU directives on accountancy harmonization have introduced British accounting traditions into continental European accounting practices. This has led, among other things, to the introduction across Europe of the notion of financial statements giving a "true and fair" view. The EU harmonization process is still at an early stage, and there have been some difficulties in blending the accounting cultures of Europe and the English-speaking world. Nonetheless, recent developments have resulted in a significant rapprochement of the two accounting traditions.

Accounting practice in command economies is very different from both the *laissez-faire* capitalist culture of the English-speaking world and the *dirigiste* market systems of continental Europe. Command economy accounting focuses on the allocation of state resources to various economic enterprises. The state drives the ultimate decisions in the planned economy, and accounting practice serves as an instrument for the state to monitor the source and application of funds. Command economy accounting therefore focuses on statistics as well as financial statements in the traditional sense: Production quantities in relation to state-determined quotas are often given as much prominence as financial data.

The concept of "fair presentation" is almost entirely absent from the command economy's accounting culture. Accounting in such a context is highly bureaucratic, heavily clerical, relatively low skilled, and resistant to theoretical innovation. Adherence to central directives is the overriding concern. Charts of accounts similar to the continental European pattern facilitate state control of the national economy. Pure command economies are now very few in number, and many postcommunist systems are currently in transition to market, or mixed, economies.

In summary, accounting differences arise because of local economic, political, and even cultural factors. Common areas of international GAAP difference include lease accounting and the treatment of employee benefits. The Appendix gives details of the accounting cultures of individual countries.

LINGUISTIC DIFFERENCES

Linguistic differences are a source of potential miscommunication, and are clearly a risk for international organizations. In the case of languages with little or no linguistic affinity, the dangers of miscommunication can be extremely serious. Take, for example, the case of a German corporation with a Japanese subsidiary. The immense linguistic barriers mean that German speakers can pick up Japanese only with great effort and commitment—and vice versa. Even written communications are mutually unintelligible, owing to the different writing systems used by the two languages. In such circumstances, the only solution is to employ staff with appropriate bilingual skills, at either the parent organization or the subsidiary (or both).

Even so, the flow of information can be tricky when all communications to and from an international entity must pass through the hands of a small number of individuals for translation.

Differences between languages that share some linguistic affinity are alleviated by common vocabulary and grammatical structures. The Romance languages can be taken as an example. These languages are the modern descendents of Latin, and are derived from Latin's fragmentation into regional dialects after the fall of the Roman Empire. They include Italian, Spanish, French, Portuguese, and Romanian. The Romance linguistic family is spoken in Southern Europe and in the former colonies of the European Romance-speaking countries—South and Central America, francophone Africa, and parts of the Caribbean, the South Pacific, and Asia.

The Romance languages are not always mutually intelligible, but a relatively small effort is generally needed by speakers of any of these languages to learn another member of the language group. In the written language, moreover, pronunciation complications disappear and differences narrow even further. All Romance languages used the Roman script and it is possible, for example, for a Spanish speaker to quickly get the gist of an Italian newspaper.

French and Italian accounting terminology can be used to illustrate the mitigating effects of linguistic familiarity within the Romance language family. In French and Italian, respectively, inventory is translated as *inventaire* and *inventario*, sales as *ventes* and *vendite*, prices as *prix* and *prezzi*, and accounting as *comptabilité* and *contabilità*. (Interestingly, this small sample of basic accounting terminology shows more than French-Italian vocabulary affinities—it also displays Latin semantic influences on English.)

A word of caution is appropriate, however. Superficial similarities between languages often disguise crucial nuances. For example, one can take the well-known *faux amis* ("false friends," similar words with different meanings) between French and English. The French verb *demander* means "to ask" in English, and not "to demand," and mistranslation can impart an aggressive tone to a request.

Another linguistic consideration is miscommunication arising from varieties of the same language. English, for example, has many varieties and dialects—the English used in the United States is quite distinct from that heard in England, Australia, India, and elsewhere. Hybrid versions of English sometimes spring up, such as Singapore's Singlish, that incorporates Malay, Chinese, and Tamil vocabulary, and Kenya's Sheng, that mixes Swahili with English. Spellings are another obvious source of difference between categories of English, and vocabulary can also be quite varied. In an auditing context, a well-known example is the British use of the term "stock" to describe what in the United States is called "inventory." Conversely, the U.S. term "stock" refers to British "shares."[9]

A final point to mention in this area is the effect of a country's literacy levels. A corporation that operates in countries with low literacy levels may have difficulty communicating with all employees. For example, posting corporate newsletters on the notice boards of warehouses where a large proportion of the workforce is illiterate is unlikely to foster adequate communication with employees. Alternative forms of communication are required, such as periodic verbal briefings.

CULTURAL FACTORS

The topic of cultural differences is complex and sensitive, and ranges from ethical values to social behavior. One should tread carefully in this territory, as it is easy to unwittingly cause offense. Nonetheless, overlooking the importance of international cultural differences would be unwise, as it is a key factor in the smooth and efficient running of an organization.

A society's shared values and behavioral patterns can be sanctioned by social custom, law, or economic circumstances, and can vary significantly between countries. For example, the offering of inducements and bribery is virtually essential in doing business in some parts of the world. Customs officials, police officers, and business contacts may be unwilling to perform their duties without the greasing of palms. It would be unfair to single out individual countries, but the organization Transparency International monitors global corruption, and produces fascinating corruption rankings of countries.[10]

Dividing lines between legitimate inducements and bribery are narrow, and international organizations must establish clear policies and monitor their actions carefully. The 1977 Foreign Corrupt Practices Act (FCPA) and its amendment, the 1988 Trade and Competitive Act, make it unlawful for U.S. organizations and individuals (and their overseas employees) to bribe foreign government officials to obtain or retain business. The FCPA distinguishes between bribes and what it terms "facilitating" or "expediting" payments. The latter categories of payment secure the performance of a routine action, and may occasionally be justified. However, whether an action constitutes a bribe or a facilitating payment is often decided in court, and severe criminal and civil penalties can arise from FCPA contravention.

The FCPA is perhaps the most sophisticated antibribery legislation in the world, although many other countries have similar provisions. In 1998, for example, the president of Pakistan promulgated the "Eradication of Corrupt Business Practices Ordinance," which was aimed at curbing corruption. However, cultural variations in readiness to obey the law vary significantly between countries. In some parts of the world, illegal evasion of tax payments is almost a national pastime. Again, it would be unfair to single out specific countries, but this trend is marked in nations that have experienced overbearing and corrupt political regimes. Some postcommunist states and developing countries, accustomed to corruption at the very highest levels of government, exhibit these cultural trends. A multinational organization that operates in such an environment clearly faces risks in keeping on the right side of local, domestic, and international law, and can suffer severe public embarrassment if unpalatable practices come to light (however far from the parent organization they are committed).

In addition to bribery, other forms of corrupt practices faced by international organizations include piracy and bootlegging. In some countries, problems of this nature are chronic. The police and other enforcement authorities may give low priority to such matters, or may lack adequate resources to address them. To take an example, in early 2002 the United States announced trade sanctions worth $75 million against Ukraine, after judging that country's compact disc antipiracy measures to be ineffective.

Other cultural concerns include nepotism, which is widespread in some cultures. In such an environment, matters ranging from employment decisions to the awarding of supplier contracts may be heavily influenced by family connections. A preference for cash payments in some countries is also another source of risk, as cash payments may facilitate improper payments or tax evasion (owing to the difficulty of unraveling the audit trails of cash transactions). Respect for hierarchy is another source of potential risk in an international context. Some countries—notably those on the Pacific Rim influenced by Confucian thought—are characterized by a respect for authority that can be positive in promoting a cohesive working environment. However, the negative side of a heightened respect for authority can be reluctance to question or criticize the actions of senior management, even when improper behavior is suspected. This is, of course, a vast generalization, although it is a point worth consideration by international organizations.

In essence, international organizations should not get embroiled in any improper behavior, irrespective of how "acceptable" such practices may be locally, and how far from the parent company any such activity may be undertaken. Of course, not all considerations of cultural differences relate to problems of this nature. Adapting products to local market preferences is another area affected by cultural differences, and variations in local recipes for international brands of soda drinks and beer are good examples.

A final area for consideration in this category is the culture of the multinational organization itself. The degree of centralization within an organization will reflect the way in which it operates: Largely autonomous branches will tend to behave far differently from ones tightly controlled by a corporate head office.

Cultural matters are discussed further in Chapter 5, "The Logistics of Auditing," in the context of the practical logistics of international audits. The Appendix also gives guidance on country-specific cultural factors and social etiquette.

OTHER MATTERS

This chapter has touched on many sources of international risk—economic, political, regulatory, accounting, linguistic, and cultural. These are not the only risks facing organizations that choose to operate globally. Natural disasters around the world kill and injure staff, destroy buildings, hamper communications, and interrupt operations. For example, several recent catastrophes—the Turkey earthquake of 1999, the Venezuelan floods of 2000, and the Indian earthquake of 2000—have each claimed over 20,000 lives. Organizations that operate in areas of volatile natural phenomena are clearly at risk from such natural disasters.

Another area of concern is the corporate culture of recently acquired entities. In any environment, it can be challenging to integrate newly acquired subsidiaries, as an acquired operation may have inherited ethical values at odds with that of the new parent organization. In an international context these challenges increase, as the acquired entity's historical baggage can be complicated by cultural, linguistic, and communication problems. Inculcating new values may be difficult, especially if the acquired entity is located far from the head office.

Another area to consider is the size of international subsidiaries. Smaller entities tend to carry inherent control risks, as segregation of duties may be difficult to achieve with low employee numbers, while charismatic individuals may be tempted to override local controls. Further, dependence on key staff and planning for employee succession tends to be a perennial concern in smaller entities. Finally, communication can be difficult internationally. In addition to linguistic and cultural matters, time zone differences, poor mail infrastructures, and power cuts can frustrate communication between countries.

International organizations face many risks, which often combine into dangerous operational cocktails. The following chapter considers some methods of risk mitigation.

NOTES

1. David McNamee and Georges M. Selim, *Risk Management: Changing the Internal Auditor's Paradigm* (Altamonte Springs, FL: Institute of Internal Auditors Research Foundation, 1998), xiii [emphasis in original].

2. McNamee and Selim, 125.

3. Available from *www.theiia.org/ecm/iiapro.cfm?doc_id=269*.

4. Christopher Nobes and Robert Parker, *Comparative International Accounting*, 7th ed. (New York and London: Prentice Hall, 2002), 22.

5. Nobes and Parker, 5 and 27–29. The authors caution that these statistics are based on the membership of professional accountancy organizations and may reflect different certification practices between the various countries. However, even allowing for some discrepancies in the definitions of accountants, the statistics are striking.

6. See, for example, Friedrich A. Hayek, *Law, Legislation and Liberty: Rules and Order* (Chicago: University of Chicago Press, 1978).

7. Details available from the OECD Web site: *www.oecd.org*.

8. Nobes and Parker, 166.

9. Differences between varieties of English can lead to severe embarrassment in the multicultural office. If a British person asked a U.S. colleague for a "rubber," there may be red faces before the realization that he or she has in fact requested a pencil eraser!

10. Transparency International: *www.transparency.org*.

3

Managing International Risks

MANAGING RISK

This chapter reviews micromanagement strategies for the individual risks facing international organizations discussed in Chapter 2, "International Organizations and Their Risks." It does not touch on broader, organization-wide risk assessment and risk management—that must wait for Chapter 4, "Organization-Wide Risk Assessment." Risks are often assessed in terms of the threats they pose to the achievement of an organization's objectives, and risk management tends therefore to focus on procedures and controls that provide reasonable assurance on the achievement of objectives.

Risk can rarely be eliminated. Moreover, even when risk elimination is possible, it is often achievable only at considerable cost. Organizations therefore seek to reduce residual risks to comfortable levels. Two basic risk management strategies are "risk acceptance" and "risk avoidance." Both terms are self-explanatory. First, as its name implies, risk acceptance refers to an informed management decision to accept the risks (and rewards) of a particular activity or market. Organizations must decide whether specific issues fall within acceptable risk tolerance parameters. For example, in the period following the Argentine financial crisis that started in late 2001, some foreign organizations may have been tempted to pull out of the country on the basis of unacceptably high economic and political risks. Conversely, other organizations may have justified continued investment and activity in Argentina on the grounds of a long-term view of that country's economic health. Pulling out of a market only to re-enter it later can be a more costly option than remaining throughout a crisis period. The strategy of risk acceptance implies an informed management judgment on the balance between the risks and rewards of a particular activity.

At the opposite end of the risk management spectrum, organizations adopt a risk avoidance strategy when they deem the risks of certain activities or markets to be unacceptably high. An organization either refrains from involvement in an activity or a market, or disengages from existing commitments. For example, many western corporations eagerly entered the Russian market following the demise of the Soviet Union. However, the difficulty of operating in a period of painful transition to democratic capitalism proved too much for some organizations, who judged it necessary to pull out.

Risk avoidance can sometimes eliminate specific risks, but it can be a costly strategy. An organization may rue the opportunity cost of not taking advantage of the future prosperity of a particular activity or market. At the end of the Korean War in 1953, for example, South Korea was one of the world's poorest countries, with per capita GDP comparable to India and Central Africa. The devastation of war had destroyed much of the country's infrastructure and industrial base. However, over the following decades the country's rapid economic growth was little short of miraculous, and by the 1990s, South Korea had become one of the most affluent countries in the world. Organizations that took on the risks of operating in war-devastated South Korea in its early years were rewarded for their risk-taking during the subsequent economic boom. Organizations that initially avoided South Korea could have faced expensive entry costs as latecomers to the model Asian "tiger" economy.

Decisions to engage or remain in a particular market can rest on more than purely economic considerations. For public relations reasons, many large multinational corporations feel obliged to have a presence in all the world's large markets, even if this means enduring a period of relatively low returns (or even losses).

Within specific markets or territories, risk avoidance strategies may be applied to individual transactions. The full hedging of foreign currency cash flows, for example, can eliminate the risks surrounding future exchange rates. This example illustrates that risk avoidance can be a costly affair, as hedged rates may turn out to be spectacularly disadvantageous.

Rather than trying to entirely eliminate risks, more popular and feasible risk management strategies involve the minimization and transfer of risks. Once a risk has been managed to acceptable proportions, the incremental costs of attempting to eliminate it may be unacceptably high. For example, an organization may significantly reduce levels of inventory shrinkage by establishing robust security measures around a warehouse. Once a shrinkage level acceptable to management has been achieved, it may be unwise to spend more on security measures, as additional investment may result in diminishing returns. Expensive measures such as increasing the numbers of security staff patrols, building higher fences, and installing additional alarms or closed-circuit television monitors may not be justified by the additional benefits. This example illustrates the importance of judgment: Achieving acceptable levels of residual risk is the key to successful risk management.

Risk minimization strategies can cover attempts to both reduce the likelihood of unwelcome events occurring, and to reduce the consequences of risks once they have materialized. For example, an organization may deem the full hedging of its foreign currency cash flows to be inappropriate, as locking into fixed future exchange rates can be extremely costly. The organization may opt instead for the selective hedging of foreign currency cash flows, or for the use of currency options that can be exercised at management's discretion.

The risk management strategy of risk transfer involves either the transfer of an entire risk to a third party or—more commonly—the sharing of risk with a third party. Insurance cover is the classic risk transfer strategy, and illustrates that risk transfer strategies can be very costly. After the September 11 attacks in the United States in 2001, for example, antiwar insurance premiums rocketed for commercial airlines around the world. As a result, some airlines suspended flights to Sri Lanka, for which premiums had increased by 300 percent. (Two months before the attacks in the United States, a rebel attack at Colombo International Airport had destroyed half the Sri Lankan commercial airline fleet.)

Potential third parties for risk transfer include insurers, customers, suppliers, agents, and joint venture partners. For example, retail organizations normally agree on returns policies with suppliers, which permit them to pass on some of the costs of customer returns. A word of caution on risk transfer strategies is necessary. The managers of an organization do not abdicate responsibility for risk management when they arrange the transfer or sharing of a particular risk. A transfer of risk does not imply a transfer of accountability, and an organization's management remains responsible for the results of the risk management strategy it has adopted.

ECONOMIC RISKS

It can be argued that organizations operating in diverse markets with different economic profiles may minimize their overall risk exposure through the balancing effect of a wide portfolio of activities. The effects of underperforming territories may be compensated by the performance of stronger economies. Nonetheless, organizations can be severely troubled by economic crises in individual countries. At first sight, economic issues may appear to be largely beyond an organization's control. Powerful forces can be at play—when the Thai currency plummeted in 1997 and the Argentine economic crisis blew up in late 2001, there seemed to be little that international organizations could do to manage such cataclysmic events.

However, there are several risk management strategies to confront economic risks. Above all, timely economic intelligence is a prerequisite for minimizing risk. Organizations may use a combination of in-house analysis and external consultancy to keep up to speed with economic developments. Economic winds can change direction very quickly, and international organizations should follow the motto of a famous Scottish soccer team:[1] "Ready." Based on up-to-date information, focused risk management strategies may be deployed.

When economic risks are severe and localized, risk avoidance is a common response. This entails avoiding an activity or a market, or disengaging from existing operations. Risk acceptance is, of course, another available strategy, and an organization may decide to ride out an economic storm in the hope of taking advantage of a future recovery. Minimization strategies of varying degrees are also available—management may decide to continue their engagement in a specific activity or territory, but may prune the level of operations as a precaution.

Other minimization policies include restrictions set down by head offices on the autonomy of local entity management to make investments. The channeling of all material international investment decisions through a central corporate office is a common mechanism of minimizing global exposure to economic swings. To address currency risks, organizations can hedge all foreign currency cash flows, use currency options, or accept prevailing exchange rates (strategies of avoidance, minimization, and acceptance, respectively). In extreme cases, some organizations circumvent currency problems by entering into barter agreements. In one case, a Taiwanese organization entered into a barter arrangement with a Russian firm to exchange food, clothing, and shoes for oil, timber, and other raw materials. This was a pure barter agreement without the exchange of funds.[2]

Decisions on currency strategies therefore tend to consume significant amounts of management time in international organizations, as decisions in this area can have a major impact on financial results. Sometimes, political agreements deal organizations a helping hand by eliminating currency risks: The euro currency used in most of the European Union (EU) has replaced major national currencies such as the German deutschmark and the Italian lira. (The elimination of currency risks between countries in the EU has not been complete, however, as one major EU country—the United Kingdom—currently retains its own currency.)

In summary, economic risks are a major concern to international organizations, and research and up-to-date economic intelligence are prerequisites for formulating appropriate risk management strategies.

POLITICAL FACTORS

"May you live in interesting times." This ancient Chinese curse played on fears that eventful periods can bring problems as well as opportunities. Political situations can deteriorate as well as improve and—as discussed in Chapter 2— political events can present significant risks and challenges to international organizations.

As with economic matters, political events may often seem beyond the control of an individual organization. The key to effective management of international political risks therefore depends on the timely monitoring of political developments. As with economic risk management, organizations may use a combination of in-house analysis and external consultancy to try to anticipate important trends and events. The motto "Ready" again springs to mind. For example, in June 2000 a global soda drinks manufacturer started operations in the hitherto closed economy of North Korea, a mere three days after the United States relaxed economic sanctions on the country. Prior research had clearly alerted the corporation to the opening of a previously untapped market.

Political intelligence findings offer organizations the raw materials from which to fashion risk management strategies. Organizations can avoid specific territories, accept the risks and rewards of operating in politically volatile regions, or flex operating and investment levels in response to perceived political risks. In April

2002, for example, a Japanese automobile manufacturer decided in principle to establish a factory in war-torn Sri Lanka, clearly judging that the risks of operating in a country ravaged by a brutal civil war justified the potential rewards. (At the time of writing, the manufacturer's planned investment will only crystallize after satisfactory due diligence, which will undoubtedly include an assessment of political risk.) Another potentially important risk management strategy is that of political lobbying. This strategy carries risks of its own, of course, and lobbying must be kept within appropriate and legal boundaries if it is not to be counterproductive.

Whatever measures organizations may take to preempt political events, turmoil and war may still occur with lightning rapidity and upset the best of plans. Organizations should therefore consider contingency arrangements to cope with the fallout of political crises. To ensure the smooth running of an entity's activities, management may negotiate alternative distribution and communication channels. In extreme cases, security arrangements to protect or evacuate local employees may be necessary. Procedures for the emergency repatriation of foreign employees are required in some volatile parts of the world.

Sensitivity to local political tensions is often an essential part of doing business. Publishers, for example, must take care when preparing international editions of books—the delineation of national borders and political jurisdictions, for example, is a notoriously tricky area. In Argentina, the failure of a published map to indicate Argentine sovereignty of the Falkland Islands may land a publisher in trouble with the authorities. Similarly, maps published in India and Pakistan must show the borders of Kashmir in accordance with the very different national policies of both countries. Contravention of politically sensitive issues of this nature can be costly, in terms of fines and damaged public relations.

Risk transfer strategies may include political risk and kidnapping insurance, although cover of this nature may not be available in all countries. Indeed, insurance cover tends to be either unavailable or prohibitively expensive in the places where it is most required.

LEGAL AND REGULATORY REQUIREMENTS

Minimization is the most common risk management strategy adopted by international organizations to address legal and regulatory risks. Once an organization decides to operate or invest in a specific territory, compliance with local laws and regulations becomes an ever-constant concern. Noncompliance can result in large penalties and damaged reputations. The burdens on U.S. international organizations are particularly onerous, owing to the antibribery provisions of the Foreign Corrupt Practices Act.

Unfamiliarity with a specific legal culture can be a major challenge. Managers accustomed to operating within a common law framework may struggle to adapt to the continental European environment, for example. A popular risk minimization strategy for local legal and regulatory compliance is the use of external advisors. External advice can be costly, but it may be lower than the potential costs of noncompliance, and each case should be assessed on its merits. Another crucial minimization strategy is the preparation of written objectives and policies that cover the planning, monitoring, and management of legal and regulatory compliance. To further minimize risks, organizations can identify employees accountable for specific compliance objectives, and provide suitable training and reporting mechanisms.

Other popular risk minimization strategies include compliance reviews by internal and external auditors; the timely reporting to head office of local information on important compliance issues; the maintenance of adequate disbursement records; and the implementation of corporate "hotlines" that allow employees to anonymously air concerns over potential breaches of laws and regulations. The regulatory complexity of some environments necessitates the risk transfer strategy of using joint ventures to negotiate safely through labyrinthine local requirements.

TAXATION

A detailed discussion of taxation risk is beyond the scope of this book. Taxation advisory services have become a huge industry, with a massive bank of resources. However, as a general observation it is worth stressing that international organizations are permitted to take reasonable steps to arrange their affairs so as to minimize their tax burdens. Naturally, reasonable steps do not include any potentially illegal measures. Taxation penalties can be enormous.

International tax planning is a complicated affair, and in-house or external expertise is a prerequisite for success in this technical minefield. Locating operations in low tax economies is an obvious risk minimization strategy. In the 1990s, for example, the Republic of Ireland attracted a significant proportion of U.S. direct investment into the EU. There were several factors behind this trend—the country's well-educated, English-speaking workforce, for example—but the country's attractive tax rates for corporations was undoubtedly a major reason.

The use of tax havens is an increasingly sensitive matter, as low-taxation territories have come under intense scrutiny in recent years. In October 2001, for example, the G8 group of industrialized nations[3] met at Washington DC and called for better exchange of information and improved supervision of assets in offshore locations and tax havens, to combat the financing of international terrorism. In addition, as discussed in Chapter 2, the Organization for Economic Cooperation and Development (OECD) has criticized some countries for allegedly poor standards of financial transparency and tax regulation, and has designated specific territories as "unco-operative tax havens."[4] The OECD's member countries include the world's major economies, and the organization has the clout to turn up the heat on specific territories through the use of what it calls "defensive measures." International corporations must therefore carefully research the risks of operating through specific low-tax territories.

Other complicating factors in tax risk minimization include the existence of mutual tax treaties that avoid double taxation, and restrictions on transfer price levels. Organizations may be tempted to use artificially low or high transfer prices to shift income to low-tax countries, but in recent years, tax authorities around the world have started to monitor such matters more closely.

GENERALLY ACCEPTED ACCOUNTING PRINCIPLES

At the time of this writing, global harmonization of accounting practice is still far from achieved, and international differences in Generally Accepted Accounting Principles (GAAP) can distort an organization's management accounts and published financial statements. Accounting transactions consolidated from inconsistent information can mislead an organization into taking inappropriate operational and investment decisions. Getting the accountancy right is therefore a crucial consideration for an international organization.

To minimize potential risks of this nature, a common strategy is the use of GAAP adjustments to the financial data reported by international entities. The GAAP adjustments can be processed either locally by international entities or centrally by the parent organization, but the latter procedure carries the risk of head office unfamiliarity with the complex GAAP details of individual countries. Most corporations therefore prefer to receive accounts from their international entities with locally processed GAAP adjustments. To minimize the risk of inaccuracy, it is common for both internal and external auditors to review the accuracy of the adjustments.

Another approach to GAAP inconsistency is the preparation of local financial statements in accordance with parent organization GAAP. However, this is not possible in all countries. Moreover, concerns over the accuracy of local GAAP adjustments are not eliminated in such circumstances—accounting judgment by local staff is always necessary, and carries risks of inaccuracy.

Other risk strategies to combat GAAP differences include the nonpreparation (where permitted by law) of published financial statements. Conversely, to minimize the risks of inaccuracy, many organizations insist on the performance of an annual external audit for specific subsidiaries, even when not required by local legislation. Another strategy open to organizations unhappy with existing or proposed accounting standards is to lobby standards-setting bodies. Indeed, feedback from industrial bodies and corporations is a normal part of the drafting process of accounting standards in most countries. There have been many examples of successful lobbying by organizations, and as one commentator has put it: "An industry with enough political clout [can] bend principles" in the drafting of accounting standards.[5] However, successful GAAP lobbying may be increasingly difficult, as national standard-setting bodies are deferring more and more to International Accounting Standards: Global harmonization is undoubtedly diminishing the discretion of national standard-setting bodies.

Once GAAP differences have been ironed out of accounts, areas of accounting risk still remain. Judgment on the application of accounting principles and the existence of alternative accounting treatments may affect the consistency of international reporting. For example, the consistent use of exchange rates to translate foreign entity accounting data is essential for quality and meaningful accounts. The use of inconsistent exchange rates leads to problems in reconciling intercompany balances, and clouds the comparative analysis of entity performance. A popular risk minimization strategy is the use of fixed, groupwide exchange rates: many corporate head offices issue exchange rate lists to their international entities, and periodically verify (e.g., through internal audit reviews) the accuracy of the rates used in group reporting.

To narrow inconsistencies in accounting judgment, international organizations commonly have groupwide accounting policies. The existence of a group accounting manual does not, of course, eliminate risks of inappropriate accounting practice, and it may require the backup of regular monitoring procedures. However, the establishment of internationally applicable policies is a good risk minimization strategy and can reduce accounting judgment in important areas such as inventory valuation methodologies.

Finally, owing to the distances—physical, cultural, and linguistic—between the entities of international organizations, accounting fraud is a constant risk. The misrepresentation of accounting data can arise from pressure on local management to achieve budgetary and bonus targets, or from attempts to disguise operational problems. Risks of contravening the Foreign Corrupt Practices Act (FCPA) are also relevant in this context. Chapter 2 made reference to the antibribery provisions of the FCPA, but the FCPA also sets out accounting and bookkeeping requirements. Accounting records maintained outside the general ledger, or the use of general ledger accounts with imprecise descriptions (e.g., "miscellaneous funds") may be mechanisms for improper activity, and may be used as evidence—in combination with other factors—of FCPA contravention.

Faced with the risks of accounting gymnastics, risk minimization strategies include periodic monitoring procedures such as internal and external audits. Some multinational corporations even adopt a groupwide chart of accounts, which parallels the charts of the accounts used at a national level by some European countries.

LINGUISTIC DIFFERENCES

The principal risk minimization strategy to encourage adequate communication between international entities is the employment of staff with appropriate linguistic skills. This should cover employees in all disciplines, to encourage smooth communication through all functional levels of an international organization.

However, this is often easier said than done. The feasibility of employing sufficient numbers of staff with linguistic ability depends on several factors—the location of an organization, its recruitment policies and compensation arrangements, and the extent to which a specific language is known among the local population. For example, a U.S. or British organization that wishes to employ large numbers of English speakers at a subsidiary in the Netherlands may have little difficulty in meeting this need. The Dutch have a deserved reputation as talented linguists, especially when it comes to English. The Netherlands' education system is strong, and the country's physical proximity to Britain allows many Dutch people to hone their English skills by watching BBC television. Conversely, the same organization's subsidiary in Italy may find it harder to recruit English speakers. English has traditionally played a secondary role to French and German in the Italian education system (although this is now changing), and Italy's distance from England precludes terrestrial English-language television broadcasts.

Other linguistic risk minimization strategies include international employee exchanges, the placing of expatriates around the world, language training for employees of both the parent organization and international entities, and the translation of important organizational documents into local languages. The selection of one language as an organization's "official" in-house language is also an increasingly common risk minimization strategy. This does not necessarily imply that the parent organization's language is adopted. A large Swiss corporation, for example, has adopted English as its "official" internal language for use in meetings and important documents, although Switzerland's main languages are German, French, and Italian. This has led to the rather curious scenario of groups of managers discussing issues in English, when none of the attendees at the meeting speak English as a mother tongue. This strategy is not without risk, however: Nonnative speakers of a language may miss crucial linguistic nuances, and idiomatic expressions can lead to confusion. As in all linguistic risk minimization strategies, risks cannot be eliminated, but merely reduced to acceptable levels.

CULTURAL FACTORS

Cultural risks are notoriously difficult to minimize. It is easy to cause offense in this area, and accusations of cultural imperialism can be damaging for international organizations. The risks of cultural dissonance can, therefore, be a very real threat to the achievement of an international organization's objectives. Risk minimization strategies are commonly adopted to combat cultural misunderstandings between staff, and to reinforce parent organization behavior in areas such as bribes and improper payments.

Popular risk minimization strategies include expatriate programs and the international employee transfers. These practices can foster cultural understanding: A successful expatriate, for example, can invigorate a foreign office and help to inculcate the wider organization's culture in a specific location. Other approaches may include country briefings for employees traveling to international entities, and the preparation of a comprehensive code of ethics, disseminated throughout the organization's international entities. Such a policy may define the parameters of sensitive practices such as the permitted value of gifts to be offered to customers, and should encourage employees around the world to act in a manner consistent with corporate policy.

Management training on ethical matters is another risk minimization strategy, and training of this nature may include practical cases of how to react in compromising circumstances—when a bribe is offered, for example. The identification of responsible officials accountable for the monitoring and management of ethical matters is another frequently encountered strategy.

Other risk minimization mechanisms include periodic reports to the parent organization of an expenditure of a potentially sensitive nature (e.g., gifts and entertaining), and head office authorization (either in advance or retrospectively) of expenditure on specific items. Many corporations also maintain central registers of sensitive management information, including potential conflicts of interest. Some large organizations also establish globally accessible, confidential "hotlines" that give international employees an opportunity to discuss any concerns. Information divulged on such hotlines may be a valuable tool in minimizing FCPA contravention.

In addition to concerns over cultural misunderstanding and the risks of improper or unethical activity, organizations face cultural challenges in adapting international products to the circumstances of local markets. Consumer preferences and cultural patterns vary around the world. In France in the 1990s, for example, a theme park owned by a U.S. corporation recognized—reluctantly at first—that its alcohol-free restaurants were unfeasible. The French tradition of drinking wine with meals was too strong, and after an initial ban, alcohol was readmitted to the theme park's restaurants. To minimize such risks, local market research and the use of external advisors for information on market peculiarities can be helpful.

OTHER MATTERS

Chapter 2 considered various additional areas of international risk—natural hazards, the entrenched cultures of acquired entities, problems related specifically to small entities, and poor communication infrastructures. Risk management strategies in these areas are large in number, and some examples are given here.

To minimize risks arising from natural hazards, organizations should carefully select their operational locations. They should avoid areas of seismic activity in a country, for example. However, if a presence in a particular territory necessitates a degree of danger, then physical protection measures such as earthquake-resistant buildings or antiflood precautions may be necessary. Further, in the event of a disaster, contingency plans should be in place to assist employees and keep operations going. An important risk transfer strategy in such circumstances is, of course, adequate insurance cover for physical damage and operational disruption.

To minimize risks relating to the potentially awkward cultural fit of acquired entities, organizations may encourage an entity's employees to visit the head office, or different parts of the international group. Alternatively, expatriates from the parent organization can be placed in a newly acquired international subsidiary, to guide local employees in the organization's practices and ethos. Naturally, care must be taken to avoid swamping an entity with head office people—this could aggravate rather than alleviate some of the cultural dissonance, and provoke a counterproductive local backlash. Other popular minimization strategies include monitoring procedures such as internal audit reviews of local operational practices, and periodic conferences that give employees opportunities for international networking.

As noted in Chapter 2, the risks associated with small entities, international or domestic, can be serious. In the case of international subsidiaries, geographic, linguistic, and cultural differences may magnify the dangers. The risks arising from the limited segregation of duties typically associated with small entities can be minimized by international policies and procedures manuals, parent organization authorization of specific transactions (e.g., disbursements over a stated threshold), internal audit monitoring of procedures and transactions, and by increasing staff numbers where necessary. To minimize the risks of overdependence on a limited number of key personnel in smaller entities, organizations can plan for employee succession by grooming internal candidates and by seeking potential candidates in the wider local market.

This chapter focused on the micromanagement of individual risks. Chapter 4 moves on to consider organization-wide risk assessment and management.

NOTES

1. Glasgow Rangers.
2. Lee H. Radebaugh and Sidney J. Gray, *International Accounting and Multinational Enterprises*, 4th ed. (New York: John Wiley & Sons, 1997), 588.
3. The original G7 (Group of Seven) nations comprised the United States, Canada, Japan, Germany, Britain, France, and Italy. The addition of Russia led to the name change to G8.
4. Details available from the OECD Web site: *www.oecd.org*.
5. William T. Baxter, *Accounting Theory* (New York: Garland, 1996), 112.

4

Organization-Wide Risk Assessment

ASSESSING RISKS

The previous chapter discussed risk assessment and risk management strategies for individual areas of international risk. This chapter briefly reviews broader approaches to risk commonly undertaken by organizations with global activities. Space does not permit a detailed overview of risk assessment methodologies, as it is a vast topic with an extensive literature.[1] It focuses instead on specific aspects of risk assessment in international contexts.

In economically developed countries, corporate governance practices normally require some form of risk assessment. Although risk assessment has arguably always been part of managing a business enterprise, at least at an informal level, modern corporate governance has encouraged the intuitive risk assessment of the past to be formalized and expressed in writing. Effective governance of an organization—be it a profit-maximizing operation or a government or charitable concern—is today inconceivable without a solid risk assessment and risk management program.

At the time of writing, the major global dynamo for audit's role in corporate governance remains the 1992 internal control framework of the Committee of Sponsoring Organizations of the Treadway Commission (COSO).[2] The COSO framework identifies risk assessment as an essential component of an effective system of internal control, and has strongly influenced subsequent corporate governance developments around the world. Risk assessment seems to be entrenched as a permanent feature of international corporate governance.[3]

Internal and external auditors both use risk assessment techniques to determine and prioritize their work. They assess risk to allocate auditing resources to meet perceived risks. Such a risk-based approach is now the norm, in contrast to the often cyclical nature of auditing in the past.[4] In the wider context of an organization, internal auditors are often the catalysts for risk assessment exercises, while external auditors often play a role in the process in a consultative capacity.

In organizations where risk assessment has not fully matured as a corporate process, auditors are often pioneers who make significant contributions to the enhancement of corporate governance.

Auditors therefore frequently contribute to their organization's risk assessments for strategic management purposes. The risk profile that drives audit planning should in principle be closely aligned with an organization's overall risk profile. In other words, the auditor's risk assessment exercise should be more than a mere audit planning tool—it should lock in to the organization's risk assessment programs at the highest levels. However, the audit risk assessment and the organization's strategic risk assessment need not necessarily be identical. There may be specific risks—in areas such as insurance and manufacturing safety, for example—that are assessed and managed by other assurance functions within the organization. The audit risk assessment may therefore be one subset, albeit a major one, of an organization's overall risk profile. Adequate coordination between the various assurance functions should ensure that the overall risk profile aggregates risk assessments from all appropriate sources.

Different organizations have different risk appetites. Some sectors are characterized by a high-risk, high-return culture. Other sectors are more conservative. Whatever the cultural background, an organization's risk assessment programs should be kept within reasonable limits. The inculcation of an excessively risk-averse culture can stifle creativity, and diminish an organization's capacity for enterprise and its readiness to respond to adversity. Moreover, risk should not be allowed to subvert the auditor's mindset. One commentator was wisely warned that "over-emphasis on risk assessment may perpetuate the traditional culture of the risk-averse internal auditor, with risk being seen as something to avoid rather than an opportunity to be exploited."[5]

For the sake of convenience, the following discussions do not distinguish between risk assessment for audit planning and for wider corporate governance purposes.

QUANTITATIVE METHODOLOGIES

Risk assessment is frequently conducted through the use of metrics and algorithms. Insofar as an organization adopts quantification methods for its risk assessment exercise (or for part of it), a "formula" can be devised to capture the risks in entities, operations, and processes. The literature on the methodologies of quantitative risk measurement is large[6] and a summary of the available approaches is beyond the scope of this book.

A word of caution is necessary when dealing with risk quantification. Numerical risk assessment is an understandable approach when attempting to come to grips with a difficult or complex environment. Some sectors have traditionally required a strong quantitative base—actuarial valuations are fundamental to the basic operations of the life assurance industry, for example. However, the spread of risk assessment beyond such traditional heartlands has sometimes led to a rather naïve reliance on number-crunching, in contexts where it may be inappropriate.[7]

On occasion, the calculation of risk assessment "formulae" seems to provide a veneer of pseudoscientific clarity to complex matters that cannot be captured purely by numbers. Numerical data can provide comfort and can reduce anxiety in a confusing and occasionally frightening world, but the advantages of such an approach are often limited. Risks are often difficult (and sometimes impossible) to quantify, and overreliance on quantified data may reduce the scope for intuitive assessment.

The risk assessor who overrelies on numbers often therefore seems to dance around the heart of the risk assessment process, never quite managing to penetrate its core. In extreme cases, overelaborate risk assessment processes can detach themselves from the organizational realities they purport to represent. A curious scenario then develops, in which risk-assessment becomes a self-referential exercise divorced from the surrounding context. In such cases, the process has as much to do with effective risk assessment as the obsessive polishing of a car has to do with maintaining its engine. As discussed later in this chapter, risk assessment in many organizations therefore requires approaches that go beyond number crunching. However, many or most organizations will be tempted to put numbers to at least a part of their risk assessments.

Despite the drawbacks of quantitative risk assessment, in international organizations "numerical" risk assessments offer many advantages. Numerical risk scores can often be readily understood across cultural and linguistic boundaries. In contrast, the vocabulary of risk assessment is still evolving and can cause confusion even in English—translation into other languages and cultural environments only magnifies problems. Terms such as "risk" and "danger" may appear alarming when rendered in other languages, especially in countries where corporate governance processes have not popularized notions of risk assessment.

When different nationalities are involved in a risk assessment exercise, therefore, quantification can assist mutual understanding. What is lost through overreliance on risk scores and risk tolerance thresholds can be more than outweighed by the gains through enhanced cross-cultural clarity of the entire risk assessment process.

Other observations on quantitative risk assessment exercises in an international context include the need to adequately reflect the geographical spread of an organization's operations. Some organizations channel risk assessment processes along geographical rather than business process lines. (Domestic organizations often tend to approach the exercise from the latter perspective.) For example, an auditor's risk assessment exercise may be used to determine the frequency of visits to international entities: The frequency of visits and amount of resources committed to particular entities is in proportion to the assessed risk under such an approach.

Control Self Assessment (CSA) workshops are often used to encourage those responsible for assets or operations to quantify the risks for which they are responsible. This approach can be fraught with linguistic and cultural complications when used in an international context. Language difficulties can hinder communication, and deference to organizational hierarchy in some cultures can hamper the free exchange of information. International organizations should be careful in rolling out such exercises to subsidiaries and branches where benefits may be outweighed by linguistic or cultural misunderstanding. Another consideration is the expense of conducting workshops around the world in organizations with far-flung operations. In such circumstances, the use of written questionnaires may be a viable alternative.

QUALITATIVE APPROACHES

As suggested in the previous section, quantitative risk assessment techniques are unlikely to adequately capture the subtleties of an organization's risk profile. Some business risks are quantifiable (e.g., the risks of credit default or the risks of adopting a foreign currency hedging position) but others are quantifiable only with difficulty. Complicated and time-consuming risk assessment formulae may be a long-winded method of arriving at fairly obvious prioritization criteria that could be derived from a more rapid intuitive approach.

Although we have said that in international contexts quantified risk assessment procedures may assist in cutting across linguistic and cultural barriers, it would nonetheless be dangerous to proceed too far along the route of quantification for certain aspects of risk assessment. In all organizations—domestic and international—unquantifiable factors come into play. Personality conflicts, departmental politics, greed, incompetence, romantic affairs, corporate disloyalty, fraud, racial harassment, and so on are the stuff of organizational risk. Formal procedures and controls nearly always carry a risk of subversion by the "human factor."

It seems therefore to be impossible to remove subjectivity entirely from risk assessment. How to quantify the risk of a lawsuit arising from one employee harassing or bullying another? Or of damage to an organization's reputation that might be caused by the unsanctioned behavior of a maverick employee? Or the risk of flooding in a particular territory? Historical trends may be indicative, but they are not always reliable guides to the future.

Qualitative risk assessment techniques should therefore be employed in international risk assessment. Any methodology employed must be rigorous, systematic, and logical. Instead of assigning precise risk scores to entities or activities, a rating system of high to low risk can be used to categorize items in a risk register. In an international environment, potential linguistic and cultural complications must be managed, as they cannot be avoided. Training in the corporate risk assessment program for international employees and translation of major documents used in the process are possible means of smoothing over potential international misunderstanding. Similarly, CSA workshops that deal with qualitative risk assessment carry the risks discussed in the "Quantitative Methodologies" section and should always be handled with care.

HOLISTIC RISK ASSESSMENT

Many organizations blend quantitative and qualitative methods in a holistic risk assessment approach. An organization that puts assets at risk around the world to achieve its objectives needs a sophisticated and flexible approach to adequately assess and manage its risks. This typically involves the quantification of financial risks where appropriate, and the prioritization of other categories of risk that lend themselves less to quantification. It is essential when using a mixed approach to group together the discrete parts of the exercise. The result may be a little messy, but then the world is a messy place, too.

Scenario planning is a common holistic risk assessment tool involving the analysis of a number of different scenarios that could affect an organization, often with the assigning of probabilities of occurrence to each scenario. A range of scenarios for a distant foreign entity may include a change of political regime, the effect of a natural catastrophe such as an earthquake, the possibility of an economic recession, and the effects of changing accounting standards. For each scenario, a review of risks and opportunities could lead to either quantitative or qualitative risks assessments (or a combination of both) that could be used to determine the organization's management strategy. Scenario planning requires a certain amount of imagination, and brainstorming activities are frequently employed to tease ideas from participants in the process. Imaginative and wide-ranging discussions are not always straightforward in organizations with linguistic and cultural differences: Inability to express complex ideas in a foreign language may hamper the input of key individuals.

Whatever approach is adopted, a thorough understanding of the organization and its activities is essential to a successful risk assessment exercise. Risks must be assessed collectively, rather than in isolation, and the sheer geographical spread of international organizations can make this a complicated affair. Further, it is unlikely that any individual or small group of individuals is able to perform an adequate risk assessment alone. Knowledge of an organization is arguably beyond the scope of any one individual.

Tapping the reservoir of information held by one's colleagues is therefore essential, but it may be difficult to achieve in some multinational organizations. Geographical distances and linguistic factors often hinder information flow in international contexts. It is likely to be difficult for, let us say, an employee in a German corporate head office to prepare the risk assessment of a branch in Indonesia. A visit to Indonesia may not suffice to pick up all relevant local factors, and local management should be at the center of the risk assessment process. However, involving local management can be problematic, with linguistic and cultural factors to be overcome. Moreover, corporate governance is at varying stages of sophistication around the world. In some countries, it may be a novel thing, and a corporate head office may find that it needs to do some explaining for the exercise to work. Nonetheless, a collaborative approach to risk assessment is needed to ensure that an organization captures the accumulated knowledge of its employees.

Risk assessment and risk management are ongoing activities, and they should be under regular—or, in some cases, continuous—review. One does not need to be an advocate of chaos theory to recognize that the risk universe is continually changing, and that surprises can come at any time. To ensure continuous review, the risk assessment process should be embedded in an organization's culture and behavior. Risk assessment should not therefore be seen as an irritating, on-off exercise: It should instead drive the daily control and financing of risks.

Enthusiasm for risk assessment should come from an organization's "top table," and it is the responsibility of various layers of management to ensure that its message is communicated through the vast reaches of an international organization. One should not underestimate the barriers—physical and cultural—that need to be overcome in such a context.

NOTES

1. Chapter 7, "Select Bibliography and Other Sources of Information," suggests useful resources on risk and auditing.
2. Committee of Sponsoring Organizations of the Treadway Commission (COSO), *Internal Control—Integrated Framework* (Jersey City, NJ: AICPA/COSO, 1992).
3. Influential international guidance on risk includes the Australian and New Zealand Joint Standards Committee's *AS/NZS 4360 Risk Management* of 1996.
4. In the 1990s, the author was a member of the internal audit department of a major multinational (United Technologies Corporation) that undertook the switch from a purely cyclical auditing program to one driven by risk assessment. This was generally perceived as radical for the times, but the reaction of the wider corporation was highly enthusiastic, and the profile and reputation of an already world-class function soared.
5. Gerald Vinten, *Internal Audit Research: The First Half Century* (London: Certified Accountants Educational Trust, 1996), 93.
6. Good summarizations of quantitative risk assessment techniques are available from David McNamee and Georges M. Selim, *Risk Management: Changing the Internal Auditor's Paradigm* (Altamonte Springs, FL: Institute of Internal Auditors Research Foundation, 1998), passim. This book also contains valuable guidance on further reading on the subject. The June 2001 issue of *Internal Auditor* focuses on risk and Enterprise Risk Management.
7. See, for example, the extensive and perhaps excessive use of risk formulae in Andrew Chambers, *Effective Internal Audits* (London: Pitman, 1992 and subsequent editions), passim.

5

The Logistics of Auditing

PLANNING FOR SAFE INTERNATIONAL AUDITING

Safety is a major concern for auditors who perform international assignments. Some organizations, especially humanitarian ones, operate in the world's most dangerous war and famine zones, and their auditors are exposed to high levels of personal risk. Nonetheless, even the auditors of organizations operating in less "extreme" environments need to be vigilant when traveling. Safety risks range from the theft of possessions to illness, injury, and death. Kidnapping, with its immense human suffering and potentially huge financial costs, is another concern in some parts of the world.

The need for sensible travel precautions has probably never been higher, as the repercussions of the attacks of September 11 in 2001 continue to reverberate around the world. Yet safety has long been an issue for international auditors. In 1997, for example, four U.S. auditors were murdered in a politically motivated gun attack in Karachi, Pakistan. However, it is unfair to single out the dangers of specific countries,[1] as safety risks in individual territories can change significantly over time.

Common sense should guide travel plans. Of paramount importance is the avoidance of territories where security risks are unacceptably high, and many nations offer continuous travel advice to their citizens. The U.S. State Department, for example, provides country-specific travel warnings to U.S. citizens,[2] while the Travel Advice Unit of the British Foreign and Commonwealth Office provides similar guidance to British citizens.[3] In times of crisis, warnings are often broadcast in the general media: In June 2002, for example, the United States and Britain publicly advised their nationals to leave India and Pakistan, owing to the risk of war between the two countries.

The auditor should therefore take advice on security matters before undertaking an international assignment. Even when official advice does not prohibit visits to a particular country, the auditor should make a personal assessment of the potential impact of local circumstances and events. Industrial strikes, political elections, street protests, and other similar events can complicate the logistics of travel and can occasionally lead to danger for the traveler. This observation is not limited to volatile developing countries, as even in mature democracies political or politicized events can lead to severe violence. During the French presidential election in April and May 2002, for example, the unexpected initial success of the leader of the far-right, antiestablishment *Front National* was met by huge street protests and serious rioting in Paris and other French cities. In July 2001 in Genoa, Italy, a summit of the G8 group of industrialized nations was accompanied by clashes between antiglobalization protestors and police that led to many serious injuries and at least one death.

In some circumstances, therefore, an auditor may decide that it is simply too dangerous to perform an assignment in a specific territory. However, once a decision is made to travel to a foreign country, the auditor should at all times remain aware of personal security. Linguistic difficulties and an unfamiliar environment can magnify security risks.

Before departure, essential arrangements include the obtaining of adequate travel insurance, the leaving of emergency contact numbers with colleagues and families, and copying important travel documentation such as passports. Even a matter as mundane as the appropriate dress code for a specific country should be investigated. Women, for example, may be expected (or required) to cover their heads in public in some Muslim countries. A little research can help to avoid embarrassment and problems with local authorities.

On arrival in a foreign country, the confusion of a crowded airport after a long, tiring flight can dull reaction times. This can increase the risk of theft of personal effects such as luggage and laptop computers. Increased vigilance is necessary at such times. Sensible precautions include the avoidance of organizational insignia and corporate logos on luggage or clothing that could draw unnecessary attention to the auditor. In addition, it is generally advisable to be met on arrival at most foreign destinations by an employee of the audited organization or by an alternative, trustworthy source. Local transport such as taxis, buses, and trains may be unsafe, but many hotels offer reliable car transfer services.

Arranging safe transportation remains a concern for the entire duration of an assignment. Car and limousine hires can be expensive, but they may be necessary to minimize security risks. In essence, the visitor to a foreign country should use discretion in selecting any form of transport, and local contacts are best placed to suggest appropriate arrangements. However, one's caution should not reach the stage where the performance of an audit suffers to an unreasonable degree. As the author has suggested elsewhere, "poor transport [arrangements] can be used as an excuse not to show the auditor a facility, such as a poorly managed warehouse, that local management may wish to keep from outside eyes. The auditor must . . . judge each situation as it arises."[4]

Outside office hours, socializing tends to play an important part in establishing good working relationships with local colleagues. In some parts of the world, it is wise to be accompanied at all times by local contacts when spending time away from the office and the hotel. Moreover, the auditor should keep any sense of adventure within reasonable bounds: Exploring an unfamiliar country may be tempting, but one should never lose sight of local risks.

Medical concerns are another important area of travel risk. Many organizations have policies covering medical arrangements for employees on foreign assignments. These typically include global medical insurance cover and guidance on timely inoculations. Some medicines must be obtained well in advance of an assignment—antimalarial protection courses, for example, tend to start several weeks before a visit to a risk zone. Documentary evidence of vaccination is sometimes required. Many African countries refuse entry to visitors who do not carry a certificate proving World Health Organization approved vaccination for yellow fever. Without a certificate, the only options are expulsion from a country or an on-the-spot vaccination. At best, this can be inconvenient. At worst, it can be potentially dangerous. Auditors traveling in rural areas far from medical facilities may wish to take a small first aid kit, as well as obtaining any necessary medicines in advance of the journey.

Natural hazards are another area of risk. This topic was discussed in Chapters 2 and 3 in relation to the disruption and danger posed to international entities, but individual auditors also face risks from natural phenomena. In recent years, for example, the author has been forced to change the timing of audit assignments owing to various natural catastrophes around the world—serious flooding in Poland and Venezuela, and earthquakes in India and Turkey. Where natural hazards are seasonal and largely predictable, the auditor should plan assignments to avoid disruptive and dangerous periods. In many countries, for example, monsoon patterns are similar from year to year and can easily be avoided.

Finally, it is sometimes argued that a basic knowledge of self-defense or martial arts skills may be useful for those whose professional duties take them to potentially dangerous places. There may be some validity in this idea. Auditors of humanitarian organizations that venture into parts of the world where others are too scared to tread may be regularly placed in risky environments. However, a little knowledge of such matters can be a dangerous thing, giving individuals a false sense of security and a dangerously unrealistic expectation of their survival skills when physically attacked. The author's personal view of the matter is that avoidance is better than confrontation—as far as possible, the auditor should avoid places where self-defense skills are deemed necessary!

PLANNING FOR EFFECTIVE AND EFFICIENT INTERNATIONAL AUDITING

"One of the great paradoxes of business today is that superficially the world is becoming more and more a single market, while in reality national differences are becoming accentuated. . . . The mere fact that one stays in the same sort of hotel almost anywhere in the world, that one drives in the same sort of car, that it is now possible to call by telephone . . . from almost anywhere in the world, all give a superficial feeling of sameness. A sameness which is desperately misleading, and which must never be taken for granted."[5]

These late twentieth century comments by the former head of a multinational corporation are a reminder of the difficulties of the cultural challenges of international assignments. Waking bleary-eyed the day after a long flight, the auditor may pull the curtains of a hotel room and experience a momentary sense of disorientation. Is it Beijing, Berlin, or Bombay? However, the superficial and misleading uniformity of international hotel and flight infrastructures should not blind the traveler to the huge range of cultural variety around the world. Understanding and adapting to the cultures of different countries is normally a prerequisite for successful auditing.

Diplomats receive training in local customs and cultural practices before a posting to a new country, and brief research into the history and culture of a country to be visited may also be invaluable to the auditor. For example, an awareness of the regional diversity of Indonesia is essential in understanding that country's business environment: The Indonesian archipelago's 6,000 inhabited islands contain immense ethnic and linguistic differences that have a range of social, economic, and cultural implications.

In addition to assisting the auditor's understanding of the contexts in which international organizations operate, an awareness of cultural matters can also assist interpersonal relations. Cultural insensitivity can inadvertently cause offense and thereby damage the relationship between the auditor and local colleagues. For example, in many Muslim countries, public physical contact between the sexes is inappropriate. Although handshaking between the sexes may be common in urban areas and among the middle classes in countries such as Pakistan and Malaysia, it is generally advisable to wait for a member of the opposite sex to initiate a handshake. Cultural sensitivity between the members of international auditing teams is essential to encourage an effective and efficient working atmosphere, and the inclusion of local auditors can give the audit team an edge in knowledge of the local environment. Given the importance of cultural factors in the smooth running of international audits, the individual country sections of the Appendix offer advice on social etiquette.

Linked to cultural matters is the topic of socializing. International auditors have unparalleled opportunities to meet people of many different nationalities, and the social aspects of international assignments are an attractive part of professional life. Nonetheless, social relations in foreign countries are fraught with potential problems. First, the auditor may be expected to socialize outside office hours, and evening meals with local colleagues can be an important part of professional duties. This can make for long days and tiring assignments. Second, the auditor should be sensitive to the distinctions between reasonable and excessive socializing. Generous entertaining at social events may compromise (or at least affect perceptions of) an auditor's independence and judgment. Further, the giving and receiving of gifts is a professional minefield and, if necessary, should be restricted to inexpensive items.

Moving beyond cultural matters, linguistic problems are a potential source of audit inefficiency. Planning for linguistic issues includes the suitable linguistic composition of audit teams and the need for additional linguistic support. The latter requires careful management, as the hiring of interpreters and translators may be expensive, and those employed may be unfamiliar with auditing terminology. Where appropriate, confirmation letters and other important documentation should be translated well in advance of an audit.

There are many other aspects of international logistical planning. The importance of timely booking of flights and hotels may seem obvious, but it can occasionally be a highly problematic area. Trade exhibitions and sporting events can temporarily overburden hotels and flights in certain cities: For example, travel to parts of Japan and Korea during the 2002 soccer World Cup was difficult and expensive owing to the high demand placed on travel infrastructures by thousands of visiting sports fans. Similarly, auditors should arrange passports and visas well in advance of international assignments, as these matters can be highly bureaucratic and time-consuming.

Other matters requiring careful planning[6] include verification of the impact of local holidays; obtaining proof of ownership of laptop computers (which is necessary in some countries); obtaining suitable international electricity and modem adapters; and the use of international call cards to avoid excessive hotel telephone charges. Finally, the auditor should travel with adequate financial resources. It is advisable to carry sufficient cash in local currencies to meet contingencies and essential expenses. When specific currencies cannot be obtained outside a country's boundaries, a suitably attractive international currency is a good replacement. Adequate credit or charge card facilities are also important, as purchasing emergency flights can be extremely costly.

This chapter's emphasis on a number of potential logistical problems was not intended to detract from the benefits of international auditing assignments. Auditing globally can be extremely rewarding, professionally and personally. However, as recognized by the professional standards of both external and internal auditors, planning is central to successful auditing. With international assignments, planning is complicated by logistical, cultural, and linguistic concerns, and careful preparation is essential to reduce the likelihood of unexpected events or situations. In addition to the hard facts of logistical planning, it is unwise to neglect the "softer" aspects of cultural differences. We can leave the final word on this topic to two giants in the field of internal auditing:

> Part of planning for an audit in a foreign country must include an understanding of that country's culture: what is accepted, what is taboo; how to work around the impediments raised by that culture to normal working methods. Knowing, for example, that in being kept waiting for appointments [in countries where punctuality is not seen as a virtue], we should stuff our briefcase with material that we can work on while cooling our heels.[7]

NOTES

1. In several visits to Pakistan, the author has encountered only courtesy and hospitality.
2. Available from: *http://travel.state.gov/warnings_list*.
3. Available from: *www.fco.gov.uk*.
4. David O'Regan, *Auditing International Entities: A Practical Guide to Risks, Objectives, and Reporting* (Altamonte Springs, FL: Institute of Internal Auditors, 2001), 83.
5. John Harvey-Jones, *Making It Happen: Reflections on Leadership* (London: Harper Collins, 1988), 117.
6. All these topics are discussed in detail by O'Regan, 75–87.
7. Lawrence B. Sawyer and Gerald Vinten, *The Manager and the Internal Auditor: Partners for Profit* (New York: John Wiley & Sons, 1996), 300–301.

6

Concluding Thoughts

THE AUDITING PROFESSION IN FLUX

This book was written in the feverish atmosphere of mid-2002, when a series of accounting and corporate governance scandals shook the foundations of the external auditing profession. The sight of major corporations such as Enron and WorldCom under Chapter 11 bankruptcy protection—and the events that brought them to such a sorry state—have eroded faith in the validity of the external audit. The Big Five global external auditing firms have already shrunk to the Big Four. An indication of the atmosphere of the times can be gauged from the title of a monograph published by a reform group—*Dirty Business: The Unchecked Power of Major Accountancy Firms.*[1]

Auditors are in the spotlight like never before, and fundamental questions are being asked about the value of auditing. Well-publicized corporate governance scandals appear to have combined creative accounting with creative audit compliance. Whatever truths will eventually emerge from the current crisis, it is clear that external auditing will be subjected to fundamental reform of some nature. It is too early to predict the new directions (if any) external auditing will take in the twenty-first century, and a full discussion of the topic is beyond the scope of this book. However, given the immensity of recent events it would be remiss not to take the opportunity to briefly reflect on some of the possible avenues of action under consideration by regulatory authorities around the world.

One common suggestion is the periodic rotation of external auditors, on the grounds that the longevity of auditor appointments can result in uncomfortably close relationships with corporate management. Some countries (e.g., Italy and Spain) have already adopted measures along these lines, but apparently with few obvious benefits. Another possibility is the imposition of restrictions on senior external auditors moving to take up posts at their clients, as some observers claim that this trend can also result in uncomfortably close relations between corporations and their external auditors. Another potential avenue of action is a reduction in the types of nonauditing services that external auditors will be permitted to provide to their clients. At the time of writing, the latter approach appears to have gained widespread support in the financial press, as the range of services provided by the external auditing profession has reached very large proportions. Conflicts of interest can potentially arise from the provision of multiple services, as an auditor may be unwilling to issue a problematic audit opinion if it would jeopardize lucrative consulting services.

A professor of accounting responsible for tendering his college's auditing contract gives amusing insight into the multitude of add-on services offered by the large accountancy firms in recent years: "All of the candidates [for the audit tender] stressed their expertise in non-audit areas, such as taxation and the design of information systems. One firm went so far as to say that its catering specialists could improve the running of the college kitchens. I was tempted to ask if they also provided painting and decorating or window cleaning services, but I decided against it for fear of eliciting a positive answer!"[2]

However, the current malaise facing external auditing may be more than just a matter of definitions of auditor independence. It could be that auditing is on the threshold of a major philosophical change, as the corporate governance scandals provoke a "return to basics." This may involve a reduction of overritualistic risk assessment processes and a reemphasizing of traditional substantive testing. This is not to suggest that risk assessment is itself at fault, but simply that high-level risk assessment must always be tempered by a willingness to undertake detailed auditing work at the level of accounting transactions.

It must be emphasized that external auditing's discomfort may be internal auditing's gain. Internal auditing is likely to continue its development into an integral part of the corporate governance framework at the highest levels. There are already signs that corporate governance is increasingly looking beyond external assurance to in-house regulation and monitoring procedures.

Internal auditing is unlikely to remain immune from any future changes in the practices of external auditing, however. If corporate governance reform encourages a "return to basics" in external auditing, then internal auditors too may be encouraged to emphasize some of their more traditional practices. Alongside the use of risk assessment, the verification of the existence of adequate internal controls may be stressed once again. One of the "postulates" of auditing articulated 40 years ago by pioneering philosophers in the field was that "the existence of a satisfactory system of internal control eliminates the probability of irregularities."[3] This is perhaps a beacon of truth to hold aloft, whatever future direction auditing may take.

AUDITING AROUND THE WORLD

As stated in the Preface, the reader will find more than just auditing information in the book's individual country sections. Once a satisfactory level of technical ability is achieved, the auditor's major challenge for international assignments is to apply expertise in various challenging contexts. It is the author's firm belief that successful international auditing requires a basic appreciation of a country's history, politics, and general culture, and that good international auditing requires a spirit of intellectual adventure. The country sections aim to provide a grounding in these topics.

This book has highlighted a number of concerns in the field of international auditing: logistical challenges, cultural differences, and security concerns. However, it would be inappropriate to finish on a negative tone. Auditing can be of immense value to global organizations, and for the individual auditing professional, the experience of performing assignments around the world can be extremely rewarding. As the author has written on the subject of global travel:

"International assignments . . . can be the most difficult aspect of auditing. Yet they can also be enjoyable and enriching, and perhaps the most rewarding of auditing experiences. Images and events remain engraved in the mind for many years. For example, the present author remembers breath-taking flights over the Tibetan plateau, shimmering sunsets by the Arabian Sea, and traffic jams caused by herds of African camels. He recalls candlelit suppers in Madrid, sheltering from tropical storms in Brazilian cafés, and the pleasurable frustrations of grappling with chopsticks in Korean restaurants. Yes, international auditing can be tough and tiring, challenging and exasperating. But it can also be highly enjoyable!"[4]

NOTES

1. Austin Mitchell and Prem Sikka, *Dirty Business: The Unchecked Power of Major Accountancy Firms* (Basildon, Essex, UK: Association for Accountancy and Business Affairs, 2002).

2. Geoffrey Whittington, *Is Accounting Becoming Too Interesting?* (Aberystwyth, Wales: University of Wales, 1995), 12–13.

3. R. K. Mautz and Hussein A. Sharaf, *The Philosophy of Auditing* (Sarasota, FL: American Accounting Association, 1961), 42.

4. David O'Regan, *Auditing International Entities: A Practical Guide to Risks, Objectives and Reporting* (Altamonte Springs, FL: Institute of Internal Auditors, 2001), 89.

7

Select Bibliography and Other Sources of Information

The sources used in the preparation of this book were diverse, and scattered through a variety of forms: books, newspaper articles, scholarly journals, Web-based resources, and personal experience. This chapter discusses some authoritative voices in the ever-expanding fields of auditing, risk management, and globalization. The sources listed here are by no means exhaustive. They are intended simply to serve as a guide to the vast topics under consideration, and the omission of a particular source is no reflection on its character. In the Appendix, individual country sections include additional information on specific countries.

Chapter 1: Introduction—International Auditing

On auditing theory, important milestones include R. K. Mautz and H. A. Sharaf, *The Philosophy of Auditing* (Sarasota, FL: American Accounting Association, 1961); Michael Power, *The Audit Society* (New York and Oxford: Oxford University Press, 1997); and Lawrence B. Sawyer and Gerald Vinten, *The Manager and the Internal Auditor: Partners for Profit* (New York: John Wiley & Sons, 1996).

A good starting point for auditing history is the *Accounting Historians Journal* of the Academy of Accounting Historians (http://accounting.rutgers.edu/raw/aah). Although focused mainly on accountancy, the journal gives good treatment to the history of auditing. A valuable book in the field is R. H. Parker and Basil Yamey's *Accounting History* (New York and Oxford: Oxford University Press, 1994).

Developments in external auditing can be found at the Web site of the American Institute of Certified Public Accountants (*www.aicpa.org*). The external auditing literature is vast and is likely to increase in size as a result of the clamor for change arising from recent corporate governance scandals. (The Web sites of the Big Four international accountancy firms are valuable sources of developments in the external auditing profession.) A thought-provoking overview of the modern profession is V. Beattie and S. Fearnley's *What Companies Want (and Don't*

Want) From Their Auditors (London: Institute of Chartered Accountants' Research Board, 1998), while Dan M. Guy and D. R. Carmichael's annually updated *Wiley Practitioner's Guide to GAAS* (New York: John Wiley and Sons) sets out external auditing standards and practices.

The best source of information on internal auditing is the Web site of the Institute of Internal Auditors (*www.theiia.org*). The IIA site has links to national IIA Web pages that can be a useful source of information on international developments in internal auditing, risk management, and corporate governance. Valuable books on internal auditing include James Roth's *Best Practices: Value-Added Approaches of Four Innovative Auditing Departments* (Altamonte Springs, FL: Institute of Internal Auditors, 2000), and K. H. Spencer's *Internal Auditing Handbook* (New York: John Wiley and Sons, 1997).

Opposing views of the globalization debate can be gleaned from John Gray's *False Dawn: The Delusions of Global Capitalism* (London: Granta Books, 1998) and John Micklethwait and Adrian Wooldridge's *A Future Perfect: The Challenge and Hidden Promise of Globalization* (New York and London: Random House, 2000). Gray's powerful critique of the effects of globalization contrasts with Micklethwait and Wooldridge's eloquent defense of the phenomenon. Samuel P. Huntington's *The Clash of Civilizations and the Remaking of World Order* (New York: Simon & Schuster, 1996) offers a fascinating and disturbing thesis that, beneath a superficial veneer of globalization, the world is fragmenting into mutually-antagonistic cultures.

The literature on international auditing is sparse, but the author's *Auditing International Entities: A Practical Guide to Objectives, Risks and Reporting* (Altamonte Springs, FL: Institute of Internal Auditors, 2001) provides a brief introduction to international internal auditing. Lee H. Radebaugh and Sidney J. Gray's *International Accounting and Multinational Enterprises,* 4th ed. (New York: John Wiley & Sons, 1997) has extensive information on global auditing.

Chapter 2: International Organizations and Their Risks and Chapter 3: Managing Risks Internationally

For economic risk, the Web sites of the World Bank (*www.worldbank.org*) and International Monetary Fund (*www.imf.org*) are valuable sources of economic information, especially for developing countries. For political matters, the member states' Web sites at the United Nations (*www.un.org*) have links to the individual Web pages of countries' Permanent Missions. These contain valuable information on politics, culture, and economics, as well as links to other sources of information, such as government bodies and national media. The Web site of the World Trade Organization (*www.wto.org*) contains details of international trade agreements.

The legal and regulatory field is constantly evolving, and there are countless potential sources of information. Owing to the fast-moving nature of this topic, Web resources are probably best. The Organization for Economic and Cultural

Development (*www.oecd.org*) mainly represents the interests of developed countries, and its Web site contains much useful information—the status of tax havens is particularly well-covered. Other useful resources include the Web sites of the International Chamber of Commerce (*www.iccwbo.org*) and the International Labor Organization (*www.ilo.org*). The latter is a UN agency and its Web site has information on international employee rights. It has links to many useful international organizations, including trade unions.

One book stands out as an excellent introduction to international accounting practice, Christopher Nobes and Robert Parker's *Comparative International Accounting*, 7th ed. (New York and London: Prentice Hall, 2002), which provides historical details of differences in global accountancy. For up-to-date information on international accounting standards and their use around the world, reference should be made to the Web sites of the International Accounting Standards Board (*www.iasc.org.uk*), the International Federation of Accountants (*www.ifac.org*), and the International Forum on Accountancy Development (*www.ifad.net*). Another useful resource is Deloitte Touche Tohmatsu's "IAS Plus" Web site (*www.iasplus.com/index.htm*).

On cultural differences, two useful books stand out: Terri Morrison, Wayne A. Conaway, and George A. Borden's *Kiss, Bow or Shake Hands: How to Do Business in 60 Countries* (Holbrook, MA: Adams Media Corporation, 1995), and Roger E. Axtell's *Gestures: The Do's and Taboos of Body Language Around the World*, rev. ed. (New York: John Wiley and Sons, 1997). Other useful titles include Wiley & Sons' *Global Etiquette* series, which covers different regions of the world.

On more serious cultural (and political) matters, Transparency International (*www.transparency.org*) is a non-governmental organization that monitors corruption around the world and aims to curb its practice. Its Web site has information on anti-corruption regulations and legislation in specific countries, and it has comparative country analyses of corruption. Amnesty International (*www.amnesty.org*) seeks to promote international human rights, and its Web site details human rights abuses around the world.

Chapter 4: Organization-Wide Risk Assessment

On risk and auditing, David McNamee and Georges M. Selim's *Risk Management: Changing the Internal Auditor's Paradigm* (Altamonte Springs, FL: Institute of Internal Auditors Research Foundation, 1998) is a primary source. Its bibliography gives many pointers to further reading. While the report of the Committee of Sponsoring Organizations of the Treadway Commission (COSO), *Internal Control—Integrated Framework* (Jersey City, NJ: AICPA/COSO, 1992), is often referred to in the auditing and risk management literature, it is worth consulting this landmark document directly. A more general (and fascinating) book on risk is Peter L. Bernstein's *Against the Gods: The Remarkable Story of Risk* (New York: John Wiley and Sons, 1996).

Chapter 5: The Logistics of Auditing

The U.S. State Department offers travel warnings at *http://travel.state.gov/warnings_list*, while the Travel Advice Unit of the British Foreign and Commonwealth Office (*www.fco.gov.uk*) provides country advice to British citizens. The Central Intelligence Agency Factbook (*www.odci.gov/cia/publications/factbook*) has an array of information on economic, political, and demographic matters for virtually all countries in the world. The EU Web site (*http://europa.eu.int*) has an enormous quantity of information on its member countries.

Global Reference Section

Africa

TAX HAVENS AND INVESTMENT CENTERS: MAURITIUS

MAURITIUS

Mauritius is an Indian Ocean island to the east of Madagascar, with a population of around 1.1 million. Famous as the former home of the dodo, the extinct flightless bird, Mauritius passed through the hands of the Dutch and French before coming under British colonial control in 1810. Mauritius gained independence from Britain in 1968, and became a republic in 1992.

The island's colonial past has resulted in an ethnic melting pot, and today Mauritius has communities of Indian, African, Chinese, and European origin. Indians account for over 50 percent of the population and Creoles (descendents of African slaves) for around 33 percent. Languages spoken include English, Hindi, French, and Creole. The country has generally enjoyed a history of ethnic harmony, but in recent years the Creole population has complained of poverty and discrimination, and riots and civil unrest have occasionally broken out.

Mauritius is one of Africa's most stable, democratic, and prosperous countries. Major industrial sectors include sugar, textiles, and tourism. In recent years, the country has also attracted a significant amount of foreign investment and is home to thousands of offshore corporations. There has also been a huge development in the offshore banking sector. Many of the offshore operations tend to have close links with South Africa and India.

The country's legal system reflects both British and French colonial traditions. Mauritius Accounting Standards are based closely on IAS and are issued by the country's Accounting and Auditing Standards Committee, which was established by legislation in 1989. The committee consists of representatives from government, industry, the accounting profession, and academia. The modeling of accounting standards on IAS reflects the country's desire to raise its profile as an international investment center. Details of Mauritius accounting standards are available online from the Companies Division section of the government's Web site (*www.gov.mu*).

Further Information

Thomas Hylland Eriksen, *Common Denominators: Ethnicity, Nation-Building and Compromise in Mauritius* (New York and Oxford: Berg, 1998). Government of Mauritius: *www.gov.mu.*

ALGERIA

Geography

Algeria is located in North Africa. The country has a Mediterranean Sea coastline and bordering countries include Libya, Mali, Morocco, Niger, and Tunisia. Algeria is a vast country, and over 80 percent of its terrain is covered by the Sahara desert. The north is mountainous in parts and has a relatively fertile coastal plain. The climate is generally very hot and dry, although temperatures are cooler and rainfall more common along the coast. Algeria's hot and dusty wind known as the "sirocco" brings daily life to a halt when it flares up in summer months, and its effects are sometimes felt across the Mediterranean Sea in southern Italy.

Brief History

The territory that comprises modern Algeria has a long history of settlement and civilization, and the indigenous Berber peoples have seen a series of invaders through the millennia. Early conquerors included the Phoenicians, who established a flourishing empire at the start of the first millennium BCE centered on the coastal city of Carthage (located in modern Tunisia). Over the following centuries, the Phoenicians clashed with the rising Roman Empire and large numbers of Berbers served in the Phoenician armies. The power of Carthage waned following military defeat by the Romans, and a number of autonomous Berber kingdoms emerged around the second century BCE. However, the Berber kingdoms soon vanished as the Romans absorbed North Africa into their empire. During the Roman era, many Berbers converted to Christianity, and through both migration and conversion, the region also had a large Jewish population.

With the disintegration of the Roman Empire in the fifth century CE, the Vandals (a Germanic tribe) invaded North Africa and established a Vandal kingdom. The Greek-speaking Byzantine Empire destroyed the Vandal kingdom in the following century, but the Byzantine conquerors were unable to establish a political grip on the region. Berber political units again emerged. The next major invasion was that of the Arabs in the seventh century. The Arab conquerors brought the Islamic faith and the Arabic language, both of which had long-lasting effects on the culture of the local peoples. However, despite converting to Islam, the Berber peoples have tenaciously preserved their distinctive culture through to the present day.

In the sixteenth century, the Spanish attempted to colonize parts of North Africa, but most of the territory of modern Algeria fell under the control of the Turkish Ottoman Empire. The next outsiders to seize power in the region were the

French, who brutally conquered Algeria in 1830. The French subsequently used the political fiction that Algeria was an inseparable part of France to justify their presence in the country. However, French Algeria was in fact a traditional colony, built on the cultural and racial arrogance of imperialism.

An Algerian nationalist movement emerged in the early twentieth century, but it was not until after World War II that armed resistance to French colonialism exploded into a major war. In 1954, pro-independence guerrillas launched a major offensive against French military establishments in Algeria. The French fought tenaciously to maintain their colony, and the war of independence was exceptionally violent. More than 1 million people died in the bitter conflict, which saw widespread massacres of civilians. Both sides were accused of atrocities and other serious human rights abuses. In the late 1950s, the French colonial authorities tried increasingly desperate measures to stem the tide of a war that was clearly turning against them. The French "resettled" around 2 million civilians in an attempt to eliminate sources of the rebels' material and moral support, and they bombarded villages suspected of being sympathetic to the rebels. The war spread to France itself, in the form of street violence and politically motivated bombings. Algeria finally gained independence in 1962, and around 1 million French colonists left the country to resettle in France. (Tens of thousands of pro-French Algerian collaborators also left the country for France, as their safety could not be guaranteed in independent Algeria.)

Following the end of colonial rule, Algeria has experienced long periods of political instability. The war of independence caused serious loss of life and physical destruction, and the French "resettlement" of 2 million Algerians severely damaged the country's social and economic structures. Some commentators argue that the country has not yet fully recovered from the impact of the war of the 1950s and early 1960s. Algeria also followed a socialist path that compounded economic inefficiencies.

In the 1990s, the country's fortunes again took a violent turn, with a vicious power struggle between Islamic militants and the broadly secular state apparatus. In 1992, the army intervened to civilian politics to cancel elections that the Islamic Salvation Front (*Front Islamique du Salut*—FIS) were set to win. Outraged Islamic groups started an armed insurgency that has claimed over 100,000 lives to date. As in the war of independence, the current civil war has seen large-scale massacres of civilians, and critics have accused both the rebels and the state of murder and other human rights abuses. The FIS disbanded its armed wing in 2000, and there is currently hope for future peace, but sporadic violence still continues at the time of writing.

In recent years, street protests between Berbers demanding more cultural autonomy and the country's police and armed forces have led to dozens of deaths.

Demographics

Algeria's population of around 32 million is mainly concentrated in coastal areas. Algerians (and those of Algerian descent) resident in the former colonial power,

France, are estimated to number over 1 million. Many Algerian migrants have taken French citizenship.

Languages

The main languages of Algeria are Arabic (spoken by approximately 70 to 80 percent of the population) and Berber (20 to 30 percent). French is widely spoken by the country's middle classes and is often used for business purposes. The Saudi Arabia country section gives details on the Arabic language, but it should be noted that the variety of Arabic spoken in Algeria is quite distinct from that spoken in the Arabian Peninsula, especially at colloquial levels. There are differences in pronunciation, and many Berber words have been incorporated into Algerian Arabic. Berber is primarily a spoken language, and is a member of the Hamito-Semitic language family. There are several Berber dialects spoken in Algeria. The country's male literacy rate is approximately 75 percent, but female literacy is only around 50 percent.

Politics

The People's Democratic Republic of Algeria has its capital at Algiers. The president serves as head of state, and the prime minister acts as head of government. The Algerian parliament is bicameral, and the members of the lower chamber are elected by popular vote. In 1992, military interference in the democratic process triggered a civil war that remains the main political issue facing the country today.

Economy

The Algerian economy is dependent on natural gas and oil, which together account for 95 percent of export revenues. Other than the obvious problem of overdependence on these economic activities, the country has other serious structural problems—the devastation and dislocation caused by two brutal wars in less than 50 years; decades of inefficient, socialist policies; and low levels of foreign investment. Recent Algerian governments have implemented market-oriented reforms, but the civil war has sapped the confidence of foreign investors. Unemployment remains high, and one in four Algerians lives in poverty. Algeria's largest trading partners are France, Italy, and the United States, and the country's currency unit is the dinar.

Legal and Regulatory Environment

Algerian law is based on a mixture of both French and Islamic law. The socialist nature of immediate postindependence administrations led to the creation of a heavily bureaucratic regulatory environment, which has been partially alleviated by market-oriented reforms in recent years.

Accountancy

Algerian GAAP is strongly influenced by the traditions of French accounting, as a result of the long period of French colonial rule. The France country section gives details on the sources of French GAAP, which rely heavily on tax law and the use of a national chart of accounts. The Algerian accountancy and external auditing profession is relatively small, numbering in the hundreds, and the main professional accountancy and external auditing organization—the *Union des Experts-Comptables*—is patterned on French lines. Algeria is not yet a full member of the International Federation of Accountants.

Cultural Background

Algeria's two main ethnic groups are Arabs and Berbers. It is difficult to obtain precise data on the relative sizes of both ethnic communities, not least as a result of intermarriage, but language is often used as an indicative measure. Some commentators estimate that around 20 to 30 percent of Algerians speak one of the Berber dialects as a first language, and on this basis an approximate split of 70 to 80 percent Arab and 20 to 30 percent Berber seems reasonable.

In general, Arabs and Berbers mix well, and the ethnic boundary between the two groups is not always a rigid one—it is thought that many Arabic-speaking Algerians are of Berber descent. However, in recent years street unrest in Berber-majority areas has broken out, as some Berbers have demanded greater recognition of Berber cultural identity. (There are several distinct Berber communities with differences in language, customs, and social practices.) Virtually all Algerians are Sunni Muslims, and Christians and Jews account for less than 1 percent of the population.

Social Etiquette

The Saudi Arabia country section has comments of general application to North African Muslim culture. In addition:

- The brutal war of independence with France remains a sensitive topic for discussion, as many Algerians lived and suffered through the conflict. To avoid distress, it is a topic best avoided by the visitor.
- Civil unrest involving young ethnic Berbers is also a highly sensitive topic.

Further Information

Michael Brett and Elizabeth Fentress, *The Berbers* (Malden, MA and Oxford: Blackwell, 1997).
Hugh Roberts, *Embattled Algeria, 1988–2001* (New York: Verso Books, forthcoming in 2003).
Martin Stone, *The Agony of Algeria* (New York: Columbia University Press, 1997).

Benjamin Stora, *Algeria, 1830–2000: A Short History* (Ithaca, NY: Cornell University Press, 2001).

National Council of Algeria (Arabic and French only): *www.majliselouma.dz*.

EGYPT

Geography

Egypt is located in the northeast corner of Africa, bordering Israel and the Gaza Strip, Libya, and Sudan. The country has coastlines on both the Mediterranean and Red Seas. Egypt's terrain comprises mainly desert, although the country is bisected by the Nile River and its fertile valley. Egypt's climate is hot and dry, with modest rainfall along the Mediterranean coast.

Brief History

Egypt was the location of one of the world's major early civilizations: The fertility of the Nile Valley supported the dynasty of the pharaohs, established around 3000 BCE. Ancient Egypt produced the world-famous pyramids, monumental structures of astonishing technological advancement for their era. The Greeks under Alexander the Great conquered Egypt in the fourth century BCE. The next conquerors were the Romans, who absorbed Egypt into the Roman Empire in the first century BCE.

With the disintegration of the Roman Empire in the fourth and fifth centuries CE, a series of other peoples were attracted by Egypt's fabled wealth and strategic location. Nubians and Persians were among outsiders who invaded the country, but Egypt remained relatively stable until the arrival of the Arabs in the seventh century CE. The Arabs brought Islam and the Arabic language. A large part of the population did not abandon its Christian faith, however, and Egypt today has a community of Coptic Christians that numbers in the millions.

From the eleventh century, Egypt fell under the control of the Turks. The traditional homelands of the Turkish people were in Central Asia, but the Turks had started to migrate toward the Mid East from the sixth century CE. They adopted Islam and established a series of powerful regimes in the region. The Turkish Mamluks were among the early Turkish rulers of Egypt, and when the Turkish Ottoman Empire took control of the country in the early sixteenth century, it left local government largely in Mamluk hands.

Over the centuries, the ancient wealth of Egypt had been slowly dissipated, and when French forces under Napoleon invaded Egypt in 1798, they found a largely impoverished country. French colonial ambitions were frustrated by the British and the Ottoman Empire, who cooperated to drive the French out of Egypt in 1801. The French incursion brought the cultural wealth of Egypt to the attention of the western world, however, and it brought the European powers into the

Egyptian political arena. The economically important and strategically located Suez Canal opened in 1869. A main beneficiary of the canal was Britain, as the canal dramatically reduced the duration of the sea journey between England and the British colony of India.

Britain and France became increasingly embroiled in Egyptian politics and economic affairs in the late nineteenth century, and an anti-European nationalist movement arose in the country. Britain triumphed over France in the colonial struggle for power in Egypt, and although it was never officially a British colony, Egypt was effectively absorbed into the British Empire.

Egypt celebrates February 28, 1922 as the date the country gained independence from Britain. However, the British continued to pull Egypt's political and economic strings, and it was only after World War II that Egypt achieved full independence. Egypt tried in vain to prevent the creation of Israel in 1948, but was unable to defeat the Israelis militarily.

In 1952, a bloodless military coup was led by Colonel Gamal Abdel Nasser (1918–1970), whose populist policies blended socialism with Arab nationalism. Nasser quickly became the leading political figure of the Arab world, and his fiery rhetoric stirred Arab pride across the Mid East. In 1956, Nasser nationalized the Suez Canal, and Egypt was attacked by Britain, France, and Israel. The United States pressured the Europeans and Israelis to withdraw, and Nasser emerged victorious. His popularity among Arabs across the Mid East soared to new heights.

Despite Nasser's victory over the Suez Canal issue, Egypt was to suffer a series of damaging defeats in wars against Israel in the following decades. Under Nasser, Egypt lost a war to Israel in 1967, while under his successor Anwar Sadat (1918–1981) there was another defeat in 1973. In addition to the loss of life caused by the wars against Israel, Egypt lost significant portions of its territory. By the mid-1970s, Egyptian national pride had been humiliated.

Sadat made peace with Israel in 1979, in return for the territories seized by Israel during the wars. Much of the Arab world was outraged by the peace deal between Egypt and Israel, and Sadat was assassinated two years later. Sadat's successor as president was Hosni Mubarak (born 1928). Mubarak has followed a generally pro-western policy, and he has suppressed Muslim fundamentalists. He has also maintained peace with Israel (through to the time of writing) and has survived a number of assassination attempts.

Major challenges for the country's political rulers include chronic poverty for a large proportion of the population, and an Islamic movement that threatens to undermine the Mubarak administration.

Demographics

Egypt's population is around 69 million, of which 99 percent live in the fertile Nile Delta area. The country's large desert areas are virtually uninhabited. Poverty and overpopulation in urban areas have driven millions of Egyptians to seek employment elsewhere in the world, mainly in the oil-rich states of the Persian Gulf.

Languages

The official language of Egypt is Arabic. (The Arabic language is discussed in more detail in the Saudi Arabia country section.) Among the middle classes, English and French are widely understood, although the popularity of the latter is steadily declining. There are small communities of Armenians, Greeks, and Nubians who have maintained their languages, but in combination these groups comprise less than 1 percent of the population. The country's literacy rate is around 60 percent for men and 40 percent for women.

Politics

The Arab Republic of Egypt is a democracy and has its capital at Cairo. The president acts as head of state, and the prime minister acts as head of government. The Egyptian parliament is bicameral, and both the main assembly and the consultative advisory council contain a mixture of appointed and popularly elected members. Despite restrictions on some of their activities, Islamic groups remain the country's most serious political opposition. Egypt has a deserved reputation as a haven for dissidents and refugees fleeing other Mid East states.

Economy

Egypt's natural resources include oil, natural gas, and cotton, and major industries include chemicals, food processing, textiles, and tourism. The economy has long suffered from the problems typically associated with developing countries—infrastructure is weak, much of industry is outdated, and population pressures have added to urban unemployment. One in four Egyptians lives in poverty. The remittances of millions of foreign workers have been an important part of the economy, but the flight to other countries of well-qualified professions has led to a serious "brain drain." The countries of the EU are Egypt's main trading partners, and the currency unit is the Egyptian pound.

Legal and Regulatory Environment

Egyptian law is a mixture of Islamic law, English common law, and the principles of the French *Code Napoléon*. The English and French influences date from the colonial activities of Britain and France in the nineteenth and early twentieth centuries. The Egyptian regulatory environment is relatively cumbersome, although structural reforms—such as revised business legislation—have reduced the amount of red tape in recent years.

Accountancy

Egyptian GAAP is based on corporate law, the accounting standards of the Egyptian Society of Accountants and Auditors (ESAA), and central bank regulations. Egyptian accounting standards are broadly in line with IAS, but Egyptian GAAP differs from IAS in areas such as accounting for combinations, accounting for leases, and the treatment of hyperinflation. When Egyptian GAAP is silent on a topic, then IAS is to be used. However, all listed corporations are required to follow IAS.

Cultural Background

Culturally, Egypt has one foot in Africa and the other in the Mid East. Although the ethnic history of Egypt is complex (it involves Africans, Arabs, Greeks, Persians, and Turks), the present-day population is relatively homogeneous. There are small communities of Armenians, Greeks, and Nubians that account for less than 1 percent of the population. The majority religion is Islam, which is estimated to be the faith of around 90 to 95 percent of the population. Most of the country's non-Muslims are Coptic Christians. The latter belong to a church independent from the other main branches of Christianity, and the Copts have their own Coptic Pope. There is also a Coptic language, although this has died out for everyday use and survives only for liturgical purposes. Violence between Muslims and Copts has broken out from time to time in recent years.

Social Etiquette

- Egyptian hospitality is legendary, and business visitors tend to be well entertained.
- Although most Muslims do not drink alcohol, many Egyptian hotels and restaurants serve wine and beer.
- Tipping is common practice.
- Women should dress conservatively at all times.
- Most Egyptians have been profoundly distressed by terrorist attacks against foreign tourists in recent years. It is a topic best avoided by the visitor.
- Relations between the country's Muslim majority and Christian minority are also a highly sensitive topic.

Further Information

Ninette S. Fahmy, *The Politics of Egypt: State-Society Relationship* (New York and London: Routledge, 2002).

Barry J. Kemp, *Ancient Egypt: Anatomy of a Civilization* (New York and London: Routledge, 1991).

Carrie Rosefsky Wickham, *Mobilizing Islam: Religion, Activism, and Political Change in Egypt* (New York: Columbia University Press, 2002).

The Egyptian Presidency: *www.presidency.gov.eg*.

ETHIOPIA

Geography

Ethiopia is a landlocked country in East Africa, bordering Djibouti, Eritrea, Kenya, Somalia, and Sudan. The country's diverse terrain consists mainly of highlands, mountains, and plateaux, divided by the massive Great Rift Valley. The climate reflects the terrain's diversity—at low altitudes temperatures are generally hot, although there are both tropical and arid conditions in parts of the country. The rainy season from June to September periodically disappoints, and Ethiopia has experienced serious droughts and famines in recent decades.

Brief History

The Ethiopian nation is something of a rarity in Africa—an independent country that has managed to avoid colonization by a western power (other than a five-year occupation by fascist Italy in the middle of the twentieth century). The country has an ancient history of settlement and civilization. Some historians have even claimed that East Africa's Great Rift Valley, which bisects modern Ethiopia and runs into Kenya, may be the location of the origins of humankind. What is beyond question is that agricultural patterns of life have existed for millennia in the territory of modern Ethiopia.

Ethiopia has a complex ethnic history. Indigenous peoples were joined in the first millennium BCE by migrants from other parts of Africa and from the Arabian Peninsula. The "Cultural Background" section indicates the complex ethnic composition of the country today. Christianity came to Ethiopia in the fourth century CE, and the Christian religion established a powerful hold over the population that it retains to this day. When Arab armies exported Islam throughout the region in the seventh century, the Ethiopian Christian culture managed to survive. Today, despite over 1,000 years of pressure from both animist and Muslim peoples, the country's Christian heritage is still largely intact.

By the eighteenth century, the Ethiopia political and cultural environments were under severe strain, and the country fragmented into small, warring provinces. The only serious attempt at colonization by a European power came from the fascist regime in Italy. The Italians were latecomers to colonization in Africa, and by the late nineteenth century, much of the continent had already been carved up among Britain, France, Portugal, and Belgium. In the 1880s, Italy lay claim to neighboring Eritrea and used that territory as a springboard to attempt to colonize Ethiopia over the following decades.

In the 1930s, Italy's fascist dictator Benito Mussolini unleashed an attempt at full colonization. Italy used its military superiority in conventional and chemical warfare to attack Ethiopia in 1935, and it seized control of the country in the following year. The Ethiopian Emperor Haile Selassie (1892–1975) fled in exile. Italian colonial rule was brutal, and many thousands of Ethiopians were executed or incarcerated. Resistance, however, bubbled throughout the country. When British troops defeated the Italians in 1941, Emperor Haile Selassie returned to his liberated country. The British assisted the Ethiopians to rehabilitate their national institutions, and by the end of World War II Ethiopia had been reestablished as a stable, sovereign state. In the 1960s and 1970s, British influence waned, to be replaced by that of the Soviet Union.

A severe famine caused internal unrest in the early 1970s and public opinion turned largely against Emperor Haile Selassie. The emperor was deposed in 1974 by a left-wing military regime, and the aged and frail Selassie died (or was murdered) in captivity the following year. Under the leadership of Mengistu Haile Mariam (born 1937), the socialist state brutally repressed opposition and turned to the Soviet Union for economic and military support. A combination of a lengthy drought, disastrous economic policies, and ill-conceived resettlement plans led to a return of famine in the 1980s. A long-running war with Eritrean rebels added to Ethiopia's economic woes and hindered the transfer of food to famine areas.

Armed opposition fighters toppled the Mengistu regime in 1991, after a brutal civil war that killed thousands. Democratic elections were held in 1995. However, although the threat of famine receded after the change of regime, old hostilities with Eritrea erupted into war in 1998. The Eritreans had established their independence in 1993, after a 30-year independence struggle, but a border dispute was the spark to further hostilities. The two countries reached a peace settlement in 2000, and the border dispute was "settled" in the international courts in early 2002. At the time of writing, relations between the two countries remain tense, and the potential for further conflict has not been entirely eliminated. The war has added to Ethiopia's desperate economic plight.

Demographics

Ethiopia has a population of around 65 million. Precise population figures are difficult to establish, partly owing to large movements of refugees between Ethiopia and neighboring Sudan and Somalia.

Languages

The main languages of Ethiopia are Amharic, Tigrinya, and Orominga, but there are over 70 languages spoken in the country. Amharic is Ethiopia's official language, and most native speakers are located in the country's central regions. Tigrinya tends to be spoken in the north, while Orominya predominates in the south. The Amharic and Tigrinya languages are written in the indigenous Ge'ez script. The "Cultural Background" section gives details on the ethnic makeup of Ethiopia, which tends to reflect linguistic patterns. The country's literacy levels are low, at around 45 percent for men and 35 percent for women, despite costly literacy campaigns run by the Mengistu regime in the 1970s.

Politics

The Federal Democratic Republic of Ethiopia is a democracy and has its capital at Addis Ababa. The country's president acts as head of state, and the prime minister acts as head of government. The parliament is bicameral in structure, and its lower chamber is elected by popular vote. Ethiopia has a large number of political parties, many of which have a regional or ethnic support base.

Economy

Ethiopia is one of the world's poorest countries. Chronic poverty is a legacy of war, famine, political upheaval, and adverse climatic conditions. Ethiopia is primarily an agricultural country, and agricultural products generate 90 percent of export earnings. Over 80 percent of the workforce work in the agricultural sector, and major products include coffee, beeswax, and sugarcane. Ethiopia's droughts are notorious, and in recent years famine has been either a reality or a near-constant threat. Millions depend on food assistance. The country has industries in chemicals, textiles, and food processing, and the exploitation of natural gas promises to be a profitable future activity, but the country relies on significant amounts of foreign aid. Major trading partners include Saudi Arabia, Germany, and Italy, and the currency unit is the birr.

Legal and Regulatory Environment

Ethiopian law is based on a mixture of indigenous practices and western-style jurisprudence. The Ethiopian regulatory environment was extremely heavy during the Mengistu years, when the command economy played such a disastrous role in the daily life of the country. Since the restoration of democracy, the level of red tape has eased considerably, but the regulatory environment remains complex and cumbersome.

Accountancy

Ethiopian accountancy practice during the Mengistu regime followed the practices of most command economies, with data analysis serving the state's allocation of resources. Since the restoration of democracy, Ethiopian accounting has moved closer toward western norms and is based largely on company and tax law. However, the country's continuing economic plight has resulted in a small accountancy and external auditing profession that numbers in the hundreds. Ethiopia is not yet a full member of the International Federation of Accountants, and the large international accounting firms have only a small presence in the country.

Cultural Background

It is difficult to obtain precise data on Ethiopia's ethnic makeup, but the main communities are Oromo (approximately 40 percent of the population), the Amhara and the Tigre (32 percent combined), and the Sidamo (9 percent). The religious breakdown is approximately 40 to 45 percent Christian and 40 to 45 percent Muslim, with the balance comprising animists and followers of other indigenous beliefs. Most Christians adhere to the Ethiopian Orthodox Church, which dates from the fourth century CE. At least 60,000 Ethiopian Jews left for

Israel in the late twentieth century, and the Jewish community has today dwindled to small numbers.

As an interesting footnote, Ethiopia's long tradition of independence from colonialism has made it a symbol of Afro-centric pride. The former emperor Haile Selassie has been revered as a divine figure by some black groups, such as the Rastafarian movement.

Social Etiquette

- Ethiopians tend to be friendly to foreign visitors, and warmly appreciate the fact that a visitor has ventured to a country so often painted negatively by the media.
- Conservative dress and calm, restrained behavior is highly recommended at all times.
- Unless necessitated by professional work, the famines of the late twentieth century are a topic best avoided. The distress caused by the famines is still very real.

Further Information

Tekeste Negash and Kjetil Tronvoll, *Brothers at War: Making Sense of the Eritrean-Ethiopian War* (Athens, OH: Ohio University Press, 2001).

Richard Pankhurst, *The Ethiopians: A History* (Malden, MA and Oxford: Black-well, 1998).

Donald N. Levine, *Greater Ethiopia: The Evolution of a Multiethnic Society*, 2nd ed. (Chicago: University of Chicago Press, 2000).

Office of the (Ethiopian) Government Spokesperson: *www.ethiospokes.net.*

KENYA

Geography

Kenya is located in East Africa. It has an Indian Ocean coastline and borders Ethiopia, Somalia, Sudan, Tanzania, and Uganda. The Great Rift Valley bisects the country, and on either side of the valley's highlands the Kenyan terrain mainly comprises plains. The equatorial climate is tropical in coastal areas and dry in the country's interior.

Brief History

Kenya's ancient history of settlement has led some historians to refer to the country as the "cradle of humanity," as some of the earliest evidence of humanity's ancestors has been found in the Great Rift Valley area. The modern Kenyan population emerged as a result of millennia of migrations from various parts of Africa. From the eighth century CE, the East African coast attracted Arab traders, but by the late fifteenth century, Portuguese explorers and traders began to assert their authority in the region. Portuguese colonialism was characterized by harsh repression, and the Arabs regained control over the East African coast in 1720.

The East African economy deteriorated in the eighteenth and nineteenth centuries, as Arab traders and sultans fought for trade supremacy. In the nineteenth century, however, there was a surge in European colonial activity in Africa—the so-called "scramble for Africa." The interior of Kenya had always stayed aloof from the coastal struggles of Arabs and Portuguese, and the warrior Maasai peoples of the interior had remained largely independent. In the late nineteenth century, however, the British negotiated with the Maasai to open a railway between Uganda and the Kenyan coastal city of Mombasa. The railway was the trigger for a surge in British influence. A large influx of British settlers carved out large farms in the country, and in 1920 Kenya became an official British colony. The British and European settler community had reached around 75,000 by the 1950s.

Kenyan independence movements gained strength in the twentieth century, and culminated in the Mau Mau rebellion. The Mau Mau was a secret guerrilla society among the country's Kikuyu people, which used brutal terrorist tactics against European settlers. The British suppressed the rebellion with equal brutality, killing thousands of Kikuyu in its 1956 defeat of the rebels.

Kenya gained independence in 1963, and the charismatic founding president Jomo Kenyatta (1891–1978) dominated the independent state's politics until 1978, when he was succeeded by Daniel arap Moi (born 1924). Under Kenyatta, Kenya became one of the region's most politically stable and economically prosperous countries. Under Moi, however, Kenya's politics took a more authoritarian turn, and in the 1990s international aid agencies (including the World Bank) suspended aid to encourage greater democratization. President Moi is due to step down from power in 2003.

In recent years, Kenya has seen an increase in fighting between ethnic groups. Commentators have accused both the Moi government and the opposition of exploiting ethnic tensions for political gain. In August 1998, terrorists bombed the United States' embassy in Kenya, killing over 230 people and injuring thousands. Although almost certainly the work of outsiders, the terrorist attacks seemed to symbolize the country's contemporary political turmoil.

Demographics

The population of Kenya is around 31 million. The "Cultural Background" section gives details of the country's complex ethnic makeup.

Languages

Kenya's official languages are Swahili and English. In addition, a number of other languages are also spoken in the country—these include Kikuyu and Luhia. Swahili has been used as a postindependence political tool to reinforce a sense of national unity. The importance of English derives from Kenya's colonial past, and a new trend has seen the emergence of Sheng, a young and trendy mixture of

Swahili and English. The country's literacy level is around 75 percent, although it is higher for men than for women.

Politics

The Republic of Kenya is a democracy and has its capital at Nairobi. The president, who acts as both head of state and head of government, is elected by the National Assembly. The latter is the country's unicameral parliament, most of whose members are elected by popular vote. Although domestic opposition leaders and international aid agencies have criticized aspects of Kenya's democratic processes under president Daniel arap Moi, the country's democratic structures remain largely intact.

Economy

Kenya faces many of the classical economic challenges of developing countries—dependence on the agricultural sector, poor infrastructure, chronic poverty, and difficult climatic conditions. Three in four Kenyans work in agriculture, and major products include tea and coffee. Other important sectors include petroleum products, textiles, and tourism. The lucrative tourism sector, largely safari-based, has been badly affected by recent political unrest and ethnic fighting.

Despite prosperity in the early postindependence years, Kenya has suffered a long economic decline over recent decades. Today there is massive unemployment in the country, and 40 percent of the population lives in poverty. In recent years, international aid donors have on occasion withheld funds to encourage greater democratization. Kenya's main trading partners are Britain and Uganda, and the currency unit is the shilling.

Legal and Regulatory Environment

Kenyan law is based on a mixture of English common law (inherited from colonial times), indigenous law, and Islamic Shari'a law. The regulatory environment is highly bureaucratic, although in recent years the country has been under pressure from aid donors to reduce red tape and to introduce more transparency into economic and political systems.

Accountancy

Kenyan GAAP is based on IAS and company law. IAS has been fully applicable since 2000. The main accountancy and external auditing body is the Institute of Certified Public Accountants of Kenya (ICPAK), which was created in 1977 from preexisting accountancy bodies dating from the British colonial period.

Cultural Background

Kenya's ethnic makeup is complex. The main groups are the Kikuyu (around 22 percent of the population), Luhya (14 percent), Luo (12 percent), and Kalenjin (11 percent). Non-African inhabitants account for less than 1 percent of the population. Nominal figures for religious affiliation are around 40 percent Protestant and 30 percent Roman Catholic, with the remainder comprising Muslims and followers of indigenous beliefs. However, this data must be treated with caution, as many nominal Christians adhere to indigenous beliefs, and estimates of the Muslim community range from 7 to 25 percent.

Social Etiquette

- The visitor to Kenya should be patient at the often slow pace of life, from business meetings to travel arrangements.
- Conservative dress is recommended for women.
- Kenyans love dining and entertaining, and are likely to shower foreign visitors with warm hospitality. Most business meals are in restaurants, rather than at people's homes.

Further Information

Mark Horton and John Middleton, *The Swahili* (Malden, MA and Oxford: Blackwell, 2001).

Keith Kyle, *The Politics of the Independence of Kenya* (New York and London: Palgrave Macmillan, 1999).

Meave G. Leakey and John M. Harria (eds.), *Lothagam: The Dawn of Humanity in Eastern Africa* (New York: Columbia University Press, forthcoming in 2003).

The Government of Kenya: *http://kenya.go.ke.*

Institute of Certified Public Accountants of Kenya: *www.icpak.com.*

MOROCCO

Geography

Morocco is strategically situated in the northwest corner of Africa, with both Atlantic Ocean and Mediterranean Sea coastlines. It borders Algeria and Western Sahara, and there are two Spanish territorial enclaves (Ceuta and Melilla) on Moroccan territory. Much of the country consists of rugged mountains and large plateaux. The climate is hot and dry, although more temperate near coastal areas.

Brief History

Morocco's indigenous Berber peoples are thought to have occupied the country's territory for millennia. The Berbers are spread throughout North Africa (and are also discussed in the "Algeria" country section), and through Phoenician and Roman periods of colonization they kept their fiercely independent culture intact. By the early eighth century CE, Arab conquerors had reached Morocco, bringing the Arabic language and the Islamic faith. These cultural changes had long-lasting consequences.

In the centuries following the Arab invasions, Berber Muslims established control over both Morocco and much of Spain. Islamic Spain was a cultural melting pot and the setting for significant architectural and cultural achievements. However, Spanish Christians ended Muslim political power in Spain in 1492, and following the loss of Spain, the Berber Muslim regimes of Morocco entered a period of steady decline. A number of political groups sought power, until the Alawite dynasty achieved supremacy in the early seventeenth century. (The Alawite dynasty remains the Moroccan royal house to this day.)

Under Alawite rule, Morocco managed to remain independent during the early centuries of European colonial expansion in Africa. Eventually, by the late nineteenth and early twentieth centuries, the French turned their attention to Morocco and took control of the country in 1912. (France had already been in control of neighboring Algeria for nearly a century by that time.) Spain had also been interested in colonizing Morocco, but had managed to obtain only a small proportion of Moroccan territory. Tangier was classified as an "international" city. Unlike in neighboring Algeria, French rule in Morocco was generally light-handed and nonviolent, but over time a nationalist movement grew in strength.

Morocco eventually obtained independence from France in 1956, but Spain refused to hand over to the newly independent Moroccan state the small enclaves of Ceuta and Melilla. In the 1960s, King Hassan II (1929–1999) emerged as a regional leader, as he led peace initiatives between Israel and other Arab countries. His diplomacy was facilitated by the fact that large numbers of Moroccan Jews had moved to Israel following Israel's creation in the late 1940s. In the late 1970s, Morocco attempted to annex the territory of Western Sahara, to the south of the country. This led to a bitter war as the Polisario Front (with Algerian assistance) fought for Western Sahara's independence. The United Nations brokered a cease-fire in 1991, but the situation is still far from resolved.

Domestic political reform led to the establishment of a two-chamber parliament in 1997, with members of the lower chamber directly elected. In 1999 a new king, Mohammed VI (born 1963), took power. Commentators assessed at the time that the new monarch was a modernizer who would continue the country's democratic reforms. Morocco still wishes to obtain sovereignty over the Spanish enclaves of Ceuta and Melilla. A minor territorial dispute with Spain in July 2002 over a tiny, uninhabited Mediterranean island involved both countries' armed forces, and highlighted the continuing tensions with Spain on territorial matters.

Demographics

The population of Morocco is around 31 million.

Languages

Arabic is Morocco's official language, and it is the first language of around 55 percent of the population. The version of Arabic spoken in Morocco differs significantly from that spoken in the Arabian Peninsula (as summarized in the "Saudi Arabia" country section), with variations in pronunciation and vocabulary. In particular, Moroccan Arabic has absorbed large numbers of Berber words. Around 45 percent of Moroccans speak one of the Berber languages, although bilingualism is common. The strongholds of the Berber languages are mainly in rural areas. The former colonial language of French is spoken widely by the middle classes and is used widely for business purposes. The country's literacy rates are 55 percent for men and 30 percent for women.

Politics

The Kingdom of Morocco is a constitutional monarchy and has its capital at Rabat. Reforms implemented from 1997 have increasingly democratized the political process. The monarch acts as the head of state, while the prime minister acts as head of government. The lower chamber of the bicameral Parliament is elected by popular vote.

Economy

The Moroccan economy is heavily dependent on agriculture, in which half the workforce is employed. Drought often leads to economic hardship for a large proportion of the population. At least one in five Moroccans lives in poverty. The country has applied for EU membership as a means of bringing modernization and economic development, but prospects for EU membership seem relatively distant. The country has mature industries in phosphate rock mining, leather, textiles, and tourism, and has tried to implement structural economic reforms, such as privatization. France and Spain are Morocco's main trading partners, and the currency unit is the dirham.

Legal and Regulatory Environment

Moroccan law is based on a mixture of Islamic law and the legacies of French (and, to a lesser extent, Spanish) law. The regulatory environment is relatively cumbersome and bureaucratic, although recent reforms aimed at increasing the competitiveness of the economy have cut red tape considerably.

Accountancy

Moroccan GAAP is based on corporate and tax law, Ministry of Finance regulations, and the accounting standards of the national Accounting Standards Board, the *Conseil National de la Comptabilité*. Areas of difference between Moroccan GAAP and IAS include accounting for business combinations, lease accounting, and the treatment of employee benefits. Morocco is not yet a full member of the International Federation of Accountants, and its main professional accountancy and external auditing organization—the *Ordre des Experts-Comptables*—is patterned on the French professional association of the same name.

Cultural Background

The ethnic makeup of Morocco is thought to approximate to the country's linguistic patterns—around 55 percent Arab and 45 percent Berber. Other communities account for less than 1 percent of the population. The ethnic division between Arab and Berber is often blurred, however, owing to intermarriage and the closeness of the two groups. Many Arabic speakers, for example, are of Berber ethnic origin. Around 99 percent of Moroccans are Muslims, and the country has small communities of Christians and Jews.

Social Etiquette

The Saudi Arabia country section has comments of general application to North African Muslim culture. In addition:

- The long-running war with the Polisario Front over the disputed Western Sahara territory is a topic best avoided, as it can raise heated debate. Although hostilities have declined recently, the return of prisoners of war is a highly sensitive subject.
- Moroccans also tend to feel passionately about the return of Spanish territorial enclaves to Moroccan sovereignty. It is best not to offer a contrary view, to avoid upsetting one's hosts.
- Tea is the national drink, but alcohol is available.

Further Information

Michael Brett and Elizabeth Fentress, *The Berbers* (Malden, MA and Oxford: Blackwell, 1997).
C. R. Pennel, *Morocco Since 1830* (New York: New York University Press, 2001).
St. John Gould, *Morocco: Transformation and Continuity* (New York and London: Routledge, 2002).
Kingdom of Morocco: *www.mincom.gov.ma/english/e_page.html.*

NIGERIA

Geography

Nigeria is located in West Africa, and has an area twice the size of California. The country has over 500 miles of coastline along the Gulf of Guinea, and borders Benin, Cameroon, Chad, and Niger. Nigeria's varied terrain consists of lowlands in the south, uplands in the center, and flat plains in the north. There is also a mountainous region in the southeast of the country, near the border with Cameroon. Nigeria has a tropical climate that tends to be drier in the northern part of the country.

Brief History

The territory that comprises modern Nigeria has been settled for millennia. The earliest known culture to leave significant traces (such as sculpture) is that of the Nok people, who flourished from the fourth century BCE to the second century CE. By around 1000 CE, the largely Islamic state of Kanem was the region's main political power, and based its economy on trans-Saharan trade. Other (largely ethnically based) political states of the centuries preceding European colonization included Yoruba kingdoms and Hausa city-states. By the end of the eighteenth century, the Sokoto Caliphate had also been established in the north.

From the fifteenth century, Portuguese explorers and traders started to explore the West African coast. They established coastal bases, and in the sixteenth century initiated the transatlantic slave trade. For around three centuries, slavery was the principal economic activity along the Nigerian coast: Indigenous political rulers organized the capture of slaves, and sold them to Europeans for transport to the Americas. Other European nations undertook slave trading in the area, largely supplanting the Portuguese, and Britain emerged as the main slave trade power in the eighteenth century. Although slavery occurred along many sections of the West African coast and was not restricted to Nigeria, it is estimated that between 3 and 4 million slaves from the territory of modern Nigeria were seized and transported across the Atlantic.

The British voluntarily abolished slavery in 1807, and the United States followed in the same year. However, other European countries were reluctant to abandon the lucrative slave trade. In a remarkable transformation, Britain switched from being a slave trading power to a country that used its navy to police the West African coast to suppress transatlantic slavery. If the British intercepted ships carrying slaves, the slaves were usually released at Sierra Leone and the slavers were tried by British naval courts.

In the nineteenth century, British commodity traders moved to Nigeria to seek its natural resources. The traders often disturbed local political power balances. In 1886, the officially chartered British Royal Niger Company (RNC) was granted wide powers by the British government in the River Niger area. The RNC successfully beat off competition from French and German traders and, as in India, the establishment of a chartered trading company was the forerunner to formal colonial control. The British were increasingly playing the role of diplomatic and military power broker in local political conflicts, and in 1899 Britain dissolved the RNC and replaced it by more direct colonial mechanisms. By the outbreak of World War I, the British had consolidated their imperial power, and had united the various ethnically distinct parts of the region into one political entity.

In the twentieth century an anticolonial movement grew slowly, expressed through church groups, trade unions, professional associations, and ethnically based cultural movements. Many anticolonial intellectuals gravitated toward pan-African nationalism rather than Nigerian nationalism, perhaps reflecting long-standing ethnic rivalries and regionalist tensions in the country. The British implemented constitutional change following World War II, introducing British-style parliamentary institutions and federal structures. Nigeria became an independent nation in 1960 and expanded its territory in the following year, after the majority-Muslim electorate of north Cameroon voted for integration with northern Nigeria.

Postindependence Nigeria has suffered many problems. Long-simmering regional and religious tensions have led to a series of civil conflicts, and in 1966, the first of a series of military regimes seized power. The country's ethnic divisions exploded into civil war in the 1960s, with the attempted secession of part of the country to create an independent Republic of Biafra. From 1967 to 1970, the resulting armed conflict shocked the world with its brutality—the death toll may have been as high as 3 million, as hundreds of thousands starved during the conflict. The federal Nigerian armed forces managed to prevent the creation of an independent Republic of Biafra, but at a huge cost in terms of lives and money.

In the 1970s, Nigeria appeared to be on the verge of economic prosperity, owing to its oil wealth. However, corruption and economic mismanagement characterized the country in the late twentieth century, and most Nigerians have remained poor. In 1999, hopes for the country's future rose with the restoration of democracy, but political freedom has so far done little to improve the daily conditions of the country's inhabitants.

In recent years, religious and ethnic tensions have frequently exploded into serious civil disorder. Major clashes between Muslims and Christians have been sparked by the implementation of Islamic Shari'a law, and thousands of people have perished in the confrontations. In just one night in February 2000, it is estimated that hundreds of civilians were massacred in intercommunal violence.

Demographics

With a population of around 125 million, Nigeria is by far Africa's most populous country. (The second most populous is Egypt.)

Languages

As a former British colony, English is widely spoken among the middle classes. Indigenous languages include Hausa, Igbo (or Ibo), and Yoruba. Language patterns are closely linked to the country's ethnic makeup, and the "Cultural Background" section indicates the sizes of the country's main ethnic groups. Nigeria's literacy rate is around 55 to 60 percent.

Politics

The Federal Republic of Nigeria has been a democracy since 1999. The capital is Abuja, located at the geographical center of the country. (Prior to 1991, the capital was the port city of Lagos.) The Nigerian president, who is elected by popular vote, acts as both head of state and head of government. The bicameral National Assembly comprises a senate and a house of representatives, and the members of both chambers are elected by popular vote. In addition to its federal administration, Nigeria also has regional political structures.

There are several serious problems facing Nigeria's civilian administrations—violence between the country's diverse ethnic communities; inequitable distribution of the wealth generated by the oil industry; massive unemployment; entrenched corruption at various levels of officialdom; and spiraling crime rates.

Economy

Nigeria is very rich in natural resources. In addition to its vast oil reserves, the country has significant deposits of natural gas, tin, iron ore, coal, lead, and zinc. Oil production is the principal economic activity, and Nigeria is the world's tenth largest oil producer. Rocketing oil prices in the 1970s offered the prospect of economic prosperity, but the country was unable to fully exploit the oil boom to the benefit of its citizens. Corruption and economic mismanagement played a large part in squandering the country's oil wealth.

Nigeria's economy has serious structural problems, such as overdependence on world oil prices, poor infrastructure, corruption, criminal violence, and intercommunity riots. One half of the Nigerian population lives in poverty. The agricultural sector, which employs around 70 percent of the workforce, is unable to feed the country's huge population, and Nigeria has to import food. The country is a major recipient of foreign aid. Nigeria's largest trading partners include the United States, the United Kingdom, and Germany. The currency unit is the naira.

Legal and Regulatory Environment

Nigerian law is based largely on English common law, reflecting the country's history as a British colony. There are also indigenous elements of civil law that have survived, and Islamic Shari'a law is used in Muslim-majority northern areas. (The use of Islamic law is a highly contentious issue, and has been one of the main causes of the riots of recent years between Muslims and Christians.) Although the Nigerian regulatory environment is notoriously bureaucratic and inefficient, recent civilian administrations have started to reduce the mountains of red tape and to clamp down on corruption.

Accountancy

Nigeria has adopted IAS with little modification. The country's main professional accountancy and external auditing body is the Institute of Chartered Accountants of Nigeria (ICAN), based on the British chartered accountancy institutes. The ICAN was created from preexisting accountancy and auditing associations in 1965, and has over 12,000 members.

Cultural Background

The ethnic makeup of Nigeria is complex, and some observers claim that the country has over 200 ethnic groups. Large ethnic groups include the Hausa and

Fulani (around 30 percent of the population), the Igbo, or Ibo (20 percent), and the Yoruba (20 percent). The religious makeup of Nigeria is approximately as follows: Muslim (50 percent), Christian (40 percent), and indigenous beliefs (10 percent). However, these figures should be treated with caution, as there is much eclectic mingling of religious traditions. Christianity is often combined with indigenous spiritual practices, for example. Conflict between Muslims and Christians has threatened to destroy the social fabric of parts of the country in recent years.

The writer Wole Soyinka (born 1934), a Nobel Prize winner, was born in Nigeria.

Social Etiquette

- Nigeria's civil conflict between Christians and Muslims has led to many deaths in recent years and, unless unavoidable, is probably a subject for the visitor to avoid in conversation.
- Nigerians like to entertain foreign visitors, and business meetings often center on restaurant meals.
- Tipping is common practice, and requests for tips may sometimes seem forthright.

Further Information

David Bevin, Paul Collier, and Jan Willem Gunning, *The Political Economy of Poverty, Equity, and Growth: Nigeria and Indonesia* (New York and Oxford: Oxford University Press, 1999).
Toyin Falola, *The History of Nigeria* (Westport, CT: Greenwood, 1999).
Ike Okonta and Oronto Douglas, *Where Vultures Feast: Shell, Human Rights, and Oil in the Niger Delta* (Berkeley, CA: University of California Press, 2001).
Wole Soyinka, *Open Sore of a Continent: A Personal Narrative of the Nigerian Crisis* (New York and Oxford: Oxford University Press, 1997).
The Presidency, Federal Government of Nigeria: *www.nopa.net.*
Institute of Chartered Accountants of Nigeria: *www.ican.org.ng.*

REPUBLIC OF SOUTH AFRICA

Geography

South Africa is located in the southern part of the African continent. The coastlines along the Atlantic and Indian Oceans total over 1,700 miles, and the country shares borders with Botswana, Mozambique, Namibia, Swaziland, and Zimbabwe. It also completely encircles the small state of Lesotho. South Africa's terrain consists of an interior plateau surrounded by hills, while the coastlines tend to be bordered by narrow plains. The climate is characterized by hot summers and mild winters.

Brief History

The territory that became modern South Africa has been inhabited for millennia. Bantu peoples had settled in much of the region by the fifteenth century, when the first European explorations arrived. The Dutch established a settlement in what was to become modern Cape Town, and by the late eighteenth century, the British had joined them in the area. Unlike the Dutch settlers, who willingly took to rural life, the British preferred an urban existence. (The division between city-dwelling English speakers and rural Dutch speakers is evident to this day in South Africa's communities of European descent.)

From the beginning, the European settlers' economic existence was based on the use and exploitation of black labor. As they expanded their territory and influence, the Europeans frequently clashed with Bantu-speaking peoples. However, the nineteenth century is remembered less for conflict between the races and more for the bitter violence that broke out between the white settlers of British and Dutch origin. The British seized territory around the Cape of Good Hope in the early nineteenth century, and thousands of Dutch settlers—known as the Boers—undertook what came to be known as the "Great Trek" north in search of political independence from the British. The Boers defeated resistance from Zulu peoples and established political control over large parts of the country's interior.

The British moved to annex the Boer territories later in the nineteenth century, motivated by the region's economic wealth and a desire to extend British colonial territory in Africa. Boer resistance to British advances was initially successful, and in the Anglo-Boer War (or South African War) of 1899–1902 the Boers employed effective guerrilla tactics to pin down the numerically superior British army. British military forces reached 500,000, and British soldiers were supplemented by volunteer troops from other countries in the British Empire, including Australia and Canada. The war was characterized by widespread human rights abuses by the British, and thousands of Boer women and children died of neglect in British-run concentration camps. Boer military resistance was finally crushed, but the Boers later maintained their fierce cultural independence through cultivation of their language and religious institutions.

While the nineteenth century was defined by conflict among the region's white settlers, the twentieth century was characterized by white oppression of the region's black majority. South Africa became independent of Britain in 1910 and established the system of "apartheid"—the separate development of the races. Independent South Africa's politics was dominated by the Boers, now known as the Afrikaners. Racially based legislation was designed to ensure the political and economic supremacy of the white minority, both Afrikaner and British. The white establishment restricted the country's black population to so-called "homelands," poverty-stricken enclaves with little infrastructure.

Black opposition took several forms, from civil disobedience to armed guerrilla activity. The white regime suppressed black rebellion by brutal methods, and did not shrink from shooting street protesters. While decolonization advanced in the late twentieth century in most parts of Africa, the racialist South African regime stood out as an anachronism and many western nations implemented sanctions against the white minority regime.

Left wing regimes rose to power in many of South Africa's bordering states in the 1970s and 1980s, and the South African regime did not hesitate to intervene militarily beyond its borders to defend its interests. Domestically, the levels of street violence rose dramatically in the 1980s. This included politicized ethnic conflict between black groups, such as the African National Congress, dominated by the Xhosa community, and the Zulu-dominated Inkatha movement. There was also a surge of purely criminal violence. The African National Congress emerged as the main opposition group, and the white minority regime eventually bowed to the inevitable and agreed to a transfer of power to the country's entire multiracial population.

In 1994, the African National Congress, under its charismatic leader Nelson Mandela (born 1918), took power in free elections. The legal framework of apartheid was dismantled. The arrival of black majority rule did not put an end to South Africa's problems, however, as economic inequality, criminal violence, and the spread of AIDS have continued to tear apart the country's social fabric. Nelson Mandela stepped down as president in 1999.

Demographics

The population of South Africa is around 44 million. One in five South Africans lives in the small Guateng region, which comprises only 2 percent of South African territory and includes the cities of Johannesburg and Pretoria.

Languages

South Africa has 11 official languages. These include Xhosa, Zulu, and seven other African languages, plus English and Afrikaans. The latter language is spoken by the Afrikaners and is a variety of Dutch. The nine African languages are all members of the Bantu language family. South Africa's official literacy rate is 80 percent, but this may be an overestimate. Educational opportunities for the majority of the population were restricted during the apartheid years, and are only slowly being rectified.

Politics

The Republic of South Africa has been a multiparty democracy since 1994. Its capital is at Pretoria. (Cape Town is the country's legislative center, and Bloemfontein is its judicial center.) The country's president acts as both head of state and head of government. The bicameral parliament comprises a popularly elected National Assembly and a National Council of Provinces—the latter replaced a former senate in 1997. The National Assembly elects the president. Since the end of white majority rule, the African National Congress has been the main political party.

Economy

South Africa is rich in natural resources and the country is the world's largest producer of gold, platinum, and chromium. Diamond extraction is another important activity. There are mature industries in the chemicals, machinery, and textile sectors, and the country's infrastructure is impressive. However, after the end of white majority rule in 1994, the disparity in income between the white minority and black majority has remained immense. Around half the population lives in poverty, and unemployment levels are high. One in three South Africans works in the agricultural sector.

The country's largest trading partners are the EU, the United States, and Japan. The currency unit is the rand.

Legal and Regulatory Environment

South African law is based on a mixture of English common law and Dutch legal traditions, with elements of indigenous African law. Following the transfer of power to majority rule in 1994, the indigenous aspects of the legal system have grown in importance. The regulatory environment is relatively heavy, which is partly a legacy of the high levels of political control implemented by the white minority regime for most of the twentieth century. In recent years, red tape has been cut as democratic governments have attempted to boost the economy by liberalization measures. However, foreign corporations must keep up to date with many aspects of legislation, not least that which requires an equitable ethnic balance of corporate workforces.

Accountancy

South African GAAP is based on the standards of the Accounting Practices Board (APB) of the South African Institute of Chartered Accountants (SAICA), company law, and stock exchange regulations (for listed corporations). The APB's policy of harmonizing South African GAAP with IAS has resulted in very few differences between the two GAAP systems.

The Johannesburg Stock Exchange is large and is serviced by a sophisticated accountancy profession. The SAICA is the country's main professional body for accountancy and external auditing, and was established in 1980 from preexisting accountancy organizations. The SAICA has been influenced by British accountancy traditions. Another professional organization is the Institute of Commercial and Financial Accountants of Southern Africa, many of whose 5,000 members work in industry.

Cultural Background

South Africa is an ethnically diverse society. Around 75 percent of the population is black, 10 percent white, and 3 percent of Indian origin. The balance of 12 percent is mainly of mixed ethnic descent, and there is also a small Jewish community. The legacy of apartheid has resulted in complex interracial tensions in the country, both between different races and among various cultural groups within racial boundaries. The black community comprises several ethnic and linguistic groups (as indicated in the "Languages" section). Around two-thirds of the white community is Afrikaner, and most of the rest are of British origin. The million-strong Indian community in South Africa arrived in the country as laborers during the British colonial period. (Before he devoted himself to the cause of Indian independence, M. K. Gandhi championed the rights of South Africa's Indian inhabitants.)

One aspect of culture that cuts across ethnic boundaries to a degree is religion. Around 70 percent of South Africans are Christians, but they often worship in community-specific churches. There are also small communities of Muslims, Hindus, and Jews (who in combination represent less than 5 percent of the population). The balance of 25 percent comprises adherents to indigenous religious beliefs.

Social Etiquette

- The visitor should tread carefully when discussing the country's complex ethnic divisions, as the scars of the white majority rule era are still painful.
- Even within racial boundaries cultural differences are strong. Above all, one should not confuse the white Afrikaners with South Africans of British descent. The Afrikaners are fiercely proud of their heritage and separate identity.
- South Africans enjoy food and drink, and delight in entertaining foreign visitors. In particular, Afrikaner hospitality is legendary and it is a considerable honor to be invited to an Afrikaner home.
- South Africans love sport, but the choice of sports is often divided along racial lines. The black majority tends to follow soccer, while the white community tends to prefer rugby and cricket. South Africa performs well in all these sports at an international level.

Further Information

Nelson Mandela, *Long Walk to Freedom* (New York: Little Brown, 1995).
G. H. Le May, *The Afrikaners* (Malden, MA and Oxford: Blackwell, 1995).
Robert Ross, *A Concise History of South Africa* (New York and Cambridge: Cambridge University Press, 1999).
Leonard Thompson, *The History of South Africa*, 3rd ed. (New Haven, CT: Yale University Press, 2001).
South Africa Government Online: *www.gov.za/index.html*.
Institute of Commercial and Financial Accountants of Southern Africa: *www.cfa-sa.co.za*.
South African Institute of Chartered Accountants: *www.saica.co.za*.
Institute of Internal Auditors South Africa: *www.iiasa.org.za*.

UGANDA

Geography

Uganda is located in East Africa. Although Uganda has no sea coastline, around one half of Lake Victoria lies inside the country. (Lake Victoria is the source of the Nile River that flows through to Egypt.) Bordering countries include Kenya, Rwanda, and Sudan. Ugandan territory consists mainly of a gently sloping plateau, with mountains to the east and west. The climate is equatorial, and temperatures and rainfall vary with altitude.

Brief History

Uganda has a long history of settlement. The country's inhabitants in the first millennium BCE included a large number of Bantu speakers, who were spreading throughout much of the African continent at that time. Bantu clans evolved a series of political entities over the centuries and by around 1000 CE the larger Bantu kingdoms in the territory of modern Uganda each governed more than a million people. In the nineteenth century, the powerful Buganda and Bunyoro states were major political rivals.

Outside pressures on the region accumulated in the late nineteenth century, owing to the wealth of the ivory trade. Traders from the Arabian Peninsula made contact with Buganda and Bunyoro, while from the north Egyptians were anxious to obtain ivory and to control the source of the Nile River. European influence first asserted itself in the form of Christian missionaries, from various countries, who sparked religious rivalry with Islamic missionaries. The British later emerged as the main colonial power, and conquered the country in the 1890s, establishing a "protectorate."

Britain left local kingdoms nominally in power, but the British dominated the country's politics and economy. The British also exploited local ethnic rivalries in a "divide and rule" policy that was to have a longstanding impact on the country's ethnic relations. In 1901, the completion of a railway from Lake Victoria to the Kenyan port of Mombasa further opened up the region to European economic development (and exploitation). Cotton and coffee became major industries. Unlike in neighboring Kenya, there was little European settlement, but a large number of settlers from the Indian subcontinent came to Uganda. The Indians—known locally as "Asians"—became prominent in the country's business life.

Milton Obote (born 1924), a former schoolteacher, led the country to independence in 1962. Obote instituted a period of autocratic rule and as the 1960s progressed, he increasingly relied on his military *protégé* Idi Amin (born 1924) to shore up his regime. In 1971, Amin staged a coup to usurp his former benefactor, and Obote fled into exile. Amin came to be known as the "Butcher of Uganda," and his regime was characterized by almost unspeakable brutality and grisly violence. Around 300,000 Ugandans died as Amin and his henchmen started to liquidate all opposition, both real and imagined. Amin is said to have personally committed many horrific murders during the 1970s. A symbol of Amin's state terrorism was the common sight of a pair of shoes left by the roadside, indicating yet another person seized by the armed forces, never to be seen again.

Uganda's economy suffered as the 1970s progressed. In 1972, Amin expelled virtually the entire Asian community—which numbered over 50,000—and seized their assets. The Asians operated much of the Ugandan economy, and without their skills the country was soon plunged into a desperate economic crisis. Many factories and farms ceased to function as Amin plundered the country's wealth to reward himself and his supporters. The "Pearl of Africa" (Winston Churchill's description of colonial Uganda) had been reduced to destitution and murderous tyranny.

In 1978, Amin tried to divert attention from his crumbling regime of terror by invading Tanzania. Amin's army was beaten back by a coalition of Tanzanian and opposition Ugandan forces, and in the following year Amin fled to exile in Saudi Arabia as his regime was toppled. His murderous eight-year regime was at a close, and Obote returned from exile to seize power in what some observers claimed was a rigged election.

Political violence continued under Obote, whose regime undertook mass arrests and massacres of opponents. It is estimated that 100,000 Ugandans were killed during Obote's second period of rule. A civil war broke out between the Obote administration and the National Resistance Army (NRA), led by Yoweri Museveni (born 1944). The Obote regime fell to an army coup in 1985, and in the following year, the NRA took the capital, Kampala, and Museveni assumed power. Since then, Uganda has slowly emerged from the dark years of the Amin and Obote regimes. Museveni has slowly introduced democratic and economic reforms and has clamped down on human rights abuses. Uganda has experienced a greater degree of political stability, and has undergone a minor economic renaissance.

Uganda still faces many problems, not least of which is containment of the armed insurgency of the so-called "Lord's Resistance Army" (LRA). This bizarre and brutal armed group of Christian fundamentalists is notorious for its use of child soldiers, and hundreds of thousands of Ugandans have been displaced by its activities, mainly along the border with Sudan. The LRA has caused international outrage by kidnapping, sexually abusing, and mutilating thousands of children. Other pressing problems in Uganda are the spread of AIDS and chronic poverty.

Demographics

Uganda's population is around 24 million. The conflicts in central Africa in recent years have led to influxes of refugees from neighboring countries such as Rwanda and Sudan.

Languages

English is the official language of Uganda, reflecting the country's history as a British colony. Other major languages include Swahili and Ganda, 2 of around 30 indigenous languages of the Bantu and Nilo-Saharan linguistic families spoken in the country. The male literacy level is 75 percent, and the female level is 50 percent.

Politics

The Republic of Uganda has its capital at Kampala. The president, who acts as both head of state and head of government, is elected by the National Assembly. The latter is the country's unicameral parliament, with a mixture of elected and appointed members. Since the tyrannical rule of Idi Amin and Milton Obote, Uganda has taken a long, slow road to democratization. Remaining constraints on the open operation of political parties may be relaxed in the future.

Economy

To a degree, Uganda has recovered from the state terror and theft of the Idi Amin regime of the 1970s. However, around one in two Ugandans still lives in poverty. The country is largely agricultural, and coffee is the main source of export revenues. Around 80 percent of the workforce work in the agricultural sector. Reform in recent decades has placed the economy on a stable footing, although the country's infrastructure remains weak. Uganda receives significant amounts of foreign economic aid.

A major reason for Uganda's economic problems was Amin's decision to expel the country's Asian population in 1972. The Ugandan Asian community included a large proportion of entrepreneurs, traders, and industrialists, and the country has never recovered from losing their skills. In recent years, the Ugandan administration of Yoweri Museveni has tried to encourage the exiled Asians to return by offering compensation for appropriated assets. Few have yet to take up the offer, however. Kenya, the EU, and the United States are Uganda's main trading partners, and the country's currency unit is the shilling.

Legal and Regulatory Environment

The Ugandan legal system virtually disintegrated under the idiosyncratic terror of the Amin regime of the 1970s. Amin's whims became law, political murder went unpunished, and legal officials were among the many thousands who "disappeared" at the hands of the military. Today, civilian administrations have rehabilitated the legal system, which is based on a mixture of English common law (owing to the British colonial history) and indigenous customary law. The regulatory environment remains relatively cumbersome and bureaucratic.

Accountancy

Ugandan GAAP is based on IAS, as mediated by the accounting standards of the Institute of Certified Public Accountants of Uganda (ICPAU). The ICPAU is the country's main professional accountancy and external auditing body, and is based on British colonial precedents.

Cultural Background

The ethnic composition of Uganda is complex. Major communities include the Baganda (around 17 percent of the population), Karamojong (12 percent), Basogo (8 percent), and Iteso (8 percent). Non-African peoples comprise less than 1 percent of the population. Around one-third of Ugandans are Roman Catholics, and one-third Protestants. The remainder of the population consists of Muslims and adherents to indigenous beliefs. Political policies of both the British colonial period and the Idi Amin regime of the 1970s often stoked up ethnic and religious divisions, which are still felt keenly today. In 1972 over 50,000 Asians—people of Indian or Pakistani descent—were expelled by Idi Amin. Only a handful of Asians remain in Uganda today, and few have been enticed back by offers of compensation for assets confiscated in the 1970s.

Social Etiquette

- Ugandans are very hospitable and enjoy entertaining visitors.
- The visitor should tread carefully when discussing Uganda's recent violent past. Many Ugandans lost family and friends during the murderous regimes of Idi Amin and Milton Obote.
- English is widely understood in business and official circles.

Further Information

Peter Allen, *Interesting Times: Life in Uganda Under Idi Amin* (Lewes, UK: The Book Guild, 2000).
Martin Jamieson, *Idi Amin and Uganda* (Westport, CT: Greenwood, 1993).
Jayati Datta Mitra, *Uganda: Policy, Participation, People* (Washington, DC: World Bank, 2001).
Government of Uganda: *www.government.go.ug*.

The Americas

TAX HAVENS AND INVESTMENT CENTERS: THE BAHAMAS, BERMUDA, AND THE CAYMAN ISLANDS

THE BAHAMAS

The former British colony of the Bahamas consists of an archipelago of 700 islands near the Florida coast, with a population of 300,000. Tourism is a major industry and around 1.5 million tourists visit the islands annually. In addition to tourism, the islands' wealth derives from a large offshore financial services sector. (The Bahamas also has one of the world's largest shipping fleet registers.)

The financial services sector has brought huge wealth to the Bahamas, but prosperity tends to be concentrated in the hands of the country's white minority that comprises less than 15 percent of the population. A significant proportion of the islands' black majority suffers chronic poverty and unemployment. The crime rate is relatively high, and is linked to narcotics, gun running, and illegal migration to the United States. In recent years, the OECD has encouraged the enhancement of regulatory controls to combat money laundering and other white-collar crime. The Bahamas' legal system is based on British colonial traditions of English common law, and the islands have their own currency, the Bahamian dollar. There are no income taxes.

Further Information

Michael Craton and Gail Saunders, *Islanders in the Stream: A History of the Bahamian People from Aboriginal Times to the End of Slavery* (Athens, GA: University of Georgia Press, 1999).

Howard Johnson, *The Bahamas from Slavery to Servitude, 1783–1933* (Gainesville, FL: University Press of Florida, 1997).

Bahamas Financial Services Board: *www.bfsb-bahamas.com*.

BERMUDA

Bermuda is a self-governing British Overseas Territory with a population of around 65,000, and consists of a group of small islands in the Atlantic Ocean. Bermuda held a referendum on independence from Britain in 1995, but the proposition was defeated. The territory's legal system is based on English common law, and the territory has its own currency, the Bermudan dollar. There are no income taxes. Bermuda has one of the world's highest per capita incomes, owing to wealth derived from tourism and offshore financial services. There is also an important banana export industry.

Many of the corporations that set up shell companies in Bermuda do so for tax minimization purposes. In recent years, the United States and the OECD have encouraged Bermuda to relax its secrecy laws, to prevent tax evasion and money laundering. U.S. politicians have also denounced as unpatriotic the practice of U.S. corporations using Bermuda and similar territories to minimize U.S. taxes.

Further Information

Virginia Bernhard, *Slaves and Slaveholders in Bermuda, 1616–1782* (Columbia, MO: University of Missouri Press, 1999).
Government of Bermuda: *www.bdagov.bm*.

CAYMAN ISLANDS

The British Crown Colony of the Cayman Islands is a small island group in the Caribbean Sea, around 450 miles south of Florida, with a population of 36,000. One in five inhabitants of the islands is an expatriate worker, attracted by the wealth of the offshore financial services sector. The Cayman Islands have no income taxes, and the country has grown extremely prosperous from its offshore activities. Tens of thousands of corporations are registered in the tiny colony. Up-market tourism is another wealth-generating sector, and the islands attract more than a million tourists every year, mainly from the United States.

As with other offshore financial centers around the world, the Cayman Islands have been under pressure in recent years from organizations like the OECD to increase regulation and to take measures against tax evasion and money laundering. In 2001, the Cayman Islands signed an agreement with the United States to share information on banking matters. At the time it was alleged that banks in the Cayman Islands, which number in the hundreds, held twice as many funds as all the banks in New York City combined. Cayman Islands' law is based on English common law, reflecting the islands' British colonial traditions. The currency unit is the Caymanian dollar.

Further Information

Roger C. Smith, *The Maritime Heritage of the Cayman Islands* (Gainesville, FL: University Press of Florida, 2000).
Government of the Cayman Islands: *www.gov.ky*.

ARGENTINA

Geography

Argentina is located in the southern "cone" of South America, bordering Bolivia, Brazil, Chile, Paraguay, and Uruguay. A huge country with a long South Atlantic Ocean coastline, Argentina is around one-third the size of the United States. It is the second largest country in South America (after Brazil). Argentina's terrain is varied, from the Andes mountain range in the west to the vast plains of the Pampas. The climate is similarly diverse and ranges from subtropical conditions in the north to sub-Antarctic weather in the south. The capital Buenos Aires experiences hot summers and mild winters.

Brief History

The early history of the territory of modern Argentina was dominated by Amerindian communities, both sedentary and nomadic. Spanish colonists conquered the region in the sixteenth century and established large cattle ranches alongside the Amerindian peoples. (Cattle ranches remain an important aspect of the Argentine economy to the present day.) The colonists' dissatisfaction with Spanish rule led to a revolutionary rebellion in 1810. Six years later, Argentina gained its independence.

The first century of independence was a promising one, as Argentina attracted millions of European immigrants and established a thriving economy. In the late nineteenth century, British economic influence was important in establishing the country's railway network and a large part of its industrial base. The British influence—always informal and never overtly colonial—can still be seen in Argentina's passion for the British-introduced sports of polo and soccer. (Many of the country's world-famous soccer teams still retain their English names.)

By the early twentieth century, Argentina was considered to be one of the top 10 wealthiest countries in the world. As the twentieth century progressed, however, Argentines saw a decline in their political and economic standing. Twentieth-century Argentine politics was often bitter and violent, and the country's military intervened regularly in governing the country. In 1943, a military coup led to the rise of the autocratic leadership of Juan Peron (1895–1974) who—with his hugely popular wife Eva (affectionately known as Evita)—dominated Argentine twentieth-century politics.

Peron was an army colonel turned president whose leadership, in its early years at least, had strong fascist overtones. His populist rhetoric was based on patriotism and anti-U.S. sentiments. Claiming to represent a "third way" between capitalism and communism, Peron and his glamorous wife gained the support of the country's working classes, which became the backbone of their power base. Peronism remains a strong and emotive political force in the country.

Eva Peron died in 1952 and was buried amid scenes of intense national mourning. Following a military coup in 1955, Juan Peron was banished to Spain. During his exile, military and civilian administrations alternated in power until he returned to regain the presidency in 1973. Peron died in office the following year, after which his third wife assumed the country's political leadership.

Following Peron's death Argentina suffered intense political violence and worsening economic conditions. A military government took power in 1976 and unleashed a reign of terror. During what has become known as the "Dirty War," paramilitary death squads and state torturers suppressed the country's left-wing opposition movements. As many as 25,000 Argentines "disappeared" in the period and many thousands more were executed, tortured, and imprisoned.

The military regime attempted to divert attention from deteriorating social and economic conditions by invading the South Atlantic Falkland Islands (known to the Argentines as Las Malvinas) in 1982. The Falkland Islands were under British sovereignty and the invasion unleashed a wave of nationalistic fervor. British military forces retook the islands in a war that cost hundreds of lives.

The humiliating defeat of the Falklands War led to the fall of the military regime. Following the restoration of democracy in 1983, Argentina has established a more open political system. Nonetheless, economic conditions have not yet stabilized under civilian administrations. In the late 1980s, the country experienced hyperinflation, with prices increasing by several thousand percent annually. Despite subsequent attempts to modernize the Argentine economy and to lock the economy into global markets, in December 2001 the economy system virtually collapsed. The country defaulted on its foreign external debt repayments, unemployment soared, the national currency depreciated alarmingly against the U.S. dollar, and serious street rioting and looting erupted. Millions of citizens were plunged into poverty as capital flight from the country reached alarming proportions. At the time of writing, both the economic and political environments remain highly volatile.

Demographics

Argentina's population is around 37.5 million, of which over 15 million live in the capital and largest city, Buenos Aires. Owing to the concentration of inhabitants in Buenos Aires, much of the rest of the vast country is sparsely populated.

Languages

Spanish is spoken as a mother tongue by virtually all Argentines. More information on the Spanish language is summarized in the "Spain" country section. There are some differences in pronunciation and vocabulary between Argentine Spanish and the Castilian Spanish spoken in central Spain, although the two languages are mutually intelligible. Small bilingual communities of other nationalities, such as Germans and Lebanese, also maintain their own languages. Argentina's literacy level is around 95 percent.

Politics

The Argentine Republic is a presidential-style democracy and has its capital at Buenos Aires. The country's president serves as both head of state and head of government, and also appoints the cabinet of ministers. The Argentine parliament has a bicameral structure, with a senate and a chamber of deputies, and members of the latter are elected by popular vote.

Although democracy was restored in Argentina in 1983, the legacy of the "Dirty War" waged by the former military regime in the late 1970s and early 1980s is a continuing source of national anguish. Some investigations into the thousands of Argentines who "disappeared" in those years have taken place, and there have been prosecutions of some of the military officials responsible for human rights abuses. However, many questions remain unanswered from those dark years. Public mistrust of politicians has increased since the start of the most recent economic crisis in late 2001. Regaining sovereignty over the Falkland Islands remains an important political issue that cuts across most ideological divides.

Economy

As described in the "History" section, Argentina in the nineteenth and early twentieth centuries successfully exploited its abundant natural resources and developed a sophisticated and diversified industrial base. The country was poised to become one of the world's most prosperous economies, and it attracted millions of European immigrants who sought to be part of the anticipated prosperity. However, the twentieth century saw economic decline on a massive scale.

At the time of writing, Argentina is suffering from a severe economic crisis that has plunged one in three of its inhabitants into poverty. A decade of pegging the Argentine peso to the U.S. dollar was blown apart by the economic meltdown that started in December 2001. Important economic sectors remain largely intact, however, and these include agriculture, consumer goods, food processing, engineering, and textiles. There is hope for a future renaissance of the Argentine economy.

Legal and Regulatory Environment

The Argentine legal culture was inherited from colonial Spain and therefore reflects the Roman legal traditions common throughout southern Europe. In the twentieth century, aspects of U.S. law were added to the Spanish system, as the role of the United States in the Argentine economy grew. By South American standards, the regulatory and tax environment is relatively light, but it is still bureaucratic in comparison to North America and Western Europe.

Accountancy

Argentine GAAP is based on corporate and tax law, the standards of the *Federación Argentina de Consejos Profesionales de Ciencias Económicas* (FACPCE), and the regulations of the National Securities Commission (NCS). NCS standards are applicable only to listed corporations, and there are additional, industry-specific standards developed by regulatory bodies such as the country's Central Bank. While Argentine standards broadly follow IAS, discrepancies remain in areas such as accounting for business combinations, lease accounting, and deferred tax.

The Buenos Aires Stock Exchange requires domestic corporations to follow Argentine GAAP, but foreign corporations may follow either IAS or a national GAAP, provided that a reconciliation to Argentine GAAP is given. The FACPCE is the country's main professional accountancy and external auditing body.

Cultural Background

Ethnically, most Argentines are descended from colonists and immigrants from Spain and other European countries. In fact, more Argentines are descended from Italian than Spanish migrants, and Argentines are sometimes described as "Spanish-speaking Italians." Ethnic minorities account for around 5 percent of the population, and include Amerindians, Germans, and Lebanese. Roman Catholicism remains the country's main religion, accounting for over 90 percent of the population—at least nominally. Minority faiths include Protestantism, Judaism, and Islam.

Argentine culture is noted for several achievements. First, the erotic tango dance is perhaps the country's main cultural export. Originally an "underground" and antiestablishment pastime, the tango emerged from the shadows in the early twentieth century to take the mainstream dancing world by storm. Argentines are also passionate about sports, especially soccer. The Argentine soccer player Diego Maradona (born 1960) is considered by many to be the most talented player the world has ever seen. Argentines are also passionate polo players—and perhaps the world's best. A well-known Argentine cultural icon is the gaucho, the tough ranch worker who excels at horsemanship and struts his machismo with unabashed pride.

Social Etiquette

- Argentines are hospitable people who enjoy food and wine, and business meetings often culminate in restaurant visits.
- The Argentines, with some justification, consider their beef to be the best in the world. They delight in introducing visitors to this source of national pride.
- Argentines are soccer-crazy and are especially passionate about the fortunes of the national soccer team.
- Discussion of the Falklands War is a topic best avoided, as memories of the conflict with Britain remain strong. Argentines of all political persuasions tend to support Argentine sovereignty over the Falklands.

Further Information

Duncan Anderson, *The Falklands War 1982* (New York: Osprey, 2002).
Deborah Norden and Russell Roberto, *The United States and Argentina: Changing Relations in a Changing World* (New York and London: Routledge, 2002).
Mark J. Osiel, *Mass Atrocity, Ordinary Evil, and Hannah Arendt: Criminal Consciousness in Argentina's Dirty War* (New Haven, CT: Yale University Press, 2001).
The Argentina Presidency (Spanish only): *www.presidencia.gov.ar.*
Federación Argentina de Consejos Profesionales de Ciencias Económicas (Spanish only): *www.facpce.com.ar.*

BRAZIL

Geography

Brazil is the largest country in South America, taking up almost half the continent. Owing to its size, it shares borders with most of the continent's countries, including Argentina, Colombia, Peru, Uruguay, and Venezuela. Around 60 percent of the land is covered by forests and woodlands, and the Amazon Basin contains the world's largest rain forest. Economic development (or exploitation) of the Amazon rain forest is a major environmental problem, with widespread deforestation and the destruction of uniquely indigenous species of plants and animals. The Brazilian climate is mainly tropical, and most of the country is hot and humid throughout the year.

Brief History

The indigenous peoples of the territory that comprises modern Brazil are thought to have numbered several million when Portuguese explorers and colonists arrived in the early sixteenth century. Although the Portuguese lost many of their early imperial conquests (such as the island of Sri Lanka) to rival European powers, they managed to hold onto Brazil despite intense rivalry with Spain, France, and the Netherlands.

The Portuguese conquerors established sugar cane plantations and initially enslaved indigenous peoples to perform the plantation work. However, from the middle of the sixteenth century the plantation owners imported African slaves. A gold rush from the 1690s led to the use of slaves in mining operations as well as cane farming.

During the Napoleonic Wars in Europe in the early nineteenth century, the Portuguese monarchy moved to the safety of Brazil. Rio de Janeiro was designated the capital of a United Kingdom of Portugal and Brazil. The monarch returned to Portugal after hostilities had ended, but his son remained in Rio de Janeiro, from where he led Brazil to independence in 1822. Three centuries of Portuguese dominance were ended without bloodshed.

In the nineteenth century, coffee supplanted sugar as Brazil's main export item. Slavery was abolished in 1888, and Italians and other European immigrants flooded to the coffee estates to seek work. A military revolt of 1889 established a republic, and until the 1980s the country's politics were dominated by alternating civilian and military regimes, many of which were autocratic. Even during periods of civilian administration the army tended to hover in the political background, and often pulled the strings of civilian politicians. Democracy was restored in 1989 and has lasted to the present day.

The Brazilian economy prospered in the latter half of the twentieth century. In the 1950s, work was begun on a new capital at Brasilia and subsequent governments started to exploit the resources of the country's interior on a vast scale. By the 1970s, the country's immense natural resources, its large population, and an increasingly diversified economic base had made it South America's leading economic power. The Brazilian economy, however, has often been extremely volatile. Further, the distribution of wealth has developed into one of the world's most unequal, and large gaps between economic and social classes has led at times to social tensions and street violence.

Demographics

The population of Brazil is around 175 million. Most Brazilians live in urbanized coastal areas, which include the massive cities of Sao Paulo and Rio de Janeiro. (The "Cultural Background" section gives an overview of the country's complex ethnic makeup.) In the 1970s, Brazil's military regimes encouraged population movements to the country's Amazon Basin interior, in an attempt to increase the economic exploitation of the vast, resource-rich region. Such migration plans have currently been scaled down or halted by Brazil's civilian administrations, but they were never sufficient to arrest the broader urbanization trends in Brazilian society.

Languages

The main language spoken in Brazil is Portuguese, a legacy of the colonial past. The "Portugal" country section gives more details on the Portuguese language. Brazilian Portuguese differs from the Portuguese spoken in Lisbon in terms of pronunciation and vocabulary, but the two versions of the language are mutually comprehensible. Spanish is also spoken in some border areas, near Spanish-speaking countries, and there are small communities who speak other languages as a mother tongue—Japanese, Korean, and indigenous Amerindian languages. Brazilian literacy rates are around 80 to 85 percent.

Politics

The Federative Republic of Brazil is a democracy and has its capital at Brasilia. The country's president acts as both head of state and head of government and appoints cabinet ministers. The Brazilian parliament has a bicameral structure, with a senate and a chamber of deputies. Members of the latter are elected by popular vote under a proportional representation system. Brazilian politics is characterized by a large number of small parties, and major political challenges include land reform (powerful pressure groups have formed to demand more equitable distributions of land) and managing environmental damage to the Amazon rain forest.

Economy

Brazil has South America's largest economy, but it has a volatile history. The Brazilian economy is characterized by periods of boom and recession, and the latter have sometimes seen serious hyperinflation. The Brazilian economy suffered knock-on effects of the Asian financial crisis that started in 1997 and was even adversely impacted by the Russian financial crisis of 1998. The economy proved resilient to these shocks, however, and has recovered relatively quickly.

Important economic sectors include agriculture, automobiles, chemicals, logging, mining, and textiles. The country also has a sophisticated software industry. Given its vast natural resources and strong industrial base, Brazil has often been labeled the "land of the future." However, although some commentators argue that significant future prosperity is achievable, such aspirations continue to remain elusive. A notoriously high inequality of income distribution remains a serious problem with severe social repercussions. Millions of people live in the *favelas* (slums) of the major cities and, as in India, thousands of children sleep rough on the streets. At least one in seven Brazilians lives in poverty, and one in four works in the agricultural sector. Brazil's largest trading partner is the United States, followed by neighboring Argentina. The country's currency unit is the real.

Legal and Regulatory Environment

Brazilian legal culture follows continental European patterns, as a result of the Portuguese colonial heritage. Governments in recent years have relaxed the country's traditionally strict bureaucratic structures in attempts to make the Brazilian economy more competitive. By the standards of South America, the Brazilian regulatory environment is generally smooth and straightforward.

Accountancy

Brazilian GAAP is based on corporate and tax law, the standards of the Brazilian Institute of Independent Auditors (*Instituto dos Auditores Independentes do Brasil*—IBRACON), the standards of the Federal Council of Accountants (*Conselho Federal de Contabilidade*—CFC), and (for listed corporations) the regulations of the Securities Commission. IBRACON standards are based on IAS, yet discrepancies remain in areas such as acquisition accounting and research and development costs. (The IBRACON standards are available, in Portuguese only, from its Web site: *www.cfc.org.br*). It should be noted that the acronym IBRACON is derived from the professional body's former name of the Brazilian Institute of Accountants—*Instituto Brasiliero de Contadores*. Although the name of the institute was changed, the acronym was so well known that it was retained.

CFC standards are based on inflation accounting, and are to be applied only when the effects of inflation are material. This a good example of a country's GAAP addressing specific local concerns, as Brazil experienced damaging hyperinflation in the late twentieth century. All corporations listed on the country's stock exchanges are required to follow Brazilian GAAP.

Cultural Background

Brazil has a very varied ethnic composition. Around 55 percent of Brazilians are of European origin, 6 percent of African origin, and 38 percent of mixed European and African descent. The remaining 1 percent comprises indigenous Amerindian peoples and Asian immigrant communities (including Japanese). There are estimated to be around only 200,000 Amerindians in Brazil today, living mainly in the rain forests of the country's vast interior.

Approximately 80 percent of Brazilians are nominally Roman Catholic, but observance is not as high as this figure would suggest. The remainder of the population adheres to a variety of religions, including evangelic Protestant churches, and indigenous and African animistic beliefs. Spiritualist groups are also popular with Brazil's middle classes.

Brazil is famous for its national soccer team, which is widely viewed as being the most naturally gifted in the world. The Brazilians have won the soccer World Cup more times than any other nation. The country is also famous for its dance music such as samba and bossa nova, and the Brazilians have a reputation for throwing extravagant parties. The world-famous annual carnival in Rio de Janiero produces a riot of color, music, and enjoyment that attracts hundreds of thousands of revelers.

Social Etiquette

- Brazilians have a well-deserved reputation as a fun-loving people, and the country is famous for its music and dancing. Visitors to Brazil are often well entertained by their hosts!
- Brazil is a sports-crazy nation, with arguably the best national soccer team in the world today. A visitor who can recognize and discuss the careers of prominent Brazilian soccer stars will find cultural barriers easier to cross.
- Brazilian interpersonal warmth is often expressed by touching others' arms or shoulders. The visitor should not be alarmed!
- Business and academic titles tend to be rigorously observed.

Further Information

Edmund Amann, *Economic Liberalization and Industrial Performance in Brazil* (New York and Oxford: Oxford University Press, 2000).

Teresa P. R. Caldeira, *City of Walls: Crime, Segregation, and Citizenship in São Paulo* (Berkeley, CA: University of California Press, 2001).

Boris Fausto, *A Concise History of Brazil* (New York and Cambridge: Cambridge University Press, 1999).

David J. Samuels, *Ambition, Federalism, and Legislative Politics in Brazil* (New York and Cambridge: Cambridge University Press, 2002).

The Brazilian Government (Portuguese only): *www.brasil.gov.br.*

IBRACON (Portuguese only): *www.ibracon.com.br.*

CANADA

Geography

In surface area, Canada is the second largest country in the world (after Russia). It is marginally larger than its southern neighbor, the United States. Much of the north of the country comprises an area of permafrost, and over 50 percent of Canadian territory is covered by forests and woodland. The climate is characterized by mild to cool summers, and very cold winters with heavy snowfalls. The far north of the country experiences arctic conditions.

Brief History

The area of North America that was to become Canada fell within the cultural and political orbit of Europe from the early sixteenth century. France was the first European power to lay serious territorial claims in the area, and thousands of French settlers had crossed the Atlantic by the late seventeenth century. The fur trade was the settlers' main economic activity. The British also took an interest in Canada in the seventeenth century, creating the Hudson's Bay Company by Royal Charter in 1670. Over time, the Hudson's Bay Company evolved from a fur-trading enterprise into a major trading and exploration company that controlled vast amounts of Canadian territory.

Conflict between the French and the British resulted in the eventual political dominance of Britain. However, the European population of Canada remained overwhelmingly French speaking until the late eighteenth century, when tens of thousands of British Loyalists fled the revolution in the United States. The arrival of the Loyalists resulted in a more or less even balance of French- and English-speakers in Canada.

Canada was increasingly locked into the British Empire in the nineteenth century. As immigration from the British Isles continued, the English-speaking population far surpassed the numbers of French speakers. Scottish influence in Canada was notable, and close cultural links continue to tie Canada with Scotland. Canada became independent in 1867, but has retained close constitutional ties to Britain: The British monarch remains head of state. Canada provided significant assistance to Britain in both twentieth-century world wars.

Canada grew in prosperity in the second half of the twentieth century. The country adopted a U.S.-style capitalist system, although with a larger emphasis on social security systems. The period also saw large-scale immigration from countries other than the traditional sources of migration (Britain and France). Among the countries from which migrants sought a new life in Canada were Italy, Korea, and India.

Separatist pressures from the 1960s have led to political tensions between the largely French-speaking province of Quebec and the rest of Canada. The separatist tendencies of francophone Canada were put to the test in a 1995 referendum on Quebec's independence, but the proposition was narrowly defeated. Despite this, future prospects for the continuing unity of Canada remain uncertain.

Demographics

The population of Canada is around 31.5 million. Most Canadians live in southern areas of the country, close to the border with the United States, and large parts of the vast country are very sparsely populated.

Languages

Most Canadians speak one of the country's two official languages, English and French. Around 60 percent of Canadians speak English as a mother tongue, and 25 percent speak French. The remaining 15 percent speak the languages of immigrant communities—such as Italian, Korean, Polish, and Punjabi—or indigenous languages. Canadian English tends to reflect U.S. rather than British influences, but some British linguistic traits remain. Canadian French is quite different from the French spoken in modern France—it contains what would be considered in modern France to be "archaic" vocabulary and expressions, and has also been strongly influenced by English. French-speaking Canadians can understand metropolitan French without any problem, however. The literacy level is around 97 percent of the population.

Politics

Canada is a confederation and a parliamentary democracy; its capital is at Ottawa. The largely ceremonial head of state is the British monarch, an arrangement that reflects continuing constitutional ties with Britain. The British monarch is represented in Canada by a governor-general. The parliament has a bicameral structure, with a senate and a house of commons. The name of the latter chamber again reflects British constitutional influence, and its members are elected by popular vote. A long-running and currently unresolved political issue in Canada is the status of Quebec, the largely French-speaking province with a powerful secessionist movement. The future political break-up of Canada remains a possibility.

Economy

Canada has a prosperous market economy similar to that of the United States, and the 1994 North American Free Trade Agreement has reinforced economic links with the United States (and Mexico). The Canadian economy is not merely a mirror version of the U.S. economy, however. In contrast to the United States, Canada places a greater emphasis on the role of the state and on maintaining a large social security system. The Canadian economy is diversified, and major industries include high-technology manufacturing, financial services, and forestry and agricultural products. Structural economic problems include increasing dependence on the U.S. economy (the United States is by far Canada's main trading partner) and a "brain drain" of young professionals across the U.S. border. The currency unit is the Canadian dollar.

Legal and Regulatory Environment

The Canadian legal system is based on English common law, which reflects the country's British colonial heritage. The Quebec legal system is based on French law, owing to that province's historical links with France. Tax rates tend to be higher in Canada than in the United States, owing to the larger role for the state in Canadian society. Canada's competitive and efficient business culture results in a relatively light regulatory environment.

Accountancy

Canadian GAAP is based on corporate law, the standards of the Accounting Standards Board (AcSB) of the Canadian Institute of Chartered Accountants (CICA), and (for listed corporations) the requirements of Canada's various securities commissions. Canadian GAAP is sophisticated and the country has played a traditionally prominent role in supranational accountancy bodies—Canada was a founding member of the International Accounting Standards Committee in 1973, for example. While Canadian GAAP has tended to be traditionally closer to U.S. GAAP than IAS, it has moved closer to IAS in recent years. The CICA Web site (*www.cica.ca*) gives details of Canadian accounting standards and their differences from IAS.

The CICA is Canada's main professional accountancy and external auditing body. Founded in 1902, it has around 70,000 members today. There are two other accountancy professional bodies, whose members focus more on industry—the Certified General Accountants Association and the Society of Management Accountants have around 30,000 and 33,000 members, respectively.

Cultural Background

To an outsider, Canada may seem superficially like a smaller version of the United States, but the country's culture is markedly different from that of its southern neighbor. Canada is North America with a British tinge (and a French tinge in Quebec). Around 30 percent of Canadians are ethnically British or Irish, and 25 percent are of French origin. Most of the remaining 45 percent of the population originated from various countries in Europe, Asia, and the Middle East—the indigenous peoples, such as the Inuit, comprise less than 2 percent of the population. There is little cultural pressure on immigrants to "assimilate" into mainstream Canadian culture, and ethnic minorities tend to proudly preserve their traditions and languages (as seen in the "Languages" section). Around 40 percent of Canadians adhere to the Roman Catholic faith, and a similar proportion to Protestant churches. The remainder of the population follows a variety of faiths, or none.

Social Etiquette

- Canada tends to be proud of its separate identity from the United States. The visitor should not collapse distinctions between the two countries.
- Canadians retain some of the cultural traits of the British—the business culture, for example, tends to be rather more formal than in the United States. The Americanization of Canadian business culture has nonetheless increased in recent years.
- The visitor should be careful to avoid causing offense when discussing the strained cultural and political relations between the country's English-speaking and French-speaking communities.

Further Information

William Cross (ed.), *Political Parties, Representation, and Democracy in 21st Century Canada* (Toronto and Oxford: Oxford University Press, 2001).

John Edwards, *Language in Canada* (New York and Cambridge: Cambridge University Press, 1998).

Jorge Niosi, *Canada's National System of Innovation* (Montreal and Kingston: McGill-Queens University Press, 2000).

Keith Archer and Lisa Young (eds.), *Regionalism and Party Politics in Canada* (Toronto and Oxford: Oxford University Press, 2001).

Government of Canada: *http://canada.gc.ca/main_e.html*.

Canadian Institute of Chartered Accountants (CICA): *www.cica.ca*.

Certified General Accountants Association: *www.cga-canada.org*.

Society of Management Accountants: *www.cma-canada.org*.

CHILE

Geography

Chile is located in the southern "cone" of South America. The country has an elongated shape and its coastline hugs the South Pacific Ocean for over 2,500 miles. Chile is a narrow country, framed to the east by the Andes mountains. It borders Argentina, Bolivia, and Peru. Owing to the country's size, the climate is very varied—desert conditions in the north give way to a temperate central zone and a cold, subarctic south. Chile experiences earthquakes from time to time.

Brief History

The territory that was to become Chile had long been inhabited by indigenous Amerindian peoples before the arrival of Spanish settlers. From the early sixteenth century the Spanish consolidated their colonial presence, and settlers established large agricultural estates. The country gained independence from Spain in 1810, under the leadership of revolutionary leader Bernardo O'Higgins (1778–1842), who was of Irish descent. The present national boundaries were established in the 1880s. While Chile achieved a relative degree of political stability (in comparison to the volatile standards of the region), the country experienced civil war in the 1890s as the land-owning aristocracy was challenged by increasingly powerful industrial classes.

Twentieth-century Chile experienced disappointing economic growth, which resulted in large-scale poverty. In 1970, a Marxist coalition took power in an increasingly polarized and militant political environment. The country implemented socialistic policies before a 1973 military coup by Augusto Pinochet (born 1915). Under Pinochet's right-wing dictatorship, tens of thousands of Chileans suffered imprisonment, exile, torture, or murder. The Pinochet regime stayed in power until 1990, after which democracy returned to the country.

The country's prosperity grew in the 1990s, as the Pinochet regime's monetarist policies had laid the foundations for a successful economy. However, the Pinochet years have continued to cast dark shadows over the country's political and social climate. In 1998, Pinochet was arrested by the British authorities during a visit to London, in response to a request from a Spanish magistrate (for alleged human rights abuses against Spanish citizens living in Chile during the Pinochet years). The former dictator was returned to Chile to face trial for the crimes committed by his military regime. In 2002, however, the Chilean authorities dropped all the charges against Pinochet, on health grounds.

Demographics

The population of Chile is 15.2 million. Around one in three Chileans lives in the capital and largest city, Santiago.

Languages

Owing to Chile's Spanish colonial legacy, the country's official language is Spanish. (The Spanish language is discussed in greater detail in the "Spain" country section.) Chilean Spanish has differences in pronunciation and vocabulary from the Castilian Spanish spoken in central Spain, but the two versions of the language are mutually comprehensible. Chile also has a handful of indigenous Amerindian languages, such as Mapuche. Literacy is over 95 percent.

Politics

The Republic of Chile has its capital at Santiago. Since the end of the Pinochet regime in 1990, the country has consolidated its democratic practices. The country's president serves as both chief of state and head of government. The bicameral parliament comprises a senate and a chamber of deputies, and members of the latter are elected by popular vote.

Economy

The Chilean economy has traditionally been heavily dependent on copper. In recent years, the country's economic reforms have enhanced diversification in sectors such as agriculture (including wine), chemicals, fishing, and textiles, but copper remains crucial to the economy. Market-oriented reforms started during the Pinochet regime have been continued by successive democratic administrations, and Chile has experienced significant economic growth since the 1980s. However, economic disparities remain large between sections of the population.

Legal and Regulatory Environment

Chile's legal system is based on continental European law, reflecting the country's history as a Spanish colony. The regulatory environment is relatively liberal, as a result of market-oriented reforms started in the Pinochet era and followed by successive administrations.

Accountancy

Chilean GAAP is based on the standards or bulletins of the Chilean College of Accountants (*Colegio de Contadores de Chile*—CCC), and—for listed corporations—on stock exchange rules. There are differences between Chilean GAAP and IAS in areas such as business combinations and employee benefits. However, since 1998, if Chilean standards do not address a topic directly, IAS is used instead. The stock exchange requires foreign corporations to follow their national GAAP and reconcile their financial statements to Chilean GAAP. The CCC is the main professional body for accountancy and external auditing.

Cultural Background

Around 95 percent of Chileans are of either European or mixed European-indigenous Amerindian descent. Indigenous peoples account for only around 3 percent of the population. Around 90 percent of Chileans are Roman Catholics, and most of the remainder are Protestants. As in other parts of South America, evangelical Protestantism is becoming increasingly popular. In view of Chile's relatively small population, the country has had a significant impact on world literary culture and has produced more than one Nobel Laureate.

Social Etiquette

- The visitor should be careful to avoid distress or offense when discussing the violent period of the Pinochet regime, during which thousands lost their lives.
- The Chilean business environment is somewhat conservative, formal, and serious.
- A good personal rapport is highly prized in business contexts, and a balanced atmosphere of discussion and negotiation should not be disturbed by any aggressive behavior.

- Visitors should wait for their hosts to initiate the use of first names in a business context.

Further Information

Robert Barros, *Constitutionalism and Dictatorship: Pinochet, the Junta, and the 1980 Constitution* (New York and Cambridge: Cambridge University Press, 2002).

Julia Paley, *Marketing Democracy: Power and Social Movements in Post-Dictatorship Chile* (Berkeley, CA: University of California Press, 2001).

Patrick Barr-Melej, *Reforming Chile: Cultural Politics, Nationalism, and the Rise of the Middle Class* (Chapel Hill, NC: University of North Carolina Press, 2001).

David Mares and Francisco Rojas Aravena, *The United States and Chile: Coming in From the Cold* (New York and London: Routledge, 2001).

Presidency of the Republic of Chile (Spanish only): *www.presidencia.cl.*

Colegio de Contadores de Chile (Spanish only): *www.colegiodecontadores.cl.*

COLOMBIA

Geography

Colombia is located in the north of the South American continent, bordering Brazil, Ecuador, Panama, Peru, and Venezuela. Colombia has around 2,000 miles of coastline along both the Pacific Ocean and the Caribbean Sea. Nearly half the country's surface area is covered by forests and woodland, and much of the country comprises hills and mountains (including the Andes Mountains). Colombia's climate is tropical, but temperatures are cooler in upland areas. Volcanic activity and earthquakes occur occasionally.

Brief History

When the Spanish started to colonize the Andean region of South America in the sixteenth century, they found a number of indigenous Amerindian peoples. The precious metals used by some of the local peoples led to the Spanish myth of El Dorado—the "golden" paradise. The Spanish fought, killed, and enslaved many thousands of Amerindians, and unfamiliar European diseases killed many more. From the mid-sixteenth to the early eighteenth centuries, the territory of modern Colombia was part of the viceroyalty of Peru. In 1739, the future Colombia became part of New Granada, which included the lands of modern Ecuador and Venezuela.

Colombia celebrates its independence from Spain in 1810. Independence led to a century of political and civil conflict, and unsuccessful attempts at region federations with neighboring countries. In the nineteenth century, ideological battles between liberals and conservatives were bloody and chaotic, and the country descended frequently into civil war. The early twentieth century was more peaceful, but in 1948 the ideological differences exploded again into a civil war that claimed hundreds of thousands of lives. In 1953, a coup led to a short-lived military regime, before a civilian administration was formed from an alliance of liberals and conservatives.

In the 1970s, a number of left-wing guerrilla groups emerged, including the Revolutionary Armed Forces of Colombia (FARC). By the 1990s, the country had again slid toward chaos, with a civil war that involved political and criminal violence. In addition to the FARC and other left-wing groups, Colombia had to face the violence of powerful drug cartels and right-wing paramilitary groups. All of these armed groups have been accused of massacres and other human rights abuses. With grim irony, the local press sometimes calls the country "Locombia"—the "crazy country."

The United States (the destination of a large proportion of illegal Colombian drugs) has supported the Colombian government's efforts to restore order, and has supplied both economic and military aid. At the time of writing, however, the FARC controls a large part of Colombian territory. Widespread violence continues to blight daily life and civilians are often the victims. In May 2002, for example, over 100 people were killed while sheltering in a church from a battle between FARC guerrillas and right-wing paramilitaries. Official statistics also report that as many as 3,000 people are kidnapped in the country every year: The soaring level of abductions has discouraged both business and tourist visitors, and has damaged the country's economic and political standing in the world.

Demographics

The population of Colombia is around 40.5 million, which makes it South America's third most populous country. The capital, Bogotà, has over 8 million inhabitants.

Languages

The main language of Colombia is Spanish. As in large parts of South America, the use of the language derives from the Spanish colonial legacy. The Spanish language is discussed in greater detail in the "Spain" country section. Colombian Spanish differs in pronunciation and vocabulary from the Castilian Spanish spoken in central Spain, but the two versions of the language are mutually comprehensible. In addition, over 50 indigenous Amerindian languages are spoken in Colombia, by 2 to 3 percent of the population. The literacy rate is around 90 percent.

Politics

The Republic of Colombia is a democracy and has its capital at Bogotà. The country's president, who acts as both head of state and head of government, is elected by popular vote. The bicameral parliament comprises a senate and a house of representatives. The members of the latter are elected by popular vote. Colombian politics is dominated by the country's long-running and complex civil war involving government forces, right-wing paramilitaries, left-wing revolutionaries, and drug cartels. The FARC currently controls a large part of Colombian territory, in which it runs a parallel state.

Economy

Colombia is rich in natural resources, including oil, gold, silver, emeralds, platinum, and coal. The country also has an important agricultural sector with coffee and sugar production, and mature chemicals and textiles industries. One in three Colombians works in the agricultural sector. The Colombian economy has suffered from the dislocation caused by the decades-old civil war. Indeed, chronic economic problems are one of the elements fueling the continuing violence: Around half the population lives below the poverty line, and one in five is unemployed. Further, the illegal drug cartels run a shadow economy worth many billions of dollars annually. Colombia's largest trading partner is the United States, and the country's currency unit is the peso.

Legal and Regulatory Environment

The Colombian legal system is based on Spanish law, as a result of Spain's historical colonial influence. In recent years, however, the legal system has incorporated U.S.-style elements, especially in criminal law. The Colombian tax and regulatory environment is generally regarded as cumbersome and bureaucratic, and diversion of the state's efforts into fighting the civil war has not been conducive to a fast pace of reform.

Accountancy

Colombian GAAP is based on corporate law, tax law, presidential decree, and the recommendations of the Technical Commission for Public Accounting (*Consejo Técnico de la Contaduría Pública*—CTCP). The CTCP's recommendations are not compulsory. Colombian GAAP is closer to U.S. GAAP than IAS, reflecting close ties between the governments of both countries.

Cultural Background

Colombia is an ethnically diverse country, with inhabitants of Amerindian, Spanish, and African origin. Around 75 percent of Colombians are of mixed ethnic background, 20 percent are of European descent, 4 percent of African descent, and 1 percent are indigenous Amerindians. Around 90 percent of Colombians are nominally Roman Catholic, but evangelical Protestant churches have grown in importance in recent years. The writer Gabriel García Márquez (born 1928) is Colombia's most famous international cultural figure.

Social Etiquette

- The pace of business life in Colombia is rather slow.
- The visitor should be careful when discussing the country's internal problems, such as armed political insurgency and drug cartels, to avoid causing offense or distress.
- The visitor should avoid referring to local colleagues or contacts by their first names, unless formally asked to do so.

Further Information

Gonzalo Sanchez and Donny Meertens, *Bandits, Peasants and Politics: The Case of "La Violencia" in Colombia* (Austin, TX: University Press, 2001).
Nazih Richani, *Systems of Violence: The Political Economy of War and Peace in Colombia* (New York: State University of New York Press, 2002).
Frank Safford and Marco Palacios, *Colombia: Fragmented Land, Divided Society* (New York and Oxford: Oxford University Press, 2001).
Presidency of the Republic of Colombia (Spanish only): *www.presidencia.gov.co*.
Consejo Técnico de la Contaduría Pública (Spanish only): *www.ccpa.org.co*.

MEXICO

Geography

Mexico is located in Central America, bordering the United States, Belize, and Guatemala. It has a coastline of over 5,800 miles. The varied terrain ranges from deserts to snow-capped volcanoes. The Mexican climate is mainly tropical, other than in the hot and barren desert areas. The country sometimes experiences devastating earthquakes—in 1985, for example, an earthquake killed over 10,000 people and destroyed hundreds of buildings in Mexico City.

Brief History

Before the arrival of Spanish colonists, Mexico had been inhabited for 20,000 years or more. Impressive civilizations predated the European presence, and the cultures of the Mayans and Aztecs are world famous. The huge Mayan pyramids remain one of Mexico's main tourist attractions. In the early sixteenth century, Spanish invaders and settlers attacked the indigenous peoples and their cultures, and local resistance soon crumbled under Spanish military pressure. Further, diseases introduced from Europe decimated local populations. Indeed, the indigenous cultures were totally devastated by Spanish imperialism: It has been estimated that the indigenous population of the area that was to become Mexico fell from around 25 million to 1 million within less than a century of the Spanish conquest.

The Spanish colonial rulers exploited various economic avenues, including ranching and mining. Eventually, the settlers of Spanish origin broke away from Spain: The Mexicans celebrate September 16, 1810, as the date on which their nation gained independence. The nineteenth century was a period of political instability and war. Conflict with the United States led in 1848 to the loss of Mexican territory, including the huge states of Texas and California to its large neighbor in 1848. In the 1860s, France attempted to colonize Mexico, but French ambitions were defeated by successful local resistance.

Mexico eventually experienced a generation of peace in the late nineteenth and early twentieth centuries, but this was at the price of dictatorial administrations that suppressed basic human rights. Political repression led to the Mexican Revolution of 1910 to 1920, a complex civil war that claimed up to 2 million lives. After the revolution, a period of relative stability returned and there were modest attempts at political and economic reform. However, inequalities in wealth remained enormous and political freedoms remained restricted. Both factors were sources of simmering popular discontent, and in the 1960s university students in Mexico City led protests in favor of social and economic reform. Clashes between police and the demonstrators led to many deaths.

As economic conditions worsened in the 1980s, Mexican governments reacted by liberalizing the economy. This led to the country joining the North American Free Trade Agreement in 1994. In the same year, however, Mexico's currency collapsed. This led to several years of economic hardship, rising crime, and a surge in illegal emigration to the United States. The 1990s were also characterized by an insurgency of indigenous inhabitants in the south of the country. Named the Zapatista uprising for a radical reformer of the Mexican Revolution, the armed rebellion involved thousands of impoverished peasants who demanded greater economic, social, and political equality. The Zapatista movement is still active at the time of writing.

Demographics

Mexico's population is around 102 million. The capital, Mexico City, is among the world's largest cities, with well in excess of 20 million inhabitants. A combination of overpopulation and economic hardship has driven millions of Mexicans to move to the United States. Much of this emigration is illegal, but it is unlikely to stop until economic push factors are alleviated.

Languages

Spanish is the main language in Mexico, reflecting the country's Spanish colonial heritage. Mexican Spanish differs from the Castilian Spanish spoken in central Spain in both pronunciation and vocabulary. In particular, Mexican Spanish has adopted a large number of indigenous Amerindian words. Mexican Spanish and Castilian are mutually comprehensible, however. Around 7 percent of Mexicans speak indigenous languages, which number more than 50. Most indigenous peoples are bilingual, although it is estimated that around 1 million Amerindians do not know Spanish. The country's literacy rate is around 90 percent.

Politics

The United Mexican States is a democratic, federal republic and has its capital at Mexico City. The country's president acts as both head of state and head of government and is elected by popular vote. The bicameral parliament consists of a senate and a chamber of deputies, and the members of the latter are popularly elected through a mixed system of direct election and proportional representation. Mexico politics was dominated from the 1930s to the late 1990s by the Institutional Revolutionary Party (*Partido Revolucionario Institucional*—PRI). From 1997, a series of coalitions have replaced the PRI as the main political force. A continuing source of political tension, rebellion, and revolution is the status of the country's indigenous peoples, many of whom are socially and economically sidelined. The armed Zapatista movement has brought these issues to the world's attention in recent years.

Economy

Mexico is a major oil producer and also has large industrial and agricultural sectors. Important industries include automobiles, chemicals, mining, textiles, and tourism. Mexico has a history of economic turmoil, ranging from the effects of falling oil prices in the 1980s to the collapse of the currency in the 1990s. Structural problems afflict Mexico's market economy: outdated industrial plants, poor infrastructure, overdependence on trade with the United States, and widespread corruption. The NAFTA agreement of 1994 has locked Mexico more closely into the prosperous economic zone of North America, but poverty remains widespread (especially among Amerindians): One in four Mexicans lives in poverty. The country's currency unit is the peso.

Legal and Regulatory Environment

The Mexican legal system is based largely on Spanish legal traditions, as a result of the country's colonial history. The Mexican regulatory and tax environment has traditionally been perceived as bureaucratic and cumbersome, although market-oriented reforms and the competitive pressures of belonging to NAFTA have eased the country's red tape in recent years.

Accountancy

Mexican GAAP is based on the accounting standards of the Mexican Institute of Public Accountants (*Instituto Mexicano de Contadores Publicos*—IMCP), tax law, and Mexican stock exchange rules (for listed corporations). The IMCP has more than 20,000 members and is the country's leading accountancy and external auditing body. Its standards are known as bulletins, and bulletin A-8 (effective from 1995) states that IAS should be used for matters not covered by IMCP bulletins. The IMCP also issues nonmandatory guidance and recommendations. Although Mexico was a founder member of the IASC, Mexican GAAP has traditionally differed from IAS in several areas, notably accounting for business combinations and employee benefits.

Cultural Background

Mexico's ethnic composition derives from two main sources—indigenous Amerindian peoples, and European (mainly Spanish) settlers. Around 60 percent of Mexicans are of mixed ethnic origin, some 30 percent are of Amerindian origin, and 9 percent are of European descent. The remaining 1 percent comprises migrants from other countries and communities. There are around 60 Amerindian communities. Around 90 percent of Mexicans are Roman Catholics, but ancient indigenous religious traditions coexist with the more formalized versions of Christianity.

Social Etiquette

- Mexicans enjoy entertaining visitors, and business dealings often involve visits to restaurants.
- Business discussions tend to be nonconfrontational. Even where disagreements are genuine, the visitor should be courteous at all times and observe appropriate social decorum.
- Mexicans like to use professional and academic titles, and these should be respected by visitors.
- Women in Mexico should generally dress conservatively.

Further Information

Martin Puchet Anyul and Lionello F. Punzo, *Mexico Beyond NAFTA* (New York and London: Routledge, 2001).
Brian R. Hamnett, *A Concise History of Mexico* (New York and Cambridge: Cambridge University Press, 1999).
Richard Snyder, *Politics After Neoliberalism: Reregulation in Mexico* (New York and Cambridge: Cambridge University Press, 2001).
The Mexican Presidency: *www.presidencia.gob.mx/?NLang=en*.
Instituto Mexicano de Contadores Publicos (Spanish only): *www.imcp.org.mx*.

PERU

Geography

Peru is located in central South America, with a Pacific Ocean coastline. The country borders Bolivia, Brazil, Chile, Colombia, and Ecuador. Peru's varied terrain ranges from the Andes Mountains to the tropical rain forests of the Peruvian

Amazon Basin. The latter accounts for around one half of the country's territory. Peru's climate varies from tropical in the Amazon Basin to arid in western desert areas. The country occasionally suffers earthquakes.

Brief History

The territory that became modern Peru was the site of millennia of continuous inhabitation before the arrival of Spanish imperialists. Today the Incas are probably the best known of the area's indigenous cultures: The sophisticated Inca Empire stretched from the present-day territories of Chile to Colombia, but from the early sixteenth century Spanish invaders took advantage of local conflict and political rivalries between the peoples of the area to undermine and then destroy the Inca Empire. The Spanish also brought with them diseases from Europe that decimated indigenous populations.

Following Spain's destruction of the Inca Empire in the sixteenth century, the region enjoyed two generally peaceful centuries. The city of Lima developed into the region's principal political and economic center. In 1780, however, a rebellion of indigenous peoples erupted in protest at their economic exploitation by Spanish colonialists. The rebellion was quickly suppressed, but the underlying tensions remained.

Peru gained its independence in 1821, but Spanish forces were not defeated for another three years. The country lost a war to Chile in 1879–1883. The subsequent history of Peru has been characterized by chronic political instability and economic weakness. The uneven distribution of wealth has been striking even by the standards of the region, and social unrest has occurred since the nineteenth century.

Successive governments (military and civilian) have failed to address social inequalities, and have thereby failed to eradicate the sources of anger and frustration that were to explode in the guerrilla movements of the late twentieth century. From the 1980s, successive governments faced worsening economic problems and serious armed rebellions from two guerrilla movements—the Shining Path (*Sendero Luminoso*) movement and the Tupac Amaru Revolutionary Movement (*Movimiento Revolucionario Tupac Amaru*). The former was motivated by Maoist ideology, and the latter by the grievances of indigenous peoples. The death toll from the insurgencies has been measured in thousands of lives. At the time of writing, the activities of both guerrilla groups have been drastically curtailed, but political and criminal violence remain widespread in the country. (In March 2002, for example, just before a visit to Peru by the U.S. President, 10 people died in a car bomb near the U.S. embassy in Lima.)

In 1990, Alberto Fujimori (born 1938), a Peruvian of Japanese descent, was elected president. Fujimori tackled the guerrilla movements with some success, and peacefully resolved long-standing territorial disputes with Ecuador in 1998 and Chile in 1999. Levels of foreign investment in Peru increased along with international confidence in the country's political stability. However, Fujimori was charged with corruption and human rights abuses and, a decade after coming to power, he fled to exile in Japan.

Demographics

Peru's population is around 27.5 million. It is thought that approximately one in four Peruvians lives in the capital, Lima.

Languages

As in other former Spanish colonies in South America, Spanish is Peru's main language. The "Spain" country section gives details on the Spanish language. Peruvian Spanish differs in both pronunciation and vocabulary from the Castilian Spanish spoken in central Spain, but the two versions of the language are mutually intelligible.

The country's indigenous peoples speak up to 70 Amerindian languages, such as Quechua and Aymara, and (other than in remote regions) they tend to be bilingual with Spanish. There are also small immigrant communities, including Japanese and Chinese, who have retained their own languages. The "Cultural Background" section indicates the relative sizes of the country's various ethnic communities, which closely reflect the numbers of speakers of the various languages. The country's literacy level is around 90 percent.

Politics

The Republic of Peru has been a democracy since 1980. Its capital is at the country's largest city, Lima. The Peruvian president acts as both the country's head of state and head of government and is elected by popular vote. The Peruvian parliament is unicameral, and its members are also elected by popular vote. The main issues facing the country's politicians in recent years have been the country's long-standing economic problems, and the armed insurgencies of guerrilla groups. The illegal drugs industry is also a major challenge for the country's politicians.

Economy

Peru is a potentially wealthy country, rich in natural resources such as copper, gold, silver, lead, zinc, and oil. Peru also has a strong fishing sector, and in the early 1960s the country was considered by many to be the world's leading fishing nation. The Peruvian economy, however, has long suffered from serious structural problems, including severe social inequalities, poor infrastructure, and corruption. In particular, the country's indigenous peoples have tended since colonial times to be socially and economically marginalized. Recent governments have undertaken privatization programs and have attempted to introduce market-oriented reforms, with some success. Peru's largest trading partner is the United States, and its currency unit is the (nuevo) sol.

Legal and Regulatory Environment

As in other former Spanish colonies in South America, Peru's legal system is based largely on Spanish law. The regulatory and tax environment is highly bureaucratic, although recent governments have sought to improve the country's free market credentials by cutting red tape.

Accountancy

Peruvian GAAP is based on corporate law, tax law, IAS, and the pronouncements of the Peruvian Accounting Standards Board (PASB). Peruvian GAAP is based on IAS, but the PASB sometimes modifies IAS to meet local conditions. There are areas of traditional discrepancy between Peruvian GAAP and IAS, such as the valuation of investment properties. Under Peruvian GAAP, where IAS is unclear on a topic, then U.S. GAAP is taken to represent accepted accountancy practice. While domestic listed corporations must follow IAS (or U.S. GAAP where IAS is silent on a topic), foreign listed corporations are required to use their national GAAP and to provide an explanation of differences with IAS. The major accountancy and external auditing professional body is the College of Public Accountants (*Colegio de Contadores Publicos*).

Cultural Background

Precise information on the ethnic makeup of the Peruvian nation is difficult to obtain, mainly as a result of intermarriage between the main ethnic groups. It is commonly thought that around 50 percent of Peruvians are indigenous Amerindians, and 15 percent are of European (mainly Spanish) origin. Of the remaining 35 percent, the vast majority are classified as being of mixed Amerindian-European descent. There are also small communities of Japanese, Chinese, and African origin that in total account for approximately 3 percent of the population. (However, some commentators would classify a larger proportion of the population as being of mixed Amerindian-European descent.)

Over 90 percent of the population is nominally Roman Catholic, although large elements of traditional indigenous belief remain. There is also a small but growing number of adherents to evangelical Protestant churches.

Social Etiquette

- The visitor should be cautious when discussing such domestic political issues as terrorism and the social status of the country's Amerindians, as it is easy to unwittingly cause offense when dealing with these sensitive and complex matters.
- The personal touch tends to be important in the Peruvian business context. This includes continuity of personnel, and too much rotation of personnel in business dealings may be inadvisable.
- Peruvians tend to value professional and academic titles, and the visitor should not dispense with them as forms of address.

Further Information

Gustavo Goritti Ellenbogen, *The Shining Paths: A History of the Millenarian War in Peru* (Chapel Hill, NC: University of North Carolina Press, 1999).
Peter Flindell Klarén, *Peru: Society and Statehood in the Andes* (New York and Oxford: Oxford University Press, 1999).
Steve J. Stern (ed.), *Shining and Other Paths: War and Society in Peru, 1980–1995* (Durham, NC: Duke University Press, 1998).
Ministry of the Peruvian Presidency (Spanish only): *www.pres.gob.pe.*
Colegio de Contadores Publicos (Spanish only): *www.ccpl.org.pe.*

UNITED STATES

Geography

The United States is located in North America, bordering Canada to the north and Mexico to the south, and between the North Atlantic and North Pacific Oceans. In terms of surface area, it is the third-largest country in the world, after Russia and Canada. The varied U.S. terrain ranges from the deserts of Nevada to the icy landscape of Alaska. The United States' climate is similarly varied, from the hot desert weather of the southwest to the arctic Alaskan climate. The northeast of the country experiences hot summers and cold winters. In recent years, forest fires in the arid west of the country (e.g., in California and Arizona) have been a major environmental problem.

Brief History

When European settlers arrived to colonize North America from the sixteenth century, they found an existing population of Native American inhabitants. These included Inuit (Eskimo) inhabitants in the north and Native American peoples throughout many parts of the country. The European settlers came mainly from the British Isles, Spain, and France. Two levels of conflict emerged—first, between the Europeans and the Native Americans; and second, among the Europeans who struggled for colonial supremacy.

Many Europeans moved to North America to flee political or religious oppression in their home countries—the Pilgrim Fathers, for example, were English religious dissenters who found the established religious authorities in England hostile to their beliefs. The United States has remained a country with a reputation for tolerance and freedom of thought, and has continued to be a magnet for peoples fleeing persecution around the world. (It also attracts large numbers of economic migrants seeking a more prosperous future.)

The British emerged as the main colonizing power, although the United States came into being in a revolutionary movement that separated the country from the

British Crown in 1776. Despite the bloodshed of the revolutionary period, the independent United States subsequently maintained friendly relationships with the former colonial power. These political and cultural links are reflected today in the so-called "special relationship" between the United States and Britain. The United States retained several important aspects of British culture: the English language, the common law, the Christian religion, a leaning toward free-market economics, and democratic government. (After the American Revolution the British retained a significant colonial presence in North America in the form of Canada, into which thousands of British Loyalists fled.)

During the nineteenth and twentieth centuries, 37 new states were added to the original 13, as the new nation expanded across the North American continent. The territory of Alaska was purchased from Russia in 1867. A number of overseas possessions were also acquired, and the United States undertook some colonization (e.g., in the Philippines). The slave trade involved the brutal transfer of hundreds of thousands of Africans to North America, and the abolition of slavery was a major issue in the country's traumatic civil war that lasted from 1861 to 1865.

The population of the United States increased significantly in the two centuries following independence, as a result of voluntary immigration from Europe (initially) and South America and Asia (more recently). In the twentieth century, the rise of the United States as the world's most powerful nation-state coincided with Britain's decline as a superpower. The United States emerged after World War I as the world's most powerful country in military, economic, and political matters. The severe economic depression of the 1930s temporarily arrested the country's rise to power, but the only serious twentieth-century challenger to U.S. dominance came in the form of the Soviet Union.

Following the United States' decisive engagement in World War II, which tipped the balance against the Axis powers of Germany, Japan, and Italy, world politics was dominated by the Cold War between the Soviets and the United States (and their respective allies). The Cold War was typified by the use of large-scale armaments as a deterrent force, and localized conflicts (e.g., in Korea and Vietnam) that reflected the global ideological war. The Cold War eventually fizzled out by the early 1990s, as the Soviet Union imploded as a result of economic weakness. The Soviet satellite states obtained their independence, and by the end of the century U.S. hegemony was established. Domestically, the United States experienced a surge in living standards in the second half of the twentieth century, as its economy proved to be the world's most dynamic. Major political events in the last half century have included the civil rights movement, the Vietnam War, and the terrorist attacks of September 11, 2001.

Although slavery had been abolished in the nineteenth century, the country's black minority still faced serious discrimination as late as the 1960s. The civil rights movement emerged amid street protests and serious rioting to end enforced segregation and other legal restrictions. The movement's best-known figure was Martin Luther King Jr. (1929–1968), who died at an assassin's hands. Although the black minority still experiences disproportionate social and economic distress, the United States now has probably the most sophisticated anti-discrimination legislation in the world.

The Vietnam War was a localized element of the Cold War. From the early 1960s to the early 1970s, the United States committed increasingly large military forces in an attempt to stem the advance of communism in Asia. Fearful of a "domino effect" if countries were to fall under Soviet influence, the United States tried to repeat its earlier successes in the Korean war of 1950–1953 in stemming the advance of communism. However, the United States was unable to defeat the communist forces based in the north of Vietnam, and agreed to a cease-fire in 1973. U.S. forces were withdrawn, and two years later the communists overran the south of the country to create a unified, communist Vietnam. U.S. military commitments to Vietnam had been huge, with more than 500,000 armed services personnel on location at the most intense point. Conscription was also introduced in the United States, fueling domestic antiwar sentiments.

In September 2001, Islamic militants undertook a series of attacks on strategic targets in the United States using hijacked aircraft. The World Trade Center in New York was destroyed, and part of the Pentagon in Washington, DC was damaged. With a death toll in excess of 3,000, this was the worst act of terrorism in the United States, and the country responded by declaring a global "war on terrorism" that has changed the climate of tolerance toward political violence around the world. At the time of writing, the threat of further attacks in the United States is considered very real.

Demographics

The population of the United States is around 278 million, which makes it the third most populous country in the world (well behind China and India). Ethnically, the United States is a melting pot of different peoples. In addition to the Native American population and the early European settlers, several waves of immigration—voluntary and involuntary—have added to the country's ethnic mix. Hundreds of thousands of African slaves were forcibly introduced into North America by European slave traders. Later, millions of Europeans moved to the United States both to seek a better material life and to escape religious persecution. Initially, most European immigration occurred from Britain, Ireland, and Germany, but the emphasis later switched to southern Europe. In addition, large numbers of Jews fled Europe to escape persecution by both imperial Russia and Nazi Germany. In recent years, immigrants from Asia and the rest of the Americas have added to the country's ethnic mix.

Languages

The former colonial language of English is the principal language of the United States. Although immigration from many countries has occurred over the past two centuries, the desire for assimilation has resulted in a willingness to learn English, and the use of foreign languages has often ended in the second and third generations of immigrant families. However, Spanish is spoken by a sizable minority, mainly recent immigrants from Central and South America. The literacy level is around 97 percent.

Politics

The United States of America is a democratic, federal republic; its capital is Washington, DC. In addition to the mainland states in North America, the country has numerous overseas dependent territories, such as Guam and Puerto Rico. The president acts as both head of state and head of government and is elected by an electoral college of delegates from each state. The bicameral Congress consists of a Senate and House of Representatives, both of whose members are directly elected.

The political culture of the United States revolves around the dual party system of the Republicans and the Democrats. The ideological differences between Republicans and Democrats are less marked than in some other two-party political systems (e.g., in Britain), and there is no strong socialist movement. However, there are major differences of substance between the two parties: The Democrats tend to be more liberal on social issues, for example. The role of the president is intended to transcend partisan political barriers, and the president is normally a focus of allegiance and pride for all U.S. citizens. The United States is well known for its strong advocacy of democracy and for its freedom of speech. The country remains a source of inspiration for peoples around the world in oppressive political circumstances.

Economy

The United States is the world's economic superpower. The country's economic system is very liberalized, with a relatively small role for the state. U.S. business culture is characterized by its dynamism, economies of scale, technological advancement, and global outlook. Industries such as aerospace, military equipment, computer software, and medical equipment are the most sophisticated in the world. The country's consumer goods sector has also been successful, but has not dominated world markets to the same degree. Japanese electronic products and automobiles, for example, have made major inroads in both U.S. and global markets. The United States is a strong advocate of free markets, although it does not hesitate to impose tariff barriers when it feels it necessary. However, in comparison to Japan and the EU, the United States tends to have a less protectionist culture.

The prosperity of the United States is one reason for its attraction to would-be immigrants from around the world. (Another reason is the country's strong tradition of tolerance and political freedom.) However, inequality of income is relatively high, and there are pockets of severe poverty in some urban areas. A disproportionate number of U.S. citizens in poverty belong to the black minority. The country's welfare state is relatively modest (e.g., in comparison with the EU). Canada, Japan, and Mexico are the United States' main trading partners. The currency unit is the dollar—the world's most powerful and prestigious currency.

Legal and Regulatory Environment

U.S. law is based on English common law, owing to the country's colonial heritage. Given the United States' long commitment to free market economics, it is unsurprising that its regulatory system is generally light on bureaucracy. Flexible markets require light administration. However, visitors to the United States may be surprised at the complexity of tax regulations for both individuals and corporations.

Accountancy

U.S. GAAP is based on the standards and guidance of the Financial Accounting Standards Board (FASB), the "Statements of Position" of the American Institute of Certified Public Accountants (AICPA), and the regulations of the Securities and Exchange Commission (SEC). The FASB's standards are extremely detailed and are generally considered to be the most sophisticated in the world. They are issued after a lengthy consultation process with interested parties. The FASB Web site (*www.fasb.org*) has details of U.S. Financial Accounting Standards. A series of accounting scandals in 2002 has led to calls for a review of U.S. GAAP, and the resulting debate is taking place at the time of writing.

The Emerging Issues Task Force looks at pressing matters and offers guidance on the application of U.S. GAAP. Domestic corporations are required to use U.S. GAAP in preparing their financial statements, while foreign listed corporations may use IAS or their national GAAP. In the latter cases, a reconciliation to U.S. GAAP is required.

Owing to the power of the U.S. economy, U.S. GAAP is frequently permitted by local standard-setting bodies around the world. In the Netherlands, for example, foreign listed corporations are allowed to report in U.S. GAAP but must reconcile the results to Dutch GAAP. The FASB is committed to increasing the international comparability of U.S. GAAP and it adopts the principles of IAS where it deems appropriate. Traditionally, however, the influence of U.S. GAAP on IAS has been significant. The FASB's "Conceptual Framework" has been particularly influential in global accountancy practice, and U.S. accounting conventions for business combinations have largely been adopted around the world.

The accountancy profession in the United States is large and sophisticated and is the world's leader. The accountancy and external auditing profession is dominated by the Certified Public Accountant (CPA) qualification, which is generally awarded by individual states. The American Institute of Certified Public Accountants (AICPA) is the profession's national body. The Institute of Internal Auditors also originated in the United States, where it is headquartered.

Cultural Background

The ethnic and cultural mix of the United States is extremely varied, as discussed in the "Demographics" section. Waves of immigration from various parts of the world have led to a cultural melting pot. Racial tension in some urban areas occasionally flares into violence, but racial discrimination has diminished significantly since the civil rights movement of the 1960s. The United States has strong legal measures to counter discrimination, and U.S. practices in this area have been copied around the world, from South Africa to India. The Native American population represents less than 1 percent of total inhabitants.

In religious terms, the country remains overwhelmingly Christian. Around one-half of U.S. citizens are Protestants, and a further 30 percent are Roman Catholics. The United States is a very religious country, and foreign visitors are often surprised at the intensity of Christian observance. A minority stream of Christian fundamentalism dates back to the early days of European settlement, when religious dissenters fled from persecution. There are small communities of other religions—Jews, Muslims, and Buddhists, for example—none of which exceeds 5 percent of the total population.

U.S. popular culture may be characterized as vigorous and optimistic. Not tied down by the historical baggage that affects other parts of the world, U.S. culture is highly innovative. In a sense, U.S. popular culture has become world popular culture—in movies, television, music, and fashion.

Social Etiquette

- U.S. business culture is relatively informal in terms of dress, language (the use of first names), and management style. There is little of the formal adherence to hierarchy seen in Europe, for example.
- U.S. business tends to move faster than in most parts of the world.
- In the United States, family names are often followed by Jr., or a roman numeral indicating the generation.
- The visitor should be careful to avoid offense when discussing the United States' often-strained race relations.

Further Information

Thomas Bender (ed.), *Rethinking American History in a Global Age* (Berkeley, CA: University of California Press, 2002).

Paul S. Boyer, *Oxford Companion to United States History* (New York and Oxford: Oxford University Press, 2001).

G. John Ikenberry (ed.), *America Unrivaled: The Future of the Balance of Power* (New York: Columbia University Press, 2002).

Jeremy Isaacs and Taylor Downing, *Cold War: An Illustrated History, 1945–1991* (New York: Little Brown, 1998).

Howard Zinn, *A People's History of the United States: 1492 to Present*, rev. ed. (New York: Harper Perennial, 2001).

The White House: *www.whitehouse.gov*.

American Institute of Certified Public Accountants: *www.aicpa.org*.

Financial Accounting Standards Board: *www.fasb.org*.

Institute of Internal Auditors: *www.theiia.org*.

Institute of Management Accountants: *www.imanet.org*.

VENEZUELA

Geography

Venezuela is located on the northern coast of the South American continent. In addition to coastlines along the Caribbean Sea and the Atlantic Ocean, the country borders Brazil, Colombia, and Guyana. The terrain of Venezuela is varied, and much of it is strikingly beautiful. In the west are the snow-capped peaks of the Andes, and in the south is Amazonian jungle. Much of the east of the country is dominated by a mountainous plateau, while palm-lined beaches hug the Caribbean coastline.

Venezuela contains the world's highest waterfall, Angel Falls. The climate is tropical and humid, although highland areas are cooler. Landslides often occur after heavy rainfall: In December 1999, thousands of Venezuelans lost their lives and serious economic damage was caused by a series of devastating landslides.

Brief History

Prior to the arrival of Spanish colonizers, indigenous Amerindian peoples had long settled the area that became Venezuela. The indigenous population of the area is thought to have been as high as 500,000 when the Spanish arrived in the early sixteenth century. The Spanish conquerors decimated the local indigenous peoples through savage military action, and unfamiliar diseases introduced from Europe also killed many thousands.

German colonizers also tried to seize territory and wealth in the area, but Spain was the main imperial power. The Spanish invaders named the country for Venice in Italy, and sought the riches of the mythical golden paradise of El Dorado. In the early nineteenth century, the revolutionary freedom fighter Simon Bolivar (1783–1830) led the struggle for the country's independence from Spain. Venezuelans celebrate July 5, 1811, as their independence day and Bolivar as their national hero. The modern boundaries of Venezuela emerged only in 1830, however, following the collapse of the state (Gran Colombia) that Bolivar had hoped would unite Colombia, Ecuador, and Venezuela.

In the nineteenth and twentieth centuries, Venezuela enjoyed a reputation for political stability in a generally volatile region. By the late 1920s, the country had become the world's largest oil exporter, but the wealth generated by the oil industry enriched only a small elite. Owing to a lack of meaningful social reform, the country was (and is still) characterized by vast social and economic inequalities.

Although Venezuela embraced democratic government in the latter half of the twentieth century, political freedom did little for the economic condition of the vast majority of the population. In 1998, former paratrooper Hugo Chavez (born 1954) was elected president. A champion of the poor, the charismatic Chavez has evoked the revolutionary spirit of Simon Bolivar in promising to eradicate corruption and to distribute the country's wealth more equitably. His period of tenure has been marked by instability, however. In April 2002, amid violent street protests that resulted in dozens of deaths, Chavez was arrested by the country's military—only to be returned to power two days later. Pressing problems facing the country include overdependence on the volatile price of oil, chronic poverty, and drug-fueled violence.

Demographics

The population of Venezuela is around 24 million, and the country is among the most highly urbanized in South America. Around one in five Venezuelans lives in the capital, Caracas.

Languages

Spanish is the main language of Venezuela, and is spoken by virtually all the country's inhabitants. Venezuelan Spanish differs from the Castilian Spanish spoken in central Spain in terms of pronunciation and vocabulary, but the two versions of the language are mutually intelligible. In addition, over 20 indigenous languages are spoken by the country's small Amerindian population that accounts for under 2 percent of the population. The country's literacy rate is around 90 percent.

Politics

The Bolivarian Republic of Venezuela is named for the country's nineteenth-century independence leader, Simon Bolivar. It is a democratic, federal republic and has its capital at Caracas. The Venezuelan president is elected by popular vote and serves as both head of state and head of government. The unicameral Venezuela parliament, the National Assembly, is elected by popular vote. In the late twentieth century, Venezuela has been one of South America's more stable democracies, but (as the "History" section describes) the period of the Chavez presidency has to date been characterized by instability.

Economy

Venezuela has huge economic potential, as it is blessed with abundant natural resources. The country has one of the world's largest known oil deposits, as well as significant quantities of natural gas, gold, diamonds, coal, iron ore, and bauxite. In addition, Venezuela has mature industries in food processing, textiles, and steel and aluminum. Despite such an apparently solid economic base, around four in five Venezuelans live in poverty. The shanty towns of Caracas' poor cling precariously to the hills around the capital, and hundreds of thousands of the flimsy dwellings risk being swept away by the country's frequently heavy rainfall. Corruption and archaic patterns of social inequality appear to be the root cause of the country's widespread poverty. Only a tiny elite has seen the benefit of Venezuela's petrodollars.

The Venezuelan economy is at the mercy of world oil prices and seems to hover continuously on the brink of crisis. The United States is Venezuela's largest trading partner. The country's currency unit is the bolivar, named for the country's nineteenth-century national hero.

Legal and Regulatory Environment

The Venezuelan legal culture was inherited from the Spanish colonial period. The regulatory environment is notoriously bureaucratic and cumbersome, although modest reforms have been made in recent years.

Accountancy

Venezuelan GAAP is based mainly on the accounting principles of the Venezuelan Federation of Colleges of Public Accountants (*Federación de Colegios de Contadores Públicos de Venezuela*—FCCPV). Listed corporations must also adhere to stock exchange regulations. In general, Venezuelan GAAP permits the use of IAS for topics not addressed directly by the FCCPV's standards or by stock exchange regulations. (Mexican and U.S. GAAP have also been sources of influence on Venezuelan GAAP.) Historical areas of discrepancy with IAS include accounting for business combinations, and accounting for property, plant and equipment. The FCCPV is the country's main professional accountancy and external auditing body.

Cultural Background

Around 65 to 70 percent of Venezuelans are of mixed Amerindian-European descent, while approximately 20 percent are of European descent and 10 percent of African origin. The indigenous Amerindians number only around 200,000. Over 95 percent of Venezuelans are nominally Roman Catholic, and there are small minorities of Protestants and adherents to indigenous religious beliefs. Venezuela is famous for its music, which is an eclectic mix of African, European, and indigenous influences. Visitors will find the infectious rhythms of salsa music pulsating through the country's restaurants, bars, and taxis.

Social Etiquette

- The pace of business life in Venezuela is relatively slow, and the visitor should be patient when faced with delays or bureaucracy. Displays of frustration tend to be counterproductive, as Venezuelans value self-control and personal dignity.
- The country's business environment is relatively formal, and appropriate social decorum is necessary.
- Venezuelans value professional and academic titles, which should not be neglected by the visitor.

Further Information

Fernando Coronil, *The Magical State: Nature, Money, and Modernity in Venezuela* (Chicago: University of Chicago Press, 1997).

Richard Gott, *In the Shadow of the Liberator: The Impact of Hugo Chavez on Venezuela and Latin America* (New York: Verso Books, 2001).

Janet Kelly and Carlos A. Romero, *The United States and Venezuela: Rethinking a Relationship* (New York and London: Routledge, 2002).

Presidency of the Bolivarian Republic of Venezuela (Spanish only): *www.venezuela.gov.ve.*

Federación de Colegios de Contadores Públicos de Venezuela (Spanish only): *www.fccpv.org.*

Asia and Pacific Region

TAX HAVENS AND INVESTMENT CENTERS: HONG KONG, SINGAPORE, AND TAIWAN

HONG KONG

Hong Kong is a Special Administrative Region of the People's Republic of China. It consists of a small portion of Chinese mainland territory and more than 200 islands, and has a population of over 7 million. A British colony from 1842, the territory reverted to China in 1997 in accordance with Anglo-Chinese nineteenth-century treaties.

During the British colonial period, Hong Kong overcame the impediment of limited natural resources to develop a freewheeling market economy with strong international links. Anxious to preserve Hong Kong's economic success, China has adopted the so-called "one country, two systems" policy that allows Hong Kong's capitalist system to function within the framework of the Peoples' Republic. Hong Kong also enjoys significant autonomy in local government and press freedom. By Chinese standards, the Hong Kong political regime is very liberal, and its newspapers print criticisms of the Chinese ruling elite that would be forbidden in the rest of China.

Although it has pockets of poverty, Hong Kong is a wealthy territory, with sky-high real estate prices. It offers business and professional opportunities for both Chinese and non-Chinese. The Asian financial crisis of the late 1990s affected the Hong Kong economy, but it bounced back to health relatively quickly.

Colonial Hong Kong's legal and regulatory environment traditionally followed British patterns. These cultural factors are still largely intact, but the influence of communist China is slowly increasing. Hong Kong's tax system remains attractive—at the time of writing the top tax rate for corporations is 16 percent, and for individuals' salaried income 15 percent. There are no sales or capital gains taxes.

Hong Kong GAAP is based on the accounting standards of the Hong Kong Society of Accountants (HKSA), and on the Listing Rules of the Stock Exchange of Hong Kong. The HKSA also issues interpretations of its accounting standards. The HKSA's traditional model for its accounting standards was British, but since the early 1990s it has declared the aim of harmonizing its accounting standards with IAS. However, differences between Hong Kong and international GAAP still remain in the treatment of employee benefits, for example. Listed corporations are permitted to use IAS, but must reconcile profit or loss to Hong Kong GAAP and explain the reconciling differences. Hong Kong accounting standards are available from the HKSA Web site (*www.hksa.org.hk*).

Further Information

Mark Roberti, *The Fall of Hong Kong: China's Triumph and Britain's Betrayal* (New York: John Wiley and Sons, 1997).

Paul McGuiness, *A Guide to the Equity Markets of Hong Kong* (New York and Oxford: Oxford University Press, 2000).

David R. Meyer, *Hong Kong as a Global Metropolis* (New York and Cambridge: Cambridge University Press, 2000).

Doing Business in Hong Kong [Government Site]: *www.business.gov.hk/english/index.htm*.

Hong Kong Society of Accountants: *www.hksa.org.hk*.

Institute of Internal Auditors Web site Hong Kong Chapter: *www.theiia.org/chapters/index.cfm?cid=165*.

SINGAPORE

Singapore, a city-state with a population of 4.3 million, is located at the southern tip of western Malaysia. The country comprises a main island and around 50 smaller islands. A former British colony with a predominantly ethnic Chinese population, Singapore joined the Federation of Malaysia in 1963, but withdrew two years later to become an independent republic. Diplomatic relations with Malaysia remain somewhat frosty, but the two countries are major trading partners.

Singapore has developed an astonishingly successful and vibrant economy. The small country has established itself as a major regional business hub, and enjoys one of the world's highest living standards. Singapore's wealth derives from the successful manufacturing and export of high technology products, and many multinational corporations have established their Asian regional headquarters in the city-state.

The British colonial heritage is reflected in a legal system based on English common law. Singapore is socially conservative, and its draconian antilitter laws are internationally famous. Singapore has relatively low tax rates—at the time of writing, tax on corporate profits is 25.5 percent, while the top rate on individuals' earnings is 28 percent. The country doesn't have capital gains taxes, but sales taxes were introduced in 1994.

Singaporean GAAP derives from the country's Companies Act and the accounting standards of the Institute of Certified Public Accountants of Singapore

(ICPAS). The ICPAS Web site (*www.accountants.org.sg*) gives details of Singaporean accounting standards, which are broadly—although not entirely—in line with IAS. The ICPAS has stated its intention to harmonize its standards with IAS, but has reserved the right to adapt standards to local circumstances. Foreign listed companies are permitted to use either IAS or U.S. GAAP, but in the latter case, reconciliation to Singaporean GAAP is required.

Further Information

W. G. Huff, *The Economic Growth of Singapore: Trade and Development in the Twentieth Century* (New York and Cambridge: Cambridge University Press, 1997).

Toh Mun Heng and Tan Kong Yam (eds.), *Competitiveness of the Singapore Economy: A Strategic Perspective* (Singapore: Singapore University Press, 1998).

Lily Kong, Martin Perry, and Brenda Yeoh, *Singapore: A Developmental City State* (New York: John Wiley and Sons, 1997).

Singapore Government On-line: *www.gov.sg*.

Institute of Certified Public Accountants of Singapore: *www.accountants.org.sg*.

Institute of Internal Auditors Singapore: *www.iia.org.sg*.

TAIWAN

Taiwan, formerly known as Formosa, is an island of around 22 million inhabitants to the southeast of China. When communists achieved power in mainland China following World War II, the opposition Kuomintang nationalists under Chiang Kai-shek (1887–1975) established a government-in-exile in Taiwan. From their island base, the nationalists declared a "Republic of China" that claimed jurisdiction over the whole of the Chinese mainland. However, Taiwan is dwarfed by China's 1.3 billion inhabitants, and the Taiwanese government's claim to be the sole legitimate Chinese government looked less credible as the years passed. In the 1990s, Taiwan made the transition from an authoritarian one-party state to a democratic regime. The question of potential future unification with China remains the island's main political issue.

The People's Republic of China continues to regard Taiwan as a renegade province, and is committed to reuniting it politically with the mainland—by military force if necessary. As the People's Republic asserts that no country can have formal ties with both Taiwan and itself, Taiwan is diplomatically isolated. It has no seat at the United Nations, and it has established formal diplomatic relations with only a handful of countries. Relations with the United States, for example, are conducted through semiofficial organizations.

Diplomatic isolation has not halted Taiwan's economic development, and the country has developed a sophisticated market economy. High-technology industries significantly boosted living standards in the late twentieth century. Some commentators assert that Taiwan shows in microcosm the vast economic potential of its giant sister nation.

Taiwanese GAAP is based on the country's company and business law, and the accounting standards of the Taiwanese Accounting Research and Development Foundation (ARDF), which differ substantially from IAS. The country's Securities and Exchange Commission also issues statements on accounting practice for listed companies. Foreign listed corporations are required to reconcile financial statements prepared under their own GAAP to Taiwanese GAAP.

Further Information

David Shambaugh (ed.), *Contemporary Taiwan* (New York and Oxford: Oxford University Press, 1998).
Government Information Office, Republic of China: *www.roc-taiwan.org*.
Federation of CPA Associations of Chinese Taiwan: *www.nfcpaa.org.tw*.
Institute of Internal Auditors Taiwan: *www.iia.org.tw/E-IIA/E-iia.htm*.

AUSTRALIA

Geography

Australia is located between the South Pacific Ocean and the Indian Ocean, and in surface area is the sixth-largest country in the world. It is also the world's smallest continent, and is slightly smaller than the United States. Australia's landscapes are varied, ranging from deserts to hills. The climate is mostly arid or semiarid, although the north is tropical and the south and east more temperate. The interior suffers severe droughts, and devastating forest fires have occurred in recent years.

Brief History

Although Dutch and Portuguese traders partly explored and mapped Australia, Captain James Cook's travels opened the door to British colonization. Of course, an indigenous population of several hundred thousand Aborigines had already been living in Australia for millennia. Some historians claim that the Aboriginal culture has the oldest continuous history of any culture in the world. The Aborigines followed a traditional life of hunting and gathering. The British and European settlers subjected them to discrimination and maltreatment. This led to a fall in the Aboriginal population, although today it has recovered to around 200,000.

Britain used Australia as a penal colony, and the original settlers were mainly convicts and soldiers. In the nineteenth century, however, large-scale voluntary settlement occurred from varied social classes in the British Isles. Australia became a commonwealth of the British Empire in 1901 and has since developed as an independent nation with close constitutional links to Britain. The nature of the British constitutional relationship is today a divisive issue, as discussed in the "Politics" section.

Australia made significant contributions to the British war effort in the twentieth century's two world wars. In recent years, however, Australia has increasingly turned away from its British connections to forge closer links with Asian countries.

Demographics

Australia's population of around 20 million is relatively small in relation to the country's vastness. Most of Australia's inhabitants are concentrated along the eastern and southeastern coasts, and are highly urbanized. Around 80 percent of Australians live in towns and cities, and much of the country is sparsely populated. Australian demographic trends are generally stable, although in recent years Asian immigration has boosted the proportion of non-European and non-Aboriginal inhabitants to around 7 percent of the total.

Languages

As one would expect from Australia's British heritage, English is the country's main language and is spoken as a mother tongue by over 95 percent of the population. Australian English combines elements of British and U.S. varieties of the language, and this is reflected in a range of spellings. Other important languages include the Aboriginal languages (spoken by around 1 percent of the population) and the Asian languages of recent migrants, such as Korean. Literacy levels are around 99 percent.

Politics

The Commonwealth of Australia is a democratic, federal state, and has its capital at Canberra. The largely ceremonial head of state is the British monarch, who is represented by a governor general. The head of government is the prime minister, who by convention is the leader of the majority parliamentary party (or the leader of the majority coalition). The lower chamber of the bicameral federal parliament is elected by popular vote.

A major political issue in Australia is the question of the remaining constitutional ties with Britain. Despite the efforts of a powerful republican lobby, a 1999 referendum narrowly supported the retention of the British monarch as head of state. The issue is likely to be raised again in the future.

Economy

Australians have a high standard of living comparable with that of the major industrialized nations, owing to the country's natural resources, a successful agricultural sector, and a prosperous capitalist economy. The importance of natural resources is reflected in the economy's sensitivity to movements in commodity prices. The Australian economy is increasingly focused on Asia, and less and less on Britain and other traditional western markets. This trend accelerated following Britain's entry into what became the EU in the 1970s. The current unit is the Australian dollar.

Legal and Regulatory Environment

Owing to the British colonial heritage, Australian law reflects English common law. Visitors from English-speaking countries will find a familiar legal and regulatory environment in Australia.

Accountancy

Given Australia's historical links with Britain, and the importance of capital markets in its economic structure, it is unsurprising that the country's accounting practices follow the patterns of the rest of the English-speaking world. Australia's accounting and auditing profession is mature, and the country was a founding member of the International Accounting Standards Committee. Australian GAAP is based on company law and the standards of the Australian Accounting Standards Board (AASB). The AASB also has an Urgent Issues Group that issues abstracts on pressing matters. Differences between Australian GAAP and IAS have narrowed since 1997, when the AASB undertook to harmonize Australian accounting standards with IAS. However, at the time of writing, differences still remain—the AASB Web site (*www.aasb.com.au*) is the best source of up-to-date information on Australian GAAP.

The country's two main accountancy bodies are CPA Australia and the Institute of Chartered Accountants in Australia (ICAA). The rival organizations have failed to agree to merger terms. While they have overlapping roles, CPA Australia is characterized by a larger proportion of its members in government service, and the ICAA tends to be more closely identified with external auditing.

Cultural Background

Australia's ethnic mix is approximately 92 percent European, 7 percent Asian, and 1 percent Aboriginal. The Asian population increased through immigration in the latter part of the twentieth century, while the sizes of the other ethnic groups have been stable in recent years. The Aboriginal population has disproportionately severe social problems, including alcoholism and drug abuse, which are partly a result of centuries of social ostracism and cultural denigration. In recent years, Australian governments have started to address some of the social problems of the indigenous peoples. Around 90 percent of Australians are nominally Christian, although religious observance is probably less than this statistic would suggest.

Although a former British colony, Australian culture differs substantially from that of the "mother country." Perhaps in conscious rebellion against the colonial experience, Australians are regarded as much less formal than their British cousins. Visitors often notice a healthy mistrust of authority, and social class divisions are less obvious than in Britain.

Australians are fanatical about sport—and successful too. The 2000 Sydney Olympics showcased Australian sport to the world, while the nation's main sporting passions are cricket and rugby. Australia has conquered the world in both sports in recent years. Because of Australia's isolation, many of its inhabitants enjoy foreign travel, and the Australian backpacker is a common sight throughout the world, from Europe to India.

Social Etiquette

- Australians are well known for their informality, and have a reputation for cutting down to size any pretentiousness shown by visitors.
- Business dealings are similarly characterized by relative informality—the Australians do not have a British-style social reserve.
- Australian honesty and straight talking can sometimes appear offensive, but visitors should not be shocked by friendly yet direct talking.

Further Information

Donald Denoon, Philippa Mein-Smith, and Marivic Wyndham, *A History of Australia, New Zealand and the Pacific* (Oxford: Blackwell, 2000).
Stuart Macintyre, *A Concise History of Australia* (New York and Cambridge: Cambridge University Press, 2000).
National Australian Library—Government Information: *www.nla.gov.au/oz/gov.*
Prime Minister of Australia: *www.pm.gov.au.*
Australian Accounting Standards Board (AASB): *www.aasb.com.au.*
CPA Australia: *www.cpaonline.com.au.*
Institute of Chartered Accountants in Australia: *www.icaa.org.au.*
Institute of Internal Auditors Australia: *http://iia.asn.au.*

BANGLADESH

Geography

The territory of Bangladesh is almost completely surrounded by that of the Republic of India. The only borders that Bangladesh does not share with India are its southern coastline on the Bay of Bengal and a small stretch of frontier with Myanmar (Burma). Bangladesh is located on the deltas of large rivers that originate in the Himalayas and finish in the Bay of Bengal. The country's topography is extremely flat, and three-quarters of the territory is arable. Virtually every year the country suffers severe flooding during the monsoon season (July to October). It is not usually a question of whether Bangladesh will be flooded in a specific year—it is more a question of the severity of the inundations. On occasions, up to one third of the country's surface area is under floodwater.

Brief History

The People's Republic of Bangladesh was previously known as East Pakistan, but it broke away from political union with West Pakistan in 1971 to form an independent state. Prior to forming part of Pakistan, Bangladesh was part of the British

Empire—the "India" and "Pakistan" country sections summarize the background to the Indian subcontinent's colonial history.

The viability of the Pakistani state as constituted in 1947 was always questionable. First, Pakistan comprised two lands separated by 1,000 miles of the Republic of India's territory. Further, West and East Pakistan were very different in terms of ethnicity, language, and culture. Within less than a quarter of a century after the creation of Pakistan, the Bengali population of East Pakistan made a bid for independence. The resulting war was extremely brutal, and West Pakistani troops were accused by the Bengalis of massacring hundreds of thousands of civilians, and of using mass rape as a means of war. Indian military intervention tipped the balance in favor of the Bengalis, and in 1971 the independent state of Bangladesh was created.

Independent Bangladesh has experienced severe political turmoil, and alternating political and military regimes. Grappling with the country's severe economic problems has been the major challenge facing politicians.

As an aside, it is worth noting the modern status of the historical region of Bengal, as it overlaps with the Bangladeshi state. The eastern part of Bengal has become modern-day Bangladesh (via East Pakistan), while West Bengal is a state in the Republic of India. Bangladesh is predominantly Muslim and West Bengal predominantly Hindu, but many families are split between the two Bengals. Movements across the political border separating the two halves of Bengal have been restricted for decades, although the Indian and Bangladeshi governments have slightly eased travel restrictions between the two countries in recent years.

Demographics

Like its neighbors India and Pakistan, Bangladesh has experienced a demographic explosion in recent decades. It is one of the world's most densely populated countries, with around 130 million inhabitants. Eight out of 10 Bangladeshis live in rural areas, and the largest city is the port of Dhaka, with over 7 million inhabitants.

Languages

Bengali (sometimes called Bangla) is the official language of Bangladesh, and is spoken by around 95 percent of the population. Other languages include the so-called "tribal" languages of remote rural areas, and Bihari. The latter is spoken by a Muslim community of several hundred thousand that originated from territory now in India.

The Bengali language is of Indic (or Indo-Aryan) origin and shares linguistic roots with languages of northern India such as Hindi and Punjabi. The Bengali spoken in Bangladesh is very similar to the Bengali spoken across the border in West Bengal in India, and uses the same script. The differences in usage between Bangladeshi and Indian Bengali are relatively minor, and may be compared to the differences between U.S. and British versions of English.

As in the other countries of the former British Raj, English is widely spoken among the middle classes. Many of the documents auditors may expect to see—such as invoices, contracts and business correspondence—are in English. Owing to Bangladesh's Islamic heritage, Arabic is also used for religious purposes. Illiteracy remains a significant problem, especially in rural areas. Estimates vary, but only around 50 percent of the population is thought to be literate.

Politics

The People's Republic of Bangladesh inherited a tradition of parliamentary democracy from the British colonial period. Although the country has flirted with periods of military rule, a democratic and civilian administration is currently in place. The unicameral parliament (the *Jatiya Sangsad*) is located in the capital, Dhaka. The head of state is the president, whose duties are largely ceremonial, while (following British parliamentary influence) the head of government is the prime minister.

The Bangladeshi political scene is often acrimonious and violent, and massive street demonstrations and national strikes are fairly common. At the time of writing, the two main parties are the Awami League and the Bangladesh Nationalist Party. Many observers consider that Bangladeshi politics reflects bitter animosity between party leaders rather than substantial ideological differences.

In terms of foreign policy, Bangladeshi's physical encirclement by the Republic of India is reflected in a rather nervous attitude to Indian influence. Although the two countries coexist relatively smoothly, relations are occasionally strained. For example, border disputes occasionally flare into small-scale armed conflicts. Other sources of tension include Bangladeshi's large trade deficit with India and disputes over the sharing of water and power resources.

Economy

Bangladesh is one of the world's least developed countries, with at least one third of its population living in poverty. Agriculture is the country's biggest employer, but it is unable to absorb sufficient numbers of the workforce: Estimates of the unemployment rate reach 30 percent. Chronic impediments to economic growth include inefficient state-owned enterprises and a demographic explosion that has overstretched the country's meager resources. Power and water supplies are often rationed and infrastructure is generally very poor. However, perhaps the greatest obstacle to economic development is annual flooding of the country. The floods regularly cause massive disruption, wrecking homes and crops. In some years, flooding leads to massive loss of life. In 1991, for example, over 100,000 people died after a cyclonic tidal wave led to extensive flooding.

Domestic economic conditions have driven many Bangladeshis to work overseas, especially in the Mideast, and remittances from expatriate workers are an important source of income for many families (and for the national economy). Beyond agriculture, Bangladesh has mature textile, jute, and leather industries. The country's currency unit is the taka.

Legal and Regulatory Environment

Bangladesh inherited from the British colonial period a legal tradition based on English common law, and English continues to be widely used for legal and business matters. Bangladesh's Islamic identity is reflected in the use of Shari'a law. As in other South Asian countries, relatively heavy bureaucracy characterizes the regulatory environment.

Accountancy

Bangladeshi GAAP is based on legislation and the accounting standards issued by the Institute of Chartered Accountants of Bangladesh (ICAB). The ICAB has declared its intention to adopt IAS as Bangladesh Accounting Standards and, by 2001, 23 standards from IAS had been adopted. Listed companies are required to use IAS.

The Bangladeshi accountancy profession developed during the British colonial period. The ICAB, formed in 1973, is the country's main accountancy and external auditing organization, with a membership of around 700.

Cultural Background

Bangladesh is a predominantly Muslim country, with around 83 percent of the population adhering to Islam. There is also a substantial Hindu minority of around 15 percent. Despite religious differences, the country is ethnically homogeneous. Bengalis are by far the main ethnic group, accounting for around 98 percent of the population. The balance consists of non-Bengali Muslims originally from India and the country's so-called "tribal" peoples.

Social Etiquette

- As in most Muslim countries, public physical contact between the sexes is a sensitive matter. Although handshaking between men and women is common in urban areas, and among the middle classes, it is best for a visitor to wait for a member of the opposite sex to initiate a handshake.
- Observant Muslims avoid pork and alcohol.
- A conservative dress code for women is advisable.

Further Information

Richard Sisson and Leo E. Rose, *War and Secession: Pakistan, India and the Creation of Bangladesh* (Berkeley, CA: University of California Press, 1991).

Hasan Zaheer, *The Separation of East Pakistan: The Rise and Realization of Bengali Muslim Nationalism* (New York and Oxford: Oxford University Press, 1996).

Government of Bangladesh Web site: *www.bangladeshgov.org*.

The Institute of Chartered Accountants of Bangladesh: *www.icab-bd.com*.

The Institute of Cost and Management Accountants of Bangladesh: *www.icmab.org*.

CHINA (EXCLUDING HONG KONG AND TAIWAN)

Geography

China is a vast country in eastern Asia, similar in surface area to the United States. China borders many nations, including Afghanistan, India, North Korea, Mongolia, Pakistan, Russia, and Vietnam, and it has around 8,000 miles of coastline. The country's vastness results in an extremely diverse climate. Most of the country is temperate, but the climate ranges from tropical heat in the south to cold temperate (even subarctic) conditions in the north. The topography is equally varied, with mountains, plateaus, deserts, and plains. China has numerous rivers, including the Yangtze and the Yellow River, both of which stretch for several thousand miles. The coast is subject to annual typhoons, and devastating floods frequently occur in the heavily populated river delta areas.

Brief History

China boasts a prestigious civilization that stretches back 4,000 years or more. The culture of ancient China was sophisticated and innovative: Paper money, the nautical compass, and gunpowder are among innovations the Chinese have given to the world. Indeed, so culturally self-sufficient were the ancient Chinese that the ideogram representing their country meant simply "Center" (in terms of "Center of the World").

It is difficult to separate myth and reality in early Chinese history. The Chinese ascribe mythological origins to their civilization, starting with the creation of the universe. Whatever the truth of the origins, a dynastic pattern emerged and Chinese history is conventionally divided into its dynasties. Some dynastic rulers, such as the Mongols and the Manchus, were ethnically different from the majority Han Chinese, but the power of Chinese culture eventually assimilated all foreign rulers to a greater or lesser extent.

From the sixteenth century the arrival of European traders and missionaries led to formidable threats to Chinese independence. By this time, the Chinese had lost their historical preeminence in technology and the country's outdated military structures were exposed by European superiority. In addition, a complacent Chinese elite refused to recognize that times had changed and continued to believe in the effortless superiority of Chinese civilization. As a result, China was unable or unwilling to prevent progressive European and Japanese threats to its independence.

As in many other parts of Asia, the Portuguese were the earliest of the European traders. They based themselves at Macao but were soon followed by other Europeans, including the French, English, and Russians. European traders paid symbolic tribute to the Chinese Emperor, as they did in Mughal India, but behind this convenient fiction they encroached progressively on Chinese economic and political independence.

During the eighteenth and nineteenth centuries, the British balance of trade with China was generally negative. Chinese tea was in demand around the world, but the Chinese appeared to show little interest in the types of western products that the British could offer. To balance their negative trade pattern, the British encouraged the importation into China of Indian opium. When the Chinese Emperor eventually moved to suppress the harmful opium trade, the British retaliated with military force. This Anglo-Chinese war (or "Opium War") lasted from 1839 to 1842. British military superiority forced the Chinese into the first of many "unequal treaties" with western powers. Under these treaties, western nations gained trading and legal privileges, with little reciprocity. (It was at this time that the British gained possession of Hong Kong, which was later to emerge as an economic powerhouse.)

Following the British, other European powers and the Japanese further eroded Chinese sovereignty. The negotiation of unequal treaties and territorial expansion in coastal areas, backed by "gunboat diplomacy," became the pattern of encroachment. Finally shaken out of their complacency, the nineteenth-century Chinese ruling classes realized the extent of the country's external threats. The nineteenth century also saw major internal unrest, such as the "Taiping Rebellion," which claimed millions of lives and reflected economic and social dislocation.

Chinese resistance to western dominance crystallized in the violent Boxer Rebellion that exploded in 1900. The Boxer Rebellion failed for many reasons. For example, many of the mystical, secret societies that had pledged to rid China of foreign and Christian influences placed their faith in weaponless martial arts techniques that proved no match for contemporary western firepower. Post-rebellion China was marked by a further extension of western influence, and yet further internal unrest.

The last Manchu emperor abdicated in 1912, following a republican revolution of the previous year. A new Chinese republic was established that espoused nationalism and economic reform, but it soon disintegrated into rebellion and fragmentation. In the following decades, a complex political struggle developed, essentially dominated by the communists and their bitter rivals, the nationalists. (This bitter rivalry still exists today, in modified form, between communist China and nationalist Taiwan.) Mao Zedong (1893–1976) emerged as the dominant force among the communists. He led thousands of followers in the famous "Long March," from 1934 to 1935. In this retreat from the nationalists, Mao cemented his preeminence among China's communists as both their practical leader and principal theorist.

The internal struggle between communists and nationalists was overshadowed in the 1930s by armed Japanese expansion into Chinese territory. Japan seized Manchuria in 1931, established a puppet regime, and used the territory as a base to push into northern China and coastal areas. The nationalist government was occupied with anticommunist campaigns and was unable to stem the Japanese advance. From 1937, Japanese military action escalated, and the notorious "Rape of Nanking" between 1937 and 1938 cost hundreds of thousands of civilian lives.

World War II brought massive Japanese military forces into China. The communists and nationalists formed a short-lived united front against the Japanese but they were unable to cooperate for long. Mao was already planning for the establishment of a communist China to follow the war, and with the postwar departure of the Japanese, China stood again on the brink of civil war. The United States gave economic (rather than military) support to the nationalists, but the communists forced the nationalists from the mainland to the island of Taiwan, where they have remained to this day.

In October 1949, the People's Republic of China was formally established. Initially, Communist economic reconstruction and reform were moderate, effective, and popular. By the 1950s, however, political attitudes had hardened, and repression of internal dissent and radical land reform made the totalitarian atmosphere harsher. In the notorious "Great Leap Forward" from 1958 to 1960, communist militancy increased still further as Mao and his comrades sought to raise the ideological temperature. Their attempted agricultural reform and the creation of rural communes led to economic disaster and food shortages.

In the late 1950s, ideological differences led to a serious deterioration in relations between China and the Soviet Union. Estrangement from the Soviets unquestionably caused economic suffering in China, as the Soviet Union withdrew economic aid and recalled its "advisers." Another ideological drive took place from 1966 to 1976—the notorious Cultural Revolution. After a period of near-seclusion in the early 1960s, Mao reemerged to increase the country's revolutionary fervor. The moderate Deng Xiaoping (1904–1997) was opposed to Mao's program, which involved further ideological indoctrination in schools and universities. Academics were forced to undertake manual labor to rid them of "counter-revolutionary" ideas, for example. Overall, the authoritarian Mao period is estimated to have cost the lives of many millions of Chinese through economic stagnation, famine, and political purges.

By the late 1970s, Deng Xiaoping had been politically rehabilitated and under his guidance, China began a long program of reform. Market-oriented liberalization and economic decentralization have continued to this day, although political reform has been much slower. The Chinese Communist Party has retained its grip on power and has continued to suppress dissent, most notably in crushing student protests in Beijing's Tiananmen Square in 1989.

Demographics

China is the world's most populous country, with a population of around 1.3 billion. Demographic pressures have prompted the Chinese Communist Party to follow strict population control programs. Late marriage and one-child families have been encouraged, sometimes through economic coercion (e.g., preferential housing allocation for smaller families). The population programs have been successful in arresting the demographic explosion and, as a result, many observers expect India's population to surpass China's during the twenty-first century.

Languages

The linguistic term "Chinese" covers several major languages and many dialects. Although there are significant differences between the various spoken Chinese languages, they are linked by a common writing system. The speakers of different

Chinese languages can therefore read the same newspaper. Standard Chinese is often called Mandarin and is spoken by over 70 percent of Chinese. Other major languages include Cantonese and Shanghaiese. They are all tonal languages. In addition, the many languages spoken by ethnic minorities (see the "Cultural Background" section) complicate China's linguistic map. The Chinese writing system is based on characters or ideograms, which can represent meanings as well as sounds. The existence of a common writing system that cuts across linguistic boundaries has undoubtedly been one of the major unifying factors in Chinese cultural history. The country's literacy level is around 82 percent, and is slightly higher for men than for women.

Politics

The creation of the People's Republic of China (PRC) is discussed in the "Brief History" section. China is a communist state and has its capital at Beijing. The head of state is the president, while the head of government is the premier. The main legislative body is the unicameral National People's Congress (NPC), whose members are forwarded from regional and provincial political bodies.

The Chinese Communist Party dominates the country's politics, and the economic liberalization of recent decades has not been matched by a comparable degree of political reform. The state is still intolerant of political dissent, and human rights campaigners criticize China for its treatment of political prisoners. In the absence of a multiparty democratic system, nonparliamentary groups such as the mystical Falungong sect have taken on a role akin to that of a political opposition.

One well-known regional political resistance movement is that of the Tibetans. The exiled Dalai Lama (born 1935) serves as the Tibetans' spiritual and de facto temporal leader, and is often compared to India's M. K. Gandhi for his espousal of nonviolent resistance to Chinese dominance in Tibet.

Economy

China has the world's second largest GDP, after the United States. The post-Mao liberalization era has transformed the Chinese economy from a stagnant, command economy to a mixed system with pronounced market orientations. Domestic privatization and massive foreign investment have opened China to the world economy, symbolized by China's successful 1999 negotiation of entry to the World Trade Organization. China still faces many grave economic problems, such as high unemployment, poverty, poor infrastructure, serious environmental damage, and the burden of uncompetitive state enterprises. Up to 10 percent of the population is estimated to live in poverty. The country's largest trading partners are Japan and the United States, and the currency unit is the yuan.

Legal and Regulatory Environment

Historically, China's imperial civil service was elaborate and sophisticated, and the country still lives under a heavy bureaucratic hand. The Chinese legal system is a complex mix of indigenous custom, criminal statute, and communist party directives. Although China's economic liberalization has led to recent changes in civil, administrative, and commercial law, inconsistencies between the laws and regulations of different regions often frustrate business practice.

Accountancy

Modern Chinese GAAP is based on company law and the accounting standards of the country's Ministry of Finance (MOF). Accountancy in communist China traditionally reflected Soviet patterns of resource allocation, with a strict chart of accounts and a strong emphasis on project analysis. However, the economic reforms that started in the 1980s and the increasing interest of foreign investors in China prompted the MOF to issue western-style accounting standards. MOF guidelines were initially modest, and included such fundamental rules as advocating the use of double-entry bookkeeping. (During the Cultural Revolution, double entry bookkeeping was attacked as a vehicle of capitalist exploitation.)

Recent MOF standards have increased in sophistication and are modeled on IAS. Discrepancies between Chinese GAAP and IAS are therefore being narrowed, and the rate of convergence is expected to increase following China's entry into the World Trade Organization. In 2001, the MOF issued a new "Accounting System for Business Enterprises" that was initially applicable only to Joint Stock Limited Enterprises, but from 2002 it applied to all foreign investment enterprises. The Accounting System sets out statements of accounting principles, and recognition and reporting criteria that are substantially in line with international practice.

The Chinese Institute of Certified Public Accountants is the main accountancy and auditing body, and was established in 1988.

Cultural Background

The Han Chinese are China's majority ethnic group, accounting for around 90 to 93 percent of the country's population. The remaining population consists of many ethnic minorities, such as Koreans, Mongols, Tibetans, and Zhuang. Minority groups often follow pastoral lives in the vast and sparsely populated border areas of the country. Tensions between the Han and some ethnic minorities have resulted from government resettlement policies that have brought large numbers of Han to areas such as Tibet. Local populations have reacted with alarm to potential shifts in the ethnic balance of such regions.

Among the Han, significant cultural differences exist in language, dress, and cuisine. However, the common written Chinese language is a strong unifier, along with traditions of political centralization stretching back to the country's ancient dynasties. Confucianism has had a significant impact on Chinese culture (and on the cultures of some neighboring states). Its philosophy stresses social stability and encourages respect for hierarchy, age, and rank.

China is officially an atheist state and precise information on the numbers of adherents to various religions is difficult to obtain. However, Daoist and Buddhist beliefs predominate. In combination, Muslim and Christian minorities are thought to comprise less than 4 percent of the total population.

Social Etiquette

- Boastful attitudes are considered ill mannered and uneducated in China. It is advisable to show a degree of humility at all times in business dealings.
- The giving of a business card is an important event in China, and any cards received should be carefully scrutinized with a suitable level of respect.
- Business meetings often respect the seniority of those present, and it may be unacceptable for junior people to express opinions too forcefully, or to speak out of turn.
- Although gifts may initially be declined, such refusals are often part of an elaborate social ritual. Depending on the circumstances, one should reiterate the offer of a gift to ensure that a refusal is really intended.

Further Information

Richard Louis Edmonds (ed.), *The People's Republic of China After 50 Years* (New York and Oxford: Oxford University Press, 2000).
Joseph Fewsmith, *China Since Tiananmen: The Politics of Transition* (New York and Cambridge: Cambridge University Press, 2001).
Dean LeBaron, *Mao, Marx & the Market: Capitalist Adventures in Russia and China* (New York: John Wiley and Sons, 2001).
Supachai Panitchpakdi and Mark L. Clifford, *China and the WTO: Changing China, Changing World Trade* (New York: John Wiley and Sons, 2002).
PRC Ministry of Finance: *www.mof.gov.cn/eng/index2.htm.*
Chinese Institute of Certified Public Accountants (Chinese only): *www.cicpa.org.cn.*
China Institute of Internal Auditors: *www.ciia.com.cn/audit/e/index2.htm.*

INDIA

Geography

India is often described as a subcontinent rather than merely a country, owing to its extremely varied geographical profile. The country's surface area is around one-third that of the United States and it includes deserts, ice-capped mountains, jungles, and palm-lined beaches. In the far north, the Himalayan Mountains include the world's highest peaks and separate India from the rest of the Asian landmass. Moving southward, the country tapers gradually to a point. Below the Himalayas are the vast and heavily populated northern plains, dominated by the Ganga (or Ganges) River, while to the west is the Thar Desert. The parched and barren Deccan plateau, bordered by ranges of hills and fertile coastal areas, dominates the south. India's immense variety makes it difficult to summarize climate patterns, but notable features are annual hot seasons followed by intense monsoon rains.

Brief History

India has one of the world's great civilizations, with astonishing cultural achievements in religion, art, literature, and philosophy. Empires waxed and waned in India's early history. Some of the empires were localized, while others covered large parts of the subcontinent. Important early political states included the Mauryan Empire (326–184 BCE) and the Gupta Empire (320–606 CE). In later centuries, Muslim incursions from Central Asia led to the establishment of several Islamic regimes, culminating in the Mughal Empire. The six "Great Mughals" reigned from 1527 to 1707, and among the Islamic architecture bequeathed by their sophisticated regime is one of the Seven Wonders of the World—the Taj Mahal, completed in the 1650s.

India fragmented politically as the Mughal Empire disintegrated during the seventeenth and eighteenth centuries. European traders obtained footholds in the subcontinent and gradually expanded their influence. The English won a struggle for supremacy among the Europeans, and the militarized East India Company conquered the subcontinent though a combination of arms and diplomacy. Following an anti-British armed uprising in 1857, colonial power was passed from the East India Company to the British Crown.

The Indian National Congress was the driving force behind India achieving independence from Britain in 1947. The two main personalities in the independence movement were M. K. Gandhi (1869–1948) and Jawaharlal Nehru (1889–1964). Although both were London-trained lawyers, they were very different characters. Gandhi is considered the "Father" of the Indian nation and is still regarded by many Indians (and even non-Indians) as a saint. This status is reflected in the respectful title of *Mahatma* (Great Soul). Gandhi rejected violence both in the anti-colonial struggle and in relations between India's Hindus and Muslims. He also advocated a simple life of economic, cultural, and spiritual self-sufficiency. Nehru, in contrast, was a pragmatic, westernized politician who sought to industrialize his country and turn it into a militarily powerful, nonaligned force. (Another major player in the independence movement—M. A. Jinnah—is discussed in the "Pakistan" section.)

Independence was accompanied by the partition of the country along religious lines into India and Pakistan. (Muslim-dominated Pakistan comprised territory in both the northwest and northeast of the subcontinent, as discussed in the "Pakistan" and "Bangladesh" sections.) Millions were uprooted by partition. Large numbers of Hindus and Sikhs moved from the newly created Pakistan to India, and many Muslims made the reverse journey. These population movements were accompanied by massive sectarian slaughter, and estimates of the dead run into hundreds of thousands.

Independent India's ambitions for superpower status soon brought rivalry with China, and the two countries fought a brief war in 1962. However, India's traditional political rival has been Pakistan, and long-running tensions between the (now nuclear) neighbors has led to several wars. The status of the disputed state of Kashmir continues to be a source of instability in South Asia.

Demographics

In the absence of concerted demographic controls such as those implemented in China, India's population almost tripled in size in the half century following independence. It currently stands at around 1 billion. At the time of writing, many observers anticipate that India will soon surpass China as the world's most populous country, and that by the middle of the twenty-first century nearly one in five of the world's inhabitants will be Indian.

The country's huge population is characterized by staggering ethnic, linguistic, and cultural diversity. While the population is overwhelmingly rural, India's urban development continues apace. Three cities have populations well in excess of 10 million: Mumbai (formerly Bombay), Kolkata (Calcutta), and the capital, Delhi.

Languages

A mere glance at an Indian bank note reveals the country's astonishing linguistic diversity. The 50-rupee note, for example, displays more than 10 languages, all in different scripts. India's linguistic map may broadly be divided into north and south. Indic (or Indo-Aryan) languages predominate in the north. This language family is probably of Central Asian origin (although this is disputed by some historians) and includes Bengali, Gujarati, Hindi, Punjabi, and Urdu. All these languages are distant cousins of English, and they all use different scripts. Dravidian languages such as Tamil and Telegu dominate the south. The Dravidian linguistic family is unrelated to the Indic languages, and its languages use a variety of writing systems.

The central government has endeavored to promote Hindi as India's national language, but speakers of other culturally prestigious languages such as Bengali and Tamil have tenaciously resisted the advance of Hindi. As a consequence, English is widely used by the middle classes throughout India, often serving as the subcontinent's de facto link language. Many of the documents auditors may expect to see are in English—invoices, contracts, business correspondence, and Indian accounting standards.

Illiteracy remains a significant problem, especially in rural areas. Estimates vary, but perhaps only 50 percent of the country's population is literate. For women, the literacy rate may be as low as 35 percent.

Politics

The Republic of India has a proud political status as the world's largest democracy. Long-established parliamentary structures inherited from the British have been fused with U.S.-style federal features. The central parliament is in the capital, New Delhi, and has a bicameral structure. The parliament's upper and lower houses are called the *Rajya Sabha* and the *Lok Sabha*, respectively, and members of the latter are elected by popular vote. As in Britain, the prime minister acts as head of government, while the president fulfills the largely ceremonial role of head of state. The Indian state governments exercise regional power through local legislative assemblies.

The Congress Party—inheritor of the Indian National Congress—dominated the early years of Indian independence. Under Jawaharlal Nehru, Congress encouraged India's development as a secular, nonaligned state with socialist tendencies. India's aspirations for superpower status were underpinned by massive industrial investment and the development of formidable armed forces with nuclear capability. Nehru died in 1964 and a dynastic pattern emerged: Nehru's daughter Indira Gandhi (1917–1984) and her son Rajiv Gandhi (1944–1991) both served as Congress prime ministers. (It should be noted that Nehru's daughter married a businessman named Gandhi—contrary to a widely held belief outside India, Indira was not related to M. K. Gandhi.) A future return to power of a member of the dynasty remains a possibility, albeit a fairly distant one.

In regional politics, notably in the states of West Bengal and Kerala, communists have traditionally been stronger than the Congress Party, but Congress' dominance at the national level has only been seriously challenged in recent years by the rise of the Bharatiya Janata Party (BJP). Unlike the secular Congress Party, the BJP promotes a Hindu nationalist agenda. Although the country's large number of political parties will probably continue to necessitate complex coalition arrangements, India's main political fault-line in the twenty-first century may turn out to be the struggle between the secular Congress Party and the Hindu nationalist BJP.

Violence frequently mars Indian politics, often in the form of sectarian (or, in Indian English, "communal") fighting. Ferocious clashes between Hindus and Muslims erupt from time to time and have claimed thousands of lives since independence. A significant flashpoint is a sacred site disputed by both Hindus and Muslims in the northern town of Ayodhya. In 1992, Hindu activists destroyed a Mughal-era mosque at the site and vowed to build a Hindu temple in its place. These events sparked serious violence throughout the country, the repercussions of which continue to rumble. In 2002, thousands died in rioting between Hindus and Muslims in the state of Gujarat.

A second source of political violence is armed insurgency by separatists. In the late twentieth century, the Soviet Union and Yugoslavia disintegrated into small, independent, and frequently warring states, and many observers predicted a similar fate for India. Although there have been serious attempts by armed groups in some border areas to break away from the Republic of India, at the time of writing no independent states have been created. The most serious of India's internal insurgencies is currently in the Muslim-majority state of Kashmir.

A sobering reflection on India's political violence is the fact that three of the country's most significant leaders have been assassinated. In 1948, M. K. Gandhi was killed by a Hindu militant infuriated at his conciliatory stance toward Muslims. In 1984, Indira Gandhi was shot by her Sikh bodyguards, following her tough crackdown on Sikh separatists in the Punjab. In 1991, a Tamil suicide bomber killed Rajiv Gandhi because of his support to the Sri Lankan government in suppressing a Tamil insurgency in Sri Lanka.

Economy

In the decades following independence, the economic philosophy of Jawaharlal Nehru and his daughter Indira Gandhi was based on national self-sufficiency. It was characterized by interventionist economic policies and the use of protectionist trade barriers that keep India aloof from the global economy. In the 1980s, Rajiv Gandhi started a slow process of economic and trade liberalization that has been followed, with mixed results, by his successors. The modern Indian economy is a curious mixture of traditional village agriculture, outdated heavy industry, and a world-class high-technology sector. India's software houses handle the transactions of many western companies, and it is with only slight exaggeration that India has been described as the "back office" to the world economy.

The fight against poverty remains India's main economic challenge. Indira Gandhi's 1970s Hindi slogan of *"Garibi hatao!"* ("Banish poverty!") awaits realization. India has a prosperous middle class and an extremely wealthy elite, yet massive disparities remain. At least one third of the population lives in poverty, and India's demographic explosion has undoubtedly added to the country's economic difficulties. India's largest trading partners are the United States and Britain, and the country's currency unit is the rupee.

Legal and Regulatory Environment

India inherited from the British colonial period a legal tradition based on English common law. The English language continues to be widely used for legal matters, especially in the higher courts. The wheels of Indian justice turn slowly, and it is not unknown for civil cases to take decades to be settled. The auditor may frequently encounter situations in which legal disputes are settled out of court, to avoid the time delays of processing cases through the legal system. Some individuals and corporations take advantage of the slow legal process by proceeding with behavior such as the improper use of a rival's brand, in the knowledge that it may take many years for the matter to be satisfactorily resolved. By then, the commercial damage may be irreversible. The slow nature of the legal system is a significant risk of doing business in India.

In addition to its British-style common law system, traditional Hindu legal practices survive at the village level, but the visitor is unlikely to come into contact with these unless specifically working in a rural context. Islamic civil law is also available to Indian Muslims.

The postindependence era was characterized by heavy state regulation, and the economy stagnated under a mountain of official paperwork. The ironic term "licence Raj" came into use, to describe the era's frustrating and corruption-ridden procedures for obtaining industrial and manufacturing licenses. In recent decades, reformist governments have pruned some of the country's bureaucracy, but the regulatory environment remains cumbersome. Similarly, the Indian taxation system has traditionally been complex and cumbersome, although this has been partially alleviated by recent reforms. Both the central government and the legislatures of individual states have offered generous tax breaks and reductions in regulatory requirements to attract foreign investment. The state of Tamil Nadu, for example, has been particularly successful in attracting significant amounts of foreign industrial investment in this manner.

Accountancy

Indian GAAP is based on company law, the accounting standards of the Institute of Chartered Accountants of India (ICAI), and (for listed corporations) the guidance of the Securities and Exchange Board of India. The ICAI's Accounting Standards Board issues English-language accounting standards, some of which apply only to listed corporations, while others apply to all organizations. At the time of writing, the use of IAS is not permitted.

Although closely linked to the accounting practices of English-speaking countries, Indian GAAP has traditionally differed quite significantly from international norms, especially in terms of disclosure requirements. The historical idiosyncrasies of Indian GAAP may have reflected India's economic aloofness from the world economy during the Nehru years, as the estrangement of Indian corporate governance from broader international developments led to a distinctive national accounting culture. However, with India's increasing participation in the global economy, pressure from both domestic and international investors has led to an increasing convergence between Indian and international accounting norms.

In recent years, therefore, new Indian accounting standards have tended to narrow the differences with international standards. Recent developments include Accounting Standard AS17 (Segment Reporting) that requires corporations to undertake extensive disclosures by business and geographical segments. Disclosure of this nature has been commonplace in international accounting for many years, but AS17 became effective only in 2001. Indian accounting standards are available in English from the ICAI Web site (*www.icai.org*).

India has a mature accountancy profession that developed during the British colonial period. The ICAI is the country's principal accountancy and external auditing organization, with around 90,000 members. In addition to accounting standards, the ICAI also produces Statements on Standard Auditing Practices that it seeks to harmonize with international external auditing standards.

Cultural Background

India has one of the most ancient and complex civilizations in the world. The diversity of religions, traditions, and cultural practices is staggering. The main religions are Hinduism (around 81 percent of the population) and Islam (12 percent), and there are smaller communities of Christians (2 percent), Sikhs (2 percent), and others. Buddhism originated in India, but its center of gravity has moved to other parts of Asia. Less than 10 million of modern India's 1 billion people are Buddhists.

Hinduism is itself characterized by wide diversity, but this diversity is often described as more apparent than real. Although many deities are worshiped, an underlying unity underpins Hinduism's practices, traditions, and scriptures. The religion's sacred books include the Vedas, early texts expounding fundamental Hindu principles, and the Mahabharata and Ramayana epics.

Hinduism's complex social framework is usually referred to as the caste system. The origins of caste are obscure, yet its presence continues to be powerful. Caste is determined by birth, and it often decides an individual's social status, occupation, and marriage partner. As with many things in India, caste is a complicated subject. Its defenders point out that caste acts as a mechanism of community support and social cohesion, which are important in a country that lacks a western-style welfare state. Detractors draw attention to the caste system's inherent social conservatism and its reinforcement of economic inequalities. Moving beyond the occupational expectations of one's caste can sometimes be extremely difficult, if not impossible. To partially alleviate problems of this nature, India has introduced politically sensitive parliamentary and civil service caste quotas.

A surviving influence of the British colonial period is the country's passion for the sport of cricket. India is among the world's elite cricketing nations, but the general public opinion is that the national side has underachieved in recent years. The sport cuts across religious and caste boundaries and acts as a unifying cultural pastime, as portrayed in the world-famous movie *Lagaan* (2002).

A final observation on Indian culture is that, perhaps more than in most parts of the world, urban and rural lifestyles vary significantly. Sophisticated cities such as Delhi and Mumbai contrast immensely with rural areas where many aspects of life have remained unchanged for centuries.

Social Etiquette

- Public physical contact between men and women is a sensitive topic. Although handshaking between the sexes is common in urban areas and among the middle classes, it is best for a visitor to wait for a member of the opposite sex to initiate a handshake.
- The traditional Hindu greeting is "namaste" (or more formally "namaskar"), spoken with the hands pressed together in a respectful, prayer-type position.
- Gift items should be given in odd numbers: 11 instead of 10, for example. Even numbers of gifted items are considered unlucky.
- Pointing with either the finger or the foot is considered offensive. It is best to use the chin or the palm of the hand.
- A relatively conservative dress code for women is advisable.
- Vegetarianism is common in India, especially in the south of the country, but many Indians eat meat and fish. Most Hindus do not eat beef, most Muslims avoid pork, and out of mutual religious respect many Indians eat neither beef nor pork.

Further Information

Judith M. Brown, *Gandhi: Prisoner of Hope* (New Haven, CT: Yale University Press, 1989).

Jawaharlal Nehru, *The Discovery of India* (Delhi, India: Oxford University Press, 1989—originally published in 1946).

Stanley Wolpert, *A New History of India* (New York and Oxford: Oxford University Press, 1977 and subsequent editions).

Government of India Web site directory: *http://goidirectory.nic.in.*

Ministry of Law, Justice, and Company Affairs: *http://lawmin.nic.in.*

The Institute of Chartered Accountants of India: *www.icai.org.*

The Institute of Cost and Works Accountants of India: *www.icwai.com.*

INDONESIA

Geography

Indonesia is the world's largest archipelago. It comprises around 17,000 islands between Asia and Australia, of which only around 6,000 are inhabited. Among the most important islands are Java and Sumatra—the former is the political and cultural center of Indonesia. Forests and woodland cover around two-thirds of Indonesia, and many of the larger islands are mountainous. The country lies on the equator and its tropical climate is hot and humid throughout the year. Earthquakes, tidal waves, and volcano eruptions are relatively common, and in recent years smoke from forest fires has emerged as a major environmental concern.

Brief History

The Indonesian archipelago has been inhabited for millennia. Around 2,000 years ago, Indian civilization was the major outside influence on the political and social culture of the islands, and traces of Indian influence can be found to this day in Indonesian folk culture. Islamic culture spread to the island around 1,000 years ago, and a large majority of the population remains Muslim to this day.

European traders expanded their influence in Indonesia in the seventeenth century, with the Dutch emerging as the main colonial power. However, it was not until around 1900 that the Dutch managed to politically unite the sprawling archipelago. During World War II, the Japanese ousted the Dutch from Indonesia. The Dutch returned after the war and attempted in vain to reassert their hold on power before Indonesia achieved independence in 1949.

The first leader of independent Indonesia was President Sukarno (1901–1970), who stayed in power until the mid-1960s. The Sukarno era was one of serious social strife and ethnic conflict. Anticommunist purges claimed hundreds of thousands of lives—many of them Chinese. General Suharto (born 1921) seized power from Sukarno in 1965 and imposed his authoritarian rule on the country. Suharto was a high profile casualty of the political fallout from the Asian economic crisis that started in 1997, and his long period of rule came to an end in 1998 amid widespread street violence.

Modern Indonesia faces many problems. Serious economic weaknesses were exposed after the 1997 financial crisis, democratic reforms have proceeded only slowly after decades of dictatorial politics, and separatist movements and ethnic tensions have exploded into violence in various parts of the archipelago. In 2002, East Timor achieved independence from Indonesia, following a period of severe military repression that provoked international condemnation of Indonesia's human rights record.

Demographics

Indonesia's population is around 230 million, which makes it the world's largest Muslim country. The government has attempted to control population growth through family planning campaigns and the resettlement of hundreds of thousands of people from crowded urban areas to sparsely populated parts of the archipelago. The "Cultural Background" section summarizes the country's complex ethnic makeup.

Languages

Indonesia's official language is Bahasa Indonesia, which is part of the Malay-Polynesian language family. Bahasa Indonesia is closely related to Bahasa Malaysia. The two languages are mutually comprehensible, and both use a Roman script. Bahasa Indonesia is seen as a unifying force in the ethnically diverse archipelago, in which there are estimated to be between 300 and 600 languages and dialects. Major languages other than Bahasa Indonesia include Javanese and Sundanese, whose native speakers account for more than half the country's population. English is widely understood among the middle classes and is often used in business contexts, but knowledge of the former colonial language, Dutch, has all but disappeared. Indonesia's literacy rate is estimated to be around 85 percent, and is higher for men than women.

Politics

The Republic of Indonesia has its capital at Jakarta, on the island of Java. The country has recently emerged from decades of authoritarian political rule and is attempting to bolster its democratic practices. The country's president acts as both head of state and head of government and appoints the cabinet. Indonesia's unicameral parliament has a mixture of elected and appointed members. Indonesia has traditionally spearheaded the nonaligned movement, yet it has arguably tended to be closer to the capitalist West, especially in economic policy. Violent ethnic conflict, terrorism, and widespread poverty are perhaps the major issues facing Indonesia's politicians in the early twenty-first century.

Economy

Already poorer than smaller neighboring countries such as Malaysia and Thailand, Indonesia was devastated by the Asian economic crisis that started in 1997. The economic crisis plunged millions of Indonesians into poverty and precipitated the fall of President Suharto. The country's oil exports have boosted the economy since the dark days of 1997 and 1998, but the International Monetary Fund has insisted on further, painful structural reform. Important industries include the petroleum sector, shoe manufacturing, and textiles. At least one in five of the population lives in poverty. Japan and the United States are Indonesia's biggest trading partners, and the country's currency unit is the rupiah.

Legal and Regulatory Environment

Indonesia's legal system broadly reflects its Dutch colonial past, and is therefore based on continental European jurisprudence. Indigenous and Islamic law have also influenced the country's legal practices. Indonesia is generally regarded as having weak business and financial laws, a legacy of years of authoritarian rule and political corruption. Many regulatory weaknesses were exposed during the Asian financial crisis of the late 1990s, and these weaknesses remain a deterrent to foreign investment. However, the country's democratizing administrations have recently responded to pressure from international financial institutions to reform the regulatory environment.

Accountancy

Indonesian GAAP is based on the accounting standards of the Indonesian Committee on Financial Accounting Standards (ICFAS), as endorsed by the Indonesian Institute of Accountants. From 1994, the ICFAS has used IAS as the basis for developing Indonesian standards. As a consequence, differences between Indonesian and international GAAP are progressively narrowing. For example, segmental analysis has traditionally been inconsistently reported under Indonesian GAAP, but from 2002 an Indonesian accounting standard (PSAK 5) has brought local practice in line with IAS 14 (Segment Reporting).

Cultural Background

Indonesia's ethnic composition is complex. The Javanese are the majority community, with around 45 percent of the total population. Other large ethnic groups include the Sundanese (around 14 percent), Madurese (8 percent), and Malays (7 percent). Cultural differences between urban and rural areas can be extreme—in some remote areas, small communities follow a Stone-Age existence of hunting and gathering. (Every few years, one reads of a new group of indigenous people that has only just made contact with the modern world.)

Around 90 percent of Indonesia's inhabitants are Muslim, but at the level of popular, "folk" culture many pre-Islamic cultural practices remain entrenched. Other religious communities include Christians (around 8 percent) and Hindus (2 percent). Bali is a well-known Indonesian stronghold of Hindu culture. Conflict between different ethnic religious groups is a distressingly common feature of Indonesian political life. Fighting between Muslims and Christians in the Molucca islands, for example, has left hundreds dead in recent years. Moreover, the small but economically successful Chinese community is targeted from time to time in violent riots.

Social Etiquette

- Observant Muslims do not eat pork, nor drink alcohol.
- Social status is highly valued and discussed frankly in Indonesian culture.
- It is advisable to avoid public displays of anger or frustration.
- Business cards are considered to be very important, and should be handled and scrutinized with respect.

Further Information

David Bevin, Paul Collier, and Jan Willem Gunning, *The Political Economy of Poverty, Equity, and Growth: Nigeria and Indonesia* (New York and Oxford: Oxford University Press, 1999).

Tim Huxley, *Disintegrating Indonesia? Implications for Regional Security* (New York and Oxford: Oxford University Press, 2002).

M. C. Ricklefs, *A History of Indonesia Since c.1200*, 3rd ed. (Palo Alto: Stanford University Press, 2002).

Investment Indonesia On-line: *www.bkpm.go.id*.

Republic of Indonesia—Dept. of Foreign Affairs: *www.dfa-deplu.go.id*.

Indonesian Institute of Accountants (Bahasa Indonesia only): *www.akuntan-iai .or.id*.

JAPAN

Geography

Japan is an archipelago nation in the North Pacific Ocean, to the east of the Asian landmass. The country's four main islands of Hokkaido, Honshu, Shikoku, and Kyushu are mountainous, with few natural resources. (Indeed, Japan's economic success is astonishing given the scarcity of its raw materials.) The country's surface area approximates in size to California. Owing to the geographical spread of the island chain, the Japanese climate is very varied. The north has long and snowy winters, while the climate of the south is hot and tropical. Japan is located in an area of considerable seismic activity, and typhoons and tidal waves are common.

Brief History

The Japanese have traditionally ascribed mythological origins to their nation. Based on archaeological evidence, the Japanese islands are thought to have been inhabited for around 30,000 years. The earliest inhabitants seem to have crossed from the Asian landmass at a time when glaciation linked the Japanese islands to Asia. Chinese records indicate that around 2,000 years ago, the islands were inhabited by hundreds of scattered tribal communities. Over the centuries, many local warlords contested control of Japan, and amid the violent fragmentation the imperial family emerged as a unifying force of political and religious significance.

In Japan's early modern history, the Tokugawa period (1600–1867) was characterized by self-imposed isolation from the world. The Tokugawa shogun rulers brought centuries of civil strife and regional factionalism to a close. They unified Japan by taming local warlords, and instituted a highly centralized and stable regime. As part of the country's culture of isolation, the rulers restricted the movement of foreigners and placed firm controls on the levels of international trade. As a consequence, the Japanese economy became relatively backward and out of touch with contemporary technological developments around the world. The political elite paid nominal homage to the emperor, but they remained in control of the country's political system.

With the end of the Tokugawa era in the late nineteenth century, Japan embarked on a period of intense constitutional change and economic and social reform. The post-Tokugawa period of self-conscious modernization is known as the Meiji restoration, as it saw the restoration of the emperor as the nation's symbol of unity (and object of divine worship). In this period, Japan reversed its previous policy of isolation and the Japanese avidly sought instruction in western technology and ideas. Many Japanese studied overseas, while westerners were invited to reform the country's infrastructure, industry, and armed forces. Japan's modernization program was successful and the country's economy advanced rapidly.

The Meiji period was characterized by a streak of nationalism that ultimately led to military expansionism throughout Asia. Following decades of encroachment on Asia, Japan entered World War II in 1940 in alliance with Adolf Hitler's Germany and Benito Mussolini's Italy. Japan's surprise attack on the U.S. base of Pearl Harbor in 1941 was, of course, the catalyst for the United States' entry into the war.

During World War II, the Japanese overran many Asian nations. Burma, China, the Philippines, and Singapore were among the countries that fell. The Japanese regime of the era declared its mission to be the liberation of Asia from western imperialism, and it drew up plans for a Japanese-dominated "Greater East Asia Co-prosperity Sphere." However, instead of liberation, Japanese expansionism was marked by large-scale massacres and human rights abuses. Perhaps the most notorious of the massacres occurred in Nanking in China between 1937 and 1938, when civilian victims numbered in the hundreds of thousands.

After initial military successes Japan soon overstretched itself, and its armed forces were forced out of occupied territories. Only after the United States detonated atomic bombs over Hiroshima and Nagasaki in August 1945 did the Japanese emperor offer unconditional surrender to the Allied powers. In January 1946, the emperor repudiated his claims to divinity. The terms of surrender led to the United States occupying Japan from 1945 to 1952, and the United States undertook a program of demilitarization and democratization.

Postwar Japan has been a model world citizen with impeccable democratic credentials, generous donations to developing countries, and an aversion to military activity. The country has also undergone an economic miracle and has become the world's second most powerful economy, after the United States.

Demographics

The Japanese population totals approximately 125 million, of which 80 percent live in densely concentrated urban areas. Some estimates claim that over half the country's population lives on around 2 to 3 percent of the land surface. Japan's prosperity and dietary patterns have contributed to a notable honor—the Japanese enjoy the longest life expectancy of any nation in the world.

Language

Other than Ainu, which is spoken by tiny groups of the dwindling indigenous ethnic minority of the same name, virtually 100 percent of Japan's population speaks Japanese as a mother tongue. Japanese is unique in the family of languages. It has very few structural similarities to other languages, although some linguists detect affinities with Korean.

Although the Japanese language is unrelated to Chinese, their use of similar writing systems has led to popular misconceptions throughout the world that the two languages are related. China's cultural prestige and its proximity to Japan led to Japan's adoption of Chinese characters—called kanji in Japanese—as a writing system. The use of Chinese characters to write Japanese proved problematic, however, owing to the very different grammatical structures of the two languages. Japanese inflectional endings, for example, could only be rendered with difficulty by a system of ideograms.

The Japanese therefore developed two phonetic alphabets (or, more technically, syllaberies) to supplement the kanji. These two writing systems, called hiragana and katakana, are used alongside the Chinese characters. Hiragana is used mainly for inflectional endings and for words for which there are no kanji, while katakana is used mainly for foreign words. For example, in a sentence such as "I am going to France," all three writing systems will typically be used. The word for "I" will usually be written in kanji, the word for France in katakana, and the inflectional endings (such as the subject marker attached to "I") in hiragana.

Japanese is a subtle language with intricate levels of politeness. Its reputation as a fiendishly difficult language to read and write is justified, owing to the simultaneous use of kanji, hiragana, and katakana. However, spoken Japanese is generally considered to be relatively straightforward to speak.

As could be expected in one of the world's most educated countries, literacy is virtually 100 percent.

Politics

Japan is a constitutional monarchy and has its capital at Tokyo. The emperor is head of state, and the prime minister is head of government. Japan's bicameral legislature is called the Diet. The Liberal Democratic Party (LDP) has dominated Japanese politics since the 1950s and has provided most of the country's prime ministers and cabinet ministers. The LDP can therefore claim credit for overseeing the country's political stability and economic renaissance following World War II. In recent years, the LDP's fortunes have waned, but it was given a new lease of life in 2001 with the appointment of its populist and charismatic leader Junichiro Koizumi (born 1942) as the country's prime minister.

In terms of foreign policy, since World War II Japan has been closely aligned with the United States. The country takes a neutral stand on some issues, however. Relations with its closest neighbors remain heavily influenced by memories of the Japanese military expansionism of the early twentieth century. For example, the Japanese Ministry of Education adopted revised school textbook guidelines in the 1980s that softened the language used to describe Japan's aggression during World War II. This caused outrage in South Korea and other Asian countries, and among Japanese liberals.

Japan is a major aid donor to developing countries.

Economy

Following crushing defeat and nuclear devastation in World War II, Japan became within decades the world's second most powerful economy, after the United States. This industrial success has been attributed to many factors—the strong work ethic of the Japanese; a "job for life" culture; top-class research in high technology sectors; low spending on national defense; and fruitful government collaboration with industry. Automobiles, electronic consumer goods, and machine tools are typical manufactured products on which Japan has built its economic success. This success has been achieved despite poor natural resources: Japan imports the vast majority of its raw materials and fuels. The country tends to be self-sufficient in rice and its fishing fleet is one of the world's largest, but it imports a large proportion of its food requirements.

The Japanese business world has long been characterized by the cooperation of various elements and stages of the industrial process, with manufacturers, suppliers, and distributors acting closely in groups called *keiretsu*. These arrangements have loosened to some degree in recent years. The United States is Japan's largest trading partner, but relations between the two countries have long been strained by disputes over alleged Japanese protectionism.

It is difficult to keep a miracle going forever, and following three decades of remarkable growth, the Japanese economy experienced a slowdown in the 1990s. The Japanese were shocked to experience deflation, industrial bankruptcies, and the collapse of real estate prices. At the time of writing, the Japanese economy remains sluggish and the government is grappling with structural economic reform. Nonetheless, Japan remains among the world's largest and most technologically advanced economies. Japanese automobiles, electronic equipment, and machine tools remain in demand around the globe. Further, the country's infrastructure is world-class and is typified by the famous speed and punctuality of the *shinkansen* ("bullet train"). Despite recent economic problems, therefore, the Japanese economy remains the envy of most other nations. The country's currency unit is the yen.

Legal and Regulatory Environment

Japan's legal culture was modeled on the German Commercial Code during the nineteenth-century Meiji restoration, although U.S. influence has been strong since the end of World War II. During the occupation years of 1945 to 1952, the United States played a prominent role in redrafting the Japanese constitution and reforming the legal system. The country's regulatory and tax environments are rather complex, but efficient.

Accountancy

Japanese GAAP is derived from several sources—the country's Commercial Code; tax law; the standards of the Accounting Standards Board of Japan (ASBJ); the pronouncements and recommendations of the Japanese Institute of Certified Public Accountants (JICPA); and (for listed corporations) the Securities and Exchange Law. The ASBJ was established in 2001 and replaced the Ministry of Finance's Business Accounting Deliberation Council, the previous standard-setting body.

Japanese GAAP has traditionally differed substantially from IAS. Examples of areas of difference include acquisition accounting, the recognition and measurement of employee benefits, and lease accounting. One reason for the differences has been the traditional reliance of Japanese corporations on debt rather than equity finance, which has led to tax law driving many areas of accounting practice. The pace of harmonization with international accounting norms was slow in the 1990s, despite the fact that from 1993 to 1995 the chairman of the International Accounting Standards Committee was Japanese. The reluctance to proceed speedily with harmonization in the 1990s was attributed by many observers to the Japanese economic slowdown of that decade—corporations feared that more rigorous accounting standards would shed too much light on corporate financial weaknesses.

The ASBJ has, however, declared its intention to converge Japanese accounting standards with IAS, and its Web site (*www.asb.or.jp/index_e.html*) gives English-language details of Japanese accounting standards.

Some Japanese companies provide English-language "convenience accounts." These are not required by law, but are often produced (normally in accordance with Japanese GAAP) for public relations or investor purposes. The Japanese accountancy profession is relatively small, and the JICPA has around only 13,000 members.

Cultural Background

China's proximity to Japan and its cultural prestige have resulted in the exertion of tremendous influence over Japanese culture. These influences range from religion (Buddhism was brought to Japan in its Chinese forms) to the Japanese writing system (as discussed in the "Languages" section). Chinese cultural imprints can also be seen in areas ranging from architecture to literature to the martial arts.

However, the Japanese have not been merely passive imitators of Chinese culture, and Chinese cultural imports have usually been given a uniquely Japanese flavor.

Over 99 percent of Japan's population is ethnically Japanese. There are small communities of other nationalities—Koreans and Iranians, for example—who have settled in the country to seek work, as well as a very small indigenous ethnic minority, the Ainu. In terms of religion, the majority (around 85 percent) of Japanese nominally observe Shinto or Buddhist practices, or usually a combination of the two. Shinto is the traditional Japanese religious system, with pantheistic kami (spirits or gods with varying degrees of power). Shinto has reached a close accommodation with Buddhism, often to the point of fusion.

Japan's advanced technology society coexists with a traditional culture that respects strong social and employment hierarchies. For example, the Japanese tend to work for the same employer for the whole of their lives, although this pattern has changed to a degree in recent years.

Social Etiquette

- As is well known, the Japanese bow is an essential social tool that equates to the western handshake. The inclination of the bow is generally related to the degree of respect intended.

- The exchange of business cards is an important event at formal meetings. To avoid causing offense, it is strongly recommended to scrutinize a business card with a suitable level of interest, rather than cursorily slipping it into one's pocket.

- The Japanese enjoy after-hours business entertaining. Socializing centers on restaurants and bars, and it is common to go straight from the office to a social venue. Long hours after the office closes may be required for the visitor to Japan!

- Politeness and avoiding "loss of face" are important in Japan, and overt displays of emotions are considered ill mannered.

- It is considered bad luck to point one's chopsticks at another person.

- Given the complexity of Japanese patterns of courtesy and ceremony, it is difficult for visitors to get things right all the time. Indeed, it is commonly acknowledged that foreigners who master the finer intricacies of social interaction can be viewed with suspicion in Japan. Most minor breaches of social decorum by foreigners will be tolerated.

Further Information

Andrew Gordon, *The Modern History of Japan* (New York and Oxford: Oxford University Press, 2002).

Yoshio Sugimoto, *An Introduction to Japanese Society* (New York and Cambridge: Cambridge University Press, 1997).

Kyojiro Someya, *Japanese Accounting* (New York and Oxford: Oxford University Press, 1996).

Stephen Vlastos (ed.), *Mirror of Modernity: Invented Traditions of Modern Japan* (Berkeley, CA: University of California Press, 1998).
Japanese Ministry of Finance: *www.mof.go.jp/english.*
Accounting Standards Board of Japan: *www.asb.or.jp/index_e.html.*
Japanese Institute of Certified Public Accountants: *www.jicpa.or.jp/n_eng/index.html.*

MALAYSIA

Geography

Malaysia is located in Southeast Asia and, geographically speaking, is a country of two parts. Western Malaysia forms a peninsula to the south of Thailand, and Eastern Malaysia consists of the northern part of the island of Borneo. (The southern part of Borneo belongs to Indonesia.) The two Malaysian territories are separated by over 600 miles of the South China Sea.

Hills, mountains, and coastal plains dominate Malaysia, and forests and woodland cover two-thirds of the country. The country is hot and humid all year round, and there are annual monsoons. In recent years, serious pollution from nearby Indonesian forest fires has caused severe fog and haze problems.

Brief History

The Malay Peninsula has been inhabited for millennia, and its strategic location on important trade routes between India and China has long made it an ethnic melting pot. Before the arrival of European colonizers, Arab traders had reached the peninsula and Muslim sultanates grew on the profits of trade and piracy. Following the arrival of European traders in the sixteenth century, the British eventually gained control over the peninsula.

During the Second World War the British were displaced by the Japanese, but they returned after hostilities ended. In line with the wishes of the majority of the population, the British suppressed a postwar communist insurgency. Malaysia gained independence in 1963, with the creation of the Federation of Malaysia. The new country comprised the states of Malaya and Singapore in the west, and Sabah and Sarawak in the east. The first years of independence were troubled, and relations were tense with Indonesia. Singapore left the federation in 1965.

Malaysia has consciously striven for rapid economic development, and in the late twentieth century the country had one of the most dynamic of the Asian tiger economies. Malaysia's spectacular economic growth was temporarily arrested by the Asian financial crisis that started in 1997, but it has since recovered.

Malaysian political history has been dominated by Mahathir Mohamad (born 1925). Mahathir trained as a medical doctor before using his power base in the United Malays National Organisation to become prime minister in 1981. A controversial and outspoken figure, he is famous for citing Asian cultural values as an explanation of the success of the Asian tiger economies. His strong condemnation of "international speculators" during the dark days of the Asian financial crisis of the late 1990s also gained him global notoriety. Mahathir has tended to see himself as an unofficial regional spokesperson on such matters.

Critics have accused Mahathir of political repression, notably in his treatment of a political rival who was convicted in 1999 on charges of corruption and sexual misdemeanors. The Malaysian leader has also indulged in grandiose building projects, such as the 1997 Petronas Towers (at the time the tallest building in the world) and a costly new capital at Putrajaya.

Demographics

Malaysia's population of around 22 million comprises a complex ethnic melting pot, as discussed in the "Cultural Background" section. Population growth is modest, although the country's economic standing in the region attracts large numbers of migrants, both legal and illegal.

Languages

Malaysia's linguistic patterns reflect the country's ethnic composition. The official language is Bahasa Malaysia, spoken as a mother tongue by the majority Malay community and taught at school to the other ethnic communities. Bahasa Malaysia belongs to the Malay-Polynesian language family, and is virtually identical to Bahasa Indonesia. It is written in a Roman script, although a traditional writing system based on Arabic is also used, mainly in rural areas.

Other widely spoken languages in Malaysia include Chinese dialects such as Cantonese and Mandarin, and Indian languages such as Tamil, Telugu, and Malayalam. In Eastern Malaysia, so-called "aboriginal" peoples speak a number of indigenous languages. English is widely understood and frequently used for business purposes, owing to the country's history as a British colony. The literacy rate is around 85 percent, and is higher for men than for women.

Politics

Malaysia is a constitutional monarchy; its capital is Kuala Lumpur. The bicameral parliament comprises a nonelected senate and an elected house of representatives. The head of state is the monarch, known as the Paramount Ruler. The Paramount Ruler is a sultan chosen by (and from) the hereditary rulers of nine Malaysian states. The Paramount Ruler is rotated every five years in a constitutional device to diffuse power between the traditionally powerful sultans, whose royal houses have ruled sultanates on the Malay Peninsula for hundreds of years. The Paramount Ruler's political duties are largely ceremonial. The head of government is the prime minister, who is normally the leader of the party that dominates the lower parliamentary house. The prime minister appoints the cabinet with the consent of the Paramount Ruler.

It is often remarked that in Malaysia the Chinese run the economy and the Malays run the political system. Like all generalizations, this is an oversimplification, yet it contains more than a grain of truth. As in several other Southeast Asian countries (e.g., Indonesia and the Philippines), the Chinese are an economically successful community. The ethnic wealth gap between the Chinese and majority Malay communities has long been a source of political tension, although there has been little serious interethnic violence since the 1970s. Current political and social arrangements include employment quotas for ethnic Malays, and the arrangements seem to be generally accepted by the country's various communities.

Economy

Malaysia was seriously affected by the Asian economic crisis that started in 1997. The country's economy contracted by 7 percent in 1997, and its currency lost one-third of its value against the U.S. dollar. High government spending and excessive corporate debt had made Malaysia vulnerable to the effects of international capital flows. Malaysia's economy has since largely recovered, and one of the late twentieth century's Asian tiger economies again looks forward to a promising future.

In British colonial times, Malaysia was known for its rubber plantations, but the modern economy has developed a much greater sophistication and diversification. In peninsular Malaysia, the traditional activities of rubber, logging, palm oil production, and tin mining remain important, but have been overtaken by electronic consumer goods, light manufacturing, and tourism. The automobile industry is young but successful. Malaysia is also an oil exporter.

The Malaysian government has publicly declared its intention of turning the country into a full-fledged developed economy by 2020, and a major plank of this official policy has been the creation of high-technology facilities. Visitors to Malaysia will hear much of ventures such as the "smart city" of Cyberjaya and the country's so-called "Multimedia Super Corridor." The projects symbolize Malaysia's aspirations to become a world center for information technology.

Around 5 to 10 percent of Malaysia's population is estimated to live in poverty. This is low by the standards of the region. Although shabby slums disfigure parts of the capital Kuala Lumpur, they are on a smaller scale than in neighboring countries.

Japan, the United States, and Singapore are Malaysia's major trading partners, and the country's currency unit is the ringgit.

Legal and Regulatory Environment

Malaysian law is based on English common law, supplemented by indigenous Malay and Muslim characteristics. Business law is broadly similar to that of other former British colonies, and the regulatory environment is generally light. Business and employment law are complicated, however, by strict business ownership and employment quotas for ethnic Malays.

Accountancy

Malaysian GAAP is based on company law and the accounting standards of the Malaysian Accounting Standards Board (MASB). The MASB has stated its intention to follow IAS in principle, but has reserved the right to tailor accounting standards to the circumstances of the Malaysian legal and economic environment. Therefore, although there are a number of areas in which Malaysian GAAP differs from IAS (such as the treatment of intangible assets and goodwill), Malaysian GAAP is broadly in line with IAS. Malaysian accounting standards are available from the MASB Web site (*www.masb.org.my*), which also indicates differences with IAS. The Kuala Lumpur Stock Exchange permits the use of IAS by foreign listed corporations.

The Malaysian Association of Certified Public Accountants was formed in 1958, and has a membership of around 2,500.

Cultural Background

Malaysian society is multiethnic. There is some disagreement about the country's precise ethnic mix, partly due to high levels of intermarriage between the various communities, but it seems that indigenous Malays account for 50 to 60 percent of the population, Chinese 20 to 30 percent, and Indians around 10 percent. Religious practices tend to mirror ethnic patterns—most Malays are Muslim, most Chinese are Buddhist or Christian, and most Indians are Hindu. Unsurprisingly, the Malaysian government has striven to create a Malaysian identity that transcends ethnic boundaries, and economic development has been a key element of this process. Prosperity has diverted attention away from ethnic tensions since serious riots erupted in the early 1970s.

Social Etiquette

- English is commonly used as the business language of Malaysia.
- Although a Muslim-majority country, Malaysia is relatively liberal. Alcohol is freely available, for example. However, the visitor should not be lulled into a false sense of cultural liberalism, as many Muslims practice a more conservative lifestyle than that seen in the wider society.
- The exchange of business cards is a formal occasion in Malaysia, and cards received should be examined and handled with respect.
- Social etiquette specific to the Chinese and Indian communities is covered in the "China" and "India" country sections.

Further Information

Edmund Terence Gomez and K. S. Jomo, *Malaysia's Political Economy*, 2nd ed. (New York and Cambridge: Cambridge University Press, 1999).
Khoo Boo Teik, *Paradoxes of Mahathirism: An Intellectual Biography of Mahathir Mohamad* (New York and Oxford: Oxford University Press, 1997).
Prime Minister's Office of the Government of Malaysia: *www.smpke.jpm.my*.
Institute of Internal Auditors Malaysia: *www.iiam.com.my*.
Malaysian Association of Certified Public Accountants: *www.micpa.com.my*.
Malaysian Accounting Standards Board: *www.masb.org.my*.
Malaysian Institute of Accountants: *www.mia.org.my/main*.

NEW ZEALAND

Geography

New Zealand is located in the South Pacific Ocean, to the southeast of Australia. It is composed of two main islands, conveniently called North Island and South Island. The country is mainly mountainous and hilly, and forests and woodland cover around 30 percent of the territory. The climate is temperate.

Brief History

It is thought that the Maori people first arrived in New Zealand around 1,000 years ago, although Maori settlement occurred on a large scale only in the fourteenth century. The Dutch were the earliest European visitors and they gave the islands their modern name. The British, however, emerged as the colonizing power. The British did not use the country as a penal colony, unlike neighboring Australia.

Increasing British settlement created tensions with the Maori people by the early nineteenth century, and the 1840 Treaty of Waitangi between the British and the Maori was intended to resolve land disputes. The treaty also made New Zealand a formal British colony. Despite the treaty, unresolved and contentious land claims led to Anglo-Maori conflict in the late nineteenth century. The British consolidated their political position, and in 1907, New Zealand became an independent dominion under the British crown. The country has remained a strong British ally since its independence, and it gave military support to Britain in both world wars.

In recent times, New Zealand's antinuclear stance has often led to friction with western powers. For example, the country has refused access to its ports to U.S. ships suspected of carrying nuclear weapons, and it has severely criticized French nuclear testing in the South Pacific. Following Britain's decision in the 1970s to join the organization that has now become the EU, New Zealand's links with its "mother country" have been weakened, and it has been forced to forge closer links with Asian countries.

Demographics

New Zealand's population is relatively small, at only 3.8 million. Three-quarters of the population lives on the North Island, and at least 8 out of 10 New Zealanders live in urban areas.

Languages

English and Maori are the official languages of New Zealand. Maori is a Polynesian language written with a Roman script. New Zealand English is characterized by a distinctive accent and a vocabulary that includes some words of Maori origin. The literacy rate is virtually 100 percent.

Politics

New Zealand is a parliamentary democracy; its capital is at Wellington on the North Island. (Wellington is the world's southern-most capital city.) New Zealand maintains close constitutional links with Britain, and the largely ceremonial head of state is the British monarch, who is represented by a governor general. The head of government is the prime minister, who is usually the leader of the main party (or coalition) in the unicameral parliament.

A recurring domestic political issue in recent years has been the historical grievances of the Maori community. Around 95 percent of land is owned by New Zealanders of British or European descent, and some Maori groups have sought compensation for nineteenth-century British land seizures. However, despite the acrimony caused by this issue, race relations in New Zealand are generally good.

Economy

The traditional base of the New Zealand economy is livestock—above all, sheep farming. The huge distances between New Zealand and Britain made historically close economic ties between the two countries difficult to sustain indefinitely, and from the 1970s the British market for livestock receded in importance after Britain's adherence to what was to become the EU. Since then, New Zealand has been forced to diversify its economy, and to forge closer economic relations with Asian nations.

From the mid-1980s, market-oriented economic reforms have increased the importance of the country's industrial base, and the tourism sector is increasingly sophisticated. New Zealand today is a prosperous country with income levels comparable to Western Europe. The country's major trading partners are Australia, the United States, and Japan, and the currency unit is the New Zealand dollar.

Legal and Regulatory Environment

Unsurprisingly, given the country's historical and continuing links to Britain, New Zealand law is closely modeled on English common law. Maori customary law operates for the minority community, but otherwise, a visitor from the English-speaking world will find little unusual in the New Zealand legal and regulatory environment.

Accountancy

Traditionally, New Zealand GAAP was patterned on British models. Modern New Zealand GAAP is based on the country's Financial Reporting Act of 1993 and on the financial reporting standards of the Institute of Chartered Accountants of New Zealand (ICANZ). The ICANZ's policy is to harmonize New Zealand's accounting standards as far as possible with IAS. For example, Financial Reporting Standard 15 (Provisions, Contingent Liabilities, and Contingent Assets), applicable from 2001, is substantially consistent with IAS 37 (of the same title).

Some differences remain between New Zealand and international GAAP—the treatment of intangible assets, for example—but differences are increasingly narrowing. Details of New Zealand's financial reporting standards are available from the ICANZ Web site (*www.icanz.co.nz*).

The country's accountancy profession is mature, and the ICANZ has around 27,000 members.

Cultural Background

Despite a common British colonial heritage, New Zealand's culture is quite different from that of Australia—New Zealand is generally considered to have retained a more "British" flavor than its neighbor. New Zealand's public culture is known for its humanitarian emphasis, which is reflected in the country's strong antinuclear stance. New Zealanders love sport, and are widely considered to be the world's leading rugby nation (especially in view of the small size of the population). The legendary rugby rivalry with Australia reflects patriotic passions.

Ethnically, two cultural groups dominate New Zealand. Inhabitants of European descent comprise around 80 percent of the population, while Maoris account for around 10 percent. (The balance is made up of other Asian ethnic groups.) Around 70 percent of the population is Christian, although 25 to 30 percent describe themselves as non-religious.

Social Etiquette

- It is unwise to mistake a New Zealander for an Australian, as New Zealanders are very proud of their separate identity.
- New Zealanders have a reputation for being down to earth and forthright in business dealings, yet they are more formal than their Australian neighbors.
- New Zealanders are sports-crazy, and like to discuss their passion.

Further Information

James Belich, *Paradise Reforged: A History of the New Zealanders From the Beginning of the Twentieth Century* (Honolulu: University of Hawaii Press, 2002).
Donald Denoon, Philippa Mein-Smith, and Marivic Wyndham, *A History of Australia, New Zealand and the Pacific* (Oxford: Blackwell, 2000).
New Zealand Government On-line: *www.govt.nz.*
Institute of Chartered Accountants of New Zealand: *www.icanz.co.nz.*

PAKISTAN

Geography

Pakistan is located in the northwest of the Indian subcontinent. Occupying historical invasion routes from Central Asia to India, its surface area is almost four times that of the United Kingdom. The country shares borders with India to the east, Iran to the west, and Afghanistan and China to the north. To the south is the Arabian Sea.

Northern Pakistan has several spectacular mountain ranges, including the Himalayas, the Karakoram, and the Hindu Kush. Much of the rest of the country comprises fertile plains and arid desert. The latter dominates the coastline and the area near the Iranian border. Summers are intensely hot in most of the country, and the period July to August sees heavy monsoon rains, often accompanied by river flooding.

Brief History

Pakistan was created in August 1947 as one of two independent successor states to the British colony of India. (The other successor state was, of course, the Republic of India.) The "India" country section has details of the subcontinent's pre-1947 history, but of particular importance to the future country of Pakistan was the impact of Muslim invasions from Central Asia. The most distinguished of these invaders founded the Mughal Empire (1527–1707), which straddled the territory of both modern-day India and Pakistan. Although many of the dynasty's most famous monuments—such as the Taj Mahal—are in India, there are many distinguished examples of Mughal architecture in Pakistan. A famous example is the seventeenth-century Badshahi Mosque in Lahore. In the northwest area of the Indian subcontinent a large proportion of the local population converted to Islam, and this Muslim community later formed the basis of the Pakistani nation.

In the early twentieth century, as Indian independence neared under pressure from the Indian National Congress of M. K. Gandhi (1869–1948) and Jawaharlal Nehru (1889–1964), many Indian Muslims viewed with dismay the prospect of being a minority community in a Hindu-majority country. Gandhi in particular tried to assuage Muslim fears, but under the inspirational leadership of Karachi-born M. A. Jinnah (1876–1948), the Muslim League pressed for the creation of an independent Muslim nation on Indian territory. It named this nation Pakistan ("Land of the Pure").

Like Gandhi and Nehru, Jinnah was a London-trained lawyer. Jinnah was an immensely talented and complex man, and his role in the founding of Pakistan has justly earned him the title of *Quaid-e-Azam* ("Father of the Nation"). Without his tenacity and political genius, it is questionable whether Pakistan would ever have been created. Jinnah was by no stretch of the imagination a religious fundamentalist, yet he left his mark on world history as the architect of one of the world's largest Islamic states. His impressive mausoleum, a dazzling monument of international importance, is in Karachi.

At its creation in 1947, Pakistan comprised two "wings" separated by Indian territory—West Pakistan in the northwest of the subcontinent, and East Pakistan in the northeast. (Following a vicious conflict that cost hundreds of thousands of lives, East Pakistan broke away to form the independent state of Bangladesh in 1971. This is discussed in the "Bangladesh" country section.) The creation of Muslim-dominated Pakistan and Hindu-dominated India was accompanied by massive sectarian slaughter that killed hundreds of thousands of people. In large-scale population transfers between the countries, millions of Muslims fled to Pakistan, while millions of Hindus and Sikhs made the reverse journey.

Ill feeling between India and Pakistan has continued to the present day, partly as a result of the memories of the sectarian violence at partition, and partly over the disputed state of Kashmir. Pakistan regularly accuses India of violent repression of Kashmir's Muslim-majority population, and it describes anti-India insurgents as "freedom fighters." India accuses Pakistan of supporting terrorist separatist groups in Kashmir. To date, Pakistan has fought three wars with India. The political rivalry has taken on increasingly dangerous overtones, as both countries have developed nuclear capabilities.

Demographics

Like India, Pakistan has a large and rapidly growing population. The population has almost tripled in size since 1947, and currently totals around 150 million. There are many ethnic groups in Pakistan, reflected in the country's linguistic complexity (as summarized in the "Languages" section). While Pakistan's population is predominantly rural, urban development continues apace. The port of Karachi is Pakistan's biggest city, with a population estimated to be over 10 million.

Languages

As in India, Pakistan's lingua franca is the former colonial language of English, especially among the middle classes. Many official documents and notices are in English, as are many of the documents auditors may expect to see, such as invoices, contracts, and business correspondence.

Of Pakistan's indigenous languages, the most important are Punjabi (spoken by around 50 percent of the population), Sindhi (12 percent), Urdu (10 percent), and Pashtu (8 percent). Most of Pakistan's languages are of Indic (or Indo-Aryan) origin, like their north Indian cousins.

The similarities between the national languages of Pakistan and India—Urdu and Hindi, respectively—deserve mention. In their colloquial registers, Urdu and Hindi are virtually identical and share a common stock of grammar and vocabulary. However, the two languages part company in their written and formal registers. Urdu uses a modified Perso-Arabic script, while Hindi uses the Nagari Indian script. In its higher registers, Urdu further distances itself from Hindi by drawing much of its learned vocabulary from Arabic and Persian, rather than from Indian sources.

Illiteracy is a significant problem in Pakistan, especially in rural areas. Estimates vary, but up to 40 percent of men and 70 percent of women are illiterate.

Politics

The Islamic Republic of Pakistan has a federal structure. Its capital is Islamabad, a new city constructed in the 1960s near the garrison town of Rawalpindi. At the time of writing, Pakistan is under military rule. In October 1999, General Pervez

Musharraf took power in a coup—he dissolved parliament, suspended the constitution, and took the title of Chief Executive. This was the most recent of a series of military interventions in Pakistani politics. Although Pakistan inherited western-style parliamentary structures from British colonial times, the country's democracy is fragile, and military regimes have ousted civilian administrations on several occasions.

Other than M. A. Jinnah, discussed in the "Brief History" section, important civilian personalities in Pakistan's political history have included Zulfikar Ali Bhutto (1928–1979) of the Pakistan People's Party and his daughter Benazir (born 1953). Benazir Bhutto in 1988 became the first woman to govern a modern Islamic state. Nawaz Sharif (born 1947) of the Pakistan Muslim League served twice as prime minister before his 1999 overthrow by Musharraf. On the military side, General Muhammad Zia-ul-Haq (1924–1988) ousted Zulfikar Ali Bhutto in a 1977 coup, and ruled Pakistan until his death in an airplane crash in 1988. (Under Zia's military regime, Bhutto was executed in 1979.) Under the current military regime both Benazir Bhutto and Nawaz Sharif—bitter rivals—are in exile.

Violence frequently mars Pakistani politics, and in recent years, there have been serious sectarian clashes between rival Muslim groups. Pakistan's foreign policy is dominated by relations with neighboring India. As discussed previously, Kashmir is the main issue dividing the two countries, although water sharing from the Indus River is another source of tension.

Proximity to Afghanistan is another source of instability. The Pakistani government exerts its authority only weakly over the heavily armed and fiercely independent inhabitants of the Afghan border area, which is notorious for its lawlessness and smuggling activities. Ethnic groups straddle the porous border with Afghanistan, and millions of Afghan refugees have fled their troubled country to seek refuge in Pakistan. The Pakistani government's assistance to the United States in tracking down anti-U.S. militant groups has also enraged Islamic fundamentalist groups in the country.

Economy

The Pakistani economy has suffered from major problems since the country's creation in 1947, and at least one-third of the population lives in poverty. Remittances from expatriate workers in the Mideast are an important source of income for many families and for the national economy. The Pakistani economy is overwhelmingly agricultural and much of its industry is outdated. However, the country's textile industry has a global reputation, and Pakistani textile goods are exported around the world.

Pakistan suffers from chronic fiscal deficits and low foreign exchange reserves, and it periodically struggles to service its foreign debts. Industrial investment has been hampered by political uncertainty caused by periodic military coups, tensions with India, and instability in neighboring Afghanistan. Black markets flourish for both smuggled consumer goods and illegal narcotics.

The country's long-standing political rivalry with India has led to huge military spending, which has been a significant drain on the country's resources. Further, the presence of millions of Afghan refugees has placed further strain on an already troubled economy. Pakistan's currency unit is the rupee.

Legal and Regulatory Environment

Pakistan inherited from the British colonial period a legal tradition based on English common law. The English language continues to be widely used for legal and business matters. As Pakistan has gradually asserted its Muslim identity, Shari'a law has increased in importance. While Shari'a law affects criminal, civil and domestic matters, western-style legal principles tend to apply in business matters. For example, some of Pakistan's banks charge interest, while others follow the stricter Shari'a banking laws that forbid the practice. Pakistan's regulatory and tax environment is generally heavy and cumbersome, as in other parts of South Asia.

Accountancy

Pakistani GAAP is based on company law and the regulations of the Securities and Exchange Commission of Pakistan (SECP). The SECP has adopted IAS as mandatory for listed companies and recommended for nonlisted companies. Where IAS does not apply, Pakistani accounting practice can be significantly different from international norms, and traditional areas of difference include consolidation accounting and the treatment of deferred tax.

Pakistan's accountancy profession developed during the British colonial period. The Institute of Chartered Accountants of Pakistan (ICAP) was formed in 1961, taking on the role of earlier accountancy bodies. Although it is the country's main accountancy and external auditing organization, it is relatively small, with a membership of around 3,000. The members of the Institute of Cost and Management Accountants of Pakistan tend to work in industry.

Cultural Background

The "Languages" section indicates the country's ethnic groups, whose numbers broadly follow linguistic patterns. Pakistan's population is overwhelmingly (97 percent) Muslim. Most Pakistani Muslims are Sunni, although around one-quarter of the Muslim population is Shia. Conflict between Sunni and Shia groups has claimed hundreds of lives in recent years. The Ahmadiyya community considers itself fully Islamic, but the disapproval of their beliefs by many other Pakistani Muslims has led to acrimony since the 1990s. Smaller religious communities comprising the remaining 3 percent of the population include Hindus and Christians.

In rural areas, social practices tend to be conservative. Women, for example, are often expected to perform a secondary role in social and economic life. In major cities like Karachi and Lahore, however, westernized cultural attitudes are in evidence, especially among the middle classes.

As is the case in other South Asian nations, Pakistan is cricket-crazy. The country's national cricket team is among the most feared in the world, and most Pakistanis follow the team's performances with keen interest.

Social Etiquette

- Public physical contact between men and women is generally frowned on. Although handshaking between the sexes is common in urban areas, and among the middle classes, it is best for a visitor to wait for a member of the opposite sex to initiate a handshake.
- Alcohol is prohibited, although foreign non-Muslims may apply for a permit to drink alcohol in their hotel rooms.
- As in all Muslim countries, pork is not eaten.
- A conservative dress code for women is advisable.

Further Information

Akbar Ahmed, *Jinnah, Pakistan and Islamic Identity* (New York and London: Routledge, 1997).
Dennis Kux, *The United States and Pakistan, 1947–2000: Disenchanted Allies* (Washington, DC: Woodrow Wilson Center Press, 2001).
Stanley Wolpert, *Jinnah of Pakistan* (New York and Oxford: Oxford University Press, 1984).
Government of Pakistan Web site: *www.pak.gov.pk.*
The Institute of Chartered Accountants of Pakistan: *www.icap.org.pk.*
The Institute of Cost and Management Accountants of Pakistan: *www.icmap .com.pk.*
Securities and Exchange Commission of Pakistan: *www.secp.gov.pk.*

THE PHILIPPINES

Geography

The Philippines consists of more than 7,000 islands in Southeast Asia. Forests and woodland cover nearly half of the country's territory, which is largely mountainous. The Philippine climate is tropical, with a northeast monsoon from November to April and a southwest monsoon from May to October. The islands are occasionally subject to typhoons and cyclonic storms, and destructive earthquakes and volcanic eruptions also occur from time to time.

Brief History

The original inhabitants of the Philippines are thought to have migrated to the islands around 30,000 years ago, from the modern-day territories of Indonesia and Malaysia. Thousands of self-contained agricultural and fishing communities established themselves throughout the archipelago, linked by common social and cultural patterns. By the end of the fourteenth century CE, Islam had arrived in the Philippines via the Indonesian islands, and small Muslim political entities emerged.

Later, both Spain and the United States colonized the Philippines. Sixteenth-century Spanish colonists established a base at Manila, which has continued to be the center of Philippine commercial and political life. The islands were named for the sixteenth-century Spanish king, Philip II. Spanish missionaries converted large numbers of local people to Christianity, which has remained a striking feature of Philippine society—of all Asian countries today, the Philippines has the highest proportion of Christians. In general, the Spanish-run colony was economically unsuccessful, but in the eighteenth century it became a world leader in tobacco production.

The Philippines were ceded by Spain to the United States in 1898 following the Spanish-American War. Other western powers (notably Germany) coveted the post-Spanish Philippines, but the United States took advantage of the postwar chaos to impose its authority. Negotiations for phased independence started in the 1930s, but the Philippines gained full independence from the United States only in 1946, following Japanese occupation in World War II. Manuel Roxas (1894–1948) was the first president of the independent Republic of the Philippines, but the dominant personality in postindependence politics was Ferdinand Marcos (1917–1989). Marcos enjoyed power for two decades before a popular rebellion caused him to flee into exile (as discussed in the "Politics" section).

Owing to their former colonial links, the Philippines and the United States enjoy a special—although occasionally stormy—diplomatic relationship. Nationalist sentiment forced the United States to close its last military bases in the Philippines in 1992, although in 2002 U.S. "advisers" were invited to assist in the government's long-running fight against Muslim insurgents in southern islands. U.S. financial aid to its former colony has been substantial.

Demographics

The population of the Philippines is around 82 million. Most Filipinos live on just 11 of the archipelago's 7,000 islands, and over 10 million live in the capital, Manila.

Languages

The Philippines' two official languages are Pilipino (based on the Tagalog language) and English, but the archipelago has a complex linguistic composition. Tagalog is 1 of 10 or more "languages" and 80 or more "dialects," although linguistic classifications vary depending on largely politicized definitions of what distinguishes a language from a dialect. Although most of the country's main languages are part of the Malay-Polynesian language family, mutual comprehension between them is low and fragmentation into dialects is extensive. Many non-Tagalog speakers question the suitability of Pilipino as a national language. English is widely used in the printed media, in advertisements, and for business purposes. The term Taglish has been coined to describe a local language that mixes Tagalog and English.

Education is important to Filipinos. Despite the country's extensive poverty, literacy is around 95 percent for both men and women.

Politics

The Republic of the Philippines is a democracy and has its capital in Manila. The president serves as both head of state and head of government. The parliament has a bicameral structure, and members of both chambers are elected by popular vote. A striking feature of Philippine politics is the role of "people power," which toppled two presidents within 15 years in the late twentieth century. In 1986, Ferdinand Marcos stepped down following massive street demonstrations, while in 2001 it was the turn of Joseph Estrada (born 1937) to be ousted from power as a result of popular protests.

Marcos dominated politics from 1965, when he was elected president. After his 1972 proclamation of martial law, he ruled as a virtual dictator. Following his fall from power he was accused of corruption amounting to billions of dollars of pocketed public funds. His ambitious wife Imelda was the subject of lurid media reports of luxurious living and huge shoe collections, and her lifestyle was contrasted with the desperately poor conditions of most of the country's inhabitants. More seriously, perhaps, democratic culture was damaged by Marcos' militarized politics, but the country's democratic credentials have started to improve in recent years.

A continuing political problem is armed Muslim rebellion in the southern islands of the archipelago. Some estimates of the death toll from this conflict in the last quarter of the twentieth century exceed 100,000. Hostage taking by separatist groups has grabbed world headlines on numerous occasions, and in 2002, the United States provided military assistance to the Philippine government in its counterinsurgency struggle.

Economy

Philippine aspirations to be one of the Asian tiger economies led the country to be one of the founder members of the Association of Southeast Asian Nations (ASEAN) in 1967. However, economic progress has been painfully slow, especially in comparison with other ASEAN members such as Malaysia. The Philippine economy is dominated by agriculture, which employs around 40 percent of the workforce, and by light industry and services. The country was badly jolted by the Asian financial crisis of the late 1990s and the government faces many problems in trying to improve the lot of its people: Infrastructure is poor and foreign debt is high. Estimates of the proportion of the population living in poverty reach as high as 40 percent. As a result, many Filipinos seek employment overseas, notably in the Mideast and the United States.

The country's Chinese community is small but punches above its weight in economic terms. This reflects a similar pattern in neighboring countries such as Indonesia and Malaysia. The Philippines' largest trading partners are the United States and Japan, and the currency unit is the peso.

Legal and Regulatory Environment

The legal system of the Philippines follows the traditions of Spain and the United States, its colonizing powers. Governments anxious to promote economic growth and direct foreign investment have increasingly abandoned protectionist policies in recent years. Similarly, deregulation and privatization have been characteristic of recent administrations.

Accountancy

Philippine GAAP derives from the standards of the Philippine Accounting Standards Council (PASC) and (for listed corporations) the rules and regulations of the Philippine Securities and Exchange Commission. Traditionally, there have been considerable inconsistencies between Philippine GAAP and IAS, in areas such as acquisition accounting, lease accounting, and the treatment of research and development costs. The PASC is now consciously framing new accounting standards in conformity with IAS, and revising old ones to ensure consistency with IAS. GAAP differences can therefore be expected to narrow in the future. Details of the adoption of IAS in the Philippines are available from the Web site of the Philippine Institute of Certified Public Accountants (*www.picpa.com.ph*), which is the country's principal professional accountancy and external auditing body.

Cultural Background

Centuries of intermarriage between the islands' ethnic groups—Malays, Negritos, Chinese, and Spanish—have led to a relatively homogenous ethnic composition. Although an important community in economic terms, the Chinese account for less than 2 percent of the population. Around 92 percent of Filipinos are Christians, and mainly Roman Catholics. Muslims total less than 5 percent of the population, but Muslim armed separatism in the southern islands has been a long-running problem.

Despite the vast scale of the country and its thousands of islands, there has been a surprisingly limited degree of cultural fragmentation. Consciousness of a national identity transcending linguistic differences emerged in the late nineteenth century in opposition to colonialism. The Christian religion is perhaps the country's main unifying factor, and centuries of intermarriage between different ethnic groups appear to have created a generally tolerant culture. Other than a serious Muslim insurgency in parts of the south, the Philippines has not suffered the fissiparous tendencies of neighboring Indonesia.

Social Etiquette

- The country's business culture is relatively hierarchical, and the visitor may be required to meet more junior employees of an organization before being permitted to approach a person of appropriate seniority.
- The use of the word "yes" is not always a precise affirmative. It may be used as a polite way to say "no," and the visitor should be careful in ascertaining the intention of the word in specific contexts!
- Business entertaining at home is very common.

Further Information

Rupert Hodder, *Between Two Worlds—Society, Politics, and Business in the Philippines* (New York and London: Routledge, 2002).

David C. Kang, *Crony Capitalism: Corruption and Development in South Korea and the Philippines* (New York and Cambridge: Cambridge University Press, 2002).

Republic of the Philippines: *www.gov.ph.*

Philippine Institute of Certified Public Accountants: *www.picpa.com.ph.*

SOUTH KOREA

Geography

South Korea comprises the southern half of the Korean Peninsula, which borders the Sea of Japan and the Yellow Sea. Covering approximately 45 percent of the peninsula, South Korea is hilly and mountainous, with coastal plains in the west and south. Forests and woodland cover two-thirds of the territory. South Korea only has one land border, with its political rival North Korea. The country experiences dry, cold winters and hot, humid summers. Annual monsoon rains and occasional typhoons sometimes lead to flooding.

Brief History

Following the Silla Kingdom's unification of the Korean Peninsula in the seventh century CE, the Koreans have tenaciously maintained their separate identity despite pressures from numerically superior neighboring populations. In modern times, the early twentieth century saw Korea subjected to colonization by Japan, as the Japanese used the Korean Peninsula as a stepping-stone for expansion in the Asian mainland.

Korea's post-1945 history was shaped by the ideological Cold War that gripped many parts of the world. The United States and the Soviet Union were unable to agree on a settlement for Korea at the end of World War II, and a civil war erupted within five years of liberation from the Japanese. International powers were drawn into the Korean War, which became a microcosm of the larger global struggle between communism and western democracy.

The U.S.-supported Republic of Korea was proclaimed in August 1948, with its power base in the south, but north-based communists invaded it two years later. The resulting war lasted from 1950 to 1953. The communist North Koreans enjoyed Soviet and Chinese backing, while the United States and its allies in the United Nations supported the anticommunist South Koreans. The United States feared that inaction in Korea would be interpreted as appeasement of communism elsewhere in the world, and was determined to protect South Korea. The United States successfully contained communism to the northern half of the peninsula, which was partitioned along ideological lines. Two antagonistic states therefore emerged from the war—communist North Korea and the western-oriented Republic of South Korea. The border between the two Koreas is often referred to by its geographical location, the 38th parallel.

The war devastated the Korean Peninsula, much of which was reduced to rubble. However, South Korea quickly bounced back and built up its industrial capacity to generate a massive rise in living standards. In contrast, the reclusive and totalitarian north fell into serious poverty, with reports of starvation by the close of the twentieth century.

In June 2000, an important and symbolic summit took place between the leaders of the two Koreas. The summit was widely interpreted as a sign of potential future reduction of tensions on the peninsula, but at the time of writing, the Korean Peninsula is one of the few parts of the world where oldstyle Cold War divisions remain intact. The 38th parallel continues to be one of the world's most politically tense hotspots.

Demographics

South Korea's population of around 48 million is ethnically homogeneous, other than for very small numbers of inhabitants of Chinese descent. The largest city is Seoul, which has more than a quarter of the country's population. The government started family planning policies in the 1960s that focused on the promotion of the one-child family. Tax breaks and other incentives for smaller families were so successful that by the 1990s, the Korean government was concerned about future labor shortages.

Language

Virtually all Koreans speak the Korean language as a mother tongue. The origins of the Korean language are disputed by scholars, as Korean is not clearly linked to any linguistic family. Korean grammar is quite distinct from that of Chinese, although up to 50 percent of Korean vocabulary is estimated to be of Chinese origin. Some scholars have identified affinities between Korean and Japanese, but a common historical origin has not been proven. The Korean language has a phonetically based writing system that dates from the fifteenth century CE. Koreans also make some use of Chinese characters, although not to the extent seen in Japan.

The Koreans are fiercely proud of their language, partially as a reaction against its suppression by the Japanese before and during World War II. In that era, Korean-language newspapers were closed and schoolchildren heard to speak Korean were punished. Unsurprisingly, the Korean language became a crucial symbol of cultural independence. Virtually the entire population is literate.

Politics

South Korea is officially called the Republic of Korea (often abbreviated to ROK), and its capital is in Seoul. In contrast to its totalitarian northern rival, it is a democracy, albeit one with a turbulent and checkered history. (The military, for example, dissolved the country's First Republic in 1960.) The South Korean parliament is unicameral and its members are elected by popular vote. The head of state is the president, and the head of government is the prime minister.

After its creation in 1948, the Republic of Korea experienced four decades of authoritarian government, including military rule. Despite these political shortcomings, the postwar era provided the political stability on which the country built its astonishing economic success. In recent years, the South Koreans have attempted to further democratize their political processes. Notable features of South Korean politics include massive (and often violent) student protests, a key role for the military, and the influence of large industrial conglomerates.

The continuing Cold War with North Korea dominates the country's political agenda. At the time of writing, more than 35,000 U.S. troops remain in South Korea to assist in the country's defense.

Economy

Following the devastation of the Korean War that ended in 1953, South Korea's rapid economic growth was little short of miraculous. By the 1990s, the country had become one of the most affluent in the world, and it became a model Asian tiger. The Korean business environment has been dominated by its oligopolistic *chaebol*. The *chaebol* are massive, diversified business conglomerates that tend to be family-controlled. They usually enjoy close political connections. The *chaebol* led Korea's export drive in the late twentieth century, through which Korean automobiles and electronic goods became popular around the globe. The country's steel and shipbuilding industries also came to be among the world's largest.

Structural economic problems were painfully highlighted during the Asian financial crisis that started in 1997. South Korea suffered a severe economic recession, caused by a combination of high corporate debt, massive foreign borrowing, and poor banking disciplines. As a result of the economic shocks of the late 1990s, the government has started a program of reforming both the *chaebol* and the wider economy.

The United States and Japan are South Korea's largest trading partners, and the currency unit is the won.

Legal and Regulatory Environment

Korean assimilation of foreign laws appears to be a long-standing cultural pattern. South Korea's current legal system combines elements of traditional Chinese jurisprudence, continental European civil law, and U.S. law. The Japanese occupiers of the early twentieth century (who were then assimilating western business culture) initially brought western influences to Korea. U.S. influence has been marked since the end of the Korean War in 1953, and is reflected in the country's Commercial Code of 1962.

Accountancy

South Korean accounting has traditionally been shaped by European norms, as introduced by the Japanese during the colonial years of the early twentieth century. In common with continental European practice, tax law has tended to drive Korean accountancy practice. However, U.S. influence after 1945 led to the establishment of a Securities and Exchange Commission, whose Accounting System Deliberation Committee issued accounting standards.

In 1999 a new accounting standards body was established, the Korea Accounting Standards Board (KASB). The KASB's Web site (*www.kasb.or.kr/eng-home.nsf*) declares its intention of converging South Korean GAAP with IAS, and it gives up-to-date details of Korean accounting standards in English. At the time of writing, there are still differences between Korean GAAP and IAS, including lease accounting and the treatment of employee benefits. Over time, however, Korean GAAP is expected to move closer to IAS.

The country's principal external auditing body is the Korean Institute of Certified Public Accountants (KICPA), founded in 1954. The KICPA currently has around 5,000 members.

Cultural Background

Geographically poised between China and Japan, Korea has tenaciously retained its separate cultural identity. However, cultural influences from its neighbors have been inevitable. Korea followed the Chinese pattern of successive dynasties rather than developing a single, Japanese-style imperial line. Korea also received important religious and philosophical ideas from (or via) China, such as Confucianism and Buddhism. In modern times, the Korean experience of Japanese occupation has reinforced a strong determination to maintain a separate national identity. Around 50 percent of South Koreans are Christians, which gives South Korea the second largest proportion of Christians in Asia (after the Philippines). Most of the rest of the population is Buddhist.

Education is of massive importance in Korean culture. Large numbers of Koreans undertake third-level education, and many Koreans take doctorates in the United States.

Social Etiquette

- Koreans enjoy after-hours business entertaining. Socializing centers on restaurants and bars, and it is common to go straight from the office to a social venue. Business visitors should be prepared for long days (and evenings)!

- One should generally avoid overboisterous behavior in Korea, although nowadays many younger Koreans often act in this manner when socializing.

- One should be careful not to overtly admire any item belonging to a business contact, as he or she may feel obliged to part with the item as a gift.

- One should avoid red ink when writing people's names, as it is a color associated with death.

- One should avoid comparisons of Korea with neighboring countries—especially Japan. Koreans are fiercely proud of their cultural identity, and take offense at being casually bracketed with surrounding nations.

Further Information

David C. Kang, *Crony Capitalism: Corruption and Development in South Korea and the Philippines* (New York and Cambridge: Cambridge University Press, 2002).

Byung-Nak Song, *The Rise of the Korean Economy*, 3rd ed. (New York and Hong Kong: Oxford University Press, 2001).

William Stuck, *The Korean War* (Princeton, NJ: Princeton University Press, 1997).

Office of the Korean President: *www.cwd.go.kr/english*.

Office of the Korean Prime Minister: *www.opm.go.kr/home/english/home.htm*.

Korean Accounting Standards Board: *www.kasb.or.kr/enghome.nsf*.

Korean Institute of Certified Public Accountants: *http://kicpa.or.kr/english/default.htm*.

SRI LANKA

Geography

Sri Lanka is a tropical island in the Indian Ocean, located to the southeast of India. It is often described as "tear-shaped." This is a sadly apt comparison, given the country's tragic recent past (as discussed in the "Brief History" and "Politics" sections). Much of the country's terrain comprises flat and rolling plains, although there are mountains in the island's interior. Forests cover one-third of the country. The climate is characterized by monsoons at different times of the year—the northeast monsoon lasts from December to March, and the southwest monsoon from June to October.

Brief History

Sri Lanka's proximity to India has resulted in strong Indian cultural influences throughout its history. Buddhism, for example, arrived in the island from India.

While Buddhism has all but vanished in its Indian homeland, it has remained the majority faith of Sri Lanka.

Sri Lanka was colonized by several European nations. The Portuguese dominated the island in the sixteenth century, to be replaced by the Dutch in the seventeenth. Sri Lanka was eventually ceded to Britain in 1802, and subsequently fell under the web of British political control that stretched over much of South Asia (modern-day India, Pakistan, Bangladesh, and Myanmar). Sri Lanka gained independence from Britain in February 1948, and changed its name from Ceylon to Sri Lanka in 1972.

An existing Tamil minority in the north of the island grew larger during the colonial period, as the British encouraged Tamils to migrate from India to work in tea production and other industries. The Tamil community is markedly different from the majority Sinhalese population, which itself originated from India. Other than differences in language and culture, most Tamils are Hindu while most Sinhalese are Buddhist.

Already-strained relations between the two communities erupted into large-scale violence in the 1980s. Tamil separatists have sought to create a separate homeland in the north and east of the island, and the separatist Liberation Tigers of Tamil Ealam (the LTTE or "Tamil Tigers") have achieved global notoriety for their use of suicide bombings. However, both sides accuse each other of committing atrocities. At the time of writing, the death toll from the conflict totals well over 50,000. A further complication in Sri Lanka's fractured intercommunity relations has been clashes between the island's Muslim community and other ethnic groups. In 1991, former Indian prime minister Rajiv Gandhi was killed by a Tamil suicide bomber, apparently in protest at military support provided by India to the Sinhalese-dominated Sri Lankan government in suppressing the separatist insurgency.

Demographics

Sri Lanka's population of around 20 million comprises two main ethnic groups. The majority Sinhalese community accounts for around 75 percent of the population, while Tamils make up around 18 percent. (The balance of 7 percent comprises several smaller ethnic groups, including a community of mixed Sri Lankan and European descent.) As a result of the civil war, several hundred thousand Tamils have left Sri Lanka for India, where most Tamils live, as well as for Europe and North America.

Languages

Sri Lanka's linguistic patterns reflect the island's ethnic mix. Sinhala is the language of the majority Sinhalese and is the mother tongue of around 75 to 80 percent of the population, while 18 percent speak Tamil. The struggle between supporters of Sinhala and Tamil reflects the ethnic tensions of the civil war, as the choice of official and national languages has a powerful political significance. Sinhala is an Indic (or Indo-Aryan) language with affinities to languages of northern India such as Bengali and Hindi. In contrast, Tamil is a Dravidian language that originates from the south of India. Sinhala and Tamil are therefore linguistically unrelated, and they use distinctively different scripts.

The former colonial language of English is widely used by the middle classes, and is spoken fluently by up to 1 in 10 of the population. Many of the documents auditors may expect to see—such as invoices, contracts, and business correspondence—are in English.

In contrast to the country's South Asian neighbors (India, Pakistan, and Bangladesh), Sri Lanka has a high literacy level, at over 90 percent of the population.

Politics

The Democratic Socialist Republic of Sri Lanka has its capital in Colombo (although Sri Jayewardenepura Kotte serves as the legislative capital). The country inherited parliamentary structures from the British colonial period, and the members of its unicameral parliament are popularly elected. In contrast to the British parliamentary traditions adopted by Sri Lanka's Asian neighbors, in which the president is head of state and the prime minister is head of government, the Sri Lankan president combines both roles. The president therefore enjoys a significant concentration of political powers that would normally be separated under the constitutions of neighboring countries.

The main issue in Sri Lankan politics is, of course, the secessionist war waged by Tamil armed groups in the north of the island. Many peace initiatives have been tried, but (at the time of writing) none has as yet succeeded. The Tamil separatists who control northern areas refuse to accept the jurisdiction of the Colombo government, and they run a parallel state. The Sri Lankan government's de facto authority does not therefore cover the entire island.

Economy

Although Sri Lanka has historically been more prosperous than neighbors such as India, Pakistan, and Bangladesh, its economy has been under strain since civil war erupted in the 1980s. The war has decimated the previously lucrative tourist industry. In particular, many tourists have avoided Sri Lanka since a July 2001 rebel attack on Colombo International Airport destroyed half of the country's commercial airliner fleet. More generally, the war has inflicted serious damage on the island's infrastructure and has eroded investor confidence.

Despite the country's socialist leanings that are indicated in the state's official name of the "Democratic Socialist Republic," the Sri Lankan government has implemented market-oriented reforms in recent years to liberalize and modernize the economy. Textiles, food processing, and financial services are now key elements of the Sri Lankan economy. It is estimated that one in five Sri Lankans lives in poverty, but this statistic would undoubtedly decrease if the current ethnic conflict ended. The country's currency unit is the rupee.

Legal and Regulatory Environment

Like many former British colonies in South Asia, Sri Lanka inherited a legal tradition based on English common law. However, the Sri Lankan legal tradition is quite complex, as it has also absorbed elements of Napoleonic and Roman-Dutch law in the periods of Portuguese and Dutch colonization. In addition, Muslim and indigenous Sinhalese law also form part of the complicated mixture of Sri Lankan jurisprudence.

As a result of the fragile security situation, the Sri Lankan government has promulgated new constitutional provisions and emergency regulations, many of which have enlarged the powers of the police and armed forces. While prompted by the valid need to deal with deteriorating public security, the legal changes have undoubtedly eroded individual civil liberties. As in other South Asian countries, Sri Lankan administration and bureaucracy is relatively cumbersome.

In areas held by Tamil separatists, the jurisdiction of the Sri Lankan constitution is contested, and a parallel system of law and justice operates.

Accountancy

Sri Lanka's accountancy profession developed during the British colonial period. The Institute of Chartered Accountants of Sri Lanka (ICASL) was formed in 1959, and has around 2,000 members. The ICASL is Sri Lanka's principal accountancy and external auditing organization, and it is the country's sole accounting and auditing standards-setting authority. Corporations listed on the Colombo Stock Exchange are required to follow Sri Lankan Accounting Standards (SLAS), and at the time of writing, Sri Lanka does not permit IAS for domestic reporting purposes.

The ICASL seeks to harmonize SLAS with IAS. For example, effective from 2000, SLAS 3 (Presentation of Financial Statements) replaces two previous standards to harmonize Sri Lankan practice with IAS in this area. Details of Sri Lankan accounting standards are available from the ICASL Web site (*www.lanka.net/ica*).

Cultural Background

Sri Lanka is culturally diverse and the island's religious communities broadly reflect the sizes of the different ethnic communities. Some 70 percent of Sri Lankans are Buddhist, 15 percent Hindu, 8 percent Christian, and 7 percent Muslim. Caste is an important factor in both Sinhalese as well as Tamil life, and is discussed further in the "India" country section.

One potentially unifying aspect of Sri Lankan culture is the island's love of cricket. As in other former British colonies, passion for this sport cuts across ethnic divides. Given Sri Lanka's modest population, its cricketing success has been phenomenal, and the country has established itself among the world's elite cricketing nations.

Social Etiquette

The social etiquette section for India is generally applicable to Sri Lanka. In addition:

- The island's ethnic conflicts mean that the visitor should be sensitive to cultural nuances between the different communities.
- Many Buddhists are vegetarians.

Further Information

Ian Bruce Watson and Sri Gramage (eds.), *Conflict and Community in Contemporary Sri Lanka* (Thousand Oaks, CA, and London: Sage, 1999).
Government of Sri Lanka Web site: *http://priu.gov.lk.*
The Institute of Chartered Accountants of Sri Lanka: *www.lanka.net/ica.*

THAILAND

Geography

Thailand is located in Southeast Asia. Often compared in shape to an elephant's head, the country borders Burma, Cambodia, Laos, and Malaysia, as well as the Andaman Sea and the Gulf of Thailand. Its territory comprises mountains, tropical rain forests, and flat plains. Thailand's climate is tropical, with rainy and dry seasons and annual monsoons.

Brief History

The Thai people migrated to their present-day lands from territory now located in modern China. Avoiding assimilation into Chinese culture, the Thais spread throughout Southeast Asia from present-day Burma to Vietnam. Over the thirteenth and fourteenth centuries CE, they established a unified kingdom with its core in modern Thailand.

In modern times, a 1932 military coup led to the establishment of a constitutional monarchy. Known as Siam until prior to World War II, Thailand was the only country in the region to successfully avoid European colonization. However, Japan occupied Thailand during World War II, as the country was strategically placed on the land routes between India and the Malay Peninsula. The Japanese occupiers used slave labor to build the notorious "death railway" through the country. Many of the slave laborers were Allied prisoners of war, and their history is famously recounted in the David Lean movie *Bridge on the River Kwai.*

In the postwar years, Thailand adopted a pro-western stance and turned its attention toward economic development. By the standards of the region (that includes countries with violent recent histories, such as Cambodia and Vietnam), Thailand has enjoyed a generally peaceful and politically stable postwar era.

Demographics

Thailand's population is around 62 million. As in many Asian countries, governmental concern at potential overpopulation has led to concerted family planning policies from the 1970s. These have successfully reduced the country's annual rate of population growth to its current level of less than 1 percent. The capital Bangkok is by far the country's largest city, and contains more than 10 percent of the country's population. An immensely crowded city, Bangkok has acquired a justified reputation for fearsome traffic congestion.

Languages

Most of the inhabitants of Thailand speak Thai or one of its dialects. Thai dialects vary significantly, often to the point of near mutual incomprehensibility. From the seventeenth century, the dialect of the country's central region was adopted as modern standard Thai, and the promotion of standard Thai was reinforced in the twentieth century through mass media and education.

Thai is a tonal language. The Thai writing system is derived from Indian scripts, reflecting the strong influence of Indian culture on Thailand (as discussed in the "Cultural Background" section). Similarly, many words entered Thai from India's ancient languages, such as Pali. In the south of the country, the influence of Malaysia is seen in an influx of Malay vocabulary and the (now receding) use of a Malay script based on Arabic.

Thailand is one of the most literate of Asian countries, with an estimated literacy rate of 95 percent.

Politics

The Kingdom of Thailand is a constitutional monarchy and has its capital at Bangkok. (As an aside, Bangkok is said to hold the world record, in the Thai language, for the longest city name.) The head of state is the king, while the head of government is the prime minister. The parliament has a bicameral structure, and both chambers are elected by popular vote. The prime minister is normally the leader of the party that dominates the lower chamber.

Periods of political heavy-handedness (such as the late 1970s and early 1980s) have been characterized by military involvement in politics, restrictions of press freedom, and the incarceration of dissidents. However, Thai democracy today functions effectively, through a complex multiparty system. Thailand is a key member of the Association of Southeast Asian Nations. Broadly pro-western in political sentiment, there has nonetheless been a rise in anti-western feeling following the financial crisis of the late 1990s. In particular, many ordinary Thais view supranational institutions such as the International Monetary Fund with suspicion, owing to their advocacy of economic austerity measures.

Economy

Thailand was at the eye of the Asian financial storm that started in 1997. The country had enjoyed a period of unprecedented economic growth, with the world's highest growth rate (around 9 percent annually) from the mid-1980s to the mid-1990s. The Thai currency came under intense speculative pressure in 1997, and lost half its value to the U.S. dollar in a matter of months. This led to a general economic crisis that affected the entire economy. Many highly geared corporations faced severe difficulties, and the real estate bubble burst. In 1998, the Thai economy shrunk by over 10 percent.

Thailand's main industries include agriculture, textiles, and tourism. A darker side to the country's tourism industry has been the development of a large sex tourist culture, which has resulted in severe social problems such as child prostitution and an explosion of AIDS.

Around one in eight of the Thai population lives in poverty, and large slums scar parts of Bangkok. Japan and the United States are Thailand's major trading partners, and the country's currency unit is the baht.

Legal and Regulatory Environment

Thailand's legal system has been influenced by many sources. Traditionally India, China, and Japan were the main sources of legal influence, but more recently British, European and U.S. jurisprudence have influenced Thai law. A significant part of administrative law consists of royal decrees and executive orders. In the south of the country, the Muslim population uses Islamic civil law. The regulatory environment is rather cumbersome, although it is considered relatively efficient in comparison with other countries in the region.

Accountancy

Thai GAAP derives from local legislation and from Thai Accounting Standards (TAS) issued by the Institute of Certified Accountants and Auditors of Thailand (ICAAT). TAS are approved by the Ministry of Commerce. Thai GAAP requires financial statements to be prepared in accordance with TAS, and the Security Exchange Commission has further rules for listed corporations. At the time of writing, IAS is not permitted for domestic reporting purposes.

Traditionally, Thai GAAP has been substantially different from IAS in areas such as lease accounting and the treatment of deferred tax. However, convergence with IAS is increasing, and the ICAAT is currently committed to revising and issuing its standards in line with IAS.

Cultural Background

Thailand is located in a region commonly referred to as Indo-China, a term that reflects the area's two most importance cultural influences. In linguistic and other cultural areas, Thai culture shows clear Chinese influence, while Indian influence is reflected in the widespread use of Sanskrit and Pali terminology and the popularity of Indian mythological tales.

The country's main ethnic groups are the Thai (around 75 percent of the population) and the Chinese (15 percent). The remainder of the population includes other Asian peoples, such as the Sikh community that migrated from India in the nineteenth century. As in many other Asian countries, the Chinese community punches above its weight economically. Many Chinese are assimilated into Thai culture and have taken Thai names. In terms of religion, Thailand is an overwhelmingly (95 percent) Buddhist country, and the second largest religion is Islam (around 4 percent).

Social Etiquette

- Thais are very patriotic. This patriotism crystallizes in reverence for the monarch, and under no circumstances should one insult the Thai royal family.
- Emotional self-control is highly prized in Thailand, and one should avoid displays of aggression or over-assertiveness.
- Thailand is often called the "Land of Smiles" and the Thai people value a pleasant disposition.
- Greetings in Thailand are similar to those in India, with the hands pressed together in a respectful prayer-like position.
- It is considered extremely offensive to touch another person's head, and to point with the foot.
- In Thai cuisine, chopsticks are not normally used. Thais prefer to eat with a spoon and fork and, conveniently, many dishes are prepared in bite-sized portions.

Further Information

Christopher Baker, *A History of Thailand* (New York and Cambridge: Cambridge University Press, forthcoming—2003).
Pasuk Phongpaichit and Christopher Baker, *Thailand: Economy and Politics* (New York and Oxford: Oxford University Press, 1997).
Royal Thai Government: *www.thaigov.go.th/index_eng.htm*.
Institute of Certified Accountants and Auditors of Thailand (Thai only): *www.icaat.or.th*.

VIETNAM

Geography

Vietnam is located in Southeast Asia, bordering Cambodia, China, and Laos. The country has an elongated shape, and is only 30 miles wide at its narrowest point.

Vietnam's long coastline runs along the Gulf of Tonkin, the Gulf of Thailand, and the South China Sea. Forests and woodland cover around one-third of the land surface. The terrain is generally low-lying, but there are hills in the center of the country and mountains in the north and northwest. The climate of Vietnam is tropical, with annual monsoons.

Brief History

Throughout their history, the Vietnamese have retained a distinct and separate identity. Vietnam survived centuries of Chinese political dominance and attempted Sinicization to emerge as a separate entity in the tenth century CE. Vietnam subsequently enjoyed nearly 1,000 years of independence until colonized by France in the nineteenth century.

Following World War II, Vietnam faced three decades of bitter military conflict with western powers, involving first France and then the United States. The French tried to hold onto colonial power after the end of World War II but were defeated in 1954 by communist forces led by Ho Chi Minh (1890–1969). The decisive and famous battle that shattered French power was at the town of Dien Bien Phu.

After the defeat of the French, Vietnam was partitioned into a communist north and a pro-western south. From the 1960s, the United States engaged increasing military assistance to the southern regime to resist the encroachment of the northern-based communists. U.S. engagement in Vietnam was intended to curb the spread of communism, and followed the pattern of earlier military involvement in the Korean War of 1950–1953. However, while the United States successfully defended the south of the Korean Peninsula, U.S. political and military objectives in Vietnam failed. The conflict in Vietnam was bloody and vicious, characterized by large-scale civilian casualties, carpet-bombing, and serious environmental contamination that continues to affect the local population. At one stage, U.S. military forces in Vietnam numbered around 500,000. Communist Viet Cong fighters tenaciously used guerrilla and jungle war tactics to wear down U.S. military forces, eventually leading to a cease-fire agreement in 1973. U.S. forces were withdrawn, and in 1975 the communists overran the entire country.

This was not the end of Vietnam's military conflicts. The Khmer Rouge regime in neighboring Cambodia was led by the fanatical ideologue Pol Pot (1925–1998), who murdered millions of Cambodians in a terrifying attempt at social engineering. The Khmer Rouge started to infiltrate the Vietnamese border in the late 1970s, and they drove thousands of ethnic Vietnamese from Cambodia. In response, Vietnam invaded Cambodia. Although China entered hostilities on the side of Cambodia, Vietnam was able to topple the genocidal Pol Pot regime. The fighting continued, however. Pol Pot and his Khmer Rouge fighters regrouped in isolated mountain and jungle areas to undertake a guerrilla campaign against both the new Cambodian administration and the Vietnamese. Vietnam withdrew its military forces from Cambodia in 1989, following a UN-sponsored peace deal.

Since the 1970s, the Vietnamese communist elite has struggled to improve the country's economic condition. Despite some market-oriented reforms, the communists keep a tight hold on political power. In 2000, U.S. President Clinton visited Vietnam in a gesture of conciliation, and although there have been moves to normalize relations, the political atmosphere between Vietnam and the United States remains frosty.

Demographics

Vietnam is a densely populated country with around 80 million inhabitants. From the early 1960s, the communist northern regime implemented family planning policies, which were extended to the entire country after Vietnam's unification in 1975. The family planning program has had limited success but population containment projections have broadly been met, and the rate of annual population growth has now fallen to under 2 percent.

Languages

Vietnamese is the official language of Vietnam. A tonal language related to Thai, it is the mother tongue of the vast majority of the country's people, and is widely understood among Vietnam's ethnic minorities. An indigenous writing system was abandoned during the French colonial period, when the Vietnamese language came to be written in a Roman script devised by European Christian missionaries. Minority languages are spoken mainly in border areas, and include Khmer. The former colonial language of French is declining in popularity as schoolchildren and students increasingly turn to English as a second language. Around 95 percent of the population are literate.

Politics

The Socialist Republic of Vietnam is a communist state and has its capital at Hanoi. The head of state is the president, and the head of government is the prime minister. The president appoints the prime minister from the members of the country's unicameral National Assembly. The National Assembly is elected by popular vote but, of course, the ruling communists control the lists of candidates eligible to stand for election.

Economy

The Vietnamese economy has suffered from the effects of inefficient command structures, the destruction of decades of war, and the loss of Russian financial support following the collapse of the Soviet Union. As in China, the communist elite realized in the 1980s that market-oriented reforms were needed to stimulate the economy, but these initiatives have to date been relatively modest. The Asian financial crisis that started in 1997 appears to have cooled the Vietnamese communists' faith in market forces. The pace of political reform has lagged behind economic reform.

Up to 40 percent of the population lives in poverty, and remittances from overseas Vietnamese (mainly in the United States and Europe) have played an important role in the economy in recent years. Around two-thirds of the workforce is employed in the agricultural sector, and Vietnam is self-sufficient in food. The country's currency unit is the dong.

Legal and Regulatory Environment

Vietnamese law is based on a mixture of communist legal theory, indigenous Confucian-based practices, and continental European jurisprudence. The French colonial period saw the introduction of the *Code Napoléon* and European-style commercial and civil legal practices. As in all communist countries, however, the legal system is in large measure a politicized tool that directly serves the communists' social and economic policies. Regulatory bureaucracy is generally cumbersome.

Accountancy

Vietnamese accountancy practice in the communist era has reflected traditional command economy patterns of resource allocation. However, the need to attract foreign investment has led to the development of more westernized accounting in recent years. Modern Vietnamese GAAP is based on the Vietnamese Accounting System (VAS), issued by the Ministry of Finance (MOF). The VAS sets out accounting principles, and recognition and reporting criteria. The MOF also issues accounting standards that consciously follow IAS, and external auditing standards that follow ISA. The standards are applicable to all corporations in Vietnam, although foreign companies are allowed to use their national GAAP provided they have MOF authorization.

Cultural Background

The Vietnamese are the largest ethnic group in Vietnam, accounting for 85 to 90 percent of the population. There are more than 30 recognized ethnic minorities, located mainly in mountainous or border areas. The Hoa Chinese are the largest minority at around 2 percent of the total population, and their economic success parallels that of minority Chinese communities in other Asian countries such as Indonesia and Malaysia. Many of the so-called "boat people" who tried to leave Vietnam by perilous sea journeys in the late twentieth century were ethnic Chinese anxious to escape an environment in which their community's economic success was viewed with suspicion.

Confucianism's respect for hierarchy, seniority, and social status has historically influenced Vietnamese culture. The communist period, however, has seen an influx of western socialist ideology that has added another complex layer to Vietnamese society. The country's communist leaders have tolerated—although hardly encouraged—religious activity. Most Vietnamese are Buddhists, but the country also has Daoist, Christian, and Muslim communities.

Social Etiquette

- Visitors should be careful when discussing Vietnam's recent wars, especially the brutal war against the United States in the 1960s and 1970s. The death and injury tolls from the war were high, and it is easy to unwittingly cause distress when discussing this sensitive topic.
- Boastful attitudes during business dealings are considered ill mannered.
- Vietnamese business culture tends to be more formal than in the West.
- Business dealings are often centered on meals.

Further Information

Binh Tran-Nam and Chi Do Pham (eds.), *The Vietnamese Economy—Awakening the Dormant Dragon* (New York and London: Routledge, 2002).

Larry H. Addington, *America's War in Vietnam: A Short Narrative History* (Bloomington: Indiana University Press, 2000).

National Assembly of the Socialist Republic of Vietnam: *www.na.gov.vn/english/index.html*.

Europe

TAX HAVENS AND INVESTMENT CENTERS: ANDORRA, THE CHANNEL ISLANDS, LIECHTENSTEIN, AND MONACO

ANDORRA

The Principality of Andorra is a tiny, landlocked state located in the mountainous region between Spain and France. With a population of around only 65,000, the country receives 9 million tourists annually, many of whom are attracted by the principality's duty-free shopping. Tourism accounts for around 80 percent of GDP. The official language is Catalan (a regional language of Spain), and Spanish and French are also widely spoken.

For centuries an impoverished backwater, Andorra has become prosperous as a result of both the tourism boom and a significant banking sector. The latter has been attracted to the principality by a light tax and regulatory environment. Andorra also benefits from membership of the EU Customs Union, although for agricultural products EU tariffs apply for food imports and exports. The currency unit is the euro.

Further Information

Jorri D. Duursma, *Fragmentation and the International Relations of Micro-States: Self-determination and Statehood* (New York and Cambridge: Cambridge University Press, 1996) [Includes a chapter on Andorra].

Laidia Armengol Vila, *Approach to the History of Andorra* (Andorra: Institut d'Estudis Andorrans, 1990).

Government of Andorra: *www.andorra.ad/angles/index.htm*.

THE CHANNEL ISLANDS

Jersey and Guernsey are English-speaking British Crown Dependencies, and the most important of the Channel Islands located off the coast of northern France. They were the only part of British territory to be occupied by Germany during World War II. Today, with a population of around 90,000 for Jersey and 65,000 for Guernsey, the two islands punch over their weight economically. The islands' legal systems are based on English common law, and UK GAAP applies. In addition to the Jersey and Guernsey pounds, British currency is accepted on the islands.

Although Jersey in particular has important agricultural and tourism sectors, the wealth of both islands is built on international financial services, which account for more than 50 percent of GDP. A light tax and regulatory regime has encouraged millions of Britons to open tax-free savings accounts. In recent years, however, both Crown Dependencies have been under pressure from Britain, the EU, and the OECD to amend its laws and regulations. The amendments are intended to increase the transparency of financial activities, and to reduce the likelihood of tax evasion.

Further Information

Charles Cruickshank, *The German Occupation of the Channel Islands* (New York and Oxford: Oxford University Press, 1979).
Government of Guernsey: *www.gov.gg.*
Government of Jersey: *www.jersey.gov.uk.*

LIECHTENSTEIN

The Principality of Liechtenstein is a tiny, landlocked country of around 33,000 inhabitants, located between Austria and Switzerland. German is the principality's main language, and the Swiss franc has served as the currency since the end of World War I. Liechtenstein has achieved considerable prosperity through its light tax and regulatory regimes and is home to approximately 75,000 so-called "letter box" companies. However, amid concern over the potential for money laundering, pressure from the EU and the OECD has encouraged the principality to beef up its regulatory controls. Banking secrecy is no longer as opaque as it once was.

Further Information

James Bentley, *The House of Liechtenstein* (London: Weidenfeld and Nicolson, 1988).
Jorri D. Duursma, *Fragmentation and the International Relations of Micro-States: Self-determination and Statehood* (New York and Cambridge: Cambridge University Press, 1996) [Includes a chapter on Liechtenstein].
Principality of Liechtenstein: *www.liechtenstein.li/lisite/html/liechtenstein/index .html.en.*

MONACO

The French-speaking Principality of Monaco is located on the French Mediterranean coast, close to Italy. It shares its land border with France. Monaco's population is only 33,000, but its wealthy and glamorous image is world famous. The principality's prosperity was initially built on gambling, and its casinos still attract a huge tourist influx. In recent years, low business taxes and a light regulatory regime have attracted significant financial services activity, and corporations and wealthy individuals have taken advantage of Monaco's banking secrecy laws. However, in recent years, France, the EU, and the OECD have all pressured the principality to make its regulatory environment more transparent, to diminish the likelihood of money laundering and tax evasion. Monaco has established a customs integration with neighboring France, and the euro is the principality's currency.

Further Information

Jorri D. Duursma, *Fragmentation and the International Relations of Micro-States: Self-determination and Statehood* (New York and Cambridge: Cambridge University Press, 1996) [Includes a chapter on Monaco].

John Glatt, *The Royal House of Monaco: Dynasty of Glamour, Tragedy, and Scandal* (New York: St. Martin's Press, 1998).

Government of Monaco: *www.gouv.mc/PortGb*.

AUSTRIA

Geography

Austria is a landlocked country in central Europe that shares borders with the Czech Republic, Germany, Hungary, Italy, Slovakia, Slovenia, and Switzerland. Austria's most distinguished physical features are the mountains of the west, which include the Alps. The eastern part of the country is comprised mainly of lowlands. Forests and woodland cover around 40 percent of the land, and the Danube river runs through the west of the country. The Austrian climate is temperate, with cold winters.

Brief History

Austria's early history has much in common with that of Germany (as discussed in the "Germany" country section). The River Danube was for many years the northern frontier of the Roman Empire. With the disintegration of the Roman Empire in the fifth century CE, Germanic tribes surged from their heartland to sweep across the former Roman territories, reaching as far as Italy, Spain, North Africa, and England. The territory of modern Austria became a center of complex ethnic movements of Germanic and Slav peoples.

In the late Middle Ages the powerful Hapsburg royal family became known as the House of Austria after moving from their ancestral home in Switzerland. The Hapsburg Empire became a multiethnic state, and it expanded through strategic marriages with other European royal families. In the seventeenth century, the Hapsburgs successfully resisted Turkish expansion into Austria.

In the nineteenth century, Austria stayed aloof from the creation of a pan-German state under Prussian leadership. The so-called "Dual Monarchy" was created that separately distinguished Austria and Hungary within the Austro-Hungarian Empire. The empire comprised two legislatures in Vienna (Austria) and Budapest (Hungary) and had common policies in matters such as foreign affairs and defense. The name of the empire is slightly misleading, as its territory also covered parts of Italy, the Balkans, and the Czech lands. The Austro-Hungarian Empire was known for its civilized and refined culture. Separatist pressures from parts of the empire resulted in periodic revolutionary outbreaks, however, and northern Italy was lost to the newly created Italian state in the late nineteenth century. After World War I, the Austro-Hungarian Empire was dismantled, and Austria became a republic with a majority ethnic German population.

Within 20 years of the creation of the Austrian republic, the country had disappeared from political maps. Adolf Hitler's Germany absorbed Austria in 1938, in a political union known as the *Anschluss*. Austrian-born Hitler had been determined to unite his birthplace with his German Third Reich, and public opinion at the time appeared to be supportive of the political union. The *Anschluss* led to Austria's participation in World War II as part of Nazi Germany.

After Germany's defeat, Austria escaped absorption behind Europe's communist Iron Curtain, and the country emerged again as an independent democratic republic. Officially nonaligned, the country tended to lean toward western Europe. Austrian living standards rose rapidly and it became one of the continent's most prosperous countries. Austria joined the EU in 1995.

Demographics

The population of Austria is around 8.2 million. Several hundred thousand ethnic Germans moved to the country following the redrawing of European boundaries at the end of World War II. In recent years, immigration from East Europe has filled the gaps caused by low Austrian birth rates and labor shortages. The capital, Vienna, is the only city with more than 1 million inhabitants.

Languages

German is the main language of Austria. There are a number of languages spoken by ethnic minorities, mainly in border areas—these include Czech and Hungarian. The country's literacy rate is almost 100 percent.

Politics

The Republic of Austria is a parliamentary democracy and has its capital at Vienna. The head of state is the president, while the head of government is the chancellor. The bicameral Austrian parliament comprises a federal council and a national council, and members of the latter are elected by popular vote.

Modern Austria has a history of political stability. However, the inclusion of the far-right Freedom Party led by the charismatic Joerg Haider (born 1950) in Austria's 2000 coalition government shocked public opinion throughout Europe. Some European states—fearing a resurgence of neo-Nazi ideology—imposed sanctions on Austria, but these were soon lifted.

Economy

Austria is a prosperous country with a sophisticated capitalist economy. The Austrian economy is closely tied to that of Germany, and membership of the EU since 1995 has further strengthened economic links with Germany. Austrian industrial success in automobile parts, chemicals, machinery, and telecommunications equipment has added to the wealth generated by the tourism sector. Germany is by far Austria's major trading partner, and the country's currency is the euro.

Legal and Regulatory Environment

Austrian law is based on Roman law, with recent influences from the EU. Austrian regulation is relatively heavy and bureaucratic, and to boost the country's competitiveness within the EU recent governments had actively sought to minimize red tape.

Accountancy

Austrian GAAP is based on the country's Commercial Code, the regulations of the Austrian Security Exchange Commission (for listed companies), and EU Directives on accountancy matters. As is the case with all EU countries, Austria is committed to harmonizing domestic GAAP for listed corporations with IAS from January 2005. However, since the late 1990s Austria has already taken a flexible approach to the use of both IAS and U.S. GAAP—a 1999 law permits Austrian corporations to follow IAS for domestic reporting, provided that financial statements explain significant differences from Austrian GAAP. In addition, in 2001 the Vienna Stock Exchange announced that both IAS and U.S. GAAP were permitted for listed corporations (and required for some larger corporations). The main Austrian accountancy and external auditing organization is the *Institut Österreichischer Wirtschaftsprüfer*.

Cultural Background

Most Austrians are ethnic Germans. Although precise statistics are difficult to obtain, estimates of the ethnic German proportion of the population range from 85 to

98 percent. The country's ethnic minorities include Croatians, Czechs, Hungarians, Roma (Gypsies), Slovaks, and Slovenians. Around 80 percent of Austrians are Roman Catholics.

The cultural achievements of the Austro-Hungarian Empire are well known, and the visitor to Vienna will be struck by the beauty of the city's imperial architecture. As in neighboring Germany, Austria has a proud musical tradition that ranges from Wolfgang Amadeus Mozart (1756–1791) to the nineteenth-century waltzes of the Strauss family.

Social Etiquette

Owing to cultural similarities between Austria and Germany, the German Social Etiquette section is generally applicable to Austria.

Further Information

Mark Allinson, *Germany and Austria, 1814–2000* (New York and Oxford: Oxford University Press, 2002).

Gunter Bischof, Michael Gehler, and Anton Pelinka (eds.), *Austria in the European Union* (New Brunswick, NJ: Transaction, 2002).

Mark Cornwall (ed.), *The Last Years of Austria-Hungary*, rev. ed. (Exeter: University of Exeter Press, 2002).

Melanie A. Sully, *The Haider Phenomenon* (New York: Columbia University Press, 1997).

Austrian Government: *www.austria.gv.at/e.*

Institut Österreichischer Wirtschaftsprüfer (German only): *www.iwp.or.at.*

BELGIUM

Geography

Belgium is located in Western Europe, with a North Sea coastline and borders with France, Germany, Luxembourg, and the Netherlands. Part of the historical Low Countries, Belgian terrain consists of flat coastal plains in the north. As in the neighboring Netherlands, some of the land is reclaimed from the sea. In the south of the country, the plains give way to hills, highlands, and the Ardennes Forest. The Belgian climate is temperate—winters and summers are mild, and there is rainfall throughout the year.

Brief History

Belgium was created from the southern Netherlands in 1830, and the Netherlands country section outlines Belgium's pre-independence history. Belgium is largely Roman Catholic, but religion has not been able to unite the country's two main ethnic communities. The north of the country (Flanders) is dominated by Flemish-speakers, while the south (Wallonia) is a predominantly French-speaking area. Regional politics has long been intertwined with language politics in Belgium, and the two communities coexist in an atmosphere of cultural and political tension.

Although a small country, Belgium's strategic location between major European powers (Germany, France, and Britain) has made it a major European battleground. In World War I, for example, heavy fighting occurred along the Belgian front lines. In World War II, Belgium was occupied by Nazi Germany. Following World War II, Belgium has emerged as a prosperous state, and as the home of major international institutions such as the EU and the North Atlantic Treaty Organization. The small Belgian colonial legacy is restricted to central Africa, in Rwanda, Burundi, and the Congo.

Demographics

Belgium has a population of 10.2 million. Owing to its small size, Belgium is Europe's second most densely populated country.

Languages

The main languages in Belgium are Flemish (spoken by around 60 percent of the population), French (32 percent), and German (8 percent). The language division is broadly geographical: Flemish-speakers are concentrated in the north, French predominates in the south, and German is spoken near the German border. Flemish is closely related to Dutch, and the two languages are mutually intelligible. Belgian French is almost identical to metropolitan French, but there are some small variations in vocabulary. Literacy is around 98 percent.

Politics

The Kingdom of Belgium is a constitutional monarchy and has its capital at Brussels. The monarch acts as head of state (a largely ceremonial role), while the prime minister is head of government. The monarchy is hereditary. The country's bicameral parliament consists of a senate and a directly elected chamber of deputies. Belgium's complex federal constitution attempts to reconcile the conflicting claims and loyalties of the country's linguistic communities. Political tensions between the speakers of different languages are so intense that, at times, some observers have feared the breakup of Belgium as a political unit. One factor that has contributed to Belgium's continuing unity is the monarch, who acts as a symbol of Belgian nationhood that transcends linguistic and regional divisions. The country has many political parties, reflecting the country's linguistic and ethnic fragmentation.

Brussels is home to the headquarters of the EU but not to its parliament, which is located in Strasbourg, in France.

Economy

Belgium has a diversified capitalist economy with a sophisticated infrastructure. The country's geographical location at the "cross-roads" of Europe makes it well situated to benefit from trade and distribution. Many multinational corporations set up their European headquarters in Belgium, and the siting of EU institutions in the country has led to a large expatriate community. The Flemish-speaking north of the country is Belgium's main industrial area, while agriculture is more important in the French-speaking south. Belgian chocolate and beer are world famous. Belgium's largest trading partner is Germany, and the country's currency is the euro.

Legal and Regulatory Environment

Belgian law is based on Roman civil law and the French *Code Napoléon*. In recent years, EU law has had a major impact on the country's legal practices. Belgium has a reputation for formidable regulation and bureaucracy—the presence in Belgium of heavily bureaucratic EU institutions may have influenced the country's broader regulatory culture. In recent years, however, governments have been partially successful in liberalizing and deregulating the economy. One successful regulatory measure in recent years has been the country's implementation of favorable tax rates for EU-wide corporate "co-ordination centers." This measure has attracted many multinationals to set up regional centers for finance and accounting in the country.

Accountancy

Belgian GAAP is based on company law, royal decree, the pronouncements of the country's Accounting Standards Commission, and EU directives on accountancy. From 1976, Belgium has used a national chart of accounts similar to the French *plan comptable général*. As an EU country, Belgium is committed to harmonizing its GAAP for listed corporations with IAS from January 2005. However, the Brussels Stock Exchange already permits the use of IAS (and even U.S. GAAP) under some circumstances. Traditional differences between Belgian GAAP and IAS have been in areas such as employee benefits and consolidation accounting.

Belgium's two professional accountancy and external auditing bodies are the Institute of Accountants and Tax Advisors (*Institut des Experts-Comptables et des Conseils Fiscaux*) and the Institute of Company Auditors (*Institut des Reviseurs d'Entreprises*). The two professional bodies are closely linked and share a common Web page, which is available in French and Dutch only.

Cultural Background

Belgium's ethnic patterns closely reflect the country's linguistic patterns. Around 60 percent of Belgians are Flemish, culturally close to the Dutch; 32 percent of inhabitants are French-speaking Walloons; and 8 percent are German-speakers. Immigration in recent years has also introduced North African communities to the Brussels area. At least 75 percent of Belgians are nominally Roman Catholic, but a common religious affiliation has done little to reduce tensions between the country's ethnic groups.

Social Etiquette

- Belgians value social status and organizational hierarchy, and this is reflected in business negotiations.
- The country's cultural and linguistic divisions are sensitive topics, and the visitor is generally wise to avoid them in conversation.
- One should not confuse the linguistic or cultural background of a Belgian, as this can cause offense.
- Belgians are justifiably proud of their culinary traditions, and business dealings often center on restaurant meals.

Further Information

J. C. H. Blom and E. Lamberts (eds.), *A History of the Low Countries* (New York and Oxford: Berghahn Books, 1999).

Catherine Labio, *Yale French Studies, Vol. 102: Belgian Memories* (New Haven, CT: Yale University Press, forthcoming in 2003).

Els Witte, Jan Craeybeckx, and Alain Meynen, *A Political History of Belgium, from 1830 Onwards* (Brussels: VUB University Press, 2000).

Belgian Federal Government On-line: *http://belgium.fgov.be./en_index.htm.*

Shared Web site of the *Institut des Experts-Comptables et des Conseils Fiscaux* and the *Institut des Reviseurs d'Entreprises* (in Dutch and French only): *www.accountancy.be.*

Institute of Internal Auditors Belgium: *www.iiabel.org.*

CZECH REPUBLIC

Geography

The Czech Republic is a landlocked country in Central Europe, bordering Austria, Germany, Poland, and Slovakia. The east of the Czech Republic consists mainly of uplands, while the remainder is a mixture of hills and plains. The country's climate is temperate, although winters can be very cold. In recent years, river flooding has been a major natural hazard: In August 2002, historic parts of the capital, Prague, were severely inundated and thousands were forced to flee to safety.

Brief History

The Czech Republic is located on some of Europe's most strategic land routes, and its territory has been a battleground many times in its history. Slav peoples moved into the area of the modern Czech Republic from the fifth century CE, and they established small political units. The Slavs were surrounded by other communities—Germans to the north and west, and the Greek-speaking Byzantine civilization to the east—and they converted to Christianity around the ninth century CE. The Roman Catholic Church predominated in the territory, rather than the Byzantine East Orthodox Church.

In the Middle Ages, Czech territory fell under the rule of the Hapsburg Dynasty, which later became the Austro-Hungarian Empire. Toward the end of the nineteenth century, the nationalist idea of a separate country for the closely related Czech and Slovak peoples gathered momentum. The independent nation of Czechoslovakia came into being at the end of World War I, with the end of the Austro-Hungarian Empire.

Adolf Hitler's Germany turned its territorial ambitions to Czechoslovakia in the late 1930s. Under the guise of protecting the country's ethnic German minority, Nazi Germany invaded Czechoslovakia in 1938. Despite serious misgivings, the western European democracies appeased Hitler and abandoned Czechoslovakia to its fate. Only with Germany's invasion of Poland in the following year did World War II begin in Europe. (Britain's role in the abandoning of Czechoslovakia remains to this day a scar on that nation's conscience, and British politicians often refer to "1938" as the classic example of cowardly appeasement.)

Following World War II, the Soviet Union dominated Czechoslovakia and incorporated the country into the Soviet communist bloc. Czechoslovakia's independence was severely limited, and a repressive and authoritarian pro-Soviet regime stifled political dissent and implemented disastrous economic policies. An attempt at Czechoslovak political liberalization in 1968 was crushed by an invasion of troops from the Soviet Union and other Soviet satellite states. Czechoslovakia finally won its freedom following the collapse of the Soviet Union in 1989. The peaceful nature of the country's transition to a democracy is reflected in the frequently used term "Velvet Revolution." The writer, philosopher, and politician Vaclav Havel (born 1936) was the main protagonist of the country's return to freedom, and his sophisticated and cultured persona symbolized for many the country's dignity in its struggle for independence.

Tensions between the two main peoples in Czechoslovakia—the Czechs and the Slovaks—resulted in the dismemberment of the country in 1993. The creation of the separate nations of the Czech Republic and Slovakia was a peaceful affair, often referred to as the "Velvet Divorce" (a parallel of the "Velvet Revolution"). In 1999, the Czech Republic joined NATO, and it is currently a candidate for EU membership.

Demographics

The population of the Czech Republic is around 10.3 million.

Languages

The main language spoken in the Czech Republic is Czech, a Slavonic language related to Russian and Polish. The Czech language is written in a Roman script, in contrast to the Cyrillic alphabet used by eastern Slavonic languages. This reflects the Czech Republic's traditionally close links with western Europe, and its Roman Catholic heritage. Minority languages reflect the presence of ethnic minorities as discussed in the "Cultural Background" section. The country's literacy rate is around 99 percent.

Politics

The Czech Republic is a parliamentary democracy and has its capital at Prague. The head of state is the president and the head of government is the prime minister. The bicameral Parliament comprises a senate and a chamber of deputies, both of which are elected by popular vote. Czech politics is characterized by a large number of small parties. The country has made a successful transition from a communist authoritarian state to a democratic republic.

Economy

Following World War II, the Czech Republic (as part of Czechoslovakia) suffered from the Soviet imposition of an inefficient command economy. Living standards fell significantly behind those of Western Europe and serious environmental damage resulted from polluting state industries. Since gaining freedom from communism, the country has made major strides in deregulating and modernizing its economy. Major Czech industries include automobiles, machinery, and beer. The country has forged close links with the EU, which it aspires to join. The Czech Republic's largest trading partner is Germany, and the currency unit is the koruna.

Legal and Regulatory Environment

Czech law was traditionally based on Roman law, but the legal system was later corrupted by the unpredictable and manipulative practices of the communist era. Following the demise of communism, the traditional legal framework has been rehabilitated and modernized. The country's rather heavy regulatory culture is undergoing reform to increase the country's competitiveness, which should strengthen its EU candidacy.

Accountancy

Czech GAAP is based on accounting law, the national chart of accounts, and the Ministry of Finance's accounting standards. Czech GAAP differs significantly from IAS in areas such as accounting for business combinations and lease accounting (most leases are treated as operating leases). However, the country's stock exchange requires the use of IAS for listed corporations. The country's main external auditing professional organizations are the Chamber of Auditors of the Czech Republic (*Komora auditorů české republiky*) and the Union of Accountants of the Czech Republic (*Svaz Ucetnich*).

Cultural Background

The ethnic makeup of the Czech Republic is predominately (at least 95 percent) Slavic, with small minorities of Germans, Hungarians, and Roma (Gypsies). There are also small numbers of non-Czech Slav peoples, such as Slovaks and Poles. In recent years, the EU—to which the country aspires for membership—has criticized the Czech Republic's treatment of the Roma minority, on the grounds of allegedly discriminatory policies.

Many Czechs (perhaps 40 percent or more) have no formal religious affiliation, while around 40 percent of the population is Roman Catholic. There are also small Protestant, Orthodox Christian, and Jewish communities (all under 5 percent of the population). The rich cultural traditions of the Czech Republic are reflected in the worldwide fame of the writer Franz Kafka (1883–1924), and the continuing popularity of musical composers such as Antonin Dvorak (1841–1904) and Bedrich Smetana (1824–1884).

Social Etiquette

- Czech business culture is relatively formal.
- Status is important in Czech corporate culture, and it is important to respect hierarchy in business meetings (e.g., in the order in which attendees speak).
- Czechs enjoy socializing and business dealings often involve visits to a restaurant or bar.

Further Information

P. M. Barford, *The Early Slavs* (Ithaca, NY: Cornell University Press, 2001).
Rick Fawn, *The Czech Republic: A Nation of Velvet* (New York and London: Routledge, 2000).
John Keane, *Vaclav Havel* (New York: Basic Books, 2001).
Parliament of the Czech Republic: *www.psp.cz/cgi-bin/eng*.
President of the Czech Republic: *www.hrad.cz/cgi-bin/win/index_uk.html*.
The Chamber of Auditors of the Czech Republic: *www.cacr.cz*.
The Union of Accountants of the Czech Republic: *www.svaz-ucetnich.cz/ predstaveni_en.htm*.

FRANCE

Geography

France is located in the northwest of Europe, and it shares borders with Belgium, Germany, Italy, Spain, and Switzerland. To the north the English Channel separates France from England, to the west is the Atlantic Ocean, and to the south is the Mediterranean Sea. Much of the north and west of the country is flat, but there are hills and spectacular mountains to the east (including the Alps) and the south (the Pyrenees). The French climate varies significantly between north and south: The north is temperate, with mild winters and summers, while the south experiences very hot summers.

In addition to metropolitan French territory, the country possesses a number of relatively small overseas administrative divisions, mainly Caribbean islands. The Mediterranean island of Corsica also belongs to France.

Brief History

The Celtic inhabitants of the territory that became France were conquered by the Romans in the first century BCE. Incorporated into the Roman Empire, many of the Celts adopted the Latin language and converted to Christianity. After the departure of the Romans in the fifth century CE, Germanic tribes overran the country. The new arrivals mingled with the existing Romano-Celtic population and also adopted Latin. The resulting linguistic blend of Latin, Celtic, and German dialects eventually coalesced into the distinctive French language. Among the Germanic arrivals were the Franks, who gave the country its name.

France became a centralized state earlier than most European countries, and Paris has remained the political and cultural heartland of the country for centuries. Indeed, modern France is arguably the most centralized of the major European countries. By far the most significant event in early modern French history was the French Revolution of 1789. This radical rebellion led to the abolition of the monarchy and the establishment of a secular, republican regime. The Revolution led to more than a century of political and constitutional turmoil, with alternating republican and monarchical regimes. The dominant postrevolutionary personality was Napoleon Bonaparte (1769–1821), a military genius of Italian extraction who proclaimed himself Emperor and undertook devastating French expansionism throughout Europe. He also increased the centralization of state power in Paris and organized the codification of French law.

Eventually, France established its identity as a secular, republican state. The country increased in wealth and cultural prestige in the eighteenth and nineteenth centuries, and acquired an overseas empire that stretched from Africa to Asia. In the twentieth century, however, France suffered immense material damage in the two world wars, in both of which it suffered invasion by Germany.

Following the devastation of World War II, France was a leading member of the move toward European political integration that resulted in the EU. Central to the EU's success has been France's postwar reconciliation with its former enemy, Germany. France experienced a traumatic decolonization period, with bloody wars in Vietnam and Algeria. In the latter conflict, the number of dead has been estimated at more than 1 million. Following Algerian independence, hundreds of thousands of French settlers left North Africa to return to France.

In recent years, France has experienced political stability and an impressive economic record.

Demographics

The population of France is around 60 million. Since the nineteenth century, successive French governments have been concerned with the low French birthrate. Without large-scale immigration in the last 100 years, the French population would undoubtedly have shrunk to a much lower level than its current size. In recent years, most new arrivals in France have come from North Africa, while in the first half of the twentieth century Italy, Poland, and Portugal were among the main sources of immigration.

Languages

French is overwhelmingly the country's main language, and it is understood by virtually 100 percent of the population. French is a member of the Romance language family, descended from Latin, although French is quite distinct from Romance cousins such as Italian and Spanish in terms of pronunciation and writing conventions. The cultural prestige of the French language in the eighteenth and nineteenth centuries made it the language of the educated classes from Russia to South America. However, the rise of English in the twentieth century has eclipsed French as an international language. Further, the influx of English words into French has alarmed France's conservative linguistic and literary establishment. The official guardian of the French language, the *Académie Française*, has attempted to bolster French by creating words as equivalents for English terms, but linguistic measures of this nature have had a minimal impact on the day-to-day use of the language.

In recent years, North African immigration has led to the presence in France of several million Arabic and Berber speakers. Regional French languages include the Celtic language of Breton, the Germanic language of Alsatian, and the Romance languages of Corsican (similar to Italian) and Catalan (similar to Spanish). Other regional languages include Basque in the southwest and Flemish in the northeast. In most cases, speakers of other languages are also fully fluent in French. Literacy in France is virtually 100 percent.

Politics

The French Republic is a parliamentary democracy; its capital is Paris. The head of state is the president, and the head of government is the prime minister. The president is directly elected, while the prime minister is normally the leader of the majority or dominant party in parliament. Unlike in most European countries, where the head of state performs mainly ceremonial duties, both the president and prime minister enjoy considerable constitutional power. In recent years, the so-called "cohabitation" of presidents and prime ministers of opposing political affiliation has been a notable aspect of French political culture.

France's parliament has a bicameral structure, with a senate and national assembly. Members of the latter are elected by popular vote. The country has a complex and fragmented political party system that covers the entire political spectrum, from communists to far right groups.

The most important twentieth century French politician was General Charles De Gaulle (1890–1970), who led the country's resistance movement in World War II and dominated the first quarter century of postwar politics. He is remembered for his fierce patriotism and conservative social policies. In the late twentieth century, socialist president François Mitterrand (1916–1996) enjoyed a 15-year period of power, and left a legacy of grandiose, modernist architecture in Paris.

The cornerstone of French politics since the end of World War II has been a firm commitment to European political and economic integration. This currently takes the form of the EU, of which France and Germany have been the major dynamos.

Economy

France has a sophisticated and successful economy, which in recent years has gradually modified its emphasis from a state-driven system to one with a greater emphasis on market forces. Deregulation and privatization have generally been slower than in English-speaking countries, however, and the state continues to play a significant role in French economic life. Governments of different political colors have tended to distrust the unrestrained "invisible hand" of the market economy, and have stressed the need to maintain social equality. As a consequence, French society is notably egalitarian, and there are significantly smaller discrepancies of wealth between its citizens than can be found in neighboring Britain.

France has world-class automobile, defense, and IT sectors. Its agricultural sector is generally archaic and survives only through elaborate subsidy mechanisms, but French agricultural and wine exports have a global reputation. Tourism is also a major contributor to the national economy. The country's main trading partner is Germany, and the currency unit is the euro.

Legal and Regulatory Environment

The French legal system is based on Roman law and is noted for its rigorous codification of legal principles. The *Code Napoléon* (CN) has influenced many surrounding countries, such as Italy and Belgium, as well as former French colonies in Africa. In terms of the general regulatory environment, France has a reputation as a heavily bureaucratic society. In particular, long-established patterns of political and economic centralization have resulted in a Paris-focused regulatory culture. The traditionally important role of the state in social and economic matters has also resulted in a complex taxation system. Visitors from English-speaking countries often find French regulations rather cumbersome.

Accountancy

French GAAP derives from several sources: the country's commercial and company law; the national chart of accounts (the *plan comptable général*); accounting standards prepared by the *Conseil National de la Comptabilité* (CNC) and approved by the *Comité de la Réglementation Comptable* (CRC); and EU directives on accountancy matters. The CNC's Urgent Issues Committee (the *Comité d'urgence*) issues guidance and clarification of existing standards. French GAAP has traditionally differed from IAS in a number of areas, such as accounting for retirement benefits and the capitalization of project set-up costs. The CNC Web site (*www.finances.gouv.fr/CNCompta*) gives details of accounting standards and the national accounting plan in French, with parts of the site translated into English.

As a member of the EU, France is committed to harmonizing domestic GAAP for listed corporations with IAS by January 2005.

The French accountancy and external auditing profession is relatively small, in relation to the size of the national economy. The two main accountancy bodies are the *Ordre des Experts-Comptables* and the *Compagnie Nationale des Commissaires aux Comptes*, with a combined membership of less than 30,000. (There is some overlap between the two organizations.) The small size of the accountancy profession reflects the historic importance in France of state regulation and debt finance, in contrast to the pattern in the English-speaking world of a large accountancy profession servicing the needs of equity markets.

Cultural Background

The French nation comprises a complex ethnic mix that is difficult to disentangle and analyze. Ancient communities of Celts, Romans, and German tribes have been joined over the centuries by immigrants from Europe, Africa, and other parts of France's former empire (such as Vietnam). France is a secular country, and most of her citizens do not actively observe any religious practices. The largest religious grouping are Roman Catholics, and there are smaller Protestant, Muslim, and Jewish communities. France's gastronomic traditions are an important aspect of French culture, and are a matter of intense national pride.

Social Etiquette

- As a daily greeting, vigorous handshaking between men and affectionate kissing of the cheeks between the sexes is highly common. It can often be observed between office colleagues.
- The French are proud of their country's gastronomic traditions. Business dealings often center on restaurant meals.
- Drinking wine at lunch is common practice in business circles.
- When speaking French in a business context, avoid using the familiar word for you (*"tu"*) unless invited to do so.

Further Information

Robert Gildea, *France Since 1945*, rev. ed. (New York and Oxford: Oxford University Press, 2002).

Colin Jones, *The Cambridge Illustrated History of France* (New York and Cambridge: Cambridge University Press, 1999).

J. R. Roberts, *The French Revolution* (New York and Oxford: Oxford University Press, 1978).

Charles Williams, *The Last Great Frenchman: A Life of General de Gaulle* (New York: John Wiley and Sons, 1995).

French Prime Minister's Office: *www.premier-ministre.gouv.fr/en*.

Compagnie Nationale des Commissaires aux Comptes (French only): *www.cncc.fr*.

Conseil National de la Comptabilité (partially in English): *www.finances.gouv.fr/ CNCompta.*
Ordre des Experts-Comptables: www.experts-comptables.com/html/countries/ gb/index.html.

GERMANY

Geography

Germany is located in Central Europe and shares borders with several countries (including Austria, the Czech Republic, Denmark, France, the Netherlands, Poland, and Switzerland). It has coastlines along the North and Baltic Seas. German territory comprises flat, rolling plains in the north, and hills and mountains in the south. The climate is temperate, with cool winters and mild summers, but short spells of severely cold weather can occur in winter.

Brief History

Germanic peoples have lived for millennia in the territory of modern Germany, and they originally comprised a number of tribes. The Roman Empire attempted to subjugate the German lands, but achieved only limited success. From the fifth century CE, following the decline of Rome, the Germanic peoples spread into surrounding territories such as modern France and England.

Before the nineteenth century, German political culture was characterized by territorial fragmentation. Under the loose, overall umbrella of the somewhat misleadingly named Holy Roman Empire, many small states existed in the territory that was later to become Germany. In contrast to France and England, therefore, a unified German state was a late development in European politics.

A major event in world history occurred in the early sixteenth century, when a professor of theology at Wittenberg University, Martin Luther (1483–1546), protested at corruption and malpractice in the Roman Catholic Church. His protest ultimately led to the Protestant Reformation, the schism of western Christendom, and the creation of churches independent of Rome. The Reformation led to violent clashes throughout both Germany and Europe between Roman Catholics and Protestants.

Otto von Bismarck (1815–1898) was the driving force behind Germany's political unification in the late nineteenth century. Bismarck used his power base in the north German state of Prussia to unite the small German states, and the Prussian king became *Kaiser* (Emperor) of unified Germany. (Austria remained a separate state, however, as part of the Austro-Hungarian Empire—as described in the "Austria" country section.) The confused territorial issues of this period sowed the seeds of the twentieth century's wars over definitions of Germany's precise borders.

Germany's defeat in World War I was followed by a period of severe economic and political crisis. From this background, the National Socialist (Nazi) party under Adolf Hitler (1889–1945) achieved power through a mixture of violence and electoral success. Hitler was a radical demagogue driven by anti-Semitism and a hatred of communism. He dreamt of a "Greater Germany" that would unite all German-speaking peoples and subjugate neighboring populations.

Hitler instigated a brutal dictatorship characterized by unbridled violence and military expansionism. In 1938, he arranged the political union of his native Austria with Germany, and his regime's subsequent military invasions of neighboring countries plunged the world into World War II.

The Nazis murdered millions of political opponents and ethnic minorities throughout Europe. In particular, the Jewish and Roma (Gypsy) populations of Nazi-occupied lands were decimated. The Nazi administration is widely considered to have been one of the most evil political regimes ever seen on earth, and its systematic crimes are referred to as the Holocaust.

The Nazi war machine initially overran much of continental Europe, but military over-ambition resulted in Germany being simultaneously at war with the United States, Britain, and the Soviet Union. Unable to defeat the combined might of the Allies, Germany succumbed to military defeat in 1945. Cold War rivalries between the Soviet Union and the United States resulted in the postwar partition of Germany. (Austria reemerged after World War II as an independent and non-aligned republic.)

Following war trials for the crimes committed by the leaders of Hitler's regime, West Germany benefited from U.S. economic aid under the Marshall Plan and developed into a prosperous and democratic member of the EU. In contrast, East Germany (the so-called German Democratic Republic) became a Soviet satellite state, with a totalitarian communist regime and a command economy that led to poverty and environmental damage. The popular anticommunist movement that swept through East Europe in the 1980s led to the formal unification of Germany in 1990. The symbol of the end of the Cold War division was the 1989 destruction of the Berlin Wall, which ran through the heart of the city. German citizens literally demolished the wall with their bare hands to end a half-century of communist tyranny.

The economic integration of East Germany has been difficult, and the eastern parts of the country continue to suffer from lower living standards and more widespread social problems than western Germany. This has been a contributory factor in the rise of far right political groups in the east of the country—a trend that has worried mainstream public opinion throughout Europe.

Demographics

The population of Germany is around 83 million, making it western Europe's most populous nation. Germany has a large surface area and population densities vary: The most concentrated urban areas are centered on western industrial cities such as Essen and Dusseldorf. Demographic changes that have resulted in an aging of the population have led governments in recent years to recruit so-called "guest workers" from foreign countries. Although initially envisioned as short-term residents, many have decided to settle in Germany.

Languages

Almost all inhabitants of Germany speak the German language, although there are significant variations in dialects. German is an Indo-European language and the wider Germanic family includes English and Dutch. Modern standard German is descended from the language used by Martin Luther to translate the Bible into the vernacular language, as the prestige of Luther's Bible cemented the prestige of the dialect of German he used. Germany has small linguistic minorities, mainly in border areas, such as Danish speakers in the country's north. The Turkish and Kurdish languages are spoken by several hundred thousand people, mainly in urban areas in which immigrants from Turkey have settled. The country's literacy rate is nearly 100 percent.

Politics

The Federal Republic of Germany is a democratic state and has its capital in Berlin. The head of state is the president, whose duties are largely ceremonial, while the head of government is the chancellor. The bicameral parliament comprises the *Bundestag*, an elected federal assembly, and the *Bundesrat*, a federal council that represents state governments. German politics is characterized by a large number of political parties, with relatively strong environmentalist groups. The extreme right in Germany is probably weaker than in other European countries such as Austria, France, and Italy.

Following World War II, Germany (initially as West Germany) has followed a policy of military restraint. However, in 1994 the country decided to permit its armed forces to participate in UN and other operations around the world.

Economy

The German economy is Europe's largest, and the third most powerful in the world (after the United States and Japan). Following the devastation of World War II, German economic recovery—in West Germany, at least—was little short of miraculous. German manufacturing has a high reputation, especially in the automobile, heavy engineering, and machine tool sectors. As in many other EU countries, heavy state regulation has resulted in generous social security arrangements.

Discrepancies in the economic performances of western and eastern Germany reflect the effects of decades of communist rule in the old East Germany. Investment has poured in from the western part of the country, but the east continues to suffer lower living standards, higher unemployment, and greater social problems. The modernization of eastern Germany may take several generations to achieve.

Germany's largest trading partner is France, and its currency unit is the euro.

Legal and Regulatory Environment

The German legal system is based on wider continental patterns derived from Roman law. German law differs substantially from English common law, as it is based on legal codification rather than on case precedent. During the Nazi period, law was subordinated to short-term political decisions, but the independent rule of law has been fully rehabilitated. Individual German states operate the lower courts, while the higher courts are established at the federal level. German regulation is generally considered heavy, as the role of the state in many aspects of the German "social market" system results in complex employment and industrial bureaucratic procedures.

Accountancy

German GAAP is based on the country's commercial and tax law, the accounting standards prepared by the German Accounting Standards Committee (*Deutsches Rechnungslegungs Standards Committee—DRSC*), and EU directives on accountancy matters. The DRSC was created in 1998 and its standards, after approval by the Justice Ministry, are applicable to consolidated financial statements. Listed corporations can use either IAS or U.S. GAAP instead of German GAAP. Germany, as a member of the EU, is committed to harmonizing its standards for listed corporations with IAS by 2005. This will eliminate traditional areas of difference such as inventory valuation, lease accounting, and the treatment of investment properties. The DRSC Web site (*www.drsc.de/eng/index.html*) has English-language information on German GAAP.

The German accounting profession is relatively small, reflecting the traditional importance of debt over equity finance. The country's main accountancy and external auditing associations are the *Institut der Wirtschaftsprürfer in Deutschland*, and the *Wirtschaftsprürferkammer*.

Cultural Background

Ethnically, the population of Germany is around 92 percent German. The largest of the minority groups are the Turks and the Kurds (around 3 percent of the population), and there are also smaller communities of Italians, Poles and immigrants—many of them refugees—from the former Yugoslavia. Around 70 percent of Germans are Christians, divided almost evenly between Protestants and Roman Catholics. The balance of the population comprises secular Germans and small religious minorities such as Muslims.

Germany has perhaps the finest classical music tradition in the world, and a small sample of Germany's composers includes Ludwig van Beethoven (1770–1827), Richard Strauss (1864–1949), and Richard Wagner (1813–1883).

Social Etiquette

- German business culture is conservative and formal, and the use of surnames between even close colleagues is common.

- German business culture tends to move at a relatively slow pace, and decision making can be a long process.
- Some Germans speak excellent English, but knowledge of English is not as widespread as in neighboring countries such as Holland or Denmark.
- Germans respect academic and professional titles, and often expect to be addressed by them.
- Germans often make points forcefully, and a raised voice is not necessarily a sign of anger.
- Continuing sensitivities over the Nazi era mean than topics related to it (such as anti-Semitism) are best avoided in conversation.

Further Information

Mark Allinson, *Germany and Austria, 1814–2000* (New York and Oxford: Oxford University Press, 2002).

Martin Gilbert, *Never Again: A History of the Holocaust* (New York: Universe, 2000).

H. J. Hahn, *German Thought and Culture: From the Holy Roman Empire to the Present Day* (Manchester, England: Manchester University Press, 1998).

Todd Herzog and Sander Gilman (eds.), *A New Germany in a New Europe?* (New York and London: Routledge, 2001).

German Federal Government: *http://eng.bundesregierung.de/frameset/index.jsp*.

German Accounting Standards Committee: *www.drsc.de/eng/index.html*.

Institut der Wirtschaftsprürfer in Deutschland (German only): *www.idw.de*.

Wirtschaftsprürferkammer (German only): *www.wpk.de*.

GREECE

Geography

Greece is located on the coast of the northern Mediterranean Sea. It borders Albania, Bulgaria, Macedonia, and Turkey, and its territory includes around 2,000 Mediterranean islands. The islands, many of which are individually small, comprise around 20 percent of Greece's total land area. The terrain is largely mountainous, and the country occasionally suffers earthquakes. The Greek climate is mild in winter and hot in summer.

Brief History

Greece lies at the crossroads of Europe, Asia, and Africa, and has played a central role in world civilization. Around the start of the second millennium BCE, the early inhabitants of Greece arrived in the territory from central Asia. They developed a civilization that laid the foundations for modern western culture. Despite political fragmentation into small and warring city-states like Athens and Sparta, ancient Greece's cultural achievements in architecture, art, literature, philosophy, and politics were astonishingly sophisticated.

The Greeks established small colonies throughout the Mediterranean area, but the spread of Greek culture took off only when the Roman Empire overwhelmed Greek political independence. The Romans eagerly adopted Greek culture and adapted it to their own needs. Therefore, Greek culture spread throughout Europe, the Mideast, and North Africa via the imperial and political mechanisms of the Romans (and through the medium of the Latin language).

Prior to the absorption of the independent Greek states into the Roman Empire, the Greek political world was not always fragmented. Alexander the Great (356–323 BCE) used his power base in the Greek territory of Macedonia to defeat the powerful Persian Empire and to conquer much of the Mideast. His armies even reached as far as India. However, following Alexander's death, the political empire he had carved out soon fragmented.

After the disintegration of the western Roman Empire in the fifth century CE, Greek culture survived through the institutions of the Byzantine Empire. The Byzantine Empire inherited the traditions of the eastern portion of the Roman Empire and was the stronghold of Eastern Orthodox Christianity. From the fifteenth century, however, the Greek communities and islands of the Mediterranean were absorbed into the Turkish Ottoman Empire.

The modern nation of Greece gained independence from the Ottomans in 1829, and since then relations between Greece and Turkey have been tense and sometimes violent. Nowhere is the antagonism more intense than in the partitioned island of Cyprus, where the two ethnic groups live separately. In recent years, relations between the two countries have warmed slightly as a result of mutual aid to civilians following devastating earthquakes. However, territorial disputes continue to raise passions on both sides.

During World War II, Greece was attacked by both Italy and Germany, and suffered a brutal Nazi occupation. Following the war, communist groups made a bid for power, but they were defeated by pro-western forces. In 1952, Greece joined NATO. A military dictatorship from 1967 to 1974 was followed by the restoration of democracy. Following a referendum, the monarchy was abolished and a republic was established in 1974. The country joined the institutions that were to evolve into the EU in 1981.

Demographics

The population of Greece is just under 11 million, and one in four Greeks lives in the capital and largest city, Athens.

Languages

Almost all Greeks speak the Greek language, an Indo-European language related distantly to English. Greek has a distinctive alphabet: The Cyrillic alphabet used for Russian (and for some other Slavonic languages in countries where Eastern

Orthodox Christianity is prominent) was derived from the Greek alphabet. Literacy levels in modern Greece are around 95 to 98 percent.

Politics

The Hellenic Republic is a parliamentary democracy and has its capital at Athens. The head of state is the president, and the head of government is the prime minister. The members of the unicameral parliament are elected by popular vote. In the decades following World War II, Greek politics were volatile and tumultuous, but following the establishment of democracy in 1974, the Greek political process has functioned smoothly. A major domestic political issue that remains unresolved at the time of writing is the status of the partitioned island of Cyprus, which has a large Greek population.

Economy

Greece is one of the poorest countries in the EU, and receives significant EU economic aid. Important industries include shipping, textiles, and tourism. However, agriculture and food processing also remain important activities. Over 15 percent of the workforce works in the agricultural sector—a very high figure by EU standards. The state plays a key role in the economy, although recent governments have made modest moves in the direction of privatization. Greece's largest trading partners are Germany and Italy, and the country has been forced to implement tough economic policies to manage its budget deficit since adopting the euro currency.

Legal and Regulatory Environment

Because of the importance of the state sector in the Greek economy, levels of bureaucracy are relatively high even by EU standards. Liberalization and deregulation measures of recent years have reduced the levels of red tape to a certain degree, but foreign organizations may still find the regulations and tax law challenging.

Accountancy

Greek GAAP is based on the country's corporate and tax law, the guidelines of the country's national accounting standards board (*Ethniko Symboulio Loeistikis*), the Greek chart of accounts, and EU directives on accountancy matters. As a member of the EU, Greece is committed to harmonizing its standards with IAS by 2005, for listed corporations. The Greek government has anticipated the 2005 deadline by adopting IAS (for listed corporations) from 2003. This will eliminate traditional areas of difference between Greek GAAP and IAS such as accounting for acquired entities, and the treatment of deferred tax. The main professional accounting and external auditing organization is the *Soma Orkoton Elegton Logiston*.

Cultural Background

Greece is ethnically very homogenous. Almost all the country's inhabitants are ethnic Greeks, but there are small communities of Albanians and North Africans. (As a lot of immigration into Greece is clandestine, it is difficult to obtain reliable statistics on their numbers.) Around 98 percent of Greeks adhere to Orthodox Christianity, and most of the remaining minority are Muslim.

As mentioned in the "Brief History" section, the heritage of Greece continues to resound throughout the world. Many important buildings in many different countries—such as the White House in the United States—consciously evoke the principles of ancient Greek architecture. The world's greatest early philosophers were Greek, of course, and the thoughts of Aristotle, Plato, Socrates, and others continue to shape the western mind.

Social Etiquette

- The speed of business life is relatively slow in Greece, and the visitor must be prepared to be patient.
- Respect is shown to elder and senior people, and the visitor should avoid over-familiarity in such contexts.
- The Greeks are proud of their culinary traditions, and with good reason. Business dealings are often centered on a restaurant meal, especially lunch.
- The history of Greece's tense relations with Turkey can arouse strong passions, and the visitor should be careful when discussing the topic.

Further Information

Richard Clogg, *A Concise History of Greece*, 2nd ed. (New York and Cambridge: Cambridge University Press, 2002).

Thomas Gallant, *Modern Greece* (New York and Oxford: Oxford University Press, 2002).

Ioannis D. Stefanidis, *Isle of Discord: Nationalism, Imperialism, and the Making of the Cyprus Problem* (New York: New York University Press, 1999).

Hellenic Republic—the Prime Minister's Office: *www.primeminister.gr/index_en.htm*.

Soma Orkoton Elegton Logiston (Greek only, although an unused link suggests future English-language content): *www.soel.gr*.

HUNGARY

Geography

Hungary is a landlocked country in Central Europe that borders Austria, Croatia, Romania, Slovakia, Slovenia, and Ukraine. The River Danube runs from north to south, cutting the country approximately in half. The center of Hungary lies in the low-level Danube Basin and the country's terrain comprises mainly plains, although there are hilly areas in the north. The climate is continental, with cold winters and warm to hot summers.

Brief History

The Magyar (Hungarian) people originated in the borders of Central Asia and Eastern Europe (approximately the territories of modern Russia), and from the fifth to the ninth century CE they migrated west, eventually settling in the area of modern Hungary. The Hungarians trace the political history of their nation from 1001 CE, when King Stephen unified the Magyar clans in an independent state. Around this time, the Magyars converted from paganism to Christianity.

Much of Hungary was later absorbed into the Turkish Ottoman Empire, before later forming one of the two nations at the heart of the Dual Monarchy of the Austro-Hungarian Empire. The Austro-Hungarian Empire disintegrated after World War I, and Hungary emerged as a separate, independent state. In the interwar years, Hungarian politics was volatile—communists initially announced the establishment of a Hungarian Soviet Republic, but by the time of World War II a hardline right wing regime was in power, and it allied the country with Nazi Germany.

During World War II, under pressure from Adolf Hitler's regime, the Hungarian state started to persecute its Jewish population. When Germany invaded the Balkans, Hungary took advantage of the situation to annex Yugoslav territory with large ethnic Hungarian communities. Hungary also participated in the German invasion of the Soviet Union starting in 1941. However, during the course of the war, Hungary was transformed from a German ally into a German political satellite, and in 1944, German dominance became outright military occupation. The persecution of Jews accelerated during the German occupation, and hundreds of thousands of Jews were deported and murdered.

At the close of World War II, the Soviet Union conquered Hungary and drove out the German military forces. Hungary subsequently fell within the Soviet sphere of influence and found itself trapped behind the Iron Curtain of communism. In 1956, under the leadership of Imre Nagy (1896–1958), the Hungarian people rebelled against Soviet control and in favor of democratic reform. The Soviet army brutally crushed the revolt, incarcerating and executing thousands of Hungarians. Nagy himself was executed by the Soviets.

Following the failed rebellion, Hungary remained within the Soviet bloc, and Soviet troops remained on Hungarian soil. In the early 1980s Hungary's relations with Romania (another Soviet bloc country) deteriorated as Hungary accused Romania of oppressing its 2-million-strong Hungarian ethnic minority. The two countries almost went to war over the issue. Ironically, in view of the bloodshed of 1956, many Hungarians were pleased at the presence of Soviet troops in their country, to help deter a Romanian attack.

Toward the end of the 1980s, Hungary played a key role in the collapse of the Soviet bloc. In 1989, the country opened its border with Austria, thereby permitting thousands of East Germans to escape through its territory to noncommunist freedom. Following the collapse of the Soviet Union in 1991, Hungary allied itself with Western Europe. It joined NATO in 1999 and it is a leading candidate for future EU membership. Hungary today is generally considered among the most modernized of the postcommunist European states.

Demographics

The population of Hungary is around 10.2 million. The largest city is Budapest, in which around one in five Hungarians lives.

Languages

Virtually all Hungary's inhabitants speak the Hungarian language. Hungarian is a member of the Finno-Ugric language family and is related to Estonian and Finnish. It is unrelated to the Indo-European languages spoken in neighboring countries, although it is written in a Latin script. As described in the "Cultural Background" section, Hungary's ethnic minorities comprise around 10 percent of the population. Most members of minority communities are bilingual, speaking their mother tongue at home and Hungarian in wider society. Hungarians are reputed to be good linguists, and it is not uncommon to meet a Hungarian with a strong command of three, four, or even more European languages. Literacy levels in Hungary approach 100 percent.

Politics

The Republic of Hungary is a parliamentary democracy and has its capital at Budapest. The head of state is the president, and the head of government is the prime minister. Members of the unicameral Hungarian parliament are elected by popular vote. There are many small political parties, encouraged by a mixed voting system of direct and proportional representation.

Economy

By East European standards, the Hungarian economy is modern and liberal. From the late 1960s (while still under communist rule), Hungary was the first of the Soviet bloc countries to embrace aspects of the market economy. Following the collapse of communism, the private sector has flourished. Hungarian industry is today competitive in EU markets, and the country aspires to EU membership. However, postcommunist hangovers remain—notably in the areas of environmental damage, corruption, organized crime, and high unemployment. The agricultural sector remains important, accounting for around 7 percent of the workforce. Hungary's largest trading partner is Germany, and the country's currency unit is the forint.

Legal and Regulatory Environment

As in all ex-communist countries, Hungary has its fair share of bureaucracy and red tape, and foreign corporations may find the country's regulatory environment heavy-handed. However, by the standards of the former Soviet bloc, its regulatory reform programs have been quite successful. Duty free zones, for example, have successfully attracted foreign investment. The legal framework is based largely on continental European patterns, and has been revised from the 1990s to facilitate the transition to a market economy. The old communist legal framework has been almost entirely dismantled.

Accountancy

Hungarian GAAP is based on the country's accounting and tax laws. Hungarian accounting has long ago shed its communist inheritance, and is western in flavor. However, differences exist with IAS, notably in the field of consolidation accounting, employee benefits, and deferred taxation. The country's aspirations to EU membership are likely to encourage ever-increasing convergence with IAS (which EU countries are obliged to adopt for listed corporations by 2005 at the latest). Indeed, the country's stock exchange regulations already require foreign multinationals and local corporations with activities in other countries to follow IAS. The main professional association for external auditing is the Chamber of Hungarian Auditors (*Magyar Könyvvizsgálói Kamara*).

Cultural Background

Hungary's location in Central Europe and its history as a melting pot for various ethnic communities have endowed it with a rich cultural heritage. Ethnic Hungarians account for 90 to 95 percent of the population, and minority groups include Roma (Gypsies), Romanians, and Slovaks. The Hungarian Roma community numbers around 500,000, and is one of Europe's largest. Around 70 percent of Hungarians are Roman Catholics, and 30 percent Protestants. Other religions have only small numbers of adherents.

Visitors to Hungary usually notice the importance of music in national life. Folk music traditions are strong, and bars and restaurants often have lively and talented musical groups to entertain customers. Many of these musicians are from the Roma community. In classical music, Hungary has produced major composers such as Ferenc Liszt (1811–1886) and Bela Bartók (1881–1945).

Social Etiquette

- Many Hungarians are good linguists, but the visitor should not assume that this holds true for all people in the country.
- Business dealings often center on restaurant meals. Hungarians take pleasure in introducing foreign visitors to the country's foods and wines.
- Professional and academic titles are commonly used by Hungarians.

Further Information

Mark Cornwall (ed.), *The Last Years of Austria-Hungary*, rev. ed. (Exeter, England: University of Exeter Press, 2002).
Miklós Molnár, *A Concise History of Hungary* (New York and Cambridge: Cambridge University Press, 2001).

Maria Schmidt and Laszlo Gy. Toth (eds.), *From Totalitarian to Democratic Hungary: Evolution and Transformation, 1990–1999* (New York: Columbia University Press, 2001).

Hungarian National Assembly: *www.mkogy.hu/parl_en.htm.*

Chamber of Hungarian Auditors (Hungarian only): *www.mkvk.hu.*

REPUBLIC OF IRELAND

Geography

The Republic of Ireland covers around 80 percent of the island of Ireland, located to the west of Britain. (The remaining territory is part of the United Kingdom.) Ireland's terrain consists mainly of plains, with hills and mountains in many coastal areas. The country's rugged beauty attracts large numbers of tourists, and the green landscape has led to the affectionate term "Emerald Isle." The country's climate is temperate and humid, with mild summers and mild winters. Rainfall is common throughout the year.

Brief History

Ireland is thought to have been settled for millennia, but early Irish history is shrouded in mythology and speculation. The Celts arrived from Europe in several waves, especially during the period when Rome dominated most of Europe. Ireland was not incorporated into the Roman Empire, and many Celts moved west to evade the advancing Roman legions. The Celts mixed with existing communities in the island.

After the fall of the Roman Empire in the fifth century CE, Christian scholarship declined in mainland Europe, and was largely kept alive by Irish monks isolated from the wars and turmoil of the continent. After a period of raids by marauding Vikings, the island was colonized by neighboring England. The record of English—and later British—colonialism is at best mixed, and at worst disastrous. The wars of the Protestant Reformation reached Irish soil and the conflict between the mainly Protestant British colonizers and the mainly Catholic indigenous population came to be framed largely in religious terms. In the nineteenth century, British neglect of its Irish colony led to several hundred thousand deaths from famine. During this period, hundreds of thousands of Irish people were forced by economic circumstances to settle in North America.

The famine was also a major factor in crystallizing Irish nationalist sentiment, and in 1916, nationalists staged a relatively small-scale revolution in Dublin. This event—subsequently called the Easter Rebellion—was the catalyst for a vicious war that culminated in independence in 1921. The island was partitioned, as the majority of the inhabitants of the northeast were descended from Protestant Scottish settlers loyal to the British Crown. Vehemently opposed to Irish independence, the northern Loyalists insisted on remaining part of the United Kingdom.

Partition went ahead, although the independent Irish state claimed jurisdiction over the territory of the whole island.

The dominant figure in post-independence Irish politics was New York-born Eamon de Valera (1882–1975). Under his controversial leadership, Ireland remained neutral in World War II, partly in protest at the continuing partition of the island, and in 1948 Ireland withdrew from the British Commonwealth. The country remained largely agricultural, relatively poor, and the Roman Catholic Church controlled social life and education.

The Irish economy changed dramatically in the late twentieth century. After the country joined what was to become the EU in 1973, the emphasis shifted from agriculture to manufacturing, and Ireland became a major location for foreign investment in the EU. In particular, many U.S. multinational corporations started operations in the country, attracted by a well-educated and English-speaking workforce, as well as generous tax breaks. Alongside the liberalization of the economy, Irish social life also became more liberal, with the Roman Catholic Church losing much of its grip on society.

The major political issue in Ireland since independence has been the continuing partition of the island. Successive governments have pursued a unification agenda through peaceful means, but illegal paramilitary groups have emerged to undertake anti-British activities in both Northern Ireland and the British mainland. In response, Loyalist paramilitary groups have also sprung up in Northern Ireland, engaging in similar violent activity in support of continuing union with Britain. The political violence has claimed thousands of lives in Northern Ireland, the Republic of Ireland, Britain, and elsewhere. In recent years, a peace settlement for Northern Ireland—the "Good Friday" agreement of 1998—has aimed at settling differences through political rather than paramilitary activity. The peace process at the time of writing remains tense, but it is still intact.

Demographics

Ireland's population is around 3.8 million, and around one-third of the Irish people live in the capital, Dublin. As a consequence, much of Ireland is sparsely populated. The country's small population reflects centuries of emigration—mainly to North America, British colonies such as Australia and Canada, and Britain itself—spurred by economic hardship and political oppression. As a result, people of Irish descent number many millions around the world. In recent years, the emigration trend has slowed, owing to the effects of the Irish economic boom.

Languages

English is the main language of Ireland, but the Celtic language of Irish (or Gaelic) holds an important place in Irish culture. Native speakers of Irish are modest in number, probably totaling less than 100,000, and are located mainly in rural areas along the western coast. However, the cultural significance of Irish as a symbol of independence gives it a prominent role in the nation's life. Official documents tend to be written in both English and Irish. The literacy rate is close to 100 percent.

Politics

The Republic of Ireland is a democracy and has its capital at Dublin. The president acts as head of state and is elected by popular vote. The prime minister acts as head of government. The Irish parliament has a bicameral structure, and the lower house (the *Dail Eireann* in Irish) is popularly elected. Two large parties dominate Irish politics—*Fianna Fail* and *Fine Gael*. There is little ideological difference of substance between the parties, which are both politically republican and socially conservative. More left-leaning and liberal parties, like the Labor Party and the Progressive Democrats, have only a small presence in parliament but they often hold the balance of power in the complex coalitions of Irish politics.

Economy

The Irish economy has shrugged off its traditional image of rural poverty. Although poverty was the trigger for massive emigration over the centuries, modern Ireland has developed a sophisticated and diversified modern economy. Manufacturing and financial services have now eclipsed the agricultural sector, and Ireland is among the most prosperous of EU countries. Tourism has also been a major factor in the Irish economic renaissance: Despite the country's appallingly rainy weather, the rugged beauty of the countryside and the easygoing lifestyle attract millions of visitors annually. Many tourists are Americans of Irish descent returning to the country of their ancestors.

Irish governments have successfully encouraged foreign investment through a series of tax breaks and similar inducements. Social partnership arrangements between employers and trade unions have attempted to safeguard the rights of workers during the boom years of the Irish economy. The country's phenomenal economic growth around the turn of the twentieth century earned it the nickname of "Celtic Tiger," although there are signs that the period of high economic growth may be slowing. As the economic boom fades, some commentators fear that the social partnership arrangements may come under strain.

Ireland's currency unit is the euro, but the country's largest trading partner is the United Kingdom, which is the largest EU country to have remained outside the euro-zone.

Legal and Regulatory Environment

Irish law is based mainly on English common law, and EU-inspired law has increased in importance in recent years. Ireland's regulatory and tax environment is relatively light by European standards, and Irish governments have successfully attracted foreign investment by simplifying such matters.

Accountancy

Irish GAAP is based on the country's Companies Acts, the Financial Reporting Standards of the United Kingdom's Accounting Standards Board (ASB), and EU Directives on accountancy. Ireland follows the British ASB's standards owing to the pragmatic realization that the country's small size makes it unfeasible to establish a domestic standard-setting body. However, the ASB's standards promulgated by the Institute of Chartered Accountants in Ireland (ACAI) are modified as necessary to take account of Ireland's specific circumstances. A member of the EU, Ireland is committed to harmonizing Irish GAAP for listed corporations with IAS by 2005. The ACAI is the country's principal accountancy and external auditing association, and was formed in 1888 during the British colonial period, but there is also an Institute of Certified Public Accountants in Ireland.

Cultural Background

Ireland's ethnic background comprises mainly Celtic and Anglo-Saxon groups, between which there has been substantial intermarriage. There is also a small Roma (Gypsy) community that numbers several thousand. Ireland's religious makeup is approximately 92 percent Roman Catholic and 5 percent Protestant, with the balance comprising non-Christian groups. These statistics, however, mask changing structures in Irish society—formal religious observance has fallen dramatically in recent years, and a large part of the population is only nominally Catholic.

Although the violence of recent Irish history has been well publicized, it gives an unfair picture of the country. The Irish people have a deserved reputation as fun-loving, talented people, who enjoy the *craic* (fun among friends). The Irish fondness for beer and whiskey is legendary. However, perhaps Ireland's greatest cultural gifts to the world have been literary. The country has produced some of the finest writers of the English language, including James Joyce (1882–1951), George Bernard Shaw (1856–1950), Samuel Beckett (1906–1989), and William Butler Yeats (1865–1939).

Social Etiquette

- The Irish are well known for their relaxed social manners, and this is generally reflected in business contexts.
- The pace of business dealings between the fast-moving capital of Dublin and the calmer environment of smaller towns is noticeable.
- It is best to avoid discussions of the political violence linked to Northern Ireland, as many people have suffered from the so-called "Troubles" and strong views tend to be held on the subject.

Further Information

Tim Pat Coogan, *Eamon de Valera: A Life* (New York and London: Palgrave Macmillan, 2002).

Robert Kee, *The Green Flag; A History of Irish Nationalism* (New York and London: Penguin, 2001).

Senia Paseta, *Modern Ireland: A Very Short Introduction* (New York and Oxford: Oxford University Press, 2002).

Government of Ireland Web site: *www.irlgov.ie.*

Institute of Certified Public Accountants in Ireland: *www.cpaireland.ie.*

Institute of Chartered Accountants in Ireland: *www.icai.ie.*

Institute of Internal Auditors UK and Ireland: *www.iia.org.uk.*

United Kingdom Accounting Standards Board: *www.asb.org.uk.*

ITALY

Geography

Italy is a boot-shaped peninsula in the Mediterranean Sea. In addition to the mainland, Italy also comprises several Mediterranean islands, of which the largest are Sicily and Sardinia. (Corsica, although culturally close to Italy, belongs to France.) Italian territory consists mainly of hills and mountains—the main mountain ranges are the Alps in the north, and the Apennines that run from north to south like the country's backbone. There are also extensive northern plains centered on the River Po.

Italy has several thousand miles of often-rugged Mediterranean coastline, and it borders Austria, France, Slovenia, and Switzerland. The climate is hot and dry in the south, while in the north it is characterized by hot summers and cold winters. Parts of the peninsula are subject to earthquakes, volcanic eruptions, and river flooding.

Brief History

The Italian Peninsula has been a cultural and political center of great importance for millennia. Following a period of dominance by the Etruscans, which lasted from around the twelfth to the eighth century BCE, the Romans emerged as the most powerful political force in the peninsula. The Romans established a huge empire that stretched from Britain to the Mideast. Despite elements of cruelty such as gory gladiatorial sports, Roman rule is generally remembered for its civilizing influence. In addition to the physical imprints of the Roman Empire—roads, irrigation schemes, and impressive civic buildings—the Romans spread Greek Hellenistic civilization throughout most of contemporary Europe and North Africa. In its later years, the Roman Empire adopted Christianity as its official religion, and it spread the religion throughout Europe.

After the disintegration of the Roman Empire in the fifth century CE, the Italian Peninsula suffered around 1,500 years of foreign invasion and political fragmentation. Perhaps the main element of cultural continuity during this period was the Roman Catholic Church. Although the Protestant Reformation that started in the sixteenth century shattered the supremacy of Catholicism in European Christianity, Italy retained its Catholic culture.

Amid the long political fragmentation of the peninsula, important city-states such as Florence arose. These small political entities became prosperous centers of high cultural achievement (as discussed in the "Cultural Background" section). Venice alone became a major power in international trade. Italy was only unified politically, however, in the nineteenth century. Unification meant both the end of foreign occupation of parts of Italy, such as territory in the north that had been incorporated into the Austro-Hungarian Empire, and the end of local, independent Italian states. The latter included the Papal States, where the Catholic Church exercised temporal as well as spiritual power. The political territory of the Catholic Church was eventually reduced to the Vatican City, a small enclave in Rome.

The nineteenth-century unification of Italy is known in Italian as the country's *Risorgimento* ("resurgence"), and its main architects were Camillo Cavour (1810–1861), Giuseppe Garibaldi (1807–1882), and Giuseppe Mazzini (1805–1872). The combined activities of these three very different men brought about Italian unification. Cavour was a statesman who engineered the political creation of the modern Italian state, Garibaldi was a guerrilla fighter who had previously fought in South America, and Mazzini was an articulate advocate of unification who galvanized public opinion through his "Young Italy" patriotic movement.

In the early twentieth century, the main political figure was Benito Mussolini (1883–1945), who established a fascist dictatorship in the 1920s. Mussolini's period of rule lasted from 1922 to 1945 and was characterized by extreme nationalism, the violent repression of dissidence, and a corporatist state that reflected many aspects of the communist ideology Mussolini professed to despise. Mussolini allied Italy with Germany and Japan in World War II, leading to Italy's disastrous defeat and invasion by U.S.-led allied forces.

The Italian state created by the *Risorgimento* had been a constitutional monarchy, but the monarchy was swept away in favor of a republic by a referendum following World War II. Postwar Italy adopted democracy and played a central role in the creation of the pan-European institutions that later became the EU. The country recovered from the devastation of war through a minor economic miracle that raised living standards to levels comparable to the major developed nations of Western Europe. However, economic discrepancies between the north and south of the country have remained an intractable problem.

Demographics

The population of Italy is around 58 million. The country has several major cities with populations exceeding 1 million, such as Milan, Naples, Rome, and Turin. The south of the country has a tradition of emigration caused by difficult economic circumstances (a situation similar to that of Ireland), and many southern Italians settled in the United States in the nineteenth and twentieth centuries.

Large-scale emigration has now ended. Indeed, in a reversal of the trend, Italy is today a magnet for legal and illegal immigration from poorer neighboring areas, such as North Africa and the Balkans.

Modern Italy has Europe's lowest birth rate, and some commentators estimate that unless the trend is reversed the population could fall by 15 million over the next half-century. Immigration may be one means of maintaining the country's population level.

Languages

Italian is by far the most widely spoken language of Italy. Italian is a descendent of the Latin spoken in the Roman Empire, and the existence of many Italian dialects reflects Italy's history of political fragmentation. The differences between the dialects of Sicily and Venice, for example, are quite significant and mutual comprehensibility is not always possible. Standard Italian is based on the language used in Florence, as Florentine literary culture became the country's most prestigious following the work of Dante Alighieri (1265–1321), author of the famous *Divine Comedy*. Minority languages spoken in border areas include French, German, and Slovene. There are also tiny, centuries-old Albanian and Greek-speaking communities in the south of the country. Italy's literacy rate is around 98 percent.

Politics

The Italian Republic, with its capital at Rome, is a parliamentary democracy. The president acts as the largely ceremonial head of state, while the prime minister is the head of government. The bicameral parliament comprises a senate and a chamber of deputies. The Italian electoral system is complex, with a mixture of direct election and proportional representation. There are also a number of senators appointed for life.

Italian politics is characterized by a large number of small parties, which tends to lead to relatively unstable governments. Since the end of World War II, there have been literally dozens of governments—almost one every year. This trend has given the country a reputation for political instability. However, much of the instability is more apparent than real, as many individual politicians remain in government despite the frequent changes of administration. The so-called instability usually has more to do with political musical chairs than radical change.

Italian politics is, rightly or wrongly, often perceived as tainted with corruption and linked to organized crime. Several former Italian prime ministers have been accused or convicted of corruption. However, from the 1990s a series of anticorruption measures and investigations have been undertaken in what has become known as the "Clean Hands" campaign. The campaign is still ongoing at the time of writing.

A major political issue in the late twentieth century was terrorism. The worst episodes of political violence included the bombing by a far right group of the Bologna railway station in 1980 that killed 85 people, and the kidnapping and assassination of Italian prime minister Aldo Moro by an extreme left group in 1978.

In recent years, political terrorism has receded in intensity, but armed extremists still operate in the country.

Economy

After the devastation of World War II, the Italian "economic miracle" transformed the country into a diversified industrial economy on a par with the major European economies. However, Italy's economy is sharply differentiated between a prosperous north and a largely low-income south. Unemployment and other social problems are more pronounced in southern Italy, and successive governments have had little success in reducing the north-south economic divide.

Major Italian economic activities include automobiles, clothing, consumer goods, footwear, and textiles. Tourism is also a major contributor to the economy. Although there are some large Italian corporations, such as the Turin-based automobile manufacturer FIAT, much Italian industry takes the form of small, family-owned businesses. Throughout both southern and northern Italy, the so-called "informal" sector is considered to be significant, although governments in recent years have attempted to reduce the black economy. Italy's largest trading partner is Germany, and the currency unit is the euro.

Legal and Regulatory Environment

Italian law is derived from Roman law, with more recent influences from the French *Code Napoléon* (Italy was invaded by France during the Napoleonic era) and the EU. Regulation and bureaucracy in Italy is cumbersome even by EU standards, and is reflected in matters ranging from relatively inflexible labor laws to a tax system of almost mind-boggling complexity.

Accountancy

Italy is the home of double-entry bookkeeping, which it took from Arabic sources and refined during the era of the city-states in the fourteenth and fifteenth centuries CE. Modern Italian GAAP derives from the country's civil code, the standards (or "principles") of the Italian Accounting Committee (the *Organismo Italiano di Contabilità*—OIC), the stock market regulations of the *Commissione Nazionale per le Società e la Borsa* (CONSOB), and EU directives on accountancy. The OIC was established in 2001 as the country's new accounting standard setter, and it is intended to represent a wide range of interests, including those of the accountancy profession, investors, industry, and the financial services sector. CONSOB is a regulatory body for listed corporations with powers similar to those of the U.S. Securities and Exchange Commission.

As a member of the EU, Italy is committed to harmonizing the country's listed corporation GAAP with IAS by 2005. Differences between Italian GAAP and IAS are therefore progressively narrowing. The Italian accounting standard 30 (Interim Financial Reporting), for example, is applicable from 2002 and is substantially in line with IAS 34 (Interim Reporting).

The main professional accountancy and external auditing body is the *Consiglio Nazionale dei Dottori Commercialisti*, which was founded in 1924 and has a current membership of around 50,000. Another professional accountancy body is the *Collegio dei Ragionieri e Periti Commeciali*, many of whose 40,000 members work in industry.

Cultural Background

Italy's ethnic makeup is complex, as the country has experienced millennia of population movements. During the Roman Empire, the circulation of people within imperial borders led to people from as far away as Britain and the Mideast reaching Italy. Ethnic diversity in modern Italy is often assessed on the basis of linguistic or religious differences. There are communities of Germans and Slavs in northern border areas, and tiny communities of Albanians and Greeks in the south. Unsurprisingly, given the traditional importance of Rome in western Christianity, most Italians are Roman Catholics. There are also small communities of Jews, Muslims, and Protestants.

Italy has an astounding cultural heritage, with monuments and works of art dating from the era of classical Rome through the Florentine Renaissance to the Baroque period. Some of the world's greatest artists have lived and worked in Italy: Sandro Botticelli (1445–1510), Leonardo da Vinci (1452–1519), Michelangelo Buonarotti (1475–1564), and Caravaggio (1571–1610) are but a handful. In music, the works of Gioachino Rossini (1792–1868), Giuseppe Verdi (1813–1901), and Giacomo Puccini (1858–1924) continue to be popular in the world's opera houses. In architecture, few cities can match the grandeur of Rome and Venice.

Social Etiquette

- Italians are demonstrative by nature, and large arm movements and excited talk are not necessarily a sign of anger or frustration.
- Italians place importance on social status, and the use of professional and academic titles is commonplace.
- Italians love food, and business dealings are frequently centered on meals.
- The Italian business environment tends to be rather formal and slow moving by the standards of English-speaking countries.

Further Information

John Gooch, *The Unification of Italy* (New York and London: Routledge, 1986).
Michael Grant, *History of Rome* (London: Faber and Faber, 1978).
Harry Hearder, *Italy—A Short History*, 2nd ed. (New York and Cambridge: Cambridge University Press, 2001).
John Whittam, *Fascist Italy* (Manchester, England: Manchester University Press, 1995).
Italian Prime Minister's Office (Italian only): *www.palazzochigi.it*.

Consiglio Nazionale dei Dottori Commercialisti: www.cndc.it/inglese/default1
  inglese.html.
CONSOB: *www.consob.it/eng_index.htm.*

THE NETHERLANDS

Geography

The Netherlands—popularly called Holland—is a country in northwest Europe
that borders Belgium, Germany, and the North Sea. The terrain is very flat and
consists mainly of lowlands and land reclaimed from the sea. As some of the
country lies below sea level, an extensive system of sea walls offers protection
from flooding. In addition, around 20 percent of the territory is covered by water,
in the form of a huge network of rivers and canals. The climate is temperate, with
mild winters and summers.

Brief History

The Dutch are descended from Germanic tribes long settled in the territory that
comprises the modern Netherlands. The flat profile of the country offers little
physical protection from invaders, and in the early modern period political control
of the area passed between Austria, France, and Spain. A sense of Dutch nationhood was spurred by two developments. First, the country's North Sea coast was
a springboard for international trade and colonization, and the resulting prosperity increased Dutch self-reliance and self-confidence. Second, the Protestant Reformation had considerable success among the Dutch, increasing a sense of
cultural separateness from Roman Catholic rule by foreign powers.

By the seventeenth century, the Dutch had established their independence.
However, relations with the mainly Roman Catholic south of the country were
tense, and in 1830 the southerners created an independent Kingdom of Belgium
(as described in the "Belgium" country section). In World War I, the Netherlands
remained neutral, but in World War II the country was invaded by Nazi Germany.
Events from the brutal German occupation remain in the Dutch collective mem-
ory and the country has been one of the most ardent supporters of postwar European reconciliation and integration, which currently takes the form of the EU.

The small Dutch colonial empire was dismantled following World War II. The
main colony was Indonesia, which achieved independence in 1949. The country's
strong traditions of international trade and global colonial activity have resulted in
a famously cosmopolitan and liberal society.

Demographics

The population of the Netherlands is around 16 million. While this may seem modest, the country's small territorial size makes it one of the most densely populated
nations in the world. A rapidly aging population has led to potential workforce

shortages, but this has been offset by immigration from former colonies and a well-deserved reputation as a welcoming country for political refugees from around the world. The largest cities are Amsterdam and Rotterdam.

Languages

The Dutch language is spoken by virtually the entire population. Some German is also spoken near the German border. Dutch is a member of the Germanic linguistic family, and is a cousin of English. The Dutch have a reputation as extremely good linguists, and it is not uncommon to meet Dutch people with a good command of three or more European languages. Literacy is nearly 100 percent.

Politics

The Kingdom of the Netherlands is a democratic, constitutional monarchy and has its capital at Amsterdam. (The Hague is the seat of government.) The largely ceremonial head of state is the monarch, and the head of government is the prime minister. The latter is normally the leader of the majority parliamentary party or the majority coalition. The parliament has a bicameral structure: The upper chamber is indirectly elected, while the lower chamber is directly elected by popular vote.

Since World War II, Dutch politics has largely been consensual, without major ideological differences between the main parties. In 2002, however, the relatively uneventful world of Dutch politics was shaken by the assassination of the far-right politician Pim Fortuyn (1948–2002), who campaigned on a controversial, anti-immigrant platform. The success of Fortuyn and his followers has been interpreted by some commentators as a sign that the traditional Dutch tolerance of large-scale immigration may be coming to an end.

Economy

For centuries, the Netherlands has been prominent in global trade, and international trade remains an important aspect of the modern Dutch economy. The Netherlands is a prosperous country, which blends free market practices with a strong welfare state. In addition to a diversified manufacturing base, the country is also a major exporter of agricultural produce. Germany is the country's largest trading partner, and the currency unit is the euro.

Legal and Regulatory Environment

Dutch law is heavily influenced by Roman law and its modern French codified descendents. By EU standards, regulation in the Netherlands is relatively light. Less inward looking than neighboring countries such as Germany, the Netherlands regulatory environment reflects a pragmatic desire to facilitate international trade. In labor matters, however, there is significant regulation, and this is reflected in the country's corporate works councils that aim to reconcile the interests of the various "social partners."

Accountancy

Dutch GAAP is based on company law, accounting pronouncements and regulations issued by the Council for Annual Reporting (*Raad voor de Jaarverslaggeving*—RvJ), and EU directives on accountancy matters. Unusual for continental Europe, tax regulations have had little influence on Dutch accounting, which has a tradition of formulating accounting practice on the basis of business economics. To a degree, Dutch accounting traditions represent a compromise between continental traditions of accounting based on tax rules, and the English-speaking world's emphasis on accounting judgment.

As the Netherlands is a cosmopolitan country with a long tradition of international trading, it has perhaps unsurprisingly tended to be amenable to the use of international varieties of GAAP. Dutch corporations, for example, are permitted to use IAS, U.S. GAAP, or UK GAAP, if they provide a reconciliation to Dutch GAAP. (Listed foreign corporations are permitted to use either IAS or U.S. GAAP without a reconciliation to Dutch GAAP.) Further, as a member of the EU, the country is committed to harmonizing its standards for listed corporations with IAS by 2005. This will eliminate traditional areas of difference such as acquisition accounting and the reporting of employee benefits.

The Dutch accountancy profession is mature, and the main professional association is the Royal Dutch Institute of Registered Accountants (*Koninklijk Nederlands Instituut van Register-accountants*—NIVRA), which has around 13,000 members. Another accounting institute—the *Nederlandse Orde van Accountants-Administratieconsulenten*—focuses on management accounting and systems consulting, and has around 5,000 members.

Cultural Background

The Dutch account for around 92 percent of the population of the Netherlands, and the balance consists of a wide variety of ethnic minorities—Indonesians, North Africans, and Turks, among others. The country's traditions as a maritime and colonial power have contributed to a cosmopolitan, liberal culture that (in Amsterdam, at least) is tolerant of prostitution and drugs. Around 50 percent of the population follows Protestant forms of Christianity, and there is a Muslim minority of around 5 percent. Many Dutch people have no religious affiliation.

Perhaps the major contribution of the Dutch to world culture has been in the field of painting, and famous Dutch artists include Rembrandt Harmenszoon van Rijn (1606–1669) and Vincent Van Gogh (1853–1890).

Social Etiquette

- The Dutch business environment is well organized, and punctuality is considered a virtue.
- The Dutch are less formal than their German neighbors, and they tend to enjoy the social aspects of business life.

- The Dutch sense of humor is famous, and often lightens business meetings.
- Knowledge of English in the Netherlands is very high.

Further Information

J. C. H. Blom and E. Lamberts (eds.), *A History of the Low Countries* (New York and Oxford: Berghahn, 1999).
Mark T. Hooker, *The History of Holland* (Westport, CT: Greenwood, 1999).
Simon Schama, *The Embarrassment of Riches: An Interpretation of Dutch Culture in the Golden Age* (New York: Vintage, 1997).
Dutch government Web sites: *www.overheid.nl/info/english.html.*
Koninklijk Nederlands Instituut van Register-accountants (NIVRA): *www.nivra.nl.*
Nederlandse Orde van Accountants-Administratieconsulenten: www.novaa.nl.

POLAND

Geography

Poland is located in Central Europe and borders the Baltic Sea, Belarus, the Czech Republic, Germany, Lithuania, Slovakia, Russia, and Ukraine. Most of the country consists of flat plains, although there are mountains in the south. The Polish climate follows the continental European pattern of mild to warm summers and severely cold winters.

Brief History

Poland's history is complex, turbulent, and often tragic. Poland disappeared from political maps for many years of its history, but the tenacity of the Poles ensured the country's survival. Slav tribes settled in what is now Polish territory in the first millennium BCE, but the Poles date their nation from the tenth century CE. It was also in the tenth century that the Poles converted to Roman Catholicism, which has remained a central aspect of national culture to the present day.

In the early modern period, Polish territory came under various influences—Austrian, Prussian, and Russian. By the nineteenth century, the country was incorporated into the Russian Empire, although a Polish nationalist movement aspired to independence. In 1918, following World War I, Poland finally gained independence after a century of Russian domination. However, in 1939 the country was invaded again—this time by Nazi Germany and the Soviet Union.

The German invasion of Poland was the catalyst for World War II, and the Nazis initially agreed to share Polish territory with the Soviet Union. Later, however, Germany attacked the Soviet Union and took over Poland's entire territory. Extreme brutality and mass murder characterized the German occupation in World War II. Over 6 million of Poland's inhabitants were killed, including 3 million Polish Jews, and millions of Poles were used as slave laborers. The Nazis also selected Poland as the main territory in which they undertook the Holocaust—the systematic murder of 6 to 8 million Jews, Roma (Gypsies), and others. The victims of the Holocaust were transported from various parts of Europe to be murdered in Poland. Today, the sites of Nazi concentration camps in Poland are reminders of some of history's greatest crimes against humanity. These sites include Auschwitz and Treblinka—names that still evoke horror and fear.

Following the end of World War II, Poland fell under Russian control again. The country was nominally independent, but its communist regime was controlled by the Soviet Union. The notorious Warsaw Pact on defense symbolized the Soviet grip on the foreign policies of all its East European satellites. During the communist era, Poland recovered from the devastation of war, in which most of the capital city of Warsaw had been reduced to rubble. However, the economy stagnated under an inefficient, corrupt, and authoritarian regime.

During the communist years, the Roman Catholic Church was a major source of resistance, and the appointment of Karol Wojtyla (born 1920) as Pope John Paul II in 1978 reinforced the country's Roman Catholic culture. The Pope was a severe critic of the Polish communist regime. Another form of resistance emerged in the form of the trade union movement called Solidarity, which gained strength under the inspirational leadership of Lech Walesa (born 1943). Described by some historians as the world's first genuinely working class revolution, Solidarity spread from its northern industrial heartland to become a national liberation movement. Solidarity eventually toppled the country's communist regime, and by 1990 it had won democratic elections. The overturning of communism in Poland was the inspiration for the liberation of much of Eastern Europe from communism.

Since the end of communism, Poland has tried to modernize its economy. At last a truly independent nation, Poland has achieved impressive economic progress (by East European standards). The country joined NATO in 1999 and also aspires to join the EU.

Demographics

The population of Poland is around 39 million, and much of the country's large territory is sparsely populated.

Languages

Polish, the official language of Poland, is spoken by 99 percent of the population as a mother tongue. Polish is a Slavonic language, closely related to Russian. However, Polish is written in a Roman script, in contrast to the Cyrillic alphabet used by Russian. This reflects Poland's Roman Catholic culture and its traditionally close links to Western Europe.

Polish appears to be a fearsome language to write, as spelling conventions often lead to odd-looking clusters of consonants. The Polish name for the Republic of Poland, for example, is *Rzeczpospolita Polska*. However, once the Polish writing conventions are learned, the language is relatively straightforward to read and write. Poland has small Ukrainian and German linguistic minorities in border areas. The national literacy level is nearly 100 percent.

Politics

The Republic of Poland is a parliamentary democracy and has its capital at Warsaw. The head of state is the president, and the head of government is the prime minister. The country's parliament is bicameral, and members of the lower chamber (the *Sejm*) are elected by popular vote under a proportional representation system. The Polish political system is characterized by many small parties. Considering Poland's long experience of totalitarian government, the country has adapted well to the demands of democracy.

A major political issue remains potential membership of the EU. Many Poles are frustrated at the slow process of obtaining membership, as the EU has expressed concern at the potential impact of outdated Polish agriculture and industry on the EU's complex agricultural subsidy arrangements.

Economy

Following the end of the communist era in 1989, Poland has followed policies of modernization, liberalization, and deregulation. By the standards of Central and Eastern Europe, the Polish economy has been successful in attempting to transform itself into a modern capitalist system. However, there are still significant structural problems: Many heavy industries are in state control and are hopelessly antiquated, while the country's infrastructure is poor. Environmental damage from the communist era is severe in some parts of the country, notably in the industrial south. Further, the agricultural sector—which employs a quarter of the workforce—is extremely inefficient. Membership of the EU requires continuing fundamental economic reform. Poland's largest trading partner is Germany, and its currency unit is the zloty.

Legal and Regulatory Environment

Polish law was traditionally based on the French *Code Napoléon*, but was later corrupted by the unpredictable and manipulative practices of the communist era. Since the end of the communist regime, the legal system has been largely rehabilitated. However, the regulatory and bureaucratic culture is still stiflingly heavy—another legacy from the communist era. To enhance the country's candidacy for EU membership, the regulatory environment is being reformed to bring it closer to Western European norms.

Accountancy

Polish GAAP derives from several sources—the country's Commercial Code; accounting and tax law; the national chart of accounts; the pronouncements of the country's Accounting Standards Committee; and the regulations of the Polish Securities and Exchange Commission (for listed corporations). Polish GAAP has traditionally differed significantly from IAS, owing to the legacy of the communist command economy. Although the desire to modernize the Polish economy has led to the gradual adoption of western accountancy practices, progress has been relatively slow and in the 1990s some of the complex legislation on accounting matters was contradictory. Such inconsistencies have now largely been resolved.

In the absence of specific Polish accounting rules in an area, compliance with IAS is generally considered appropriate. Foreign listed corporations may follow Polish GAAP, IAS, or U.S. GAAP. The Polish accountancy profession is small, and the main accountancy and external auditing organizations are the National Chamber of External Auditors and the Accountants' Association in Poland.

Cultural Background

Poland is ethnically homogenous: 98 percent of the population are ethnically Polish, and the balance comprises small communities of Germans, Roma (Gypsies), and Ukrainians. The Jewish community of Poland numbered several million before World War II, but most Jews were either murdered during the Nazi occupation or left for Israel soon after the end of the war. Only small numbers of Jews are left in Poland today. At least 95 percent of Poles are nominally Roman Catholic, but observance has fallen dramatically in recent years. However, although the Church's influence has waned in urban areas, it remains a strong force in rural parts of the country.

The Polish education system is strong, and (as in many other East European countries) visitors are often struck by the high level of culture and education of the general population.

Social Etiquette

- The Polish business environment is relatively conservative, with respect for authority and seniority.
- Poles enjoy a drink and are generally not shy about indulging in alcohol at social events.
- Despite recent modernization of the Polish economy, the business culture remains generally slow.

Further Information

P. M. Barford, *The Early Slavs* (Ithaca, NY: Cornell University Press, 2001).
Norman Davies, *Heart of Europe: The Past in Poland's Present* (New York and Oxford: Oxford University Press, 2001).
University Jerzy Lukowski and Hubert Zawadzki, *A Concise History of Poland* (New York and Cambridge: Cambridge University Press, 2001).
The Chancellory of the (Polish) Prime Minister: *www.kprm.gov.pl.*
Accountants' Association in Poland: *www.skwp.org.pl.*

PORTUGAL

Geography

Portugal shares the Iberian Peninsula with its larger neighbor Spain. Portugal's northern and eastern borders are with Spain, while the west and south of the country have North Atlantic Ocean coastlines. The Tagus River cuts the country in half: North of the Tagus the terrain is mountainous, while the south consists mainly of plains. The Portuguese climate is temperate, with cool winters and warm summers. In the country's interior, however, summers can be very hot.

Brief History

The Iberian Peninsula has been settled for millennia. Early inhabitants of the area of modern Portugal included the Iberos, Lusitanians, Phoenicians, and Celts. With the arrival of the Romans in the third century BCE, the Iberian Peninsula was incorporated into the Roman Empire. During the Roman period, the Latin language and the Christian religion were adopted by most of the Iberian peoples.

Following the disintegration of the Roman Empire in the fifth century CE, the area of modern Portugal suffered further invasions. Germanic tribes that included the Vandals and Visigoths swept into the Iberian Peninsula and were assimilated into the local population. In the eighth century CE, Arabic-speaking Muslim Berber invaders from North Africa established political control over most of the peninsula. Muslim political power was extinguished by the end of the fifteenth century CE, mainly by Spanish Christian forces (as discussed in the "Spain" country section). The independent Portuguese monarchy emerged during the Christian reconquest of the peninsula, and Portugal became one of modern Europe's earliest nation states.

A traditional alliance with England went hand in hand with Portugal's political ascendancy from the fourteenth century. Indeed, even before Muslim power had been extinguished in the Iberian Peninsula, Portugal had entered its "golden age." The country was a pioneer in the European voyages of discovery, and established a global empire that stretched from South America to India. However, owing to Portugal's small size, the country was ultimately unable to compete with more powerful colonial competitors such as England and France. The only sizeable former colonial territory with remaining Portuguese cultural influence is Brazil. Elsewhere, Portuguese imperial possessions tended to be small territories such as Goa in India and Macau in China. The Portuguese, however, also colonized large parts of Africa.

In 1755, Portugal's capital Lisbon was destroyed by an earthquake, which contributed to the country's decline. In 1822, the colony of Brazil became independent, and in 1910, a revolution overthrew the Portuguese monarchy. In most of the twentieth century, Portugal was administered by autocratic regimes. The main political figure in the twentieth century was Antonio de Oliveira Salazar (1889–1970), who dominated Portuguese politics from the 1930s until the late 1960s. Salazar was a ruthless and arch-conservative dictator, who studied to be a

Roman Catholic priest before switching to a career as an academic economist. He never married and followed a rather austere lifestyle. He translated his interpretation of conservative Christianity into a political system based on patriotism and social conservatism, with strong fascist overtones. Salazar kept Portugal neutral during World War II, and the country joined NATO in 1949.

Portuguese decolonization in the late twentieth century was often turbulent and violent. In 1961, Indian troops "liberated" the colonial enclave of Goa, while in 1976 Indonesia annexed the Portuguese territory of East Timor. (As described in the "Indonesia" country section, East Timor finally became independent in 2002.) In Africa, Portugal fought bitter wars to remain in control of territories such as Angola and Mozambique, but it granted independence to all of its African colonies in 1975. In the previous year, a military coup had introduced democratic reform. In 1999, Portugal returned its last overseas territory, Macau, to China. Portugal democratized itself in the post-Salazar era, and joined what was to become the EU in 1985.

Demographics

Portugal's population is around 10 million. The country's traditionally low population has been reinforced by long traditions of emigration. Portuguese settlers spread throughout Portugal's colonial empire, but Brazil was by far the main destination for emigration. Other countries settled by large numbers of Portuguese include Canada, France, and the United States. In the late nineteenth and early twentieth centuries, the country experienced the highest per-capita emigration levels of any European country, other than Ireland. As in Ireland, economic factors were the major stimulus for the massive population movements. Following decolonization and improvements in living standards in the late twentieth century, the rate of emigration has decreased significantly. In a reversal of the trend, it is estimated that up to 800,000 Portuguese returned to the country following the independence of the African colonies in 1975.

Languages

Portuguese is a member of the Romance language family. It is a descendent of Latin, which arrived in what was to become Portuguese territory during the Roman Empire. Portuguese shares close similarities of grammar and vocabulary with Spanish and Italian. The period of Muslim political domination of the Iberian Peninsula resulted in the adoption of around 600 words of Arabic origin into Portuguese. Literacy is low by European standards, at around 90 percent (although some observers estimate that functional literacy may be nearer 80 percent). Improving the country's educational infrastructure is widely seen as a priority.

Politics

The Portuguese Republic has its capital at Lisbon. For much of the twentieth century, the country lived under the autocratic Salazar dictatorship, as described in the

"Brief History" section, but the current parliamentary democracy is well established. The head of state is the president, and the head of government is the prime minister. There are numerous political parties in the unicameral parliament, covering a wide political spectrum.

Economy

Portugal has traditionally been one of Western Europe's poorest countries, and per-capita wealth remains significantly below that of the major European economies such as Britain, France, and Germany. The country receives significant economic assistance from the EU. Major industries include agricultural produce (including wine), footwear, textiles, and tourism. Portugal's economy has made significant advances in recent decades, and this has led to the end of mass emigration. Spain and Germany are Portugal's largest trading partners, and the currency unit is the euro.

Legal and Regulatory Environment

Portugal's legal system is based on Roman civil law, and is similar to that found in other Mediterranean European countries such as Spain and Italy. The country's regulatory and tax environment has a reputation for being rather bureaucratic, even by EU standards. Recent governments have attempted to reform tax laws and regulations to improve the competitiveness of the Portuguese economy.

Accountancy

Portuguese GAAP is based on accounting and tax law, the national chart of accounts, the standards and guidelines of the country's Accounting Standards Board (the *Comissão de Normalização Contabilística*—CNC), and EU directives on accountancy matters. The CNC is financially and administratively the responsibility of the Ministry of Finance, but it represents a wide variety of views from the public and private sectors.

As a member of the EU, Portugal is required to harmonize listed corporation GAAP with IAS by 2005. Portuguese GAAP has traditionally been significantly different from IAS, but in advance of 2005 the CNC has been progressively narrowing discrepancies. For example, the CNC has issued Accounting Directive 28 (Income Taxes), which is based on IAS 12 (Accounting for Taxes on Income) and is applicable from 2002. The main professional external auditing body is the *Ordem dos Revisores Oficiais de Contas*.

Cultural Background

The inhabitants of Portugal, as described in the "Brief History" section, are derived from numerous ethnic groups that have settled in the Iberian Peninsula over the millennia. The country's colonial history has also led to relatively small communities of African, Indian, and Chinese descent—in total, such communities probably amount to less than 100,000 individuals. Portugal has also long been home to a large Roma (Gypsy) population, numbering perhaps 100,000.

The Portuguese have a reputation for racial tolerance, and there was significant intermarriage between communities throughout Portugal's colonial empire. (This trend is perhaps most evident in the multiethnic nature of the former colony of Brazil.) Many Portuguese who returned to the country following the decolonization processes of the late twentieth century were of mixed ethnic backgrounds. Most Portuguese are Roman Catholics, and religious observance remains high by European standards.

Social Etiquette

- It is crucial to avoid confusing Portugal with Spain. Despite the two countries' geographical proximity, the Portuguese are very proud of their separate identity within the Iberian Peninsula.
- The pace of business life is relatively slow in Portugal.
- Business dealings are frequently centered on restaurant meals, and the Portuguese are deservedly proud of their culinary and viticultural traditions.

Further Information

C. R. Boxer, *The Portuguese Seaborne Empire* (New York: Knopf, 1969 and subsequent editions).

Antonio Costa Pinto, *Salazar's Dictatorship and European Fascism* (New York: Columbia University Press, 1996).

Peter Russell, *Prince Henry "The Navigator": A Life* (New York: Yale University Press, 2000).

Portuguese Government Web site: *www.portugal.gov.pt/en.*

The Presidency of the Portuguese Republic: *www.presidenciarepublica.pt/en/main.html.*

Ordem dos Revisores Oficiais de Contas (Portuguese only): *www.cidadevirtual.pt/croc.*

The Portuguese Accounting Standards Board: *www.cnc.min-financas.pt/sitecnc1_EN.htm.*

RUSSIA

Geography

In surface area, Russia is the largest country in the world. It spans 10 time zones and stretches from northern Europe to northern Asia. Owing to its vastness, Russia has many borders. A sample of bordering nations includes China, Mongolia, and North Korea in Asia, and Finland, Poland, and Ukraine in Europe. The country also has coastlines on the Arctic and Pacific Oceans.

Russian territory is characterized by immense plains west of the Ural Mountains, which are often seen as the dividing line between Europe and Asia. East of the Urals, tundra and forest dominate the vast area of Siberia. Uplands and mountains predominate in the south, as in the Caucasus Mountains. The Russian climate ranges from arctic in the north to temperate in the south, and much of the country experiences heavy winter snowfalls.

Brief History

Slav peoples have traditionally dominated the territory of western Russia, and Slav political entities have existed in the region from the ninth century CE. Kiev was the focus of early Slav political power, and was the core of the future Russian nation. The peoples of the Kiev region converted to Christianity from the tenth century. Kiev later declined in importance following the devastating and bloody Mongol invasions of the thirteenth century, and the focus of future Russian power shifted to Moscow. (Kiev later developed into the political center of the Ukrainian people, who—culturally and linguistically—are closely related to the Russians.)

Mongol political domination lasted from the thirteenth to the late fifteenth centuries, after which Moscow consolidated its independent power. The Muscovites resisted the advances of Turks and other peoples, and by the early eighteenth century, Russia had developed into a powerful imperial state with western European-style armed forces. Culturally, the country began in the eighteenth century to move closer to Western European traditions of technology, social customs, and culture. However, there was a large part of Russian society that advocated a return to indigenous as opposed to Western European culture. (The debate about the degree of involvement in European politics and culture remains a lively one to the present day.)

In the early nineteenth century, Russia survived an invasion attempt by the French emperor Napoleon, and the country established the administrative and economic foundations for its later twentieth-century status as a world superpower. Russian settlers moved east into Asia, claiming territory as far as the Pacific Ocean coast. The western spread of Russian political control over large parts of Asia in the nineteenth century mirrored the spread of U.S. political control over much of the North American continent in the same era. Increasingly, Russia came to see Asia as its sphere of influence, and it coveted the British Indian empire—but without success. The country did not yet have the economic or military resources to challenge the world's major powers, such as Britain, the United States, and an increasingly modernized Japan.

At the end of World War I, following years of severe social tension and class conflict, the Russian Empire was transformed by a communist revolution. The communists executed the Russian royal family, and the state took over many aspects of economic and social life. The country changed its name to the Union of Soviet Socialist Republics (abbreviated to USSR, or the Soviet Union). Under the ruthless and dictatorial leadership of Josef Stalin (1879–1953), the Soviet Union became an autocratic and totalitarian state that did not shrink from using violence against its own citizens to repress political dissent. In the 1930s, Stalin brutally "purged" the country of millions of political opponents through assassinations, executions, and deportations to remote areas of Siberia. Inefficient agricultural collectivization projects led to millions of deaths by starvation.

In World War II, Nazi Germany invaded the Soviet Union and committed human rights abuses on an immense scale. Millions of Russians died or were forced into slave labor. The Soviet Union had initially tried to appease Adolf Hitler's anticommunist fanaticism by signing a mutual nonaggression pact, but Hitler later set out to destroy the Russian state. The Soviets were initially unable to resist the German military advances, as Stalin's repression of the Soviet people had involved the execution of many army officers who could have played an important role in the country's defense.

The Germans quickly overran huge swathes of Soviet territory, and reached the outskirts of Moscow. However, in the course of time the Soviets turned the direction and momentum of the war. Allied with the United States and Britain, they forced the German armies back to Berlin. The cost of the war in human terms was immense, and it is estimated that more than 20 million Soviet citizens lost their lives. The successful Soviet resistance at the siege of Stalingrad became an important symbol in Soviet—and later Russian—national identity.

The World War II alliance with the United States turned into one of hostility after the end of the war. The period of frosty relations became known as the Cold War. Most of the world was divided into territories influenced by the two ideologically opposed superpowers of the Soviet Union and the United States. In some locations—such as Korea and Vietnam—superpower rivalry influenced local conflicts, and both Soviet and U.S. military forces were deployed (directly or indirectly) in proxy wars. The two superpowers avoided direct conflict, however, largely owing to the deterrent effect of huge nuclear arsenals. The United States was largely successful in containing Soviet influence to its satellite states behind the so-called "Iron Curtain" in Eastern Europe, and to other enclaves in Africa, South America, and elsewhere. Ideological differences meant that the Soviet Union was unable to maintain friendly relationships with its sister communist regime in China, and Sino-Soviet relations were always tense.

In 1979, Soviet forces invaded Afghanistan to prop up an unpopular pro-Soviet government, and over the following decade Afghan resistance dealt a severe blow to Soviet military prestige. Meanwhile, domestically the Soviet Union remained an autocratic and totalitarian regime: Persecution of dissidents and an anti-Semitic state policy were symptoms of the continuing repression of human rights. Stalin died in 1953 and his successors, including Nikita Khrushchev (1894–1971), were more moderate. However, it was only with the arrival in the 1980s of Mikhail Gorbachev (born 1931) that reform of the country's political regime began in earnest. Gorbachev instigated a period of fundamental reform, known by the terms *glasnost* (openness) and *perestroika* (restructuring). The country's economy had fallen significantly behind western standards, owing to the inefficiencies of communist central planning. In the absence of transparent market mechanisms, corruption and black marketeering were rampant by the late twentieth century.

In 1986, an explosion at the Chernobyl nuclear power plant (in Ukraine) covered large parts of the Soviet Union and neighboring countries with a cloud of radioactive material. The regime's poor management of information about the disaster led many to doubt the true effectiveness of the Gorbachev reforms. However, Gorbachev's modernization programs unleashed powerful democratic forces, domestically and internationally. The Soviet Union lost its East European satellites in the late 1980s and early 1990s. The most dramatic example of the liberation of eastern Europe was the unification of Germany, with the destruction of the communist-constructed Berlin Wall in 1989.

The independence of Soviet satellite states was followed by the political disintegration of the Soviet Union itself. The federal communist state fell apart and long-repressed local nationalisms resurfaced. By early 1992, the Soviet Union had splintered into 15 independent republics. Russia reemerged as a nation state as part of this process, and it has since struggled to establish a democratic administration and reform its problematic economy. Some observers estimate that the legacies of the political totalitarianism and economic mismanagement of the communist era may take generations to eradicate.

Demographics

The population of Russia is around 148 million. Owing to the vast size of the country, the overall population density is very low. As described in the "Languages" and "Cultural Background" sections, there are many ethnic and religious groups in modern Russia.

Languages

Russian is a Slavonic language, related to Czech and Polish. However, unlike those languages, Russian does not use the Roman alphabet. The country's historic attachment to the Eastern Orthodox Church led to the early adoption of the Cyrillic alphabet, which is based on the Greek alphabet. Minority languages in Russia are numerous, owing to the country's size and its multiethnic character, and include Finnish, Iranian, Mongolian, and Turkish. Around 10 percent of the country's inhabitants speak a language other than Russian as their mother tongue. The country's literacy levels are nearly 100 percent.

Politics

The Russian Federation is a democracy and has its capital at Moscow. The head of state is the president, and the head of government is the prime minister. The federal parliament has a bicameral structure, with a federal council and the popularly elected *Duma*. There are many political parties, covering the entire spectrum from communist to neo-fascist. It is probably fair to describe Russian politics as volatile, as the country's experience of democracy is only very recent—even before the long communist era, Russia experienced centuries of autocratic monarchic government.

A major recent issue has been an armed separatist insurgency in the southern province of Chechnya. Many thousands of combatants and civilians have lost their lives in the bitter conflict, which remains unresolved at the time of writing.

Economy

In the postcommunist era, Russia has struggled to establish an open, efficient economy. The corruption and idiosyncrasies of the old Soviet regime continue to cast shadows over the modern economic system, and Russia has generally been slower than former Soviet satellite states such as Poland and Hungary to implement meaningful reform. A decade of economic uncertainty crystallized in the financial crisis of 1997 and 1998. In August 1998, the Russian government was forced to devalue the ruble, and millions of Russians were plunged further into poverty.

However, the country has mature industries in the chemicals, defense, and engineering sectors, and it is rich in oil and natural gas. The importance of oil makes the Russian economy notably dependent on world oil prices, and rising oil prices assisted the postdevaluation recovery of the Russian economy in 1999 and 2000. At the time of writing, serious economic problems include corruption, capital flight, environmental damage, terrorism, poor infrastructure, and inadequate public services. As many as one in three Russians lives in poverty, and many public sector workers face interruptions in payments of their salaries. The Russian currency unit is the ruble, and Germany and the United States are key trading partners.

Legal and Regulatory Environment

The Russian legal system is based largely on the civil law culture associated with countries in which the Eastern Orthodox Church has been traditionally dominant. However, Russia's communist past was characterized by a distortion of the rule of law, as the communist regime manipulated the legal system as part of its economic and social engineering. As a heavily politicized tool, the law was employed to suppress dissent and to prevent challenges to the decisions of the bureaucratic elite. Russia's recent market-driven reforms have led to the rehabilitation of many aspects of the legal system. However, the legal and regulatory environments remain cumbersome and highly challenging to foreign organizations.

Accountancy

During the communist era, Soviet accounting consisted of highly standardized routines for reporting the data that underpinned the planned economy. Soviet accounting was characterized by strict reporting formats and the use of rigid charts of accounts. Modern Russian GAAP derives from the country's Civil Code, accounting and commercial law, and the accounting standards and regulations of the Russian Federation's Ministry of Finance (MOF). The MOF establishes accounting standards for nonfinancial institutions. Russian GAAP has traditionally differed significantly from IAS, but market reforms of recent years have started to narrow the discrepancies. The use of accruals—rather than cash—accounting is now normal practice, for example. Indeed, in 1998 (encouraged by the American Chamber of Commerce in Russia) the MOF stated its intention to draft Russian accounting standards in line with IAS. However, in practice many discrepancies with IAS remain: accounting for business combinations and lease incentives are two of the major areas of difference. Banks and other financial institutions are regulated by the Central Bank of the Russian Federation (CBRF), and not by the MOF. The CBRF currently permits cash (rather than accruals) accounting. It is anticipated that Russia will fully adopt IAS by 2004.

The major Russian accounting and external auditing body is the Russian Collegium of Auditors (known under the Russian acronym of RKA).

Cultural Background

Around 80 to 90 percent of Russia's population are estimated to be ethnically Slav. The remainder comprises a number of other ethnic groups, including Koreans, Mongolians, Roma (Gypsies), and Turks. However, intermarriage between various communities makes precise ethnic data difficult to obtain. Russia's Jewish and German communities have significantly fallen in size after the collapse of the Soviet Union, when many took the opportunity to emigrate. Eastern Orthodox Christianity is the country's main religion, but decades of atheistic communist rule have eroded the importance of religion for many Russians.

Russia has rich literary and musical traditions. Authors such as Fyodor Dostoyevsky (1821–1881), Aleksandr Pushkin (1799–1837), and Lev Nikolayevich Tolstoy (1828–1910) have produced some of the world's finest literature, while the music of Russian composers such as Pyotr Il'yich Tchaikovsky (1840–1893), and Sergei Prokofiev (1891–1953) remains popular around the world.

Social Etiquette

- Russians are quite direct in social interaction. A curt handshake and the stating of a person's name is a common means of introducing oneself.
- Gifts are often an important part of doing business.
- Many Russians enjoy drinking, and the visitor should be wary of matching the vodka intake of local colleagues and associates!
- The business environment can at times appear to be somewhat chaotic, and the visitor should stay cool despite delays and other bureaucratic frustrations. Displays of frustration are unlikely to speed things up.

Further Information

P. M. Barford, *The Early Slavs* (Ithaca, NY: Cornell University Press, 2001).

Dean LeBaron, *Mao, Marx & the Market: Capitalist Adventures in Russia and China* (New York: John Wiley and Sons, 2001).

Neil Robinson, *Russia: A State of Uncertainty* (New York and London: Routledge, 2001).

Robert English, *Russia and the Idea of the West: Gorbachev, Intellectuals, and the End of the Cold War* (New York: Columbia University Press, 2000).

Russian Federation Web site: *www.gov.ru/main/page8.html*.

The Russian Collegium of Auditors (Russian only): *www.rka.org.ru*.

SPAIN

Geography

Spain shares the Iberian Peninsula with Portugal. Much of the country is surrounded by water—the Bay of Biscay, the Atlantic Ocean, and the Mediterranean Sea—while there are land borders with Andorra, France, and Portugal. Spanish territory consists mainly of rugged and arid highlands, and the Pyrenees mountain range separates the country from France. The climate of the south and the interior is hot and dry in summer, and mild in winter. Coastal areas tend to be cooler in summer.

In addition to mainland Spain, the country also possesses external territories—two enclaves in North Africa, the Balearic Islands in the Mediterranean, and the Canary Islands in the Atlantic Ocean. Gibraltar, the southern tip of Spain, belongs to the United Kingdom.

Brief History

Following the disintegration of the Roman Empire in the fifth century CE, the Iberian Peninsula was invaded by Germanic tribes, including the Vandals and the Visigoths. The Germanic invaders were absorbed into the local, Latin-speaking population. The next major wave of invasion came from North Africa and started in the eighth century. Large parts of the peninsula fell under the control of Arabic-speaking Muslim Berbers. The Berbers established an Islamic regime that left a wealth of outstanding architecture. Other cultural imprints of the Muslim period of Spanish history can be seen today in cuisine, language, and music.

Spanish resistance to the Muslim invaders crystallized in the fifteenth-century royal marriage of Ferdinand of Aragon and Isabella of Castile. Under the leadership of Isabella and Ferdinand, the Castilian royal family became the dominant power of Christian Spain. By 1492, Muslim political power in Spain had been destroyed in a process known as the *Reconquista* (reconquest). The new Christian regime persecuted non-Christians, and the notorious state-controlled Inquisition attempted to enforce conversion through torture. Muslim inhabitants who refused to convert to Christianity were expelled from the country.

The *Reconquista* was followed by the rise of Spain as an international power, as the crusading energies of Spain's domestic struggle against the Muslims were directed to other parts of the world. The Spanish explored and colonized the Philippines and large parts of South America. Spain's main colonial rival was Portugal, and in 1493 the Pope declared a division of the unexplored world between the two countries. This agreement eventually led to Portuguese dominance in Brazil, and Spanish dominance elsewhere in South America. The Spanish *conquistadors* (conquerors) brutally subdued local populations in South America at the cost of millions of lives, and extracted huge wealth in the form of local precious metals.

Through dynastic royal marriages, Spain also came into possession of significant European territory, from Italy to the Netherlands. The country was even briefly united with Portugal in the later sixteenth and early seventeenth centuries. A planned invasion of England in 1588 failed, however, and Spain's power began to wane from the sixteenth century. England eclipsed Spain as Europe's main colonizing power. Spain lost most of its European possessions, Portugal gained independence, and the economy declined. After the French revolution, Spain fell under French temporary occupation until the defeat of Napoleon in the early nineteenth century. In the early nineteenth century, most of Spain's South American colonies gained independence, while later in that century Spain lost the Philippines to the United States.

Following the dismantling of the Spanish empire, the country faced domestic fragmentation in the twentieth century. Regional movements advocating autonomy or even independence gained strength, notably in the Basque region and in Catalonia. A violent movement for Basque separatism exists to this day.

The principal historical figure in twentieth-century Spain was Francisco Franco (1892–1975), the fascist dictator who ruled Spain from 1939 to 1975. Franco's rise to power came after victory in a bitter civil war (1936–1939) between nationalists and republicans. The civil war, in which hundreds of thousands of Spaniards died, was the outcome of ideological divisions in Spanish society that had simmered in the early 1930s. Franco was a general by the age of 33, and his military ability played an important role in the nationalist's defeat of the republican forces. Mussolini's Italy provided thousands of troops to assist the nationalists, and Hitler's Germany provided air support.

Following the civil war, the Franco regime was characterized by authoritarian rule and self-imposed international isolation. Spain remained neutral during World War II. Franco's dour, humorless personality was stamped on the country as a whole, and Spain fell behind much of the rest of Europe in terms of social and economic sophistication. Franco died in 1975, after which his authoritarian regime was slowly transformed into a parliamentary democracy. As head of state, King Juan Carlos (born 1938) assisted Spain's transition to democracy. In 1981, for example, he personally intervened in the political process to avert an attempted right-wing coup.

Spain's conversion to democracy led to the opening of the country to the world. Living standards increased substantially and the country joined what would later become the EU in 1985. However, political violence remains a major problem in Spain, above all in the Basque region.

Demographics

The population of Spain is around 40 million, which is significantly lower than the populations of the main European nations (Germany, Britain, Italy, and France). Much of the country is sparsely populated, although there are several large cities—Madrid (the capital), Barcelona, Valencia, and Bilbao.

Languages

The main language of Spain is Castilian Spanish, which is spoken by around 75 percent of the population. Spanish is a modern descendent of Latin, which entered the Iberian Peninsula during the era of the Roman Empire. Spanish has also been influenced by the country's other invaders—Germanic tribes and North African

Muslims. There are many Spanish dialects, and language politics in Spain tends to be acrimonious. Recognition of regional dialects tends to be a matter of political prestige, and is often linked to regional political sentiments. Non-Castilian languages include the Romance languages of Catalan (spoken by around 15 percent of Spain's inhabitants) and Galician (8 percent), and the unrelated language of Basque (3 percent).

Basque is something of a linguistic anomaly, which is unrelated to the Indo-European language family. Indeed, despite attempts by some scholars to link Basque with other language groups, the evidence for any linguistic affinities is thin. Basque appears to be a genuinely unique language. During the Franco period, the use of both Basque and regional Romance languages was suppressed. Since the establishment of democracy, however, regional languages have grown in strength.

The country's literacy rate is around 99 percent.

Politics

The Kingdom of Spain is a constitutional monarchy and has its capital at Madrid. The head of state is the monarch, and the head of government is the government's president. The monarchy is hereditary. Members of the lower chamber of the bicameral parliament are elected by popular vote. After the long fascist dictatorship of General Franco, Spanish democracy is relatively young. There are a large number of political parties, among which the right-of-center Popular Party and the Socialist Party have dominated in recent years.

Major political issues include the armed separatist movement in the Basque region, demands for the return to Spanish sovereignty of the British territory of Gibraltar, and the economic and social ramifications of the country's stubbornly high unemployment rate.

Economy

The state has a strong role in the Spanish economy—the importance of the state originated in the Franco era and was reinforced by the socialist administration of the 1980s. The Spanish economy has relatively severe structural problems that have resulted in the EU's highest unemployment rate. Although Spain has introduced liberalization and privatization measures from the 1990s, the economy has yet to resolve its stubborn employment crisis.

Major Spanish industries include automobiles, consumer goods, and heavy machinery. The tourism and agricultural sectors are also important, and Spain is a major exporter of fruit and vegetables within Europe. Spain's main trading partners are France and Germany, and the country also retains strong economic links with former colonies in South America. The currency unit is the euro.

Legal and Regulatory Environment

Spanish law is derived from Roman law, with more recent influences from the EU. The Spanish legal system is similar to those of neighboring countries such as

Portugal and Italy. The regulatory environment has traditionally been perceived as highly bureaucratic by EU standards. Although recent governments have been partially successful in their attempts to deregulate the economy, employment legislation and regulations are still areas of considerable complexity.

Accountancy

Spanish GAAP is based on the country's Commercial Code, company law, the national accounting plan, accounting standards issued by the Institute of Accountancy and Audit (*Instituto de Contabilidad y Auditoria de Cuentas*—ICAC), and EU directives on accountancy matters. The ICAC has been committed since 1998 to minimize differences between Spanish GAAP and IAS, and as a member of the EU the country is committed to harmonization with IAS by 2005 (for listed corporations).

The Spanish accountancy and external auditing profession is relatively modest in size—the *Instituto de Auditores-Censores Jurados de Cuentas de Espana* has only around 7,000 members.

Cultural Background

In the late twentieth century, Spain made a rapid transition from a conservative, heavily controlled society under Franco to a modern, liberal democracy. Many of the strains of this sudden change are apparent in modern Spain, with social problems ranging from rampant drug abuse to large-scale prostitution. The country remains predominantly Roman Catholic, but observance has fallen dramatically following the end of the Franco era. Ethnically, the Spanish population comprises a mix of Latin, Germanic, and North African peoples. The Basque community is considered by many to be an ethnically separate group. Around 500,000 people speak the Basque language.

Social Etiquette

- In comparison with the English-speaking world, the pace of business is rather slow in Spain.
- Professional and academic titles are widely used in Spain, and the visitor should respect them.
- Spanish business dealings often center on meals.
- In Spain, the business dress code is generally smart, even stylish.

Further Information

Raymond Carr (ed.), *Spain: A History* (New York and Oxford: Oxford University Press, 2002).

Sheelagh Elwood, *Franco: Profiles in Power* (New York and London: Longman, 2000).

Bernard F. Reilly, *The Contest of Christian and Muslim Spain* (Oxford: Blackwell, 1995).
Presidency and Government of Spain: *www.la-moncloa.es.*
Instituto de Auditores-Censores Jurados de Cuentas de Espana (Spanish only): *www.iacjce.es.*
Instituto de Contabilidad y Auditoria de Cuentas (Spanish only): *www.icac.mineco.es.*

SWEDEN

Geography

Sweden is located in northern Europe, in the eastern part of the Scandinavian Peninsula. It borders Finland and Norway. The country is mountainous in the west, but much of the rest of the terrain comprises lowlands. Forests and woodlands cover two-thirds of the land. Sweden has cold winters, with subarctic conditions in the north, and mild summers.

Brief History

The peoples of the Scandinavian Peninsula left their mark on world history in the form of Viking expansion in many parts of Europe. The Vikings were a pagan, seafaring warrior people who started to attack richer settlements in northern Europe from the ninth century CE. The British Isles and Russia were victims of many destructive Viking raids. Some historians claim that the Vikings also reached North America, long before fifteenth-century European explorers.

The Vikings moved to some of their conquered territories and adopted more settled ways of life. One group, the Normans, settled in northern France and adopted the French language. The Normans invaded England in 1066, and the French-speaking Norman imprint on British culture is still evident, not least in the large amount of English vocabulary of French origin. (The Normans later extended their political power to territories as far away as Sicily in the Mediterranean Sea and the Canary Isles near the African Atlantic Ocean coast.)

For centuries during and after the Viking era, Scandinavia remained politically fragmented, and local regimes came and went. The Swedish date the formal origins of their country to 1523, when Gustavus I (1496–1650) was elected king. Gustavus I is regarded as the founder of the modern Swedish state, and he made Lutheran Protestantism the state religion. It was under Gustavus II (1594–1632), however, that Sweden became a major European power and expanded its territory. By the eighteenth century, Swedish power was waning. The country lost territory to Russia and the German states in the nineteenth century, and in 1905, Norway peacefully gained independence from Sweden.

Since participation in the early nineteenth century Napoleonic Wars, Sweden has adopted a strategy of neutrality and has not been involved in any armed conflicts. Sweden's neutral stance kept it aloof from both twentieth-century World Wars. Sweden joined the EU in 1995, but it has declined to join NATO.

Demographics

Sweden has a population of just under 9 million, which makes it Scandinavia's most populous nation.

Languages

Nearly all Swedes speak Swedish as a mother tongue. Swedish is a member of the Germanic language family, and it is closely linked to neighboring Danish and Norwegian. (Indeed, Swedish, Danish, and Norwegian are mutually comprehensible.) The north of the country has small minorities of Lapp and Finnish speakers, which together account for around 3 percent of the population. The literacy rate is virtually 100 percent.

Politics

The Kingdom of Sweden is a constitutional monarchy and has its capital at Stockholm. The monarch fulfills the largely ceremonial role of head of state, and the head of government is the prime minister. The country's parliament (the *Riksdag*) is unicameral, and its members are elected by popular vote under a proportional representation system. In 1986, the Swedish prime minister Olof Palme (1927–1986) was assassinated. His murder is still unsolved at the time of writing.

Sweden's political system is stable, and is noted for its promotion of a strong social security system and for its liberal views on immigration and asylum. Sweden's politicians are also well known for their commitment to neutrality, and they often accept mediating roles between conflicting groups around the world. A major political issue is the potential adoption of the EU's euro currency.

Economy

Sweden has a high standard of living, which has been achieved through a successful mixed economy. The country's infrastructure is world class and the workforce is highly educated. Important sectors include automobiles, engineering, furniture, and telecommunications. However, toward the end of the twentieth century the Swedish economy started to feel structural strains, partially caused by the funding requirements of high social security benefits. Despite this, the Swedish economy remains one of the EU's most prosperous, and the country remains a large aid donor to developing countries. Sweden's largest trading partners are Germany and the United Kingdom, and the currency unit is the krona.

Legal and Regulatory Environment

Sweden has a continental-style civil law system that coexists with customary indigenous law. Since 1995, membership of the EU has led to the increasing importance of EU-inspired law. Sweden's legendary attachment to large-scale social warfare programs has contributed to a rather bureaucratic regulatory culture. Tax rates have traditionally been among the highest in Europe.

Accountancy

Swedish GAAP is based on corporate law, the accounting standards of the Financial Accounting Standards Council (*Redovisningsrådet*—RR), and EU directives on accountancy. As a member of the EU, Sweden is committed to harmonizing domestic GAAP with IAS for listed corporations by 2005. This should lead to the elimination of traditional areas of difference with IAS, such as accounting for employee benefits and investment properties. However, Swedish GAAP is already broadly in line with IAS, and Sweden's stock exchange allows foreign listed corporations to follow IAS or a major national GAAP (provided that the results are reconciled to Swedish GAAP).

The RR's accounting standards are applicable to listed corporations, while the Swedish Accounting Standards Board (SASB) issues separate standards for unlisted corporations. The SASB standards tend to be similar to those of the RR, although generally simplified.

The main accountancy and external auditing professional bodies are the *Föreningen Auktoriserade Revisorer* and the *Svenska Revisorsamfundet*, with a combined membership of around 5,000.

Cultural Background

Sweden has small ethnic and linguistic minorities of Lapps (sometimes called Sami) and Finns, as well as more recent immigrant communities of Greeks, Turks, and other nationalities. Sweden has a well-deserved reputation as a country that welcomes political refugees. Most Swedes (over 85 percent) are Lutheran Protestants, and the remaining population includes Roman Catholics and the religions of various immigrant communities. The country has a reputation for liberalism and social tolerance.

Social Etiquette

- The Swedes are reputed to be serious and undemonstrative, but this is probably a little unfair—they enjoy socializing and entertaining, and a visit to a restaurant is often an important part of business dealings.
- Business meetings tend to be characterized by directness and little preliminary small talk.
- In Sweden, losing one's temper is considered to be an indication of unreliability and untrustworthiness.
- Swedes tend to maintain eye contact, and this is not a sign of aggression or intimidation.

Further Information

Arthur Gould, *Developments in Swedish Social Policy: Resisting Dionysus* (New York: St. Martin's Press, 2001).
Byron J. Nordstrom, *The History of Sweden* (Westport, CT: Greenwood, 2002).
Peter Sawyer (ed.), *The Oxford Illustrated History of the Vikings* (New York and Oxford: Oxford University Press, 2001).
The Swedish Government: *www.sweden.gov.se.*
Redovisningsrådet (Swedish only): *www.redovisningsradet.se.*
Svenska Revisorsamfundet: www.revisorsamfundet.se/srs.cs.
Föreningen Auktoriserade Revisorer: www.far.se/english.asp.

SWITZERLAND

Geography

Switzerland is a landlocked country in Central Europe that borders Austria, France, Germany, Italy, and Liechtenstein. The terrain is mainly mountainous, and includes the breathtaking and world famous Alps. The climate is continental, but is also affected by the altitude. Cold winters with heavy snowfall alternate with warm summers.

Brief History

The modern Swiss state traces its origins to August 1, 1291, which is celebrated as a national holiday. This was the date on which the Swiss Federation was founded, from territories that formed part of the central European Holy Roman Empire. (The Holy Roman Empire was a German-speaking political unit, and is not to be confused with the Latin-speaking Roman Empire that disintegrated in the fifth century CE.)

As surrounding European nations such as France, Germany, and Italy coalesced over the centuries into largely centralized nation states, the Swiss preserved their political arrangement of a federation of semi-autonomous cantons. At various times in Swiss history, cantons joined or threatened to leave the federation. The federal constitution of 1848 guaranteed cantons a degree of autonomy that held the country together, despite its marked linguistic and cultural diversity.

Despite its location in the geographical heart of Europe, Switzerland has stayed aloof from war in the last 200 years. The country's last experience of armed conflict was during the Napoleonic Wars of the early nineteenth century. Since then, the country has kept a rigidly neutral status, which has contributed to political stability and the accumulation of wealth. Switzerland is today one of the world's most prosperous nations.

The country stayed neutral during both world wars of the twentieth century. The absence of war has resulted in Switzerland enjoying the benefit of a relatively uneventful history by the standards of the surrounding countries, which have been so often devastated by armed conflict. The country has been a bastion of democracy in a continent where autocratic politics has so often been dominant.

In a referendum, the Swiss voted in 2002 to formally join the UN. In fact, Switzerland already had cordial relations with the UN, and a number of UN institutions have been based in the country for many years. Indeed, the country's traditions of neutrality have resulted in it being chosen as the location for many international organizations, such as the World Trade Organization. However, the Swiss continue to remain aloof from Europe's greatest political development of the last half-century—the EU.

Demographics

The population of Switzerland is around 7.3 million. There are also up to 1 million foreign workers, mainly from Italy and other southern European countries.

Languages

The Swiss linguistic map is complex. The main languages spoken are German (around 73 percent of the population), French (20 percent), Italian (6 percent), and Romansch (1 percent). The latter is a Romance language, sometimes called Rhaeto-Romanic, spoken today only by small numbers of people. Many Swiss speak more than one language, which is often a necessity in such a relatively small, multilingual country. The literacy level is virtually 100 percent.

Politics

The Swiss Confederation is a federal republic and has its capital at Bern. The country's president acts as both head of state and head of government. The federal parliament has a bicameral structure, with a Council of States and a National Council. Members of the latter are elected by popular vote under a proportional representation system. Swiss politics is known for its stability, and coalition governments have tended to follow broadly similar policies over decades. Important decisions—such as the one to join the UN—tend to be put to the electorate in the form of a referendum.

A major political issue in recent years, and one has that caused the Swiss much discomfort, is the disclosure that some Swiss financial institutions were less than helpful in returning looted gold and funds to the victims of Nazi persecution following World War II. At the time of writing, victim support groups continue to lobby Switzerland for a full settlement of the issue.

Economy

Switzerland is a very prosperous country, with a sophisticated market economy. It is a major financial center, and has mature industries in chemicals, electronics, and precision instruments. Swiss watches are considered by many to be the world's finest. Although the country is not an EU member, it has concluded major trade agreements with the EU that tie it closely to the surrounding economies. Many foreign workers flock to Switzerland, mainly from Italy and other southern European countries.

Switzerland's largest trading partner is Germany, and the country's currency unit is the franc.

Legal and Regulatory Environment

Swiss law follows continental European patterns. The country is famous for the traditional secrecy surrounding its banking laws, and this secrecy (or confidentiality) has been an important contributory factor to the prosperity of the country's financial services sector. In recent years, however, Switzerland has been under pressure from other nations to relax and reform some of its secrecy laws. The Swiss banking system has been accused of avoiding transparency, thereby allowing the unhindered flow of the funds of terrorists, criminals, and corrupt politicians from around the world. The fight by victims of Nazi Germany to recover their looted wealth from some Swiss banks has also added to the pressure on the regulatory sector.

Accountancy

Swiss GAAP is based on the country's commercial and tax law, and the Accounting and Reporting Recommendations (ARR) of the Swiss Foundation for Accounting and Reporting Recommendations (*Fachkommission für Empfehlungen zur Rechnungslegung*—FER). Swiss GAAP has tended to follow EU developments, but rather more loosely than if it had been an EU member. The standards of the FER elaborate commercial law, and are broadly in line with IAS (although less detailed). Listed corporations are required to comply with ARR, but are also permitted to use IAS. If IAS is used, additional disclosure is normally needed to comply with Swiss GAAP. Disclosure for the financial services sector has traditionally been low, to preserve secrecy (or confidentiality, if one prefers that term). Details of Swiss accounting standards are available in English from the FER Web site (www.fer.ch/inhalteng.htm).

Swiss accounting has a reputation for conservatism, which is perhaps a reflection of the national character. The accounting and external auditing profession is small, as in neighboring Germany, and the main organization is the *Treuhand-Kammer*.

Cultural Background

The linguistic complexity of Switzerland reflects the country's diverse ethnic makeup. The country's ethnic communities broadly follow the usage patterns of the four main languages, as discussed in the "Languages" section. Despite the diversity of Switzerland's communities, commonly recognized aspects of the Swiss national character include stability, conservatism, and a fierce attachment to independence. Most Swiss are Christians, with slightly more Roman Catholics than Protestants.

Social Etiquette

The country sections for Germany, France, and Italy offer guidance on the social characteristics of Switzerland's main communities. As Germans form the country's largest ethnic group, the culture of Switzerland may be described as broadly Germanic, but there are significant variations between Switzerland's non-German communities. In addition:

- The Swiss business environment tends to be rather serious, with little room for levity or informality.
- Despite the general conservatism of Swiss business culture, Swiss men in particular often wear brightly colored attire—even in the most formal business context.

Further Information

Philippe Braillard, *Switzerland and the Crisis of Dormant Assets and Nazi Gold* (New York: Columbia University Press, 2000).
Michael Butler, Malcolm Pender, and Joy Charnley (eds.), *The Making of Modern Switzerland* (New York and London: Palgrave Macmillan, 2000).
Jonathan Steinberg, *Why Switzerland?* 2nd ed. (New York and Cambridge: Cambridge University Press, 1996).
The Federal Authorities of the Swiss Confederation: *www.admin.ch/ch/ index.en.html*.
Institute of Internal Auditors Switzerland: *www.svir.ch/en/index.html*.
Swiss Foundation for Accounting and Reporting Recommendations: *www.fer.ch/ inhalteng.htm*.
Treuhand-Kammer (German and French only): *www.treuhand-kammer.ch*.

UNITED KINGDOM

Geography

The United Kingdom consists of an island in northwest Europe, plus the northern portion of the island of Ireland. (A number of small islands in northern Europe are also under British sovereignty.) The territory of the main island comprises low mountains in the north and west, and flat plains in the center, east, and south. The British climate is temperate and is characterized by frequent rainfall throughout the year. Winters can have severe cold spells, and summers occasionally experience hot periods, but the weather tends to revert rapidly to the temperate mean.

Brief History

Celtic peoples settled in the British Isles in the first millennium BCE, mingling with indigenous peoples of whom little is known. The expansion of the Roman Empire over much of the island of Britain began under Julius Caesar in the first century BCE. The Romans brought the country within the orbit of the leading civilization of the day, and significantly developed its infrastructure. Following the collapse of the Roman Empire, the Romans left Britain in the fifth century CE and the country soon reverted to a low-technology society of warring Celtic tribes.

Over the following centuries, Germanic invaders from northern Europe and Scandinavia settled in Britain, driving the Celtic inhabitants to the fringes of the British isles, where they later established the nations of Scotland, Wales, and Ireland. (The county of Cornwall in southwest England has also retained a Celtic culture to this day.) The Germanic invaders belonged to several tribes, such as the Angles and Jutes, and they eventually coalesced to create the English people. The Angles gave their name to England.

A further layer of cultural influence on Britain occurred in 1066 with the Norman Conquest of England. The Normans were a Scandinavian people who had settled in northern France and adopted French culture and language. The Normans established themselves as England's ruling class, although over time they learned English and were absorbed into the local population. Some historians have identified in the division between a French-speaking ruling class and an English-speaking majority population the seeds of Britain's famous (or notorious) class system that is still evident today.

Britain is the political union of the nations of England, Scotland, and Wales. The United Kingdom comprises the union of Britain with Northern Ireland. England and Wales were united in the thirteenth century CE, and Scotland joined England in the eighteenth century. British conquest of Ireland brought it into the union in the nineteenth century. Following a war of independence, the Republic of Ireland broke free in the early twentieth century, but Northern Ireland remains in the United Kingdom.

The British colonial empire expanded throughout the world, and by the nineteenth century it covered territory in Africa, Asia, and North America. British maps colored imperial possessions in red, and the red parts of the maps were very large indeed. Around 25 percent of the world's surface area was under British rule at one stage. During the height of the British Empire, Britain was the world's unrivaled superpower, with immense military and political clout, and a huge industrial base. British institutions and culture—including the English language—spread around the globe. However, victory in both World War I and World War II sapped Britain's wealth, and the country was eclipsed by the United States (of course, a former British colony) as the world's superpower in the twentieth century.

Following World War II most British colonies achieved independence, but British culture has survived in many former colonies in the form of parliamentary structures, legal practice, and the use of the English language. One positive aspect of British influence in the world has been the importance of democratic, parliamentary government, to which many countries pay at least lip service. The Commonwealth is a political organization of former British colonies, and it is an important networking mechanism for the countries of the former empire. At the time of writing, around 30 percent of the world's population lives in Commonwealth countries.

Following World War II, the United Kingdom combined the dismantling of its colonial empire with a broadly socialistic path at home. Many industries were nationalized, and comprehensive social security mechanisms were introduced that included an extensive welfare state and free medical care. Although prosperity increased, Britain fell behind many of its European neighbors in economic matters. By the 1970s, Britain had a feel of crisis, owing to inefficient state-run enterprises, massive industrial unrest, and an increasingly volatile economy.

In reaction to the crises of the 1970s, Prime Minister Margaret Thatcher (born 1925) emerged as the dominant postwar politician. A close ally of the United States, Thatcher instigated free market reforms and privatized many ailing state industries. She initiated a "supply-side revolution" that reformed the country's sluggish economy. In 1982, under Thatcher's leadership, Britain fought a war with Argentina over the territorial dispute of the Falkland Islands. Several hundred troops died as Argentina's invading forces were ousted from the South Atlantic islands.

The United Kingdom joined what is now the EU in the 1970s. This marked a change of emphasis from historic links with the United States and the Commonwealth to closer ties with Europe. The country has often struggled to adapt to the tenor of the EU, and it has remained aloof from initiatives such as the euro currency. The United Kingdom's traditional "special relationship" with the United States remains strong, and was reflected in the diplomatic support given to the United States following the attacks of September 11, 2001.

Demographics

The United Kingdom has a population of around 60 million, of which the majority lives in England. Population density is skewed to the southeast of England, around London. London has between 7 and 9 million inhabitants, depending on definitions of the city's boundaries. "Green field" rural sites have enforced building restrictions to curb urban sprawl in the congested southeast.

Languages

English is the main language of the United Kingdom. Other important languages include the Celtic languages of Welsh, spoken by about 500,000 inhabitants of Wales, and the closely related Scottish and Irish Gaelic languages, spoken by several thousand inhabitants of Scotland and Northern Ireland. In the late twentieth century, immigration from Commonwealth countries led to the introduction of several ethnic minority languages. For example, languages from the Indian subcontinent such as Bengali and Punjabi are spoken in some British cities. The country's official literacy rate is near 100 percent.

Politics

As described in the "Brief History" section, the United Kingdom of Great Britain and Northern Ireland is the political union of England, Wales, Scotland, and Northern Ireland. In practice, however, the terms Britain and the United Kingdom are used interchangeably. The country is a constitutional monarchy and has its capital at London. The monarchy is hereditary, and the monarch serves as the largely ceremonial head of state. The head of government is the prime minister, who by convention is the leader of the majority party (or majority coalition) in parliament.

The parliament has a bicameral structure. The lower chamber, the House of Commons, is elected by popular vote, while the upper chamber, the House of Lords, is a curious mixture of hereditary peers, political appointees, and members of the clergy. The British are proud of their parliamentary traditions, but the British constitution is quite outdated in many respects. The anachronisms of the House of Lords are under review at the time of writing and it is widely expected that more elected and appointed members will replace the hereditary peers.

The main political parties are the Conservative and Labour parties, who have tended to alternate power in the last 100 years. (The historically strong Liberal Party is today a minor force in British politics, and its best hope of governing is to hold the balance of power between the Conservatives and Labour in a coalition.) Traditional ideological divisions between Conservative and Labour have diminished as both parties have embraced the market economy, privatized industry, and an increasingly modest welfare state. There are regional and nationalist parties in Northern Ireland, Scotland, and Wales.

In recent years, the United Kingdom has devolved powers to Scotland, Wales, and Northern Ireland, and there is talk of the creation of regional English assemblies. Northern Ireland has been scarred by serious sectarian violence from the 1960s to the present day. This has seen the rise of paramilitary groups advocating either the continuing attachment of Northern Ireland to the United Kingdom or its adherence to the Republic of Ireland. The "Good Friday" peace agreement of 1998 has lessened tensions and reduced paramilitary violence, but at the time of writing, the peace process is still fragile.

Other than Margaret Thatcher, the major twentieth-century British political figure was Winston Churchill (1871–1947), who led the country through World War II. Thatcher and Churchill shared many traits in common, not least a fierce and stubborn patriotism.

Economy

The United Kingdom is a major trading and financial power, with a commitment to free market economics that is somewhat unusual in the EU. The City of London has survived the loss of the British Empire to remain a financial center of global significance. The United Kingdom's economy was traditionally based on heavy manufacturing, and the modern Industrial Revolution started in Britain. However, the main characteristic of the modern British economy is its emphasis on the service sector, and manufacturing has experienced decades of steady decline. The agricultural sector is highly efficient in comparison with EU practices, but it has been affected by outbreaks of "mad cow" and foot-and-mouth diseases. Britain's North Sea oil reserves are significant, but high extraction costs have reduced their profitability.

From the 1980s, both Conservative and Labour governments have introduced market-oriented reforms that have reduced the numbers of state-owned enterprises. The country's economic problems include poor transport infrastructure and the persistence of significant levels of poverty. By EU standards, Britain's problems in both areas are severe. Britain's largest trading partners are Germany and France, and the currency unit is the pound.

Legal and Regulatory Environment

English law is based on the common law of case precedent, while Scottish law draws more heavily from continental influences. EU-inspired law has increasingly influenced the British legal system. By EU standards, regulation is light, as the market-oriented reforms of the late twentieth century have discouraged red tape and bureaucracy.

Accountancy

British GAAP is based on the country's Companies Acts, the Financial Reporting Standards of the Accounting Standards Board (ASB), and EU directives on accountancy. The Companies Act requires financial statements to be prepared in accordance with applicable accounting standards (the ASB's standards are considered appropriate) and to give a "true and fair" view. Tax rules have little effect on accounting practice, as separate tax accounts are prepared alongside investor-oriented financial statements.

As a member of the EU, the United Kingdom is committed to harmonizing domestic GAAP with IAS for listed corporations by 2005. However, the ASB has committed to anticipating the harmonization program before the 2005 deadline. Harmonization of UK Financial Reporting Standards with IAS will cover both listed and unlisted corporations.

The British accountancy profession was the world's earliest, with associations established in Scotland in 1854 and England in 1870. As a consequence, the British accounting and external auditing profession is large and mature. In addition to the Institute of Chartered Accountants in England and Wales and the Institute of Chartered Accountants of Scotland, other accountancy bodies include the Association of Chartered Certified Accountants (ACCA), the Chartered Institute of Management Accountants (CIMA), and the Chartered Institute of Public Finance and Accountancy (CIPFA). Chartered accountants have tended to dominate external auditing, while the ACCA and CIMA members have focused on management accounting, and CIPFA members on public finance. However, boundaries between the accountancy institutes are gradually narrowing and there is periodic talk of mergers. The ACCA has been successful in attracting large numbers of international students to its certification programs.

Cultural Background

The English are descended from Germanic peoples, while the Scots, Irish, and Welsh are mainly of Celtic origin. However, intermarriage makes analysis of the

United Kingdom's ethnic makeup extremely difficult. An approximate split is as follows: 80 percent English, 10 percent Scottish, 3 percent Irish, and 2 percent Welsh. The balance of 5 percent consists of other ethnic minorities, including those of Caribbean, Indian, Pakistani, and Chinese origin. The United Kingdom's population is multicultural, especially in urban areas, as a result of immigration from Commonwealth countries.

In matters of religion, Britain is a largely agnostic country. The established Anglican (Episcopal) church nominally has 25 to 30 million adherents, but this figure hides large patterns of nonobservance. Other Christian groups include other Protestant churches (e.g., Methodists and Presbyterians) and Roman Catholics. There are also Hindu, Jewish, Muslim, and Sikh minorities. Religious observance tends to be highest in Northern Ireland, Wales, and parts of Scotland, and lowest in England.

In addition to a respected literary high culture, dominated by William Shakespeare (1654–1616), the United Kingdom has been a major force in popular music. In particular, the 1960s and 1970s saw a "British invasion" of the U.S. popular music scene by the Beatles, the Rolling Stones, and Led Zeppelin, among others.

Social Etiquette

- Traditionally, a certain amount of social reserve is associated with the British. This reserve still exists, but visitors may also be surprised at the boisterousness of modern British social behavior.
- British understatement and restraint in business dealings should not necessarily be interpreted as indifference. It can often serve as a self-defense mechanism while digesting information and reaching a decision.
- Although the United Kingdom is a member of the EU, most British people feel ambivalent toward their European neighbors. In general, they do not share the enthusiasm for the EU evident in such nations as France and Germany.
- A two-fingered victory sign should not be done with the palm facing inward, as this is a highly offensive gesture.

Further Information

Eric J. Evans, *Thatcher and Thatcherism* (New York and London: Routledge, 1997).
Roy Jenkins, *Churchill: A Biography*, rev. ed. (New York: Farrar, Strauss and Giroux, 2001).
Simon Schama, *A History of Britain* [3 volumes] (New York: Talk Miramax Books, 2000 to 2002).
T. O. Lloyd, *The British Empire*, rev. ed. (New York and Oxford: Oxford University Press, 1996).
10 Downing Street (Prime Minister's office): *www.number-10.gov.uk*.
Commonwealth Secretariat: *www.thecommonwealth.org*.
Accounting Standards Board: *www.asb.org.uk*.
Association of Chartered Certified Accountants: *www.acca.org.uk*.

Chartered Institute of Management Accountants: *www.cimaglobal.com.*
Chartered Institute of Public Finance and Accountancy: *www.cipfa.org.uk.*
Institute of Chartered Accountants in England and Wales: *www.icaew.co.uk.*
Institute of Chartered Accountants of Scotland: *www.icas.org.uk.*
Institute of Internal Auditors UK and Ireland: *www.iia.org.uk.*

FEDERAL REPUBLIC OF YUGOSLAVIA

Geography

The borders of Yugoslavia have changed significantly since the 1990s, as summarized in the "Brief History" section. At the time of writing, the Federal Republic of Yugoslavia consists of several states in the Balkans, in southeast Europe. The states are Serbia, Montenegro, Vojvodina, and Kosovo. The state of Montenegro borders the Adriatic Sea, while the other states are landlocked. Bordering countries (including former Yugoslav republics) are Albania, Bosnia and Herzegovina, Bulgaria, Croatia, Hungary, Macedonia, and Romania.

Yugoslavia's varied terrain includes mountains, fertile lowlands, and forests. The climate is similarly varied: Winters are cold, while summers are hot and humid. Coastal areas benefit from a milder Mediterranean climate.

Brief History

Yugoslav territory is a complex historical patchwork of frequently warring communities. It has been a meeting place of major cultures and religions—Islam, Roman Catholicism, and Eastern Orthodox Christianity—and has often been a battlefield throughout its history. The Serb and Croatian peoples moved to the region several centuries after the birth of Christ. Although ethnically and linguistically close (the two peoples are Slavs and speak virtually the same language), the two communities differentiated themselves through religious affiliation. The Serbs adopted Eastern Orthodox Christianity and used the Cyrillic alphabet to write their language, while the Croatians followed Roman Catholicism and used the Roman script.

By the fourteenth century the Serbs were the dominant community in the region, but Turkish occupation of the Balkans characterized the following centuries. Serbian resistance against the Ottoman Turkish Empire is an important aspect of Serb national sentiment, and it was not until the late nineteenth century that most Serbs were free from Turkish rule. (Some parts of southern Yugoslavia remained part of the Turkish Ottoman Empire until the early twentieth century.) The period of Turkish dominance also led to the creation of a community of Muslim inhabitants of the Balkans, mainly Slav converts to Islam, whose descendants live mainly in Bosnia.

In 1912 and 1913, Serbia, Bulgaria, and Greece joined forces to oust Turkey from its remaining Balkan strongholds. As a result, Serbia doubled the size of its territory. However, as Turkish power diminished the Austro-Hungarian Empire stepped into the Balkans as the dominant political force. In 1914, the heir to the throne of the Austro-Hungarian Empire was assassinated in Bosnia. This triggered a series of political dominoes that dragged the major European countries into World War I.

At the end of World War I, the Austro-Hungarian Empire collapsed, and in 1918, the Kingdom of Serbs, Croats, and Slovenes was formed. The newly formed country changed its name to Yugoslavia in 1929. However, in World War II Nazi Germany invaded the Balkans. The German occupation was severely brutal and stoked hatred between the region's ethnic groups. The Germans established a puppet Croatian administration that massacred thousands of Serb civilians, as well as Jews and Roma (Gypsies).

Yugoslav resistance to German occupation took the form of many groups, including communist partisans. Among the latter was Josip Tito (1892–1980), who took political control of the country at the end of World War II and established a communist regime. The Tito regime was somewhat distant from the Soviet Union, and Yugoslavia did not endure the degree of Soviet dominance experienced by other East European communist states such as Poland and Czechoslovakia.

Tito was successful in dampening rivalries between Yugoslavia's ethnic groups. However, after Tito's death in 1980 the Yugoslav federation started to unravel, and long-suppressed ethnic divisions started to reassert themselves in a series of bloody conflicts. In 1991, Slovenia, Croatia, and Macedonia declared independence, to be followed in 1992 by Bosnia and Herzegovina. In 1992, the republics of Serbia and Montenegro declared a new Federal Republic of Yugoslavia, and under the leadership of President Slobodan Milosevic (born 1941) undertook military campaigns to reassert Serbian authority. The resulting wars in Croatia and Bosnia included massacres of civilians and other human rights abuses that commentators blamed on all participants.

In 1998, a rebellion in the mainly Muslim and ethnically Albanian province of Kosovo was put down by force by Milosevic's Serbian armed forces. International pressure on Milosevic included NATO air strikes against Yugoslavia in 1999, and the Serb military forces were obliged to withdraw from Kosovo. Milosevic lost power in 2000, and the succeeding administration agreed to extradite the former president to an international court to face charges of alleged war crimes. In early 2002, Serbia and Montenegro agreed to form a looser political federation that is expected at the time of writing to be called "Serbia and Montenegro." The name "Yugoslavia" may soon vanish from maps.

Demographics

The Balkans' ethnic conflicts have resulted in large-scale population movements in the region, which have complicated the reliability of population data for individual countries. Of the hundreds of thousands of refugees who crossed the borders of the former Yugoslav states in the 1990s, some have started to return in recent years to their former places of residence. Indicative population statistics suggest that Serbia and Montenegro (including Kosovo) have a combined population of around 10.7 million.

Languages

The main language of the Federal Republic of Yugoslavia is Serbian, which is a Slavonic language related to Russian. Like Russian, Serbian uses the Cyrillic alphabet. In neighboring Croatia, a similar language uses the Roman script. In the past, one often encountered the linguistic term "Serbo-Croat," which indicated the close relationship between the Serbian and Croatian languages. However, following the ethnic division of the old Yugoslavia, both communities prefer to identify their languages separately. (For a comparable linguistic separation, see the notes on Urdu and Hindi in the "Pakistan" country section.)

Perhaps 95 percent of the population of modern Yugoslavia speak Serbian, with an Albanian-speaking minority (mainly in Kosovo). In the neighboring states, the Slavonic languages of Croatian, Slovenian, and Macedonian are used. Other minority languages in the Balkans include Bulgarian, Hungarian, Romanian, and Turkish. Literacy is around 95 percent, and higher in the Serbian community than in the Albanian community.

Politics

The Federal Republic of Yugoslavia is currently undergoing a democratization process. The capital, Belgrade, is in Serbia. The head of state is the president, and the head of government is the prime minister. The parliament has a bicameral structure, with a chamber of republics and a chamber of citizens. Yugoslav politics is characterized by a large number of small parties, and by increasing cooperation with western nations in bringing alleged war criminals to justice. The latter is seen as a means of achieving the political rehabilitation of the country in the post-Milosevic era.

The current Federal Republic of Yugoslavia dates from 1992, but the two main states, Serbia and Montenegro, are (as discussed in the "Brief History" section) considering a change to the federal structure that would eliminate the term "Yugoslavia."

Economy

The devastation of the wars that accompanied the collapse of the former Yugoslavia in the 1990s resulted in severe economic disruption. Trade in the region was interrupted, and the emerging Balkan states were effectively war economies burdened by massive military spending. The surges in postcommunist affluence seen in states such as Poland and Czechoslovakia were not therefore reflected in Yugoslavia. Further, the bombing of the country by NATO during the 1999 Kosovo conflict further degraded the country's infrastructure and industrial base. In recent years, powerful criminal gangs have emerged to control black markets in smuggled consumer goods.

Yugoslavia's best hope for economic recovery is reengagement with the wider global economy, which the current administration is attempting to achieve alongside a program of political reform. The country's currency unit is the dinar.

Legal and Regulatory Environment

Yugoslav law is largely based on Byzantine civil law, although the legal practices of the communist period still influence the current system to a degree. The regulatory environment is heavy and complicated, reflecting both the communist legacy and the recent years of war activity, when the state played a major role in the day-to-day life of the country.

Accountancy

In 1998, the Association of Accountants and Auditors of Yugoslavia voted for the direct implementation of International Accounting Standards for all the country's listed corporations.

Cultural Background

The Balkan Wars of the 1990s led to large population movements along ethnic and religious lines. As a result, Yugoslavia is today an overwhelmingly Serbian and Eastern Orthodox Christian country, other than in the mainly Muslim and Albanian province of Kosovo. Ethnic divisions and attitudes have, unsurprisingly, hardened as a result of the conflicts. There is a Hungarian minority of several hundred thousand in Vojvodina province, near the Hungarian border, and the Roma (Gypsy) population is estimated to be several hundred thousand strong.

Social Etiquette

- Discussion of the Balkan Wars of the 1990s and the 1999 NATO bombing campaign should be avoided unless necessary. The wounds of war remain painful, and many Yugoslavs have lost family members in the conflicts. It is easy to unwittingly cause offense or distress.
- Despite the country's recent reputation as a violent place, the Yugoslavs are generally a well-educated and hospitable people.
- The pace of business life in Yugoslavia tends to be slow, as in all former communist countries with a tradition of heavy state planning.

Further Information

P. M. Barford, *The Early Slavs* (Ithaca, NY: Cornell University Press, 2001).

John K. Cox, *The History of Serbia* (Westport, CT: Greenwood, 2002).

Ian Jeffries, *The Former Yugoslavia at the Turn of the Twenty-First Century* (New York and London: Routledge, 2002).

Louis Sell, *Slobodan Milosevic and the Destruction of Yugoslavia* (Durham, NC: Duke University Press, 2002).

Serbia and Montenegro Governmental Web site: *www.gov.yu/start.php?je=e&id=10.*

The Mideast

TAX HAVENS AND INVESTMENT CENTERS

There are no significant tax havens or investment centers in the Mideast, as the tax-free oil states of the Persian Gulf offer many of the advantages of the classic tax haven.

IRAN

Geography

Iran is strategically located between the Arab world and Central Asia. It has coastlines on the Persian Gulf and the Gulf of Oman in the south, and on the Caspian Sea in the north. Iran shares borders with several important nations in the region, including Afghanistan, Armenia, Azerbaijan, Iraq, Pakistan, and Turkey. The country's terrain comprises a central plateau surrounded by mountains and uplands, and much of the land consists of arid desert. The climate is hot and dry, and devastating earthquakes occur from time to time.

Brief History

Iran has an ancient history of continuous civilization, and its cultural achievements have been among the finest in the world. In the second millennium BCE, Aryan invaders from Central Asia moved into the territory that would become Persia (and modern Iran), bringing agricultural skills far more sophisticated than those in use by the region's existing peoples. The first great political power in Persian history was the Achaemenid Empire, which established political power in Persia from the sixth century BCE. The empire became a world power, conquering large parts of the Mideast. (As a footnote, the Achaemenians captured Babylon and freed Jewish captives, as recounted in biblical records.)

The Achaemenians clashed frequently with the Greeks, and in the fourth century BCE the armies of the Greek military leader Alexander the Great invaded Persia. Alexander's legacy led to the disintegration of the Achaemenid Empire. One of Alexander's Greek generals was Seleucus (died 280 BCE), who ruled over much of Persia and established the Seleucid Dynasty. This Seleucids were ousted in the third century BCE by the Parthian Dynasty. The Parthians ruled Persia until another dynasty, the Sassanids, seized power in the third century CE. Sassanid rule was to last until the seventh century CE, and it reestablished the frontiers of Persia broadly in line with those of the old Achaemenid Empire. It also clashed frequently with the Roman Empire. Zoroastrianism became the state religion during the Sassanid era.

In the seventh century the Arabs invaded Persia and toppled the Sassanid Dynasty. The Arabs brought Islam, and over the following 200 years most of the local population converted to the newly introduced faith. Despite Arab and later Turkish cultural dominance, the Persians retained a strong sense of their distinct identity by retaining their own language and adhering to the Shia interpretation of Islam. Persian achievements in art, philosophy, science, and theology were admired throughout the world.

In the early thirteenth century, Persia was ransacked by invading Mongol armies. Cities were devastated, irrigation systems were destroyed, and the population decreased dramatically. As if this were not enough, in the fourteenth century the fierce Mongol-Turkic warrior Timur (1336–1405) conquered Persia and left another trail of death and destruction.

Stability returned to the country with the rise of the Safavid Dynasty in the sixteenth century, which was the first indigenous Persian dynasty for nearly 1,000 years. Shia Islam became the state religion, and artistic achievements reached new levels. Safavid power was challenged by the Ottoman Turks and by Afghans, but it lasted until the early eighteenth century. Post-Safavid Persia was volatile and politically unstable, before the Qajar Dynasty took control. The Qajar Dynasty ruled Persia from the late eighteenth century until 1925. The Qajars lost territory to Russia in the nineteenth century as the Russians consolidated their presence in Asia, and it lost its territorial claims in Afghanistan to the British Empire.

In the twentieth century, Persia's rulers moved the country in a secular direction, allied broadly with western interests. The country changed its name from Persia to Iran in 1935. Iran's economic prosperity grew as a result of the oil sector, but religious opposition to the secular regime also grew. The Iranian monarch, the shah, was propped up diplomatically and militarily by the United States, but local opposition to his pro-western rule hardened in the 1970s. Radical Islamic and Marxist groups used guerrilla tactics to try to overthrow the shah.

By the late 1970s, Iran was at a social, economic and cultural crossroads. Increasing social unrest and street protests created a climate of fear and instability, and the shah's regime was accused of serious human rights abuses in its attempts to suppress the growing dissent. The shah finally fled the country in January 1979, and within weeks the Islamic opposition leader Ayatollah Khomeini (1902–1989) returned from exile to establish a militant Islamic theocracy. The Islamic Republic of Iran came into being on April 1, 1979.

The new Islamic regime wasted no time in reversing the western, liberal agenda of the shah and his predecessors. Western-style clothes and music were among cultural artifacts outlawed by the new rulers, and a strict dress code for women was introduced. From the earliest days of the Islamic Revolution, Khomeini used hard rhetoric to denounce the United States as an enemy of Islam. Militant students seized the U.S. Embassy in Tehran and held U.S. hostages from November 1979 until January 20, 1981. Relations with the United States were strained, and the United States alleged that the Iranian regime sponsored terrorism.

In addition to strained relations with the United States, postrevolutionary Iran soon found itself at war with Saddam Hussein's Iraq. After an Iraqi attempt to seize disputed territory, the Iran-Iraq war lasted from 1980 to 1988 and cost more than 1 million lives. The Iranian regime caused international outrage by using child soldiers and "human wave" attacks at Iraqi lines. (Most western powers supported Iraq during the 1980s war, but Iraq was later to eclipse Iran in its antiwestern stance.) Partly as a result of the war with Iraq, the Iranian economy suffered in the late twentieth century and millions of Iranians were plunged into poverty.

In recent years, an internal power struggle has emerged between conservatives and liberals. The struggle essentially centers on the degree to which Iran should accommodate itself to the influences of the outside world. Relations with the United States remain very strained, and in 2002 the United States claimed that Iran (along with Iraq and North Korea) formed part of a political "axis of evil."

Demographics

The population of Iran totals around 66 million. The largest city, Tehran, has over 12 million inhabitants. The Iranian population is growing rapidly, and over 50 percent of the population is under the age of 25.

Languages

The main language of Iran is Farsi (sometimes called Persian), spoken as a mother tongue by around 60 percent of the population. Farsi is an Indo-European language that is related distantly to English. It is quite distinct from Arabic, but Arab cultural influence led to Farsi's adoption of a modified version of the Arabic script. Farsi also absorbed many Arabic words. There are many dialects of Farsi spoken in modern Iran, and other major languages spoken in the country include Turkic dialects (25 percent) and Kurdish (10 percent). There are also small numbers of Arabic speakers. Most non-Farsi speakers know Farsi as a second language. Literacy is around 70 percent, and is higher for men than for women.

Politics

The Islamic Republic of Iran is a rare phenomenon—a modern theocratic state. Its capital is at Tehran. The head of state is the Leader of the Islamic Revolution, Iran's supreme spiritual authority, who is appointed for life. The head of government is the country's president. The Iranian parliamentary body is the unicameral Islamic Consultative Assembly, whose members are elected by popular vote. There are reserved seats for religious minorities. Iranian politics is essentially driven by religious considerations, and in recent years there has been a power struggle between conservative and liberal interpretations of the Islamic Revolution.

Economy

Iran has many natural resources—oil, natural gas, coal, copper, iron ore, lead, manganese, and zinc. Oil accounts for around 85 percent of the country's export revenues. In addition, Iran has important industries in the carpet manufacturing, defense, food processing, and textile sectors. Centralized state planning plays an important role in the Iranian economy, but modest market reforms have been made in recent years.

Despite the country's oil reserves, the Iranian economy has severe structural problems—infrastructure is poor, unemployment is high, and foreign investment has been deterred by the radicalism of the political regime. One-third of the workforce is occupied in the agricultural sector, and around 40 percent of the population lives in poverty.

Iran's main trading partners include Japan and Germany. Owing to frosty political relations, the United States has little trading activity with Iran. The country's currency unit is the rial.

Legal and Regulatory Environment

Iranian law is based on Islamic Shari'a law. The charging of interest, for example, is forbidden. The regulatory environment is considered to be relatively cumbersome, although market reforms of recent years have partially alleviated the amount of red tape.

Accountancy

Iranian GAAP is based on the regulations of the Ministry of Economic Affairs and Finance, and in particular on the National Accounting Standards (NAS) of the ministry's Audit Organization. Stock exchange regulations require listed corporations to follow NAS. The NAS are based broadly on IAS, but there are areas of discrepancy between the two GAAP systems in areas such as lease accounting, deferred tax, and the treatment of employee benefits. The country's main professional association for accountancy and external auditing is the Iranian Institute of Certified Accountants (IICA). The IICA was established in 1972 and has a membership of around 1,800.

Cultural Background

The ethnic composition of Iran is approximately as follows: Farsi, or Persian (60 percent), Azeri (25 percent), and Kurdish (10 percent). There are also small communities of Arabs, Armenians, and Jews. Around 99 percent of Iranians are Muslim—approximately 90 percent are Shia, and 9 percent Sunni. There are small numbers of Christians, Jews, and Zoroastrians.

Iran's Islamic culture pervades everyday life, and drives cultural aspects varying from social behavior to dress codes. Iran is famous for its arts and crafts, and Persian carpets are exported throughout the world.

Social Etiquette

- Observant Muslims avoid pork and alcohol, and alcohol is forbidden.
- A conservative dress code for women is advisable.
- The visitor should be careful to respect Iranian religious sensibilities.

Further Information

Christiane Bird, *Neither East Nor West: One Woman's Journey Through the Islamic Republic of Iran* (New York: Simon & Schuster, 2001).
Bager Moin, *Khomeini: Life of the Ayatollah* (New York: St. Martin's Press, 2000).
Malise Ruthven, *Islam: A Very Short Introduction*, rev. ed. (New York and Oxford: Oxford University Press, 2000).
Elaine Sciolino, *Persian Mirrors: The Elusive Face of Iran* (New York: Free Press, 2000).
Behzad Yaghmaian, *Social Change in Iran: An Eyewitness Account of Dissent, Defiance, and New Movements for Rights* (New York: State University of New York Press, 2002).
Presidency of the Islamic Republic of Iran: *www.president.ir*.
Iranian Institute of Certified Accountants: *www.iranianica.com/iica.html*.

IRAQ

Geography

Iraq is located at the geo-politically strategic head of the Persian Gulf. The country borders Iran, Jordan, Kuwait, Saudi Arabia, Syria, and Turkey. A large part of the terrain consists of desert plains, with marshlands in the south. The Iranian and Turkish border areas are mountainous. The Iraqi climate is a typical desert one, with dry, hot summers and mild to warm winters. Mountain areas experience cold winters with heavy snowfalls.

Brief History

The borders of modern Iraq approximate to the lands of the ancient Mesopotamian civilization. Mesopotamia gave the world many of its finest early cultural achievements, such as literacy. The region has subsequently been home to a series of further impressive civilizations—Persian, Greek, and Arab. In the seventh century, Arab invaders brought the Islamic faith to Iraq, whose population at the time was predominantly Christian. The population adopted the Islamic faith and the Arabic language. Under the Abbasid Caliphate that lasted from the eighth to the thirteenth centuries, Iraq was at the political and cultural center of the Islamic world, which stretched from Morocco to India.

Mongol invasions in the thirteenth century led to huge loss of life and the destruction of the Abbasid Caliphate. The influence of Baghdad started to wane. By the seventeenth century Iraq had been reduced from its position of former preeminence to a war-torn buffer zone between the Turkish and Persian empires. Violent conflict on Iraqi soil between the Sunni-majority Turks and the Shia-majority Persians exacerbated religious divisions still evident in Iraq today. The Ottoman Turks gained political control of Iraq and remained in power for almost three centuries, until World War I. However, the extent of Ottoman control was not always very strong, and certain parts of Iraq—Kurdish areas in particular—remained virtually autonomous.

Resentment against Ottoman "Turkification" policies in the late nineteenth and early twentieth centuries led to the emergence of a mainly middle-class Arab nationalist movement. In World War I, the Ottoman Empire sided with Germany, and British forces from India invaded the Ottoman territory of Iraq. The British captured Baghdad in 1917. The British intervention raised Arab hopes for an independent Iraq, but Britain and the other victorious war allies decided to carve up large parts of the Mideast into so-called "mandates," or administrative districts. Britain was given a "mandate" in Iraq, which effectively meant that the country was under British colonial control. Civil unrest and nationalist agitation united various ethnic and religious Iraqi groups and undermined the British administration. The British tried various political tricks to hang onto Iraq while giving the country a veneer of independence, but they were ultimately unsuccessful. In 1932, Iraq finally became an independent nation.

Despite its oil wealth, the newly independent Iraqi nation was politically unstable, and after a series of uprisings, the Iraqi monarchy was overthrown by a 1958 military coup. The new republic has since been dominated by a series of powerful and often ruthless military rulers. In the 1960s, armed Kurdish separatists started an insurgency, while long-standing ethnic and religious divisions exploded into violence in other parts of the country. The country seemed to be heading toward chaos.

In 1968, another coup saw the rise to power of the Arab nationalist Baath Party, which subsequently suppressed all political opposition. This period also introduced Saddam Hussein (born 1937) to the world. Saddam became president in 1979, and in the early years of his autocratic rule the country became prosperous from its oil wealth. Saddam had ambitions to turn Iraq into a regional power. He denounced the 1979 peace agreement between Egypt and Israel, and his use of strong anti-Israeli rhetoric was designed to reinforce his claims to pan-Arab leadership.

Saddam's rule soon came to be characterized by war. The Iraqi regime fought bloody conflicts against Kurdish separatists in the north of the country, and against neighboring countries. Saddam initially attempted to negotiate with Kurdish separatists, and offered them a semi-autonomous region within the Iraqi state. However, he accompanied negotiation with more brutal tactics of forced resettlement.

Over time, the conflict became increasingly bitter, and in 1988 Saddam outraged world opinion by using chemical weapons to kill thousands of Kurdish civilians.

In 1980, Saddam took advantage of the turmoil caused by the Iranian Islamic Revolution of the previous year to invade Iran. He was motivated by a desire to settle a long-running territorial dispute, and by fears that the radical policies of Shia-dominated Iran could spread to Iraq's Shia communities. The resulting war lasted until 1988 and cost more than 1 million lives, but it did not achieve any conclusive results. Iraq's superior military equipment was balanced by the Iranian's numerical advantage and sheer fanaticism.

In 1990, Iraq invaded Kuwait and announced that it had annexed the territory. The world feared that Saddam would go on to invade Saudi Arabia and thereby control a large proportion of the world's oil reserves. The United States led a broad coalition of countries that successfully ousted the Iraqis from Kuwait in 1991.

The cumulative devastation of the wars against Iran and the U.S.-led coalition left Iraq in economic ruin, but Saddam did not relinquish power. International sanctions increased the country's economic plight, and child mortality rates soared. At the time of writing, the United States is threatening to topple Saddam by military action if necessary, alleging that the Iraqi regime is developing weapons of mass destruction.

Demographics

The population of Iraq is around 23 million.

Languages

Iraq's main languages are Arabic and Kurdish. Arabic is spoken by between 75 and 80 percent of the population, and Kurdish by 15 percent to 20 percent. (The Arabic language is discussed further in the "Saudi Arabia" country section.) Kurdish is an Indo-European language unrelated to Arabic. Other minority languages include Armenian and various Turkic languages. The country's literacy rate is around 50 percent, and is higher for men than for women.

Politics

The Republic of Iraq is a one-party state ruled by the largely secular Baath Party and has its capital at Baghdad. The country's president acts as both head of state and head of government and is elected by the Revolutionary Command Council. The country has a unicameral parliament, but the government does not tolerate political dissent. Political opposition often takes the form of extra-parliamentary movements, some of which are in exile.

Economy

The Iraqi economy is based on the oil sector, which has traditionally provided the vast majority of exports. The country's late-twentieth-century prosperity disappeared in the 1980s and 1990s, however, as a result of costly wars against Iran and the U.S.-led coalition that ousted the Iraqi army from Kuwait. Politically motivated economic sanctions have also strangled the Iraqi economy and standards of living have plummeted. Millions—perhaps even a majority of the country's inhabitants—now live in poverty. The United Nations has relaxed some sanctions for humanitarian purposes, but economic conditions remain grim.

Iraq's largest trading partners are Germany and Japan. Russia also remains an important trading ally, reflecting old Cold War links with the Soviet Union. The country's currency unit is the dinar.

Legal and Regulatory Environment

Iraqi law is a mixture of continental European legal practice and Islamic law. French legal traditions were introduced to the country during the long period of Turkish Ottoman rule that ended with World War I. The regulatory environment is heavy, reflecting the pervasive role of the state in the economy and in many areas of public life. At the time of writing, severe political tensions and economic sanctions have reduced the activities of foreign corporations in Iraq to a trickle.

Accountancy

Little information is available on Iraqi accountancy and auditing practices, owing to the virtual closure of the country's economy to the rest of the world following the wars and economic sanctions of recent years. It is assumed that company and commercial law drive Iraqi accountancy practice, with influence from the period of the British "Mandate" of the early twentieth century. The country's Association of Public Accountants and Auditors is, however, a full member of the International Federation of Accountants.

Cultural Background

The main ethnic groups in Iraq are Arabs (75 to 80 percent of the population) and Kurds (15 to 20 percent). There are also small communities of Armenians, Jews, and others. Most Iraqis are Muslim, with around 60 to 65 percent Sunni and around 35 percent Shia. Christians account for less than 5 percent of the population.

The Kurds live in the northern region of Iraq and are mainly Sunni Muslims. The Iraqi Kurds are part of a regional Kurdish population that covers parts of Iran, Syria, and Turkey. Many Kurds aspire to an independent homeland of Kurdistan that would unite the Kurdish peoples currently scattered between different Mideast states. Kurdish nationalism is a major political issue across the region, and the Kurds have tenaciously maintained their cultural identity despite their fragmentation across modern state boundaries.

Social Etiquette

The Saudi Arabia country section has comments of general application to Muslim culture in the Mideast. In addition:

- Visitors should be careful when discussing the country's recent wars against Iran and the U.S. coalition that ousted the Iraqi army from Kuwait. It is a sensitive topic that can easily inflame passions and cause distress.
- It is important to distinguish between the country's Kurdish and Arab inhabitants. The Kurds are fiercely independent and proud of their separate cultural identity.

Further Information

Majid Khadduri and Edmund Ghareeb, *War in the Gulf, 1990–91: The Iraq-Kuwaiti Conflict and its Implications* (New York and Oxford: Oxford University Press, 1997).

Sandra MacKey, *The Reckoning: Iraq and the Legacy of Saddam Hussein* (New York: W. W. Norton, 2002).

Charles Tripp, *A History of Iraq*, 2nd ed. (New York and Cambridge: Cambridge University Press, 2002).

The Iraqi Presidency (official government Web site): *www.uruklink.net/iraq/epage1.htm.*

ISRAEL

Geography

Israel is located between Lebanon and Egypt, and also shares borders with Jordan, Syria, and Palestinian territories whose political status remains unresolved at the time of writing. Israel has a Mediterranean Sea coastline. The country's terrain comprises a heavily populated coastal plain, the Negev desert in the south, and highlands and mountains in the north and center. The Negev desert accounts for around 50 percent of the country's territory. The climate is hot and arid in the desert areas, but more temperate in other parts of the country.

Brief History

The modern state of Israel was created in the aftermath of World War II, and represented the culmination of the aspirations of the Zionist movement of the nineteenth and early twentieth centuries. The Zionists desired an independent state for the Jewish people, who had settled in many countries following the destruction of their state and religious institutions by the Romans in the first century CE. A major figure in the Zionist movement was Hungarian-born Theodor Herzl (1860–1904). Herzl was converted to Zionism after observing the "Dreyfus Affair" in France of the 1890s, in which a Jewish army officer was convicted of treason by an anti-Semitic establishment. At one stage, the British touted Uganda in Africa as a possible location for a Jewish state. However, the Zionist movement turned to the ancient biblical territories as the natural homeland of the Jews, and worked toward establishing a Jewish state in the Mideast.

The Zionists realized their dream following World War II, when centuries of European anti-Semitism crystallized in the mass murder of millions of European

Jews by the regime of Nazi Germany and its allies. The State of Israel was created in 1948, as Britain withdrew from its UN administrative mandate in Palestine. The United Nations recognized Israel in 1949.

The creation of Israel led to violent hostilities with the region's Arab nations. The city of Jerusalem was divided, and hundreds of thousands of Muslim Arab Palestinians were displaced from Israeli territory. To this date, the refugees and their descendants live either in neighboring Arab states or in territories of continuing uncertain political status (the West Bank and the Gaza Strip) alongside Israel. Timely arms shipments from Czechoslovakia helped Israel to survive early attempts to destroy it, but the country's subsequent history has been one of frequent armed conflict with neighboring countries. Major conflicts broke out in 1956, 1967, 1973, and 1982. The legendary fighting abilities of the Israeli military led to victory over Arab forces on all these occasions, which took on a Cold War flavor. The United States supported Israel while the Soviet Union backed Israel's Arab enemies. Despite its military superiority, Israel has not been able to fully contain the region's violence. At the time of writing, serious violence continues between Israel and various armed Arab organizations.

In the 1956 ("Six Day") war, the Israeli armed forces defeated the Egyptian army to gain control over large parts of the Sinai Peninsula. Underlying tensions erupted again in 1967, when Israel defeated the combined military forces of Egypt, Jordan, and Syria. Israel was able to occupy the remainder of the Sinai Peninsula east of the Suez canal, as well as Jordan's West Bank (including East Jerusalem) and the Syrian Golan Heights. In the 1973 war, a coordinated Egyptian and Syrian offensive caught Israel by surprise on the Jewish religious festival of Yom Kippur. The Arab nations made swift advances, but the Israeli armed forces again proved victorious. In 1982, Israel invaded southern Lebanon, in response to attacks from fighters of the Palestine Liberation Organization (PLO). Lebanon was already experiencing a bitter civil war among its complex mix of ethnic and religious communities. The Israelis drove the PLO—regarded by some Arab nations as the legitimate representative of the Palestinian people—out of Lebanon and into exile.

Israel has had some success in achieving peace with neighboring countries. In 1979, the Camp David agreements led to peace between Israel and Egypt, and Israel handed the Sinai Peninsula back to the Egyptians in 1982. In 2000, Israel withdrew from southern Lebanon, ending an occupation that dated from the invasion of 1982. However, the longest-running challenge has been the search for peace between Israel and the Palestinians. With a view to ending decades of political violence, the two sides have engaged in talks of exchanging land for peace since the 1990s. This involves Israel giving up occupied territories such as the West Bank and Gaza Strip to create a Palestinian state, and returning the Golan heights to Syria (as it returned the Sinai Peninsula to Egypt in 1982). In response, Israel would obtain peaceful coexistence with its Arab neighbors.

At the time of writing, the peace process is under severe strain, and Israelis and Palestinians are caught in a deadly cycle of violence. Armed groups operating from Palestinian territories have undertaken a series of suicide bombings deliberately targeted at civilians, which have horrified world opinion. Israel has responded by temporarily reoccupying Palestinian land, imposing curfews, and arresting or assassinating Palestinian military opponents.

Demographics

Israel's population is just under 6 million. Following the creation of the modern Israeli state in 1948, Jewish immigration has occurred from many parts of the world, including Europe, the Mideast, and Ethiopia. Following the collapse of the Soviet Union, many Russian Jews have also moved to Israel. Around 80 percent of the Israeli population is Jewish, and the remainder are mainly Arab Muslims. Israel's literacy rate is around 95 percent.

Languages

The main language of Israel is Hebrew, which is an official language of the country. Other important languages include Arabic, the official language of the country's Muslim minority, and Russian, which is the first language of many recent immigrants from the former Soviet Union. Hebrew and Arabic are linguistically related but use different writing systems. Other languages such as Yiddish (a derivative of German) are spoken by immigrants from various parts of the world, a reflection of the diverse origins of Israel's inhabitants. English is widely spoken among the middle classes.

Politics

The State of Israel is a parliamentary democracy and has its capital at Jerusalem. However, not all countries recognize Jerusalem as the Israeli capital, and many foreign embassies are located in the city of Tel Aviv. The head of state is the president, and the head of government is the prime minister. The prime minister selects the cabinet from the Knesset, the unicameral parliament elected by popular vote. The main Israeli political parties are the Labor Party and Likud, but Israel also has numerous small parties that often hold the balance of power in coalition governments.

Israeli politics has long been dominated by the country's fight for survival in a hostile region. The country's main political ally is the United States, from which it derives financial, military, diplomatic, and moral support. Israel has also developed a nuclear defense capability.

Domestically, tensions between secular and religious Jews have been a feature of Israeli politics since the creation of the modern state.

Economy

Israel has a sophisticated mixed economy that blends free enterprise with a large role for the state. The country has limited natural resources, but is more or less self-sufficient in agriculture (other than grains). Despite an arid climate, the agricultural collectives of the pioneering kibbutz movement laid the foundations of agricultural self-sufficiency in the early years of the state's existence. Today, agricultural products—especially fruits—are a major category of exports. Israel also has successful industries in the high-technology manufacturing and defense sectors. High defense spending is assisted by military aid from the United States.

Tourism is another traditionally important element of the Israeli economy. Jews, Christians, and Muslims all trace religious and cultural roots to Israeli territory, but Israeli-Palestinian violence has deterred many potential visitors in recent years. Israel's major trading partner is the United States and the country's currency unit is the shekel.

Legal and Regulatory Environment

Israeli law is based largely on English common law, which reflects the influence of the British "Mandate" of the early twentieth century, as well as on more recent influences from the United States. Domestic law reflects the religious cultures of Jews, Muslims, and Christians. In general, Israeli regulation and bureaucracy are relatively cumbersome, reflecting both the country's security needs and the state's significant role in the country's economic life.

Accountancy

Israeli GAAP is based on company law and the accounting standards of the Israel Accounting Standards Board (IASB). The IASB was established in 1997 and took over standard-setting responsibilities from the Institute of Certified Public Accountants in Israel (ICPAI), the country's main accountancy and external auditing body. The IASB encompasses a range of interests, including the ICAPI, the Tel Aviv Stock Exchange, and investor groups.

Although Israeli GAAP has traditionally tended to follow U.S. GAAP, the IASB has declared its intention to harmonize Israeli GAAP with IAS, although it has reserved the right to modify IAS to fit the circumstances of the local environment. For example, the Israeli Accounting Standard 8 (Discontinuing Operations), valid from 2002, is based on IAS 35 of the same name. The IASB Web site (*www.iasb.org.il*) has details of Israeli accounting standards in English.

Cultural Background

Around 80 percent of the population of Israel is Jewish, but the Jewish community is very varied. As discussed in the "Demographics" section, many Israelis were born outside the country and originate from Africa, the Americas, Asia, and Europe. The two dominant Jewish ethnic groups are the Ashkenazim, who originate from Central and Eastern Europe, and the Sephardim, who originate from the Mediterranean and Mideast regions. The remaining 20 percent of the Israeli population consists mainly of Muslim Arabs, although there are also a number of relatively small Christian communities.

One of the Jewish people's outstanding cultural achievements has been in the field of classical music, with contributions by many of the world's greatest classical musicians and conductors. Examples include pianist Artur Rubinstein (1887–1983), violinist Itzhak Perlman (born 1945), and conductors Sir Georg Solti (1912–1997) and Daniel Barenboim (born 1942).

Social Etiquette

- There are significant cultural differences between Israel's Jewish and Muslim communities—one aspect among many is the Muslim prohibition on alcohol. Both communities avoid pork.
- The Jewish working week runs from Sunday to Thursday.
- The speed of business in Israel is somewhat slower than in the west.

Further Information

Dan Cohn-Sherbok and Dawoud El-Alami, *The Palestine-Israeli Conflict: A Beginners' Guide* (New York: Oneworld, 2001).

Martin Gilbert, *Never Again: A History of the Holocaust* (New York: Universe, 2000).

Michael B. Oren, *Six Days of War: June 1967 and the Making of the Modern Middle East* (New York and Oxford: Oxford University Press, 2002).

Harry Orlinski, *Ancient Israel*, 2nd ed. (Ithaca, NY: Cornell University Press, 1960).

Israeli Government: *www.pmo.gov.il/english*.

Israel Accounting Standards Board: *www.iasb.org.il*.

Institute of Certified Public Accountants in Israel: *www.icpas.org.il/eng/index.html*.

Institute of Internal Auditors Israel: *www.iia.org.il/English/First_page.htm*.

KUWAIT

Geography

Kuwait is a small country, but its wealth and strategic location at the center of a volatile region make it an extremely important nation. Located between Iraq and Saudi Arabia at the head of the Persian Gulf, Kuwaiti territory comprises desert plains. The climate is intensely hot and dry in summer, although winters are cooler.

Brief History

The territory of modern Kuwait has been inhabited for only around 300 years, despite the fact that the region in which Kuwait is located has been a center of civilization for millennia. (The "Iraq" and "Saudi Arabia" country sections give information on the wider region's history.) Kuwait developed as a moderately prosperous port, which flourished on the overland caravan trade as well as on the Persian Gulf sea trade. In contrast to many neighboring countries, Kuwait was not constructed as a state by twentieth-century colonialists. It has been an autonomous or semi-autonomous political entity from the eighteenth century.

In the nineteenth century, the Kuwaitis managed to keep the Turkish Ottoman Empire at arm's length, and the territory was ruled by the Al Sabah royal house. To protect the sea routes from England to India, the British provided naval defenses to Kuwait around the turn of the twentieth century. British involvement deterred the Ottoman Empire from enforcing its territorial claim over Kuwait, and Britain also helped to combat piracy in the Persian Gulf.

In the early twentieth century, the house of Al Saud tried to incorporate Kuwait into the United Kingdom of Saudi Arabia, but the British negotiated a treaty that kept Kuwait under British economic control. The Kuwait Oil Company (KOC), a joint British and U.S. venture, started operating in the 1930s. It soon became clear that Kuwait had massive oil reserves. The KOC interrupted its activities during World War II, but in the latter half of the twentieth century the oil sector led to a boom in living standards.

Indian independence following World War II meant that Britain no longer had a strong incentive to maintain its interests in the Persian Gulf. The Kuwaitis gained independence in 1961, but the Iraqis soon claimed sovereignty over the territory. British and later Saudi troops were invited to Kuwait to deter an Iraqi invasion. When the Arab League recognized Kuwaiti independence, the Iraqis were temporarily forced to back down on their territorial claim.

Kuwait developed as a small but prosperous oil state, and it kept aloof from the 1980s war between Iran and Iraq. However, the country's peaceful existence was shattered in 1990 by an Iraqi invasion. Iraqi leader Saddam Hussein had resurrected his country's old claim to sovereignty over Kuwait. The world was outraged, and feared that the Iraqi invasion of Kuwait was a prelude to an invasion of Saudi Arabia. With UN approval, a coalition of nations led by the United States ousted Iraqi forces from Kuwait early the following year, in the so-called "Operation Desert Storm." The military operation to retake Kuwait was preceded by intensive bombing of Iraq that left large parts of Iraq's military and civilian infrastructures in ruins. Kuwait also suffered serious damage during the war, and the retreating Iraqis set alight hundreds of Kuwaiti oil wells.

Kuwait has successfully rebuilt its country following the destruction caused by the Iraqi invasion. The country has also made modest democratic reforms, including the promise of extension of the franchise to women.

Demographics

The population of Kuwait is around 0.9 million. There are also over 1 million foreign expatriate workers in the country, attracted by the country's oil wealth. Following the Iraqi invasion of 1990, Kuwait expelled hundreds of thousands of Palestinian workers, because of perceived Palestinian sympathy for Iraq and the alleged collaboration of many Palestinians with the Iraqi invasion forces. These Palestinian workers have been replaced by other nationalities.

Languages

Arabic is the official and main language of Kuwait. (The "Saudi Arabia" country section gives more details on the Arabic language.) A small minority of the population (perhaps 5 percent or less) with historical roots in Iran speaks Farsi as well as Arabic. English is widely understood. The country's literacy rate is approximately 80 percent, and is higher for men than for women.

Politics

The State of Kuwait is a constitutional monarchy that has become increasingly democratized following the 1990 Iraqi invasion. The country's capital is Kuwait City. The Al Sabah house controls the highest political offices, with the monarch acting as head of state, and the prime minister (by tradition, the crown prince) as head of government. Members of the unicameral parliament are elected by popular male vote, and women have been promised the franchise.

Economy

The oil sector dominates the Kuwaiti economy. Other major industries include natural gas, fishing, and food processing, but the petroleum sector accounts for 90 percent of export revenues. Kuwait has around 10 percent of the world's oil reserves. Other than fish, nearly all food has to be imported. Following the 1990 Iraqi invasion, the Kuwaiti economy has been fully rebuilt, and the country remains a prosperous one that attracts foreign workers from around the world. Kuwait's largest trading partners are the United States and Japan, and the currency unit is the dinar.

Legal and Regulatory Environment

Kuwaiti law is based on Islamic law, above all in personal and domestic matters. The country's commercial law has a broadly secular nature. Taxation is nonexistent. The regulatory environment is relatively cumbersome, especially in employee-related matters—there are strict rules on the indigenization of the workforce in corporations, for example.

Accountancy

Since 1990, Kuwaiti GAAP has been based on IAS (with the use of additional explanatory information to give details on the local regulatory environment). The Kuwait Association of Accountants and Auditors is a full member of the International Federation of Accountants, and owing to the country's oil wealth, the major international accounting firms are all represented in the country.

Cultural Background

The inhabitants of Kuwait—excluding foreign expatriate workers—are almost entirely Arabs, although as many as 5 percent are thought to be of Iranian origin. Sunnis account for around 80 to 85 percent of Kuwaitis, and the Shia population is estimated to be around 15 to 20 percent. Most Iranian-origin Kuwaitis who speak Farsi as well as Arabic are Shia Muslims.

Social Etiquette

The Saudi Arabia country section has comments of general application to Muslim culture in the Mideast. In addition:

- Visitors should be careful when discussing the country's 1990 invasion by Iraq, as this sensitive topic is still distressful for many.
- Kuwait is relatively liberal by Mideast standards, but visitors should not be misled about the extent of the country's liberalism. Alcohol is still strictly forbidden, for example.
- Conservative dress for women is advisable, although not to the extent of neighboring Saudi Arabia.

Further Information

Frederick F. Anscombe, *The Ottoman Gulf: The Creation of Kuwait, Saudi Arabia and Qatar* (New York: Columbia University Press, 1997).

Majid Khadduri and Edmund Ghareeb, *War in the Gulf, 1990–91: The Iraq-Kuwaiti Conflict and Its Implications* (New York and Oxford: Oxford University Press, 1997).

Malise Ruthven, *Islam: A Very Short Introduction*, rev. ed. (New York and Oxford: Oxford University Press, 2000).

Mary Ann Tétreault, *Stories of Democracy: Politics and Society in Contemporary Kuwait* (New York: Columbia University Press, 2000).

Kuwaiti Ministry of Finance: *www.mof.gov.kw*.

SAUDI ARABIA

Geography

Saudi Arabia is the largest country in the Arabian Peninsula. It has coastlines along the Persian Gulf in the west and the Red Sea in the east, and it borders Iraq, Jordan, Kuwait, Oman, Qatar, the United Arab Emirates, and Yemen. Most of the terrain is sandy desert, and the climate is hot and dry. Humidity is high in coastal areas.

Brief History

The Arabian Peninsula has been inhabited for millennia. Sea trading along the peninsula's coasts brought a degree of wealth to the area, but living conditions in the dry interior were always difficult. The peoples of the interior adopted a nomadic or semi-nomadic lifestyle, and the camel-based caravan trade led to the establishment of trade routes between the peninsula's oases. Jews and Christians were drawn to the area by the trading economy.

By far the most significant event in the history of the Arabian Peninsula was the advent of Islam, following the birth of the Prophet Muhammad in 570 CE. Muhammad instituted a new spiritual and social order that altered subsequent world history. Following Muhammad's death, a series of caliphs oversaw the expansion of an Islamic empire. Arab conquests took Islam throughout much of the Mideast and North Africa. However, in the centuries following Muhammad's death, the center of gravity of Islamic civilization and political power shifted from the Arabian Peninsula to the wider Muslim world—to the territories of modern Syria, Iran, Iraq, and Turkey. However, the Arabian Peninsula retained its position as the spiritual focus of Islam owing to the crucial importance of the Muslim pilgrimage to Mecca.

The modern history of Saudi Arabia is closely linked to the royal house of Al Saud, and its unification of the country under the principles of the relatively strict Wahhabi interpretation of Sunni Islam. After a long and complex struggle, the Al Saud defeated Turkish and Egyptian political interference in the peninsula to establish the modern nation state of Saudi Arabia in 1932.

In the 1930s, the discovery of oil transformed Saudi Arabia's economy. The newly found oil wealth gave the country both economic and political clout, as evidenced during the Arab oil crisis of the early 1970s, which had severe repercussions on the world economy. Relations with neighboring countries were often strained. Following the Iranian Islamic Revolution of 1979, religious rivalry between predominantly Sunni Saudi Arabia and predominantly Shia Iran was a source of potential instability in the Mideast. Tensions rose after Saudi security forces battled Iranian pilgrims in 1997, in fighting that cost hundreds of lives. However, the main threat to Saudi Arabia in the late twentieth century came from Saddam Hussein's Iraq.

Following the 1990 Iraqi invasion of Kuwait, the Saudis invited the armed forces of the United States into Saudi territory, as part of a coalition of anti-Iraqi western and Mideast forces. The war was successful, but many Saudis were deeply unhappy at the presence of non-Muslim troops in their country. The 1990s saw a rise of militant, anti-western guerrilla groups, some of which were based outside the peninsula.

The country's economic miracle has soured a little in recent years. The effects of population growth, volatile oil prices, high unemployment, and a ballooning budget deficit have taken their toll. However, Saudi Arabia remains one of the world's richest countries. Pressures for political reform have also increased in recent years as the Saudis attempt to reconcile conservative religious beliefs with the modernizing pressures of an oil-boom society.

Demographics

The population of Saudi Arabia is around 17 million. Owing to Saudi Arabia's hot, desert terrain, much of the country is uninhabited. There are also around 5 million foreign workers in the country, mainly from other Mideast countries and the Indian subcontinent. The population of foreign workers also includes hundreds of thousands of Europeans and North Americans attracted by generous tax-free salaries.

Languages

The language of Saudi Arabia is Arabic, a member of the Semitic language family that is related to Hebrew. Arabic is written with a cursive script, from right to left. Owing to the role of Arabic in the Islamic religion, the language has great cultural prestige around the world. Even unrelated Indo-European languages such as Farsi (in Iran) and Urdu (in India and Pakistan) have adopted modified versions of the Arabic writing system. Literacy is around 65 percent, and it is higher for men than for women.

Politics

The Kingdom of Saudi Arabia is a monarchy and has its capital at Riyadh. The monarch acts both as head of state and head of government. There are no western-style, democratic elections. The monarch appoints a Council of Ministers and a consultative council to assist in governing the country.

Economy

The petroleum sector is Saudi Arabia's main economic activity and the source of its staggering wealth. Petroleum and petroleum-related products account for 90 percent of the country's exports. The country has around a quarter of the world's known oil reserves. Other resources include natural gas, gold, copper, and iron ore, and major industrial sectors include cement and construction. The prosperity generated by the oil industry has attracted millions of foreign workers to seek employment in the country.

As discussed in the "Brief History" section, the country's pressing economic problems include high unemployment and budget deficits. Saudi Arabia remains a wealthy country, however, and it is a major donor to developing Muslim countries. The United States and Japan are Saudi Arabia's main trading partners, and the currency unit is the riyal.

Legal and Regulatory Environment

Saudi law is, of course, based strictly on Islamic Shari'a law. The charging of interest by banks, for example, is prohibited. Criminal punishments including executions and amputations are administered in public, and the deterrent effect of these draconian measures has resulted in generally low crime levels. The country's economic growth since the middle of the twentieth century has resulted in the introduction of secular legal principles in commercial and business. There is no taxation in the country, which is a reflection of its immense prosperity. The regulatory environment is relatively cumbersome, as the state plays a large part in the economic life. In addition, strict controls over many aspects of Saudi life have added to the country's red tape. Recent moves toward privatization are expected to reduce the levels of state involvement in economic affairs.

Accountancy

Saudi GAAP is based on regulations of the Ministry of Commerce, and on the accounting standards of the Saudi Organization of Certified Public Accountants (SOCPA). The SOCPA has issued only a limited number of accounting standards, but has stated that where its standards do not cover a topic, then U.S. GAAP (adjusted for the context of Saudi Arabia) should be used. There have traditionally been a number of areas of discrepancy with IAS, in areas such as employee benefits and the treatment of goodwill. At the time of writing, the use of IAS is not permitted.

Cultural Background

Around 90 percent of the inhabitants of Saudi Arabia are ethnic Arabs, and the remainder are of African or mixed Arab-African descent. (This analysis excludes the millions of foreign workers who live on a temporary basis in the country.) All Saudis are Muslims, and overt displays of other religions by foreign workers are forbidden. Indeed, Islam dominates Saudi life and is reflected in strict dress codes for women in public, the banning of alcohol, and constraints on the range of women's employment.

Social Etiquette

- Visitors should respect the Islamic faith and avoid any hint of disrespect to the country's religious practices. Contravention can land the visitor in trouble with the country's religious and civil authorities.
- Alcohol is forbidden and contravention is severely punished.
- The pace of business life is generally slower in Saudi Arabia than in the west, and elaborate negotiations often accompany business dealings.
- Arabic hospitality is legendary, and visitors are often treated with great ceremony.
- Saudis are justifiably proud of their cuisine, which includes spicy meat dishes and fine breads. Under no circumstances do observant Muslims eat pork.

Further Information

Frederick F. Anscombe, *The Ottoman Gulf: The Creation of Kuwait, Saudi Arabia and Qatar* (New York: Columbia University Press, 1997).

Daryl Champion, *The Paradoxical Kingdom: Saudi Arabia and the Momentum of Reform* (New York: Columbia University Press, 2002).
Madawi al-Rasheed, *A History of Saudi Arabia* (New York and Cambridge: Cambridge University Press, 2002).
Malise Ruthven, *Islam: A Very Short Introduction*, rev. ed. (New York and Oxford: Oxford University Press, 2000).
Majlis Ash Shura (Government Web site): *www.shura.gov.sa/EnglishSite/ EIndex.htm.*

TURKEY

Geography

Geographically (and culturally), Turkey straddles the Mideast, Europe, and Asia. It has coastlines on the Black Sea, the Aegean Sea, and the Mediterranean Sea, and it shares borders with—among other countries—Armenia, Greece, Iran, Iraq, and Syria. Turkey's terrain is mountainous, with a high central plateau. The climate in coastal areas is Mediterranean, while the interior experiences hot summers and cold winters. Turkey experiences devastating earthquakes from time to time.

Brief History

The territory of modern Turkey has been inhabited for millennia, but the Turkish people arrived only around the eleventh century CE. The Turks' original home was in Central Asia, and they had migrated slowly westward from the sixth century CE. A series of peoples had taken political control of what was to become Turkey prior to the arrival of the Turks, including Persians, Greeks, Celts, and Romans. The Romans introduced Christianity to the region, and when the Roman Empire split into two halves in the third century CE, the capital of the Greek part of the Roman Empire was established at Byzantium. The city of Byzantium was embellished and renamed Constantinople, and for over 1,000 years it remained the center of Greek Christendom and the Byzantine (Eastern Roman) Empire. With the rise of Islam in the seventh century CE, the Byzantine Empire successfully resisted the advances of Arab armies.

Later, in the eleventh century, the Seljuk Turks established control over the modern territories of Turkey, Iraq, and Iran. The Seljuks had adopted the Islamic faith before achieving political power in the Mideast. They championed the Sunni interpretation of Islam and they managed to withstand the brutalities of both crusading Christians and invading Mongols.

In the fifteenth century, the city of Constantinople finally fell to Turkish forces. However, the Seljuks had been replaced by a new Turkish regime—that of the Ottomans. The Ottoman Empire turned out to be one of the most powerful political states the world has ever seen. Sultan Suleyman the Magnificent (1520–1566) transformed Constantinople into an Islamic city, and the days of Christian Byzantium were finished.

The Ottoman Empire stretched over much of the Mideast, but by the nineteenth century it was under severe strain from resurgent nationalism in its many territories. The Greeks obtained their independence from the Ottomans in 1832, to be followed over the next century by Albanians, Arabs, Bulgarians, Serbs, and other nationalities. Greek independence was accompanied by massive, so-called "population transfers" between the two countries. This enforced migration involved millions of Greeks and Turks.

The Ottoman Empire finally collapsed at the end of World War I. During World War I, the Ottomans deported the largely Christian Armenian population of eastern Anatolia. At least 500,000 (and possibly many more) Armenians died during the forced marches that followed. The Armenians regard this catastrophe as genocide, although the Turks have generally denied that the large-scale Armenian deaths were deliberately planned.

Out of the ruins of the Ottoman Empire, the nationalist reformer Kemal Ataturk (1881–1930) created the modern Turkish state in 1923. Ataturk is today revered in Turkey for ensuring the survival of the country in its present-day form, and for his reforming zeal. He turned Turkey in a secular direction. The country was neutral in World War II and joined NATO in 1952. The country's strategic location at the junction of Europe, Asia, and the Mideast has made it an important regional power.

In 1974, Turkish forces moved into northern Cyprus, to defend the Turkish population amid the island's civil war that set Greek against Turk. The international community has generally refused to recognize the legitimacy of the Turkish state in northern Cyprus, but it remains a heavily garrisoned fortress. On the mainland, the late twentieth century saw a brutal insurgency by Kurdish separatists seeking a separate homeland called Kurdistan. The Turkish state met brutality with brutality in repressing the Kurdish rebellion, and the death toll has reached 30,000 or more. Critics accused both the Turkish state and the Kurdish rebels of committing human rights abuses. Indeed, allegations of human rights abuses appear to be among the main reasons for the delays surrounding Turkey's candidacy for membership of the EU. At the time of writing, there appear to be glimmers of hope for resolution of the bloody conflict.

Demographics

Turkey has a population of around 67 million. The country's surface area is large, however, and the overall population density is low. There are significant concentrations of inhabitants in some urban areas, especially around the cities of Istanbul, Ankara, and Izmir. Hundreds of thousands of Turks and Kurds moved to Germany to seek work in the latter part of the twentieth century.

Languages

Around 85 percent of the population of Turkey speaks Turkish, and 12 percent Kurdish. The balance is made up of small communities of speakers of Arabic, Armenian, and Greek. Turkish is a member of the Ural-Altaic language group and is unrelated to the region's neighboring Indo-European and Semitic languages. Prior to the reforms of the Ataturk period, Turkish was written with a modified Arabic script, but it is now written with a Roman alphabet. The change of writing system was a key part of the secular reforms of the early twentieth century. Kurdish is an Indo-European language closely related to Farsi (Persian), and several Kurdish dialects are spoken in Turkey. Successive Turkish governments have done little to promote the Kurdish language, and have at times been accused of suppressing its use for public and official purposes. The country's literacy rate is around 80 to 85 percent, and is higher for men than for women.

Politics

The Republic of Turkey is a parliamentary democracy and has its capital at Ankara. The country's president acts as head of state, and the prime minister as head of government. The unicameral parliament is elected by popular vote. Since the Ataturk era, the Turkish military have not been shy to interfere in politics, ostensibly to defend the country's secular traditions. The country's main political issues are a long-running struggle between secularists and Islamists, and the armed Kurdish separatist movement.

Economy

Turkey's main industries include clothing, iron and steel, textiles, and tourism. The country's agricultural base is strong and around one-third of the workforce is employed in the agricultural sector. The Turkish economy is volatile and erratic, and its structural problems include poor infrastructure and chronically high inflation. The country's hopes of joining the EU have been frustrated, and the economy has continued its topsy-turvy trajectory. In late 2000, Turkey experienced a severe financial crisis that still casts its shadow over the economy. The country's largest trading partner is Germany, and the currency unit is the lira.

Legal and Regulatory Environment

The Turkish legal system is based largely on continental European legal principles. The reformists of the Ataturk era replaced Islamic law with secular law, and looked to Europe to provide the necessary templates. The regulatory environment has a reputation of being cumbersome, despite attempts in recent years to alleviate the amount of red tape.

Accountancy

Turkish GAAP is based on tax and accounting law, the country's uniform chart of accounts, and the accounting standards of the Ministry of Finance's Capital Markets Board (CMB). CMB standards apply to public companies, banks, and corporations with more than 100 shareholders. CMB standards are generally in line with IAS, although there are areas of difference such as consolidation accounting and the treatment of employee benefits. Where CMB standards are quiet on a topic, the

CBM recommends the use of IAS. Stock exchange regulations permit foreign listed corporations to use either IAS or a national GAAP. Where a national GAAP other than those of the United States and the United Kingdom are used, reconciliation to IAS is normally required. Turkish listed corporations must follow Turkish GAAP.

Turkey's main professional accountancy and external auditing body is the Union of Chambers of Certified Public Accountants of Turkey (known under the Turkish abbreviation of TURMOB).

Cultural Background

Modern Turkey has generally been reluctant to acknowledge the existence of the country's ethnic minorities. In the 1980s, for example, the Kurds were often referred to as "Eastern Turks." However, the country is far from homogeneous: Around 85 percent of the population is ethnically Turkish, and a further 12 percent Kurdish. (Approximately 50 percent of all Kurds worldwide live in Turkey—the rest live mainly in Iran, Iraq, and Syria.) The Kurdish separatist insurgency of recent years is discussed further in the "Brief History" section. Turkey also has small communities of Arabs, Armenians, Greeks, and Jews. Around 99 percent of the Turkish population is Muslim.

The ethnic Turkish population consists of various groups that differ in terms of social customs, dress, and use of dialects, but urbanization is tending to reduce these differences. Similarly, the Kurdish population is also split into different social and religious groups.

Social Etiquette

- The pace of Turkish business life is generally quite slow by western standards.
- Turkish hospitality is famous, and business dealings often involve visits to restaurants and bars.
- For a Muslim majority country, Turkey is relatively liberal. Alcohol is freely available, for example.
- Conservative dress is advisable for women.
- A polite demeanor is valued at all times during business discussions.

Further Information

Bernard Burr, *The Emergence of Modern Turkey*, 3rd ed. (New York and Oxford: Oxford University Press, 2001).

Lord Kinross, *Ottoman Centuries: The Rise and Fall of the Turkish Empire* (New York: William Morrow, 1988).

Andrew Mango, *Ataturk: The Biography of the Founder of Modern Turkey* (New York: Overlook Press, 2000).

Office of the Prime Minister (of Turkey): *www.byegm.gov.tr.*

TURMOB: *www.turmob.org.tr/english/index.html.*

UNITED ARAB EMIRATES

Geography

The United Arab Emirates (UAE) is located on the Arabian Peninsula, along the coast of the Persian Gulf. The UAE borders Oman and Saudi Arabia. The territory consists mainly of desert, with coastal plains and mountains in the east. The UAE climate is hot and dry, although mountainous areas are considerably cooler owing to the effects of altitude.

Brief History

The "Saudi Arabia" section gives an overview of the history of the Arabian Peninsula, including the rise of Islam. This section concentrates on the emergence of the UAE as a separate political entity. The coast of the Persian Gulf has been coveted by outside powers for centuries, not least by the European colonizing nations that took an interest in the region from the sixteenth century. The Portuguese were the first Europeans to arrive in the territory of the modern UAE, but they were soon supplanted by the British. Britain was anxious to control the Persian Gulf, as it was strategically located between England and the British colony of India.

In the late nineteenth and early twentieth centuries, Britain acted as the Persian Gulf's "policeman," suppressing sea piracy and slave trading in addition to maintaining its strategic interests. The British also negotiated a series of treaties or "truces" with local political leaders, on account of which the British called the coast the "trucial coast." The British left local rulers nominally independent, but pulled the strings of the local economy. The British also effectively dominated the small Gulf States' foreign affairs. (A similar situation occurred in neighboring Kuwait.)

When the house of Al Saud created the modern state of Saudi Arabia in the early twentieth century, they wished to incorporate the coastal Gulf States into their nation. Only British intervention allowed the future UAE to remain independent from the Kingdom of Saudi Arabia.

As the twentieth century progressed, the economic dynamics of the region shifted. The Persian Gulf States had been characterized by sea trade, fishing, and pearl diving, but they took advantage of the oil boom to transform themselves into highly prosperous economies. The UAE came into existence in 1971 as the so-called "trucial" states gained independence from Britain. A federal structure binds the UAE's seven states of Abu Dhabi, Dubai, Ajman, Fujayrah, Ra's al-Khaymah, Sharjah, and Umm al-Qaywayn. The UAE has become a major international business center and one of the Mideast's most politically stable entities.

Demographics

The UAE's indigenous population of around 500,000 is considerably outnumbered by 1.5 to 1.7 million foreign expatriate workers. The UAE's oil wealth attracts foreign workers from around the world. In particular, the Indian subcontinent is the source of a large proportion of the expatriate workers, and workers' remittances from the UAE play an important role in the subcontinent's economy. The UAE's settlement patterns are highly urbanized and concentrated in coastal areas.

Languages

The language of the UAE is Arabic, of which the "Saudi Arabia" section gives an overview. There are also small numbers of Farsi (Persian) speakers in Dubai, which has had traditionally strong links with Iran. Literacy levels are around 80 percent and, unusual for the region, are evenly balanced between men and women.

Politics

The United Arab Emirates is a federation of seven emirates (sometimes referred to as sheikdoms) and has its capital at Abu Dhabi. Each state retains a degree of independence. The president acts as head of state, and the prime minister as head of government. There are no western-style democratic elections, and the rulers of the UAE's seven states appoint members of the unicameral Federal National Council.

Economy

The UAE's prosperity is based on the oil and natural gas sectors. Although there are important fishing, boatbuilding, pearl, and tourism industries, the economy's performance is driven by fluctuations in the prices of oil and gas. The UAE's wealth has attracted an influx of foreign workers who dwarf the local population. Japan is the country's largest trading partner, and the currency unit is the Emirati dirham.

Legal and Regulatory Environment

UAE law is based on Islamic law in personal and domestic matters, but there are many secular elements of business and commercial law. Taxation is nonexistent, and the regulatory environment is relatively light by the standards of the region.

Accountancy

From early 1999, all banks and financial institutions in the United Arab Emirates are required to prepare their financial statements using IAS, but IAS is not applicable at the time of writing to nonfinancial organizations. Owing to the country's oil wealth, the major international accounting firms are all represented in the country, and the Accounting and Auditing Organization for Islamic Financial Institutions is based in Bahrain.

Cultural Background

Virtually all of the UAE's inhabitants are Arab Sunni Muslims. There is a Shia population of around 15 percent, of which a section is of Iranian descent. By the standards of the region, the UAE is liberal, and it is generally tolerant toward the cultures and religions of its expatriate workers. However, the country is still rather conservative by western standards.

Social Etiquette

The "Saudi Arabia" country section has comments of general application to Muslim culture in the Mideast. In addition:

- The UAE is relatively liberal, and alcohol is available in certain areas. However, visitors should avoid assuming that liberalism runs deeply and should be careful not to offend Islamic customs and sensibilities.

Further Information

Sayyid Hamid Hurriez, *Folklore and Folklife in the United Arab Emirates* (New York and London: RoutledgeCurzon, 2002).

Frauke Heard-Bey and Geoffrey Arthur, *From Trucial States to United Arab Emirates* (New York and London: Longman, 1996).

Malise Ruthven, *Islam: A Very Short Introduction*, rev. ed. (New York and Oxford: Oxford University Press, 2000).

Rosemarie Said Zahlan, *The Origins of the United Arab Emirates: A Political and Social History of the Trucial States* (New York and London: Palgrave-Macmillan, 1996).

Government of the United Arab Emirates: *www.uae.gov.ae*.

Accounting and Auditing Organization for Islamic Financial Institutions: *www.aaoifi.org*.

Index